SERVANTS
OF THE
SERVANT.

A BIBLICAL
THEOLOGY
OF LEADERSHIP

SERVANTS OF THE SERVANT.

A BIBLICAL THEOLOGY OF LEADERSHIP

By
DON N. HOWELL, JR.

Wipf & Stock Publishers
Eugene, Oregon

Wipf & Stock Publishers
199 West 8th Avenue, Suite 3
Eugene, OR 97401

Servants of the Servant.
A Biblical Theology of Leadership
Copyright©2003 by Don N. Howell, Jr.
ISBN: 1-59244-422-9
Publication Date: 11/14/03

TABLE OF CONTENTS

Introduction: Biblical Leadership

Importance

Leadership is a concept of immense importance, one that has gained increasing visibility in the past two decades. The number of books, monographs, journal articles and even doctoral dissertations devoted to some aspect of leadership is staggering. There has been almost exponential growth in the number of seminars offered to help people develop as leaders and to nurture their skills in training others. If one does a search of *amazon.com* for books with the term "leader" or "leadership" in the title, the number of entries that come up are 1,902 and 4,628 respectively. When one expands the search to "leadership" as the subject or category of the book, 10,244 entries are available to scroll through. Clearly those in the political, corporate, educational, and ecclesiastical worlds are looking for help as to how to effectively lead others and they are getting an abundance of advice.

Countries, companies and churches rise or fall with the quality of their leadership. Over the past twenty-five years in vocational Christian ministry, primarily as a church planter and theological educator, this writer has encountered numerous examples of both constructive as well as unhealthy patterns of leadership. What has stood out is that effective leadership is critical to the success of any organization or group in accomplishing its mission.

Definition

But how does one define leadership? There are almost as many definitions of the subject as there are published works dedicated to it. In a broad, functional sense, what seem to be central to every level and context of true leadership are **initiative** and **influence**. One sees a need and, based on one's governing convictions, exercises initiative to address that concern; influence is then brought to bear on others to join in and contribute to the accomplishment of a stated objective. Whether the exercise of such leadership is constructive or unhealthy depends on the leader's **character, motive(s)** and **agenda**.

The subject of this work is *biblical leadership*. We could use, and will use at times, other synonymous descriptive terms for this manner of leadership such as pious, spiritual, or godly. However, we prefer the term "biblical" because our goal is to seek to understand those precepts, principles, and examples related to leadership that are set forth in the Bible. Our purpose is to construct a profile of what kind of leadership effectively promotes the kingdom of God in the world and meets with God's approval. Before offering a working definition of biblical leadership, we set forth two presuppositions of this study.

1. First, it is the bedrock conviction of this writer that Holy Scripture, comprised of the Old and New Testaments, is the authoritative guide for the Christian believer in every realm of life, including how one grows into and conducts oneself as a leader of others. Admittedly, the Bible is not a textbook on the practice of leadership, but is a truthful record of the saving acts of God and his

interpretive word. However, in this drama of the progress of redemption, God raises up and uses human leaders to accomplish his saving purposes. Those who are set forth in Scripture as godly leaders exercise their derived powers under the authority of God's holy word. Joshua, as he succeeds Moses, is commanded to meditate day and night on the book of the law, for its precepts are the path to prosperity for the nation (Josh 1:8). Samuel reminds the nation of Israel as it institutes a monarchy that the king and his subjects will stand or fall depending on their fidelity to the commands of God. Will their leader adopt the customary role of the oriental despot or subject his rule to the covenant (1 Sam 12:13-15)? In the waning years of Israel's experience as a free nation, weighed down by the seductive forces of idolatry, the boy king Josiah, under his godly mentor Hilkiah, recalls the nation to its covenantal obligations by reading from the rediscovered book of the law (2 Kg 23:1-3; cf. 22:8). He is marked out as a leader like no other because he led the nation "in accordance with all the law of Moses" (23:25).

The criterion of a leader's success remains the same for new covenant leaders. Timothy is instructed at the outset of his pastoral ministry to study the word of truth, the Holy Scriptures, which, by their power to instruct, rebuke, correct and train in righteousness, will thoroughly equip him to lead the church (2 Tim 2:15; 3:14-17). Timothy's mentor, the apostle Paul, is the preeminent example of one who leads from the conviction that "everything that was written in the past was written to teach us, so that through endurance and the encouragement of the Scriptures we might have hope" (Rom 15:4). From the historical narrative of the Bible emerge normative principles. These, along with authoritative precepts from the didactic portions of Scripture, establish a consistent set of priorities that must govern authentic spiritual leadership.

2. Our second presupposition is that biblical leadership is not limited to particular models related to style, role or setting. This writer's study of Scripture has created and nurtured the conviction that God's priorities focus on the **character** of the leader, the **motives** that drive his or her practice of leadership, and the **agenda** that the leader pursues. This threefold set of priorities can be applied to all styles, roles and settings. Secular leadership theory (even those that purport to be biblically based, but all too often incorporate biblical principles into secular frameworks) tends to concern itself with the narrower domains of leadership style, role, and setting. The style could assume an almost unlimited number of possibilities: the leader as entrepreneur, strategist, mobilizer, facilitator, organizer, team leader, coach, mentor, administrator, activist, developer, provocateur, executive, resource-provider, vision-caster, exhorter, or consensus-builder. The role, if we focus on a ministry setting, could be pastor, elder, staff member, chairman of the board or president of an institution, director of an agency, Sunday school teacher, or discipleship group leader among many others. The setting could be the church or the parachurch organization, including institutions for ministry training. All of these styles, roles and settings can function as the context of biblical leadership because the latter is concerned with character, motive, and agenda rather than a particular application.

Scripture teaches that God is about the business of extending his lordship over the hearts of people who respond with faith and repentance to his offer of forgiveness (Mt 4:17, 19). God is calling people to himself, and to community with others under his rule, and bringing them into conformity to his holiness so that they can declare his excellencies and bring others out of darkness into his marvelous light (1 Pet 2:9). His redeemed and transformed children are commanded to go forth in obedience to their Lord's testamentary commission and make disciples of people from all nations (Mt 28:18-20). Those who would lead others, at least in the Scriptural definition of the term, must align their practice of leadership with these most essential priorities on the expressed heart of God.

With these two presuppositions and the divine blueprint in mind, we now offer a definition: **"Biblical leadership is taking the initiative to influence people to grow in holiness and to passionately promote the extension of God's kingdom in the world."** Biblical leadership, then, is defined in a way that is proactive, purposive and comprehensive.

1. Proactive: Leadership involves taking the initiative to influence others. Since it is impact for the kingdom that is at the core of the definition of biblical leadership, the godly leader looks for, pursues and follows up opportunities to positively move others toward holiness of character and obedience to the divine agenda. The godly leader aspires to decisively influence the character and life-direction of others. That aspiration must translate into a Spirit-energized determination to seize the day of opportunity, whether great or small.

2. Purposive: The biblical leader focuses on helping people individually, and the church collectively, to grow in godliness and to obey God's declared agenda of extending his dynamic rule (i.e. his kingdom) over the peoples of all nations. There are two corollaries of this. First, biblical leadership is people-oriented rather than program-driven in that it focuses on the spiritual maturation of individuals and communities of faith (Col 1:28-29). Second, it is kingdom-oriented rather than organization-driven in that it seeks to help people find their niche where they can make their most significant and satisfying contribution to the extension of God's saving rule in the world (Rom 12:4-8). Leaders bring God's people in line with God's mission.

3. Comprehensive: Because it is kingdom impact on the character and conduct of others that one seeks, this kind of leadership can be exercised in both formal and informal settings, in both secular and vocational ministry contexts. Some are thrust into formal leadership positions by the dramatic call of God— Moses, Gideon, Samuel, and Paul. Others are appointed to formal roles by human leaders—Joseph as vice-regent of Egypt by Pharoah, Nehemiah as governor of Judea by Artaxerxes, and Titus as the pastor in Crete by Paul. Many, if not most, who rise to positions of prominence begin by taking the initiative to use their God-given gifts initially in small and obscure settings— Joseph as a slave in Potiphar's house, Joshua as Moses' young apprentice, Barnabas as a generous giver to his church, and Timothy as a witnessing teenager in his home town of Lystra. Virtues are nurtured, skills are honed, and the opportunities for leadership are expanded. It is a good thing, Paul writes, to

3

aspire to leadership, if its underlying intent is to impact people for the glory of God (1 Tim 3:1; cf. 1:17; 6:16).

Methodology

This study of the theme of leadership in the pages of Scripture seeks to follow the progressive record of the drama of redemption. Those who stand out in Scripture as leaders are designated, first of all, "servants of the Lord." The unfolding record of those individuals that God uses to further his saving purposes in the world demonstrates what we call a servanthood pattern of leadership. Our study begins with a study of the biblical language of the servant. The intent is not to establish a preconceived framework in which to force the biblical data, but to clarify what the Bible means by this term "servant," one that it uniformly assigns as the designation of choice for its finest leaders, including Moses, David, Paul and above all the Lord Jesus Christ. We profile eleven Old Testament and five New Testament personalities who are given significant enough coverage that one can draw principles from their successes and failures as leaders (or leaders-in-training). Our profile of Jesus Christ focuses on three motifs that governed his training of the twelve apostles for kingdom ministry. These motifs—harvest through sacrifice, righteousness through freedom, and greatness through servanthood—are those dimensions of his theology of the kingdom of God that he sought with great intentionality and repetitiveness to impart to his disciples as future kingdom leaders. He equipped them to be equippers of others. The data of the Pauline letters is mined for those convictions that governed Paul's practice of leadership—both of his mission team and of the communities of faith that grew out of that mission. This data is organized into two areas: (1) characteristics of his approach to influencing people; (2) criteria for those who would qualify as leaders of the emerging churches. The treatment of each leader, from Joseph to Paul, begins with a series of "preliminary questions for consideration" and concludes with a mini-profile that correlates the biblical data with these questions. The final chapter offers a summary profile of the "servant-leader."

PART ONE

Language of the Servant: From Deprivation to Dignity

Chapter 1.
Old Testament: From slave of man to servant of the Lord

The Bible takes the term for slave, both the Hebrew עֶבֶד and its equivalent in the Greek language, δοῦλος, and transforms it into a designation for one bestowed with the unparalleled honor of being called "the servant of the Lord." In order to appreciate fully this remarkable metamorphosis, it is necessary to briefly explore the background of the term. Slavery was part of the social fabric of the Ancient Near East. From Mesopotamia to Egypt slavery was an institution that provided servants for the estates of free citizens and heavy labor for public works projects. The slave class came from those captured as prisoners of war, from those forced to sell themselves due to crushing debt, and from those born into slave families. Though their treatment depended on the disposition of the master, slaves were viewed as property much like animals and land.[1]

Israel reflected her oriental setting by adopting slavery as a social institution. The term עֶבֶד frequently refers to a household slave or domestic servant: Abraham owned servants, the chief of which was Eliezer (Gen 24:2); Isaac owned many servants (Gen 26:14, 19); Gideon had ten servants, the chief of which was Purah (Jdg 6:27; 7:10-11); Saul's father Kish owned servants (1 Sam 9:3); Ziba was a servant in Saul's household (2 Sam 9:2, 9); Gehazi was Elisha's servant (2 Kg 5:25). The book of Proverbs employs the term slave as a metaphor for lowly status and deprivation of rights in many of its wisdom sayings (12:9; 14:35; 22:7; 29:19, 21; 30:22). However, the Mosaic law provided for the protection and welfare of slaves, particularly those fellow Hebrews forced to become slaves due to default on their debts. The laws of Exodus 21:2-6 and Deuteronomy 12:15-18 require that a Hebrew slave be released after six years of service, though the slave could voluntarily refuse freedom and become a slave for life. The Jubilee year was established to prevent the existence of a permanent class of Hebrew slaves and the permanent transfer of landed property from one tribe to another (Lev 25:8-13). The Israelites' experience under their Egyptian taskmasters seared into the consciousness of the nation the harshness endemic to slavery (Ex 1:11-14; 2:23-25; 5:1-21). After the miraculous deliverance of the nation—from slaves to adopted sons (Ex 4:22-23; 6:1-8)—the Lord repeatedly calls on his people to remember that they were slaves in Egypt, and thus to treat their own slaves, both native and alien, with just and kind consideration (Deut 5:14-15; 15:12-15; 16:11-12; 24:17-18, 21-22).[2]

It is the character of God and his covenantal mercies to Israel, then, which

---

[1] *TDOT*, X: 389-390. The Code of Hammurabi, an 18th c. B.C. Mesopotamian law code, offers many parallels with the Mosaic legislation on the protection and welfare of slaves.

[2] Roland de Vaux, *Ancient Israel: Its Life and Institutions*, transl. John McHugh (London: Darton, Longman, and Todd, 1961): 80-90, provides a thorough and readable account of slavery in the life of the nation Israel.

6

account for the shift of meaning from bonded "slave" to redeemed "servant." The word for slave, with all of its associations of oppression, dependency, and servility, becomes a favorite self-designation for those who delight to call themselves "servant of Yahweh," their King and Redeemer. Two other uses of the term עֶבֶד prepare the way for this decisive shift. First, the most frequent use of the word עֶבֶד in the Old Testament is as a term of humility when one person addresses another as "your servant:" Abraham to his three visitors (Gen 18:3, 5); Judah to Joseph (Gen 44:18); Ruth to Boaz (Ruth 3:9); Hannah to Eli (1 Sam 1:16); and David to King Achish (1 Sam 27:5). This deferential language is common to many oriental languages and was employed as a matter of courtesy. Second, this term often refers to the "subjects" of a greater personage, usually a king such as Abimelech of Gerar (Gen 21:25) or Pharaoh of Egypt (Gen 41:10). After the rise of the monarchy the leading officials or closest attendants of Kings Saul (1 Sam 18:24; 19:1), David (2 Sam 11:13; 15:15), and Solomon (1 Kg 10:5) are designated "servants." While the nuances of dependency, respect, and obedience are certainly present, the designation is an honorable one, no longer degrading and pejorative. It signifies those who promote the interests and welfare of their ruler.

The great leaders of the Old Testament are commonly designated "servant of the Lord." This is the title of honor par excellence for those who discover a joyful abandonment to the will of the Lord.[3] The two leaders who most clearly represent the ideals of the servant-leader are Moses and David. These two are singled out for special emphasis in the pages of Holy Scripture, first, because they exemplify a passion for God's glory and a concern for the spiritual welfare of the covenant nation, and second, because they prefigure the great Prophet (Deut 18:15-18) and King (2 Sam 7:16; Isa 11:6) respectively who comes to consummate redemption as the suffering Servant. However, it is not only prominent leaders called to specific tasks that receive this title. The use of "servant" for Israel, the people of God, prepares for its wider application to ordinary believers who submit their lives to the divine purposes. The Psalmist is a prime example of one who expresses in supplication the trusting dependence of the willing servant. Finally, it is the Servant of the Lord, so graphically depicted in the songs of Isaiah, that brings all of the promises of redemption to fruition through his vicarious sacrifice. It is evident in its manifold application that the term "servant of the Lord" is in essence one who

---

[3] The term "servant (of the Lord)" is applied to many of the leading personalities of the Old Testament, either as a title of honor in the historical narrative, a humble self-designation when addressing God in prayer, or a direct ascription from the Lord himself: Abraham (Gen 26:24; Ps 105:6, 42); the three patriarchs Abraham, Isaac and Jacob (Ex 32:13; Deut 9:27); Caleb (Num 14:24); Joshua (Josh 5:14; 24:29; Jdg 2:8); Samson (Jdg 15:18); Hannah (1 Sam 1:11); Samuel (1 Sam 3:9-10); Solomon (1 Kg 3:7, 8, 9; 8:28-30, 52, 59; 2 Chron 6:19-21); Elijah (1 Kg 18:36; 2 Kg 9:36; 10:10); the prophets Jonah (2 Kg 14:25) and Ahijah (1 Kg 14:18; 15:29); Hezekiah (2 Chron 32:16); Nehemiah (Neh 1:6, 11); Job (Job 1:8; 2:3; 42:7-8); Isaiah (Isa 20:3); Eliakim, the leading official under Hezekiah (Isa 22:20); Daniel (Dan 6:20; 9:17); the three friends of Daniel (Dan 3:26, 28); Zerubbabel (Hag 2:23); the pagan king of Babylon, Nebuchadnezzar (Jer 25:9; 27:6; 43:10). The guild of true prophets is corporately labeled "my/his/your servants the prophets" (2 Kg 9:7; 17:13, 23; 21:10; 24:2; Jer 7:25; 25:4; 26:5; 29:19; 35:15; 44:4; Ezek 38:17; Dan 9:6, 10; Zech 1:6; Amos 3:7; cf. 2 Kg 10:23; Isa 44:26). The angels (Job 4:18; Ps 103:21) and the natural elements (Ps 104:4) are servants of the Lord because they contribute to the fulfillment of the divine purposes.

aligns his or her life direction with the divine agenda, the redemptive program that centers on revealing God's glory to the nations by consecrating a people that honor his name (Isa 42:6-9; 49:6b).

1. Moses: Moses adopts the posture of a servant at his initial call (Ex 4:10) and during his trials as a leader (Num 11:11). In the exodus event the Lord vindicates Moses as his true servant before the nation (Ex 14:31). The Lord rises to Moses' defense against his slanderous siblings, Aaron and Miriam, reminding them that they are speaking against his faithful servant (Num 12:7-8). Moses pleads with the Lord to reverse his judgment against "your servant" and allow him to enter the promised land, a plea that is refused (Deut 3:24-26). The account of Moses' death inscribes on his epitaph, as it were, "servant of the Lord" (Deut 34:5). In the annals of Israel's history Moses is memorialized as one whose passionate pursuit of God's presence (Ex 33:12-16) and selfless intercession for his people (Ex 32:11-14) set him apart as the "servant of the Lord" (Josh 1:1, 2, 7, 13, 15; 8:31, 33; 9:24; 11:12, 15; 12:6; 13:8; 14:7; 18:7; 22:2, 4, 5; 1 Kg 8:53, 56; 2 Kg 18:12; 21:8; 1 Chron 6:49; 2 Chron 1:3; 24:6, 9; Neh 1:7-8; 9:14; 10:29; Ps 105:26; Dan 9:11; Mal 4:4; cf. Rev 15:3).

2. David: From his early years as a fugitive the future monarch nurtures the habit of dependent prayer as the Lord's servant (1 Sam 23:10-11; cf. Ps 144:10). After his accession to the throne of Israel the Lord speaks an unparalleled word of promise to "my servant David" (2 Sam 7:5, 8), namely, the pledge of an eternal dynasty from his offspring (7:11-16). David expresses, through the prayer of a servant (2 Sam 7:19, 20, 21, 25, 26, 27, 28, 29), his overwhelming sense of wonder at God's gracious purposes. His sense of unworthiness ("Who am I?" [7:18]) is matched only by his exaltation of God's majesty ("How great you are" [7:22]). He prays that his throne will be established, in accordance with the promise, so that the surrounding peoples might recognize the greatness of Israel's God (7:25-26). Later when his military census invites divine judgment, David pleads for the Lord to "take away the guilt of your servant" (2 Sam 24:10). Solomon praises, but fails to imitate, his father's servant model (1 Kg 3:6; 8:24-26, 66; cf. Ps 89:39). In the aftermath of the catastrophic disruption caused by Solomon's apostasy, the nation will recall the promises to David, and remind itself that the dark present will one day give way to a glorious kingdom under Messiah's rule "for the sake of my servant David" (1 Kg 11:13, 32, 34, 36, 38; cf. 2 Kg 8:19; 19:34; 20:6; Ps 89:3, 20, 50; 132:10; Isa 37:35; Jer 33:21, 22, 26; Ezek 34:23-24; 37:24-25; cf. Zech 3:8). David is memorialized as the servant-king who departed from the standard practice of oriental monarchs and submitted his rule to the will of the Almighty (1 Kg 14:8; Ps 78:70-72).

3. Israel: It is in the waning years of her existence as a free nation that the prophets, especially Isaiah, anticipate a time when the Lord will draw Israel back to himself, lovingly care for her, and once again make her a people of joyful witness. Even in fearful exile the Lord promises to strengthen and uphold (Isa 41:8-9), renew and revitalize (44:1-5), and liberate (48:20) Israel/Jacob, "my/ his servant." Though his servant is presently blind and deaf to his overtures of

love (Isa 42:19), the Lord will never forget her (Isa 44:21). He will bestow on her a title of honor, probably the very title, "servant of the Lord" (45:4). Jeremiah and Ezekiel similarly predict that the Lord will restore from exile his banished servant, consecrate her as a holy people, and return her to the land of promise (Jer 30:10; 46:27-28; Ezek 28:25; 37:25; cf. Jer 2:10; Ps 136:22; 1 Chron 16:13). When the first stage of those hopes come to fruition, Nehemiah the servant prays not just for the community as a whole but for his fellow servants (pl.) who are in distress in the holy city (Neh 1:6, 10). He galvanizes the will of this servant people to complete the rebuilding of the city walls (Neh 2:20). All of these prophetic and prayerful images together confirm that Israel can fulfill her destiny as the Lord intended only when she once again assumes the role of "my servant" and "my witnesses" (Isa 43:10, 12).

4. Psalmist: It is in the Psalms, the prayer and praise book of Israel, that one can listen into the petitions of the individual believer who assumes the posture of a humble servant and earnestly pleads for the Lord's favor.[4] The Psalmist petitions the Lord to grant "your servant" protection from sin (19:13), exemption from judgment (143:2), his abiding presence (face) (27:9; 31:16; 69:17; 119:135), joy (Ps 86:4), strength (86:16), goodness or favor (119:17, 65), unfailing love (119:76, 124; 143:12), the fulfillment of the promises of protection and preservation (119:38, 49, 84), personal well-being (35:27; 119:122), discernment (119:125), and enabling for obedience (119:176). The Psalmist-servant is warned by (19:11), meditates on (119:23), and lovingly embraces (119:140) the promises and precepts of the law. He rejoices to be called the Lord's servant, freed from the chains of fear and despair (34:22; 109:28; 116:16). Those dignified to be entitled his servants praise the name of the Lord forevermore (113:1-2).

5. Isaianic Servant: The prophet Isaiah testifies through four "servant songs" of a figure who endures the extremity of humiliation, suffering and even death in order to remove transgression and provide release from captivity to sin (42:1-7; 49:1-7; 50:4-11; 52:13-53:12). Yahweh introduces his chosen servant as the Spirit-endowed emissary who tenderly stoops to free those locked in the dungeon of spiritual darkness, both in Israel and among the Gentiles (Isa 42:1-7; cf. Mt 12:17-21).

The second song describes a servant who is at once "Israel" (49:3), and yet who testifies of his dependence on God's strength as he undertakes his appointed mission to restore Israel (49:4-5) and to bring salvation to the nations of the earth (49:6). The dual application of the appellation "servant" to the nation (v. 3) and to a divinely commissioned individual (vv. 5, 6) probably means the suffering Servant acts like the ideal Israel, fulfilling the promise of salvation to the nations that the empirical nation could not and would not mediate.[5] The terminology of the servant's weakness (v. 4a), dependency (v. 5), and rejection (v. 7) anticipates the fuller exposition of his suffering in the fourth song.

The third song develops further the themes of the earlier descriptions of

---

[4] The noun עֶבֶד occurs 57 times in the Psalms (14 times in Ps 119). See *TDOT*, X: 393-394.
[5] John N. Oswalt, *The Book of Isaiah*, NICOT, 2 vols (Grand Rapids: Eerdmans, 1998): 2: 290-291.

the servant: his suffering (50:6), determination to complete his appointed role (50:7), final vindication (50:8-9), and authoritative word of salvation for those who dwell in spiritual darkness (50:10).

The fourth song graphically portrays the suffering of the servant in its truest colors, deeper and darker than the muted shades of the earlier depictions (49:4, 7; 50:6-8). The servant suffers appalling humiliation in his redemptive mission to the nations and is vindicated by God (52:13-15). In a careful progression the song laments the servant's lowly demeanor and career of sorrows (53:1-3), expounds his vicarious death as a penal substitute for wayward transgressors (53:4-6), marvels at his silence before his accusers (53:7-9), and celebrates the justification of many (53:10-12). Here is the preeminent picture of a servant, one whose pleasure is to fulfill the divine will for his life (53:10c).[6] Though his vicarious death is singular and unrepeatable, his self-defacing commitment to the divine purpose qualifies him as the servant whose character compels imitation.[7] The servant who delights to obey God's will (Isa 53:10c) is the servant of God's delight (Isa 42:1).

To conclude, the Old Testament transforms the term for oppression, "slave," into a title of honor, "servant." Its manifold usage as a designation for preeminent leaders such as Moses and David, for the covenant people Israel, and for the messianic Servant of Isaiah's songs adumbrates a wider application to the individual believer who joyfully submits to the authority of the covenant Lord, and walks before him in humility, so clearly exemplified by the Psalmist.[8]

---

[6] This is the meaning of the exquisite declaration in the Hebrew, literally, "the will (or delight/ pleasure) of the Lord will prosper by his hand (i.e. by his mediatorial work [cf. Num 36:13])." The subject of the sentence, חֵפֶץ, which means "that which one takes delight or pleasure in" (cf. Isa 44:28; 46:10; 48:14; 58:3, 13), is cognate with the main verb of v. 10a (חָפֵץ): The Lord "willed" (i.e. delighted, took pleasure) to crush him. The servant in turn delighted to accomplish the divine will, which was to offer himself as a guilt offering for transgressors (53:10b). The servant is thus one whose entire being is committed to fulfilling the Lord's purpose for him (cf. Jn 4:34; 17:4; 19:30; Heb 10:7, 9, quot. Ps 40:8 [MT 40:9]: "I desired [Heb. חָפָצְתִּי] to do your will, O my God").

[7] The normal term used in the LXX to translate the Hebrew עֶבֶד for the Isaianic Servant is παις (42:1; 49:6; 50:10; 52:13). However, the translators chose δουλος for עֶבֶד in Isa 49:3, 5 (v. 7, pl.) and the substantival participle of δουλευω in 53:11. These two Greek terms for "servant" seem interchangeable in 49:5-6. In the texts we have applied to Israel proper (above), the LXX also normally renders עֶבֶד by παις (41:8, 9; 43:10; 44:1, 2, 21; 45:4). However, δουλος is used in Isa 48:20 and there is a curious interchange of the plurals παιδες and δουλοι in Isa 42:19. While παις is the definitive Christological term for the messianic Servant in the early apostolic preaching (Acts 3:13, 26; 4:27, 30), δουλος is the term of choice in the Carmen Christi (Php 2:7), a hymn that supports the command to imitate the mind of Christ (2:5). Do not the two terms together point to two dimensions of the work of the suffering Servant: (1) the exclusivity of his vicarious sacrifice (παις), and yet (2) the attitude of self-sacrificial abandonment to the divine purposes that demands imitation (δουλος)? We affirm both the exclusive messianic (vicarious sacrifice) and the shared paradigmatic (selfless obedience) nature of the portrait of the Servant in Isaiah.

[8] The Old Testament authors employ the cognate verb עָבַד (290 times) for the obedient response of the covenant people, both corporately and individually, to the redemptive mercies of the Lord. To "serve" (often rendered "worship") the Lord is a theological and ethical disposition that encompasses a person's entire being. To serve the Lord is a joyful, reverential, willing, and wholehearted commitment to his person (worship), his word (obedience), and his purposes (witness) (Ex 3:12; 4:23; 10:26; Deut 6:13; 10:12-13, 20; 13:4; 28:47; Josh 24:14-24; 1 Sam 12:14, 20, 24; 1 Chron 28:9; Ps 2:11; 22:30; 100:2; Jer 30:9).

Chapter 2.
New Testament: Servant of the Lord and servant of others

When we come to the New Testament, the family of terms related to δουλος, the Greek term for slave, takes on the same meanings that the עֶבֶד-word group does in the Old Testament. This is because the translators of the Greek Old Testament, the Septuagint, normally rendered the Hebrew עֶבֶד by δουλος, so the latter becomes a Greek term with a Hebrew meaning. Its biblical sense contrasts markedly with its use in Hellenistic writings where the δουλος-word group (which includes δουλεια [service] and δουλευω [to serve or worship]) is almost exclusively pejorative. The Greeks placed great value on personal autonomy, that is, freedom from subjection to the will of someone or something outside of oneself. Plato, Aristotle, the Stoic philosopher Epictetus, and Philo all employ the δουλος-group in a derogatory sense, as the forfeiture of opportunity for self-determination that is at the heart of meaningful existence. To be subject to the will of another is to be stripped of one's dignity and is thus a condition that is contemptible.[9]

An important corollary here is that the δουλος-word group is not used in Greek literature to describe religious devotion. The Greek pantheon consisted of gods who acted like distant cousins of their human counterparts, and did little to interfere with the latter's quest for personal freedom. Devoted service or humble worship of the gods would diminish human autonomy and thus has no place in the domain of this family of terms.[10] By stark contrast, it is the majesty of the Judeo-Christian God that transforms the values, and thus the language that gives expression to those values, attested to in the New Testament writings. God is a transcendent Creator and Lord who deserves the worship of those he has made and redeemed (1 Tim 1:17; 6:15-16). Dependent obedience, humble submission, reverent worship, and wholehearted commitment to the will and purposes of Another are qualities that, far from destroying human dignity, bring about its restoration. Here is a Hebraic world-view poured into the linguistic vehicle of the Greek language.

1. Slavery and the gospel: First, the *doulos*-terms retain their secular usage to refer to slavery as a social institution in the Roman empire of the first century. In his parables Jesus often refers to the context of household slaves whose service is designed to promote the welfare of their masters: the servants who are perplexed at the weeds growing in their master's field (Mt 13:27-28); the unmerciful servant who is punished for his callous treatment of his fellow servants (Mt 18:23-32); the servants who attempt to collect payment from tenant farmers (Mt 21:34-36); the servants dispatched to invite guests to the

---

[9] *TDNT*, 261-264; *NIDNTT*, 592-593.
[10] Ibid., 264-265.

wedding banquet of their master's son (Mt 22:3-10); the servant responsible to manage the household during his master's absence (Mt 24:45-50); and the servants entrusted by their master with talents to multiply on his behalf (Mt 25:14-30). Although they belong to their master, and owe him unquestioned obedience (Mt 8:9) and exclusive allegiance (Mt 6:24), with no expectation of reward for their service (Lk 17:7-10), there is no thought of slaves as a degraded lower class of people devoid of inherent value.[11]

The class distinctions between slaves and freedmen (1 Cor 7:20-24; 9:19; 12:13; Gal 3:28; Col 3:11) and between slaves and sons/heirs (Gal 4:1, 21-31) are assumed in Paul's epistles. The apostle addresses the slave-lord relationship in the ethical sections of several of his letters. He commands believing slaves to obey their masters with respect and sincerity (Eph 6:5-6), and believing masters to treat their slaves with kind consideration (6:9a). In both cases the institution of slavery, which is never commended, is transcended by the new position in Christ. Paul views the social setting as the context for Christian masters and slaves to live out their religious convictions (6:7-8, 9b; Col 3:22-4:1; 1 Tim 6:1-3; Tit 2:9-10). Peter goes further and implores believing slaves to obey even harsh masters, for in so doing they imitate their Lord who suffered unjustly and so invite God's commendation (1 Pet 2:18-23). Paul appeals to Philemon to forgive and receive back his runaway slave, Onesimus, who had escaped to Rome and subsequently been led to Christ by Paul. The basis for the appeal is Onesimus' new standing in Christ, so that Philemon should regard him no longer as a slave, but as a beloved brother (Phm 16).[12] Once Paul raises the possibility of slaves gaining their freedom, which they should pursue if the opportunity arises (1 Cor 7:21).[13] What is striking is that the apostles show no interest in mobilizing political support to overthrow what was obviously an unjust social institution. Their policy could be called one of 'respectful subversion' of the institution by calling believers, both slave and free, to view themselves and others from their new vantage

[11] Joachim Jeremias, *Jerusalem in the Time of Jesus*, transl. F. H. and C. H. Cave, 3rd ed., (London: SCM, 1969): 110-111, 312-316, describes slavery, both Gentile and Jewish, as it existed in Palestine in the time of Jesus.
[12] It is unclear whether Paul is requesting that Philemon restore Onesimus without punishment to his former social standing as a slave, yet now regarded as more than that, a brother in Christ, or is asking Philemon to release Onesimus from his slavery. James D. G. Dunn, *The Epistles to Colossians and to Philemon*, NIGTC (Grand Rapids: Eerdmans, 1996): 333-336, rightly concludes that whether the request is for forgiveness or manumission, the new standing of Onesimus as a brother "in the Lord" should govern Philemon's attitude toward him.
[13] The Greek of the apodosis of 1 Cor 7:21b, which follows the condition (protasis), "but if you indeed (ἀλλ εἰ καὶ) are able to become free," reads literally "rather make use of" (μαλλον χρησαι). Most English versions render this with the sense of the Amplified Bible: "avail yourself of the opportunity (to become free)" (see KJV, NASB, NIV). Alternatively, the protasis could be taken concessively, "even if you can gain your freedom;" the apodosis would then read: "make use of your present condition (i.e. to promote the gospel while remaining a slave) now more than ever" (NRSV). The former rendering seems to this writer the more natural sense of the Greek text, while the latter perhaps has a slightly stronger contextual fit where Paul is urging both believing slaves and freedmen to live out their Christian faith in their present life context (1 Cor 7:17-24). For a full discussion, see Anthony C. Thiselton, *The First Epistle to the Corinthians*, NIGTC (Grand Rapids: Eerdmans, 2000): 553-559.

point as fellow members of the body of Christ and brothers in the family of God (Gal 3:28; Col 3:11).

The approach of Paul to the institution of slavery emerges out of his theological conviction that there is a deeper and darker dimension to slavery that encompasses all people regardless of social class. This kind of slavery has eternal consequences, unlike social slavery whose domain is temporal and provisional. All people are under the suffocating authority of sin (Rom 3:9). The Greek ideal of human autonomy is nothing more than a mythological construct, for all people are in one of two binding relational fields: (1) slavery to the controlling and condemning power of sin and exclusion from the redeeming grace of God, or (2) freedom from sin's power and subjection to the righteous rule of the Lord Jesus Christ (Rom 6:16-18, 20-22). Paul apologizes, as it were, for using the metaphor of slavery to describe Christian submission to the lordship of Christ, for the former denotes deprivation that is certainly not true of the latter (6:19a; cf. Rom 8:15a). Christ's vicarious death on the cross secured redemption, that is, the purchase of the slave's freedom through payment of the required ransom (Gal 3:13; 4:5; Rom 3:24; 1 Cor 1:30; Eph 1:7; Col 1:14; 1 Tim 2:6; Tit 2:14; cf. Heb 9:12, 15; 1 Pet 1:18-19).[14] The result is that redeemed believers are the possession of their Lord and offer to him willing service and wholehearted obedience (Rom 6:17-19; 1 Cor 6:19-20). When the believer is thus called δουλος (or δουλοι [pl.]) it is best to translate "servant(s)" rather than "slave(s)," for the entire personality is now a voluntary rather than compulsory participant in the act of obedience (1 Cor 7:22-23; Eph 6:6-7). This is especially clear in Paul's employment of the active verb "serve" (δουλευω) where God (1 Thess 1:9), the Lord Jesus Christ (Rom 12:11; 14:18; 16:18; Eph 6:7; Col 3:24), the gospel (Php 2:22), and other believers (Gal 5:13) are the intentional objects of the service rendered. The theological framework of the gospel, then, provides the basis for the transformation of a term of degradation, "slave (of man, sin, the law)" to a badge of honor, "servant of God."

2. Jesus, the model servant: We have already noted that Jesus repeatedly used the analogy of the household slave who actively promotes the interest of the master. This was designed to teach his disciples about their responsibility to use all of the resources given them to faithfully promote the kingdom of their Lord (Mt 24:45-51; Lk 12:35-48; 17:7-10; 19:12-27).

The Lord Jesus took the slave metaphor and then extended its significance to a new arena, the relationship of his followers to one another. He began by setting them an example of what servanthood in the new covenant would involve, an application of the metaphor without precedent in the Old Testament.[15] During

---

[14] Leon Morris, *The Apostolic Preaching of the Cross*, 3rd ed. (London: Tyndale, 1965): 39-59, provides a detailed exposition of the language of redemption contained in these crucial texts.

[15] The closest the Old Testament comes to the idea of one who is in authority acting as a servant to others is when King Rehoboam is told by his advisers: "If today you will be a servant to these people (i.e. the northern tribes who suffered hardship under Solomon) and serve them and give them a favorable answer, they will always be your servants" (1 Kg 12:7, NIV). His subsequent actions made the offer only an unfulfilled hypothesis and proved the self-destructive nature of autocratic leadership (1 Kg 12:8-19).

that last meal with his disciples on Thursday night, the Lord arose from the table, removed his tunic, wrapped himself with a towel, filled the basin with water, and began to wash his disciples' feet one by one, drying them with the towel (Jn 13:4-5). This was a lowly act performed only by non-Jewish slaves in a Jewish household.[16] Jesus pressed the application to his stunned disciples: just as I have acted as a slave to serve you, so you must do to one another (Jn 13:15-17). Jesus spoke of their bound duty to imitate him as a slave would one's master (13:16).

Later that same evening in his extended farewell discourse to them, Jesus reminds them that their allegiance to him as Lord, like a slave to a master, will invite for them the same treatment that he receives (Jn 15:20-21). Jesus admits the slave analogy is an imperfect one by affirming that he considers them friends not slaves (Jn 15:15; cf. Rom 6:19a). First century slavery meant to perform one's appointed duties without questioning their necessity or requesting their rationale (Mt 8:9). The context of service was one of obligation not relationship. Jesus, however, invited his followers to intimate communion with him, and invited them to participate in the mission of extending the Father's kingdom, which he has openly communicated to them. The δουλος of the new covenant, then, offers absolute allegiance to one Lord, enjoys personal intimacy with one's Master-Friend, and willingly carries out menial tasks for the benefit of one's fellow servants. In this case, imitation becomes the sincerest form of worship.

The horizontal dimension of service in the new covenant is central to a second set of terms attested in Jesus' teaching: διακονος (servant), διακονια (service), and διακονεω (to serve). The original meaning of this word group is serving others during a meal ("table-waiting").[17] Though the Greeks disdained such lowly service, Jesus once again turns a concept of disrespect into an ethic of noble opportunity. Their Lord is like the master who when he returns from a long absence reverses the customary role and serves a meal to his reclining servants (Lk 12:37). The disciples' oriental hierarchy of greatness esteems the one who sits at the table and enjoys the lavish meal prepared by another (cf. Lk 17:7-8), "but I am among you as one who waits at the table" (Lk 22:27). The two terms δουλος and διακονος thus complement one another. The δουλος has offered the entire life to promote the welfare of one's Lord; the διακονος, in humility and love, expresses that surrender by pursuing the welfare of one's fellow servants. This involves adopting countercultural values and assuming the less esteemed positions in order to cede prominence to others (Mk 9:35; Mt 20:26/Mk 10:43; Mt 23:11; Lk 22:26).[18]

---

[16] *TDNT*, II: 271, 277.

[17] Ibid., II: 82-83.

[18] Several other Greek terms for domestic or personal servant in the New Testament should be noted, each of which also occurs in the LXX to render the Hebrew עֶבֶד: (1) ὑπηρετης occurs 20 times in the NT, frequently of an assistant or servant to a superior (Mt 26:58; Lk 4:20; Jn 18:3; Acts 13:5; cf. LXX: Prov 14:35). It refers to Paul as the Lord's servant in Acts 26:16; 1 Cor 4:1 (cf. Lk 1:2). (2) οἰκετης (Lk 16:13; Acts 10:7; 1 Pet 2:18; cf. LXX: Gen 9:25-26; 44:16; 50:18) and οἰκετεια (Mt

3. Paul, servant of Christ: Though his heart had been liberated from the yoke of the law and released from the grip of sin, the apostle Paul delighted to call himself the "servant of Christ" (Rom 1:1; Gal 1:10; Php 1:1) and "servant of God" (Tit 1:1). Despite the fact that δοῦλος meant bond-slave, in Paul's case the service of his Lord was one of voluntary surrender to the divine agenda. Like the slave who chose to remain in the lifelong service of a kind master (Ex 21:5-6; Deut 15:16-17), Paul was the "redeemed servant" (1 Cor 6:20; 7:22-23) who chose to relinquish his rights to a loving family and a lucrative career so that his Lord's name might be magnified among the Gentiles (1 Cor 9:19-23). As the Lord's "servant," Paul stands in solidarity with the other great figures like Moses and David who fill the record of redemptive history.[19] Those who participate with him in sacrificial dedication to church pioneering work, like Timothy (Php 1:1; cf. 2 Tim 2:24), Tychicus (Col 4:7), and Epaphras in Colosse (Col 1:7; 4:12), he honors with the title "servant (or fellow servant) of Christ." He and those of his mission team stand as servants who honor Jesus by dedicating their energies to edify rather than lord it over his church (2 Cor 4:5).

    Paul employs several other terms that complement the foundational term δοῦλος and disclose his self-understanding as a servant-leader.

    (i)   διάκονος: The word that originally meant "table-waiter" is Paul's term of choice when he wants to emphasize the calling to serve the people of God. Paul attaches this noble designation to his associates who proclaim the gospel and build up the church, one that accents loving service: Phoebe (Rom 16:1); Apollos (1 Cor 3:5); Tychicus (Eph 6:21; Col 4:7); Epaphras (Col 1:7); Timothy (1 Tim 4:6). This becomes the technical term for the secondary level of church leadership that cares for the practical needs of the members, that is, the deacons (Php 1:1; 1 Tim 3:8, 12). When Paul uses this term of himself, it speaks of the governing values of dependency (2 Cor 3:6), sacrifice and hardship (2 Cor 6:4; 11:23), and thanksgiving for the privilege of assisting the spread of the gospel and the growth of the church (Eph 3:7; Col 1:23, 25).

    (ii) ὑπηρέτης: This term originally meant a rower or galley slave.[20] In the New Testament it refers to an assistant who carries out the tasks assigned by a higher authority: the attendants in the courtyard of the high priest

---

24:45) mean the "household slave" that can be appointed to manage the affairs of the master's household. In Rom 14:4 Paul uses the term for a fellow believer who is accountable as a servant to one Lord. (3) θεράπων (Heb 3:5; cf. LXX of Moses: Ex 4:10; 14:31; Num 12:7-8) and θεραπεία (Lk 12:42) also refer to the "household slave." (4) παῖς occurs 24 times in the NT and can be a generic term for children or adolescents (Mt 2:16; 17:18; 21:15), or as an equivalent to δοῦλος meaning a household slave (Lk 12:45; 15:26).

[19] The New Testament refers to leading figures of the old covenant era (Moses [Rev 15:3]; the prophets [Rev 10:7; 11:8]) and the new covenant era (Mary [Lk 1:38, 48]; Simeon [Lk 2:29]; James the brother of the Lord [Jas 1:1]; Peter [2 Pet 1:1]; Jude [1:1]; John the apostle [Rev 1:1]) by the term δοῦλος (or the feminine form δούλη), in continuity with its Hebrew ancestor, עֶבֶד (see f.n. 3). Other terms to designate these servants include (1) παῖς (Israel [Lk 1:54]; David [Lk 1:69; Acts 4:25]; Jesus [Mt 12:18; Acts 3:13, 26; 4:27, 30]) and (2) θεράπων (Moses [Heb 3:5]).

[20] *EDNT*, 3: 400.

(Mt 26:58); the temple guards to the Jewish ruling council (Jn 7:32, 45, 46); the disciples to Jesus (Jn 18:33); John Mark to Barnabas and Paul (Acts 13:5). In the prologue to his first volume Luke employs this term to designate the apostles as "servants of the word," that is, witnesses who stand under the authority of the revealed truth about Jesus and proclaim his death and resurrection (Lk 1:2). When Paul stands before Agrippa II he relates the words of the Lord's commission to him: "I have appeared to you to appoint you as a servant (ὑπηρετης) and as a witness of what you have seen of me and what I will show you" (Acts 26:16). The Lord directly assigns Paul the task of proclaiming to the Gentiles the forgiveness of sins through Jesus' name (Acts 26:17; cf. 9:15-16). The background of this language is Isaiah's prophecy of a servant who will bring salvation to the ends of the earth (42:1, 6-7; 49:6b). From the outset of his commission Paul is designated as one who must suffer in order to witness to the Servant-Lord whose image he bears (Acts 9:16; cf. Gal 6:17; 2 Cor 1:5; 4:10-11; Php 3:10). In a representative and testimonial sense, then, Paul takes on the role of the Isaianic servant.

Paul uses the term ὑπηρετης as a self-designation once in his letters (1 Cor 4:1). Significantly he combines this term, which originally meant the lowest of slaves, a rower in the galley of a Roman ship, with another term, ὀικονομος, which signified the servant appointed as steward or manager of his lord's estate (cf. Lk 12:42; 16:1, 3, 8).[21] Servant-leadership for Paul means humble status and privileged stewardship. To one of lowly position has been committed a sacred trust, namely, to plant churches among the Gentiles on the foundation of the gospel of Christ crucified. The criterion of faithfulness will determine whether his service receives the divine approval (1 Cor 4:2-5).

(iii) ὀικετης: This is the simplest term for the "household slave," one who is bound to obedience to one master (Lk 16:13; Acts 10:7; 1 Pet 2:18). Paul applies this metaphor to the relationships in the church: each believer is a "servant" whose personal standards on external matters will be assessed by the Lord (Rom 14:4). To judge one's brother, as the Roman Christians were doing, is to interfere in the line of accountability that runs solely from servant to Lord. Paul clearly places himself under this image of a "household slave" when he joins himself to other believers ("each of us") as one who will render an account of his works at the judgment seat of Christ (Rom 14:12).

(iv) λειτουργος: This word, which in its Hellenistic setting referred to fulfilling one's public duties such as paying taxes or performing political service, was transformed in the Septuagint into a term for the service of priests and Levites in the temple (cf. Neh 10:39; Isa 61:6).[22] Paul employs this term of his apostolic ministry under the image of a priestly servant who brings to God acceptable and consecrated offerings, in this case the

---

[21] *EDNT*, 2: 498-500.
[22] Ibid., 2: 348-349.

Gentile believers who have been obedient to the gospel (Rom 15:16). This is particularly significant since Paul is on the verge of delivering the funds collected from the Gentile churches for the relief of the Jerusalem saints (Rom 15:25-27, 30-31). Leaders appointed by the churches to handle those funds will travel with him to the holy city in this final act of his eastern Mediterranean ministry (Acts 20:4; Rom 15:23, 28). It is very possible that Paul views his ministry in Jerusalem as the eschatological fulfillment of Isaiah 66:19-20 where the prophet anticipates a day when God's glory will be universally proclaimed and redeemed people from all nations stream to Jerusalem to offer worship to the Lord. The inestimable dignity of being granted such a vocation moves Paul to exult in his service to God (15:17).[23]

To summarize, Paul frames his leadership of the Gentile churches within the language of servanthood: submission to one Lord (δουλος); sacrifice and hardship for the sake of others (διακονος); suffering as a witness to the greater Servant (ὑπηρετης); accountability to faithfully carry out his mission (οἰκετης); and the priestly offering of worship to God (λειτουργος). Here is the multi-faceted self-portrait of Paul, the servant-leader.

4. The imitation of Christ Jesus (Php 2:5-11): The dignity with which the New Testament clothes the Greek term for slave, δουλος, reaches a climax in its stunning application to the incarnation of the Son of God in Philippians 2:7. The poetic masterpiece in which this text is situated is one of a number of primitive christological hymns (Eph 5:14; Col 1:15-20; 1 Tim 3:16; 2 Tim 2:11-13; Tit 3:4-7) or confessions (Rom 1:3-4; 4:24-25; 10:9; 1 Cor 12:3; 15:3-8) that Paul inserted into his letters. Such passages are a powerful testimony to the early church's worship of Christ as Lord, its faith directed toward the exalted Jesus as one standing alongside God the Father as co-recipient of praise and adoration (2:9-11).

The poem proper (2:6-11) supports Paul's injunction for the believers to adopt the mindset of Christ Jesus (2:5).[24] The flow of the argument in the preceding and subsequent contexts forcefully supports an ethical understanding of this passage, that is, Paul describes the attitude of the preincarnate Christ as the supreme example of self-sacrificing humility that he wants these believers to inculcate in their relationships with one another. Philippians 1:27-30 can be seen as a literary unit under the theme, "conduct worthy of the gospel."[25] Even under external threat of persecution, the Philippians must contend for the progress of the gospel (1:27-30). The manifold benefits of their standing in Christ are the requisite motivation behind such unity of purpose (2:1-2). In order to realize unity, an attitude of mutual humility, which places others' needs above one's own, is paramount (2:3-4). As an example of such humility there stands Christ, who for a time surrendered the exercise of his divine prerogatives in order to die for mankind on the

---

[23] The conjunction οὖν (Rom 15:17) makes his joyful exultation consequent upon the priestly (or levitical) service he is privileged to render (15:15-16).
[24] The need to supply some verbal form to the elliptical ὁ καὶ ἐν Χριστῷ accounts for the wide variety of possible translations.
[25] Moises Silva, *Philippians*, WEC (Chicago: Moody, 1988): 16-17, 89-90, 153-154.

cross (2:5-8), and was consequently exalted by God (2:9-11). Three leaders who have emulated Christ and provide further models of the servant's sacrificial humility are Paul (2:17-18), Timothy (2:19-24) and Epaphroditus (2:25-30). Throughout the letter to the Philippians unity is a central concern, for persecution from the secular authorities (1:27-30), external pressure from false teachers (3:1-2, 15, 18-19), and internal dissension between two influential women (4:2) together threaten to sever the believers' bonds of loyalty. Paul's message is that the preservation of unity depends on moral courage and a humble spirit, the latter exemplified by Christ.

The hymn proper begins by describing the preexistent Christ as existing "in the form of God." Whether the Greek term rendered "form" means nature, essence, condition, mode status, or glory,[26] this prepositional phrase is further qualified and explained by the following expression "to be equal with God."[27] Further, the same term is used later in the contrastive phrase, Christ took "the form of a servant" (v. 7). These two contextual factors indicate that Christ's mindset in his preexistent state as God the Son is the setting for his self-abnegation. Just as he actually became a servant, so he actually possessed deity.[28] What is meant by Christ's decision to "not consider" his equality with God as "something to be grasped" (NIV)? Again, the interpretive proposals are vast and varied.[29]

The following two finite verbs, "he made himself nothing" (v. 7)[30] and "he humbled himself" (v. 8), however, can be seen as the positive counterparts to the negative statement in v. 6. To put it together, Christ refused to act selfishly, to misuse his divine prerogatives, to clutch at his preexistent glory (2:6); on the contrary, he made himself nothing, as it were, by becoming a man, a servant, a sacrifice (2:7-8).

The humility of Christ is enacted in two descending levels.[31] First, the

---

[26] Ralph P. Martin, *Carmen Christi. Philippians 2:5-11 In recent interpretation and in the setting of the early Christian worship* (Grand Rapids: Eerdmans, 1983): 99-133, gives an extended survey of proposals for the background of the term μορφη. The three major views are its classical sense of essence (roughly equivalent to οὐσια), various religionsgeschichtliche parallels such as Kasemann's "mode of being" (Daseinsweise), or the LXX usage, which equates μορφη with δοξα (and perhaps εἰκων), so that Christ possessed the visible divine glory that manifested his oneness with the essential being of God the Father (cf. Jn 17:5).

[27] In the expression το εἰναι ἰσα θεω the definite article το is taken as an anaphoric article, that is, to denote previous reference: "the (previously referred to—as being in the form of God) being equal with God."

[28] L. D. Hurst, "Re-enter the Pre-existent Christ in Philippians 2:5-11?," *New Testament Studies* 32:3 (1986): 449-457, has leveled seven telling criticisms of the attempt of scholars to interpret the details of the hymn as referring exclusively to the human being, Jesus of Nazareth, with no thought of preexistence.

[29] Silva, *Philippians*, 117, provides a helpful chart of the array of choices one has in rendering ἁρπαγμος in its present context, a term which occurs only here in the Greek Bible.

[30] Kenotic theologians have traditionally been guilty of reading too much into the verb κενοω, which in Paul simply means to nullify, to render void, to make of no effect (Rom 4:14; 1 Cor 1:17; 9:15; 2 Cor 9:3).

[31] The two verbs in 2:7-8, ἐκενωσεν and ἐταπεινωσεν, are each modified by two aorist participles. The transition between the two stages of descent is marked by και (v. 7b). The third participial phrase, σχηματι εὑρεθεις ὡς ἀνθρωπος, summarizes the previous thought and introduces the second main verb, ἐταπεινωσεν.

preexistent Christ made himself nothing by becoming a man and a servant (δοῦλος). There is no emptying of divine attributes, but rather an assumption of humanity and servanthood (2:7). Second, the incarnate Christ then humbled himself, demonstrating the full extent of obedience to his Father by dying on the cross (2:8). The lowest point in the descent is now reached. From the prerogatives of deity to the abasement of a shameful death Christ voluntarily passed.

Why did Paul choose the term δοῦλος for Christ's role in the incarnation? First, as the word for a common slave it denotes one who is without rights, advantages or privileges, though in the case of Christ it is a state willingly assumed for the sake of others.[32] Second, the term sets the stage for its counterpart, "Lord," to which status Jesus was exalted by the Father as a result of his obedience (2:11). Third, we believe that Paul uses a term that can be applied both to Christ and to believers, as he often does, to underscore the imitational solidarity of the servants with the Servant.[33] If you aspire to be a true servant of God and of your brothers in Christ, Paul is saying, here is the paradigm of servanthood against which you should measure yourself.[34] Fourth, the concept of the Servant's humiliation is matched by the exaltation of Jesus to lordship (2:9-11). The ethical purpose of the hymn carries with it the implication that believers, in imitation of their Lord, will be rewarded and vindicated for voluntarily yielding their rights as he did (cf. Mt 16:24-27; 18:3-4; Mk 8:34-35; 10:28-31).

To conclude our study of the servant language of the Bible, the Old Testament sets the stage by taking the Hebrew term for slave, עֶבֶד, and transforming it into a designation for the person who is granted the inestimable privilege of leading the covenant people to live according their holy calling, namely, "servant (of the Lord)." The New Testament raises the dignity of the term one level further by assigning its Greek equivalent, δοῦλος, as the term of signification for the Lord Jesus Christ, the fulfillment of Isaiah's portrait of the suffering Servant. As the servant par excellence, he takes the place of a common slave and sacrifices himself for the welfare of his people. New covenant servant-leaders learn, by imitating their servant-Lord, to abandon their own agendas and preferences in order to seek the good of their fellow servants (Jn 13:13-17). Through such imitation they become servants of the great Servant.

[32] Gordon D. Fee, *Paul's Letter to the Philippians*, NICNT (Grand Rapids: Eerdmans, 1995): 212-213.
[33] It must remain an open question whether or not the Isaianic suffering Servant is in the background of Philippians 2:7. We have shown above (f.n. 7) that while παῖς is the normal rendering for עֶבֶד in Isaiah's servant songs, δοῦλος (or its cognates) is employed in Isa 48:20; 49:3, 5, 7; 53:11. We suggest that Paul employs δοῦλος at least in part because it captures that dimension of the humiliation of Christ which believers can and must imitate, namely, sacrificing their own rights for the sake of others.
[34] Gerald F. Hawthorne, *Philippians*, WBC (Waco, TX: Word, 1983): 78-79, points out the impressive parallels between Jn 13:3-17 and Php 2:6-11. This suggests that Jesus' striking act of condescension in washing the disciples' feet may well have informed the language of the hymn. In addition to the flow of the argument, as traced above, the terminological links with the surrounding context point to the ethical purpose Paul had in mind in quoting the hymn: φρονεω (2:2, 5; cf. 2:3, ταπεινοφροσυνη); ἡγεομαι (2:3, 6); κενοω (2:7) and κενοδοξια (2:3); σχημα (2:7) and ταπεινοω (2:8; cf. 4:12) with μετασχηματιζω (3:21) and ταπεινωσις (3:21) respectively; ὑπηκοος (2:8) and ὑπακουω (2:12). The very words of the hymn link Christ's attitudes and actions to what Paul elsewhere predicates of believers.

PART TWO

Old Testament Profiles
in Leadership

Chapter 3.
Joseph: Character refined through suffering

Preliminary questions to consider:
1. *How is one's leadership authenticated and what is the true measure of a leader's success?*
2. *What preparations can leaders make that will enable them to resist temptations to compromise their integrity?*
3. *What conviction(s) will nurture a leader's vision for the future in the midst of harsh circumstances that might otherwise create a sense of victimization?*

Preparation through hardship (Gen 37:2-38:30)

The first member of the patriarchal family to assume a leadership role of major proportions is Joseph, the eleventh son of Jacob and first by his beloved Rachel (Gen 30:22-24). He is introduced as a seventeen-year-old tattletale who brings reports to his father about his brothers' unsavory actions (37:2). Jacob unwisely favors Joseph, seen in the richly ornamented robe he makes for him, which deepens the bitterness the older sons harbor against their half-brother (37:3-4). This jealousy grows into murderous hatred when Joseph relates to his brothers two dreams that presage his exaltation and their humiliation. Though he rebukes his son (37:10), Jacob is hesitant to reject the dreams outright (37:11b), for his own transforming encounter with Yahweh came in a dream years earlier at Bethel (Gen 28:10-22). Joseph's immaturity, Jacob's partiality, and the brothers' hostility become the instruments in God's hand to orchestrate his redemptive purposes.

Joseph is sent by his father to check on his brothers who are tending their father's flocks near Dothan. Their plot to murder Joseph is prevented only by Reuben's plea, perhaps an attempt to regain his father's favor after being discredited for his incestuous act with Bilhah (Gen 35:22). Ishmaelite traders purchase the boy for twenty shekels of silver and take him to Egypt where he is sold as a slave for the household of Potiphar, a royal official of the Pharaoh (37:36).[1] Joseph's life shifts from favored son in the land of promise to destitute slave in a foreign land. The focus of the unfolding narrative will be not on Joseph's inner struggles, but on his stunning rise to prominence, despite repeated setbacks, according to the unconquerable divine plan.

The grave danger of the covenant family being amalgamated, by intermarriage, into Canaanite culture is underscored in the Judah-Tamar incident of Chapter 38. Judah's forfeiture of covenant values is proved by his shocking behavior: intermarriage with a Canaanite woman (38:2); nurture of wicked sons who imitate their father's selfishness (38:7, 10); sexual engagement with an apparent prostitute

---

[1] The Hebrew word translated "guard" (טַבָּח) in Gen 37:36 (NIV) can mean either executioner or cook. Thus Potiphar was either in charge of the royal prisoners or he was the chief cook. See *TDOT*, V: 284.

22

(38:16, 21); acceptance of shrine prostitution (38:21); lying to Tamar about her prospects of marrying Shelah (38:11, 14, 26); brazen hypocrisy and cruelty upon the discovery of Tamar's pregnancy (38:24). The sin of the Amorites was filling up (Gen 15:16) and rapidly pulling the chosen race into its vortex. With Judah joining Simeon and Levi (Gen 34) and Reuben (35:22) as discredited leaders, God would now raise up Joseph in order to transfer the covenant family to segregationist Egypt, where their identity could be preserved and their numbers increased (Gen 43:32; 46:34).

Integrity tested in Potiphar's house and the king's prison (Gen 39:1-41:40)

When the narrative returns to Joseph we find him serving in Potiphar's household with distinction. He is twice promoted: (1) from indoor slave to personal attendant (39:2-4a); then (2) to steward of the household where he managed Potiphar's entire estate (39:4b-6a). Potiphar's implicit trust in Joseph to direct his affairs (39:6a) may well hint at the latter's personal integrity as well as administrative skills. The text, however, explicitly attributes Joseph's success in leadership not to latent talent or personal charisma, but to the divine blessing. "The Lord was with Joseph" is the refrain of explanation behind Joseph's prosperity (39:2, 21, 23).

Joseph's vocational success, however, does not render him immune from moral temptation. Rather it provides the setting for exposure to it. His manly physique and handsome features attract the unwanted attention of Potiphar's wife, whose repeated attempts to seduce Joseph end in frustration. In the white-hot moment of temptation Joseph is protected by, first, his deep sense of stewardship to Potiphar (39:8-9a) and, second, his accountability before a holy God (39:9b). His character is tested and refined, strongly contrasting with Judah's failure. With his refusal to compromise, Joseph must bear the hatred of the spurned woman who falsely accuses Joseph of attempted rape (39:16-18). Once again Joseph's destiny seems to be manipulated by human evil and he ends up in prison.

God's covenant loyalty and unmerited favor (39:21) sustain Joseph and ensure his success.[2] He gains the complete trust of the warden (39:23), as he did with Potiphar, who places him in charge of the other prisoners. The narrative highlights God's sovereign disposition of the events of those prison years: Joseph's favor with the warden (39:21-23); the two dreams of the cupbearer and the baker, the interpretations and fulfillments of which belong to God (40:8); the cupbearer's failure to remember Joseph for two years, then his sudden recollection (40:14, 23; 41:9); Pharaoh's dreams in the intervening years and their interpretation (41:16, 25, 28, 32). Joseph is vindicated before Pharaoh as a man "in whom is the spirit of the gods" (41:38).[3] Joseph, like Daniel later, is elevated above the wise men of the

---

[2] These two Hebrew terms, חֶסֶד and חֵן, are of major import in the OT and refer, in this context, to the loyal love shown Joseph as an instrument of God's covenant purposes and the gracious favor God grants him in the eyes of the warden to accomplish those purposes. See *TDOT*, V: 24-25, 54-57.

[3] This is Pharaoh's way of describing a person with supernatural insight that transcends mortal limits. The Babylonian kings Nebuchadnezzar (Dan 4:8, 9, 18) and Belshazzar (Dan 5:14) ascribe the same powers to Daniel when they confess that "the spirit of the (holy) gods" is in him. Alternatively, the rendering could be "the Spirit of God," in which case Pharaoh, in a kind of *sensus plenior*, utters a deeper theological truth beyond his comprehension (cf. Num 27:18; Deut 34:9).

land and moves from interpreter to chief adviser, second-in-command to Pharaoh (41:39-43). Joseph, now thirty years old, has moved in the space of thirteen years from slave to household steward (39:6a), from prisoner to prison manager (39:23), and now to vice regent of Egypt (41:40).[4] Such a stunning reversal of fortune and meteoric rise to prominence could ruin a young leader, but in the case of Joseph his sufferings have nurtured a meek spirit. He will prove a worthy leader who acts for the welfare of his subjects. "The vale of tears has proved to be the valley of soul making."[5]

Discernment and tenderness as Vizier of Egypt (Gen 41:41-47:26)

Vast, sweeping powers are given to Joseph as minister of internal affairs, including management of the budget and taxation. This "discerning and wise" leader (41:33, 39)[6] carries out the bold yet painful program of taxing and storing 20% of the harvest produced in the seven years of abundance (41:46-52), and the strict rationing of grain that follows during the seven years of famine (41:53-57). In the early years two sons are born to Joseph, whose names capture his theocentric interpretation of the setbacks and successes of his Egyptian sojourn: Manasseh, "God has made me forget all my trouble and all my father's household," and Ephraim, "God has made me fruitful in the land of my suffering" (41:50-52). In the birth of his sons Joseph celebrates the goodness of God. The torments of the past, especially his brothers' betrayal, have released their grip on his heart.

Joseph's discerning policy to store and ration earlier harvests brings provision for the surrounding nations as well (41:57) and draws the sons of Jacob to purchase grain for their starving family. The first two journeys of his brothers to Egypt are given extensive coverage. They reveal a leader who balances shrewdness with sensitivity, toughness with tenderness. Five times the narrative records the weeping of the vice regent of Egypt (42:24; 43:30; 45:2; 45:14-15; 46:29). On the first visit (42:1-38) Joseph shows special interest in the youngest son left behind, his own full brother Benjamin (42:15, 16, 20, 34). He weeps in private, takes Simeon hostage, demands Benjamin as ransom, and secretly returns their silver. On their return visit (43:1-45:28) Joseph asks about their father (43:27) and shows special favor toward Benjamin (43:29-30, 34). In the silver cup deception the brothers are reduced to desperation (44:1-15), but Judah's intercession, which stresses Jacob's special tie to the sons of Rachel, one taken away and one remaining (44:16-34), breaks Joseph's resolve to maintain secrecy. In an outburst of tears Joseph reveals himself to his brothers who are at first terrified at the revelation (45:1-3), but then reassured that his intentions are reconciliation not revenge. His unconditional offer of forgiveness toward his brothers is grounded in the profound

---

[4] Joseph's birth is dated 1915 B.C (Gen 30:22-24). He is sold into slavery at age seventeen (37:2; 1898 B.C.) and becomes Vizier of Egypt at the age of thirty (41:46; 1885 B.C.). He dies at the age of 110 (50:22; 1805 B.C.).

[5] Gordon J. Wenham, *Genesis 16-50*, WBC (Dallas, TX: Word, 1994): 399.

[6] These two terms, נָבוֹן and חָכָם, appear together a number of times in the Old Testament (Deut 4:6; Prov 10:13; 14:33; 16:21; Hos 14:10). In this context they refer to the ability to perceive the problem ahead and to envision a solution (discernment), and the ability to implement the solution (wisdom or applied knowledge) respectively.

conviction that God has superintended the affairs of his life to accomplish the deliverance of the covenant family (45:4-9). Joseph manifests a remarkable capacity, especially for one in a place of leadership, not to be victimized by a troubled past. He refuses to exploit his position of authority to redress grievances against former offenders.

With the migration of Jacob and his family to Egypt, the covenant nation is preserved both from moral corruption and from starvation and so begins to prosper (47:27). As with Potiphar (39:6) and the prison warden (39:23), Joseph has gained the complete trust of Pharaoh who grants his family freedom to settle in Goshen and to pursue their vocation of shepherding livestock (47:1-12). With requisite skill Joseph manages the economy of Egypt during the famine years and expands Pharaoh's ownership of currency, land, livestock, and people (47:13-26).

Keeper of the Covenant (Gen 47:27-50:26)

Though his entire adult life (age 17 until his death at 110) is spent in a pagan land and he serves in the upper echelons of leadership in a secular government, Joseph maintains his spiritual identity as a loyal son of Israel. First, Joseph swears to Jacob to bury his father in the land of promise (47:28-31), which he faithfully carries out (50:4-14). Second, he brings his sons Manasseh and Ephraim to their grandfather for the patriarchal blessing (Ch 48). Third, he receives Jacob's final benediction as the prince among his brothers (49:22-26). Fourth, he reassures his brothers that their present amnesty is no temporary measure to satisfy Jacob only to be reversed upon his death, but is a permanent settlement founded on his bedrock belief that "you intended to harm me, but God intended it for good" (50:19-20). Fifth, he predicts the future deliverance of the sons of Israel, in accordance with the patriarchal promises (50:24-25), and commands at such a time that his bones be deposited in the land of promise (50:25b). Joshua will one day bury Joseph's bones in Shechem in the heart of Canaan (Joshua 24:32).

Leadership profile of Joseph

1. *The presence of God: The biblical text has scant interest in the inner turmoils Joseph faced in the betrayal of his brothers, the slanderous attack on his integrity by Potiphar's wife, or the languishing years in prison. Genesis is no psychodrama, but a record of the steady progress of God's redemptive program. What the record stresses is the triumph of Joseph at every turn. His repeated promotions and success is attributed not to strength of will or superiority of intellect, but to the divine favor. "The Lord was with Joseph" was the sine qua non of his success as leader.*

2. *Integrity before God and man: A defining moment for Joseph came when he was alone with the beautiful wife of Potiphar. The sexual act would have been consensual and the brief pleasure intense. But Joseph knew that the long-term consequences would be disastrous: a spoiled stewardship of his master, a violated conscience, and, above all, an offended and dishonored God. The power of refusal lay in Joseph's ability to perceive that to indulge the present would be to sacrifice the future.*

25

3. *Confidence in God's sovereign grace:* Joseph proved resilient in setbacks, forgiving when wronged, and faithful in stewardships because of his profound belief in a God who was working through him to accomplish the deliverance of the chosen family (Gen 50:19-20).[7] The tiny slice of history he occupied was thus dignified with greater meaning beyond the immediate. Joseph's overwhelming sense of privilege and accountability ruled out the petty agendas, manipulative techniques, and controlling maneuvers so endemic to leadership patterns both past and present. He was thus free to act for the benefit of his masters and the welfare of his subjects.

---

[7] Did Joseph understand further that God's redemptive agenda for the nations was being worked out when he said, "to accomplish the saving of many lives" (v. 20b)? The climactic promise of universal blessing was given initially to Abraham (12:3; 15:1; 17:4, 16; 18:18; 22:18) and repeated to Isaac (26:4b) and to Jacob (28:14b; 35:11; 48:4). Joseph's final testamentary words affirm his connection to the three patriarchs (50:24-25).

Chapter 4.
Moses: Persevering advocate for a stubborn people

Preliminary questions to consider:
1. *Where does a leader's love for a difficult people find concrete expression?*
2. *What governing values enable a leader to fight off the natural desires for status and power?*
3. *If the opportunity of leadership brings with it a heightened accountability, how does this impact the leader's relationship with God and personal moral standards?*
4. *How does a leader learn to release one's present enjoyment of recognition and authority into the hands of a worthy successor?*

Prepared but not yet ready (Ex 1:1-2:25)

In the intervening years between Joseph's death and Moses' birth Israel grew from a family of seventy to an "exceedingly numerous" (1:7) people filling the land of Goshen (1:1-7).[1] Alarmed at their growth and worried over their independence, Pharaoh adopted draconian measures to eliminate the threat: (1) adults reduced to slave labor (1:11-14); (2) genocide by systematic destruction of new born boys, first by mid-wives then by all Egyptians (1:15-22). The strategy failed due to God's overruling (1:20-21).

Born of Levite parents, a Hebrew baby boy is hidden for three months (Heb 11:23), rescued along the Nile bank, and adopted by Pharaoh's daughter who names him Moses, the one she "drew out" of the water (2:1-10). The delivered one is to become the deliverer. Providence is quietly at work: "The omission of any reference to God in these verses is surely intentional."[2]

Raised like an oriental prince, "Moses was educated in all the wisdom of the Egyptians and was powerful in speech and action" (Acts 7:22). However, like Joseph, his secular environment failed to erase his true identity. At age 40 (Acts 7:23) Moses defends a persecuted Hebrew, "one of his own people" (2:11), killing the Egyptian oppressor. This decisive action is the "great forsaking" driven by faith (Heb 11:24-27). It reveals a courageous yet impulsive man, one who mistakenly reckoned the people even now would follow him to freedom (Acts 7:25). But neither he nor the people were ready.[3] One who is called and gifted to lead must first be tested and validated. The discovery of his act of murder forces

---

[1] There are approximately 280 years between the death of Joseph (1805 B.C.) and the birth of Moses (1526 B.C.). Moses' life is divided into three 40 year periods and his death at the age of 120 is dated 1406 B.C. The Exodus event is dated 1446 B.C.

[2] John I. Durham, *Exodus*, WBC (Waco, TX: Word, 1987): 17.

[3] The question from the eyewitness to his act of murder is full of irony: "Who made you ruler and judge over us?" (Ex 2:14a). The divine purpose and the divine timetable will ultimately converge, but not until the leader has been duly prepared. The covenant people must also be readied as followers.

him to escape Pharaoh's anger by fleeing to the desert of Midian (2:15). Here he will remain forty years until the age of 80 (Ex 7:7), long years of family building (2:15-22) and shepherding the flocks of Jethro (3:1). This extended period of forced obscurity tempers his excesses and prepares him to confront Pharaoh and to lead Israel. Both roles will require an abundance of patience. Meanwhile, back in Egypt the Israelites groaned and God "remembered his covenant with Abraham, with Isaac and with Jacob" (2:24).

Holy calling and initial reluctance (Ex 3:1-4:17)
In the familiar confines of the desert of Midian, at the not uncommon sight of a flaming thorn bush, Moses encounters the holy God (3:5), the God of the patriarchal promises (3:6), and the eternal, self-existent Yahweh (3:14-15). The vision of God is the prerequisite for the leader's self-understanding. The mission is clear: "I am sending you to Pharaoh to bring my people the Israelites out of Egypt" (3:10). Moses is incapacitated by fear, perhaps recalling his earlier rejection, and quickly protests. But God will not be worn down by a reluctant leader and meets each objection with special provision: (1) Insecurity—"Who am I?"—is met by the promise of his presence and a successful outcome (3:11-12); (2) Ignorance—"What shall I tell them?"—is countered by clarifying his name and by validating wonders (3:13-14, 20); (3) Skepticism—"What if they do not believe me or listen?"—is answered by three signs of confirmation (4:1-9); (4) Escapism—"Please send someone else to do it"—is accommodated by the provision of Aaron as his spokesman (4:10-17).

First exercise of leadership (Ex 4:18-7:7)
The assurances of the Lord prove superior to the forces of self-doubt and Moses resolves to return to Egypt (4:18-20). The initial steps are encouraging: Aaron agrees to accompany him, Moses performs authenticating signs, and the elders and people of Israel worship the Lord for his covenant mercies (4:27-31). The exercise of leadership, however, is rarely a straight line of progress. Moses' initial approach to Pharaoh is rebuffed. Pharaoh, in rejecting the Lord, passes even harsher measures against Israel—a full quota of bricks, but without a supply of straw. Moses' obedience has made Israel's plight worse and he experiences the first of many complaints against him by those he is appointed to lead (Ex 5:20-21). The always-transparent Moses spills out his disappointment with God in a series of why's (Ex 5:22-23). Leadership is producing a feeling of isolation and the Lord answers the prayer of complaint with a series of "I will"'s that encompass the full scope of his redemptive plan past, present and future (Ex 6:1-8).[4] Still, the lingering doubts about his gifting for the task remain: "I speak with faltering lips" (6:12, 30). The Lord reminds Moses that Aaron will speak for him. Further, the deliverance will rest with the Lord not with his servant (7:1-5). Moses moves forward in obedience (7:6).

---

[4] Seven verbs in the first person singular reiterate God's determination to fulfill the covenant promises to Israel: I will bring out, free, redeem, take, be (your God), bring to, give (Ex 6:6-8). Another series of "I will"'s follows in 7:3-5: harden, multiply, lay my hand on, bring out, stretch out, bring out.

Chapter 4. Moses: Persevering advocate for a stubborn people

Confrontation, obedience, and prayer (Ex 7:8-11:10)

By faith Moses overcomes his natural tendency to shy away from his appointed role and enters into a series of direct confrontations with the ruler of Egypt. As the ten plagues of water to blood, frogs, gnats, flies, death of livestock, boils, hail, locusts, darkness, and death of the firstborn are poured out upon Egypt, the cycle of judgment, desperation, relief, and the hardening of Pharaoh's heart is a monotonous one. During the first five plagues Pharaoh hardens his heart (7:13, 14, 22; 8:15, 19, 32; 9:7, 34-35), while God hardens Pharaoh in the latter plagues (4:21; 7:3; 9:12; 10:1, 20, 27; 11:10; 14:4, 8). What stands out in the narrative is, above all, the relentless obedience of Moses in the face of Pharaoh's broken promises of conditional release,[5] Pharaoh's hollow words of feigned remorse (8:8, 15; 9:27-28, 34; 10:16-17, 20), and his repeated hardenings. Moses resolutely refuses any offers of compromise and demands that all of Israel be released to worship and sacrifice to the Lord in the desert (8:26-27; 10:9; 10:25-26). Second, Moses has grown into a powerful intercessor before God (8:8, 12-13, 28-31; 9:28-33; 10:17-19). "And the Lord did what Moses asked" (8:13, 31; cf. 9:33; 10:19) is the sequel to his intercessions. Such divinely fortified courage, tenacity, and intercession bring Moses esteem before the royal officials of Pharaoh, in spite of the havoc wrought on their land and people (11:3). Moses concludes the contest with one final terrible prediction of death (11:5-6). He storms out of the court "hot with anger" (11:8). His wrath is directed at a ruler whose recalcitrance will lead to the death of so many innocent firstborn children.

Steadfastness in crisis (Ex 12:1-15:21)

Moses carries out the Lord's instructions regarding the Passover event (12:21-28) and its annual commemoration (13:3-16) with precision (Heb 11:28). He is now served by elders and obeyed by the people as accredited leader of an emerging nation (12:21, 28, 35, 50). He anticipates the realization of the promise of inheritance in the land (13:5, 11) and, upon departure, takes care to bring along the bones of Joseph in accordance with the oath his brothers swore to him (13:19; cf. Gen 50:24-25). The journey toward Canaan begins with God leading his people by a pillar of cloud by day and of fire by night (13:21-22).

Opportunity is accompanied by danger and the pursuing army of Pharaoh pins the nation against the waters of the Red Sea (14:5-9). Threatened by his enemy and slandered by his fear-paralyzed brothers (14:10-12), Moses possesses a defiant faith in God's sure deliverance: "The Lord will fight for you; you need only to be still" (14:14). The people respond to Moses' faith by imitating it and they pass safely through the waters, while the Egyptian pursuers are drowned (14:21-30; cf. Heb 11:29). The result is a nation that reverences God and is confident in its leader (14:31). The people know, though their memories will prove short, that Moses' sole concerns are God's glory (14:18; 15:1-18) and their physical and spiritual welfare.

---

[5] Pharaoh first offers Israel the chance to worship in the desert of Egypt only (8:25, 28). When he does permit departure from Egypt, Pharaoh limits it to men only, without wives and children (10:8, 10-11). Finally, he will release all the people to worship, but they must leave behind their flocks and herds (10:24).

Patient shepherd of a grumbling flock (Ex 15:22-17:15)

The burdens of leadership immediately fall on God's servant in the journey from Egypt to Sinai. The reader of the narrative would expect a deeper level of confidence in God and his appointed leader from a people redeemed in such a spectacular way, but is disappointed to find that the first experience of deprivation elicits not trust but complaint. At the waters of Marah they grumble at Moses over lack of fresh water, a distress relieved by Moses' intercession (15:23-25). In the desert of Sin the people's yearning for the culinary delights of Egypt is condemned by Moses as grumbling against the Lord (16:2, 7-9, 11). The provision of sufficient manna for one day's needs (16:4, 18) creates a test of faith, which the people fail. Moses is angry and administers the Lord's rebuke (16:20, 27-30). Quarreling again breaks out against Moses at Rephidim over lack of water (17:1-2a) and they question his intentions (17:3). Having failed the Lord's tests (15:25b; 16:4b), the congregation now tests the Lord (17:2b, 7) by doubting his presence: "Is the Lord among us or not?" (17:7b). Here is a shocking failure to remember the recent Passover and Exodus events. The unrealistic expectations of people who demand of the human instrument what only God can supply makes the weight of leadership nearly unbearable: "What am I to do with these people?" (17:4). Each complaint is met by Moses' pleading and God's provision, this time with water from a rock (17:5-6). External attack from Amalekites is also countered by the great intercessor, whose uplifted hands express appeal to and dependence upon the Lord (17:11-12, 15-16a; cf. 9:29).

Wisdom in delegation (Ex 18:1-27)

The strains of leadership have reached a breaking point. Besides the rigors of the journey and the incessant complaints of the people were the legal disputes Moses was forced to settle. Jethro, his father-in-law, correctly perceives that an overworked Moses will soon reach the point of utter exhaustion (18:13-18). His advice is to appoint judges to handle the simpler cases so that Moses can be freed to concentrate on the more difficult disputes (18:22, 25-26). The qualifications for the judgeships are threefold: (1) capable representatives of the people; (2) reverence for God; (3) trustworthy men who abhor dishonest gain (18:21). Worthy exercise of leadership among the people of God falls to those with godly character, unblemished integrity, and proven capability. Jethro sets forth the threefold benefits of delegation: (1) Moses will be preserved from excessive strain; (2) younger leaders will be developed who will "share the load;" (3) the legal cases will be expedited, bringing greater satisfaction to the disputants (18:22-23). While Moses' responsibility to instruct the people in the decrees of the law remains undiminished (18:20), he possesses the meekness to recognize the soundness of Jethro's advice and proves capable of delegating responsibility to others (18:24-26).

Mediator with God and lawgiver (Ex 19:1-24:18)

Moses' unique role in Israel's history as mediator of the Torah cannot be replicated in any other levels of leadership, but his participation in the Sinai theophany reveals much about the character of the man. For eleven months Israel remains camped at the foot of Mount Sinai (Ex 19:1-2; Num 10:11). That which

Chapter 4. Moses: Persevering advocate for a stubborn people

God instructs Moses is communicated without addition or subtraction to the community (19:7, 8, 9, 14, 25). Moses' status is confirmed by divine utterance in order to inspire the peoples' trust in him (19:9). On the first day God charges Moses with the task of reminding Israel of her unique identity as a kingdom of priests and holy nation (19:3-8). On the second day Moses prepares the people for God's visitation by consecration and separation from the mountain (19:9-15). On the third day he is called up into the awesome presence of God while the people remain at the foot of the mountain (19:16-25). To a nation terrified by God's visitation Moses speaks words of comfort: this is a test to cause you to fear God and eschew sin (20:18-21).

Moses' third ascent of Mount Sinai reveals several concentric circles of intimacy, which gradually narrow until Moses alone approaches the Lord directly (24:1-2). First, the people remain at the foot of the mountain where Moses administers the covenant ratification ceremony through blood (24:4-8). The circle narrows to 75 men, including the 70 elders, Aaron and his two sons, along with Moses and Joshua, who climb the first stage and celebrate the presence of God with a covenant meal (24:9-11). Third, Moses and his young aide Joshua climb nearer (24:12-14). Finally, Moses is left alone to remain with God forty days and forty nights where he receives the tablets of the law (24:15-18). Are the degrees of access permitted by God related to the heart condition of the recipients? The glory of God, like a consuming fire (Ex 24:15-18; cf. Heb 12:18-21, 29), settles on Mount Sinai, a prelude to the tabernacle construction where the shekinah glory will dwell (Ex 40:34-35), but cannot be contained in any structure (Ex 33:18-23).

Intercessor for a rebellious people (Ex 32:1-33:6)

Moses' most thrilling encounters with God's awesome power, at the Red Sea and Sinai, are each followed by sobering doses of human depravity. This time it is not grumbling but full-scale apostasy. The people's impatience at Moses' delay on the mountain nurtures the ultimate sin—violation of the first and second commands (20:3-6)—and makes their promise of obedience ring hollow (Ex 19:8; 24:7). Aaron's accommodation to the peoples' demand for gods (32:1), his aggressive complicity in fashioning golden calf-idols (32:2-4), even attempting to sanitize its worship with an altar to the Lord (32:5), and his permissive stance toward the peoples' revelry (32:25) comprise one of the most egregious cases of failed leadership in Scripture. Only the fervent intercession of Moses can avert the Lord's threat to annihilate Israel. His prayer discloses a heart consumed with God's glory with no thought of personal status or power:[6] These are "your people" with whom you have covenanted and whose destruction would efface your reputation among the nations (32:11-13). With such doxological pleading the Lord relents from the threat (32:14).

Moses storms down the mountain, hurls the two tablets to the ground breaking them to pieces, symbolic of covenant violation, burns the image, grinds it to powder (but cannot remove it from their hearts), scatters it on the water, and makes the

---

[6] Moses never even mentions in his prayer the offer of God to exalt him as father of a new nation (32:10b).

Israelites drink from it (32:15-20). The Lord's anger (32:11) has become Moses' anger (32:19). Aaron, the failed steward of Israel during Moses' absence, is confronted by his brother, but resorts to multiple rationalizations, transferring the blame to people and circumstances (32:21-24). Moses forthrightly deals with the crisis by compelling the Levites to execute judgment on the offenders (32:27-29). Beyond the immediate measures, Moses prays and fasts forty days for the full restoration of the nation to its covenant pathway (Ex 32:30-35; Deut 9:18, 25). The Lord renews Moses' call to lead Israel to inheritance in the land of the Canaanites (32:34), though he reverses the earlier promise of his presence with them (33:3b; cf. 23:21). "Stiff-necked people" (32:9; 33:3, 5; cf Acts 7:51) becomes the nickname of the people Moses has been called to lead.

Intimate friend of God (Ex 33:7-34:35)
At the tent of meeting outside the camp, not the later tabernacle in the center of the camp, where the people would gather to inquire about disputes (Ex 18:15-16), the Lord spoke to Moses "face to face, as a man speaks to his friend" (33:11). Moses' intimacy with God, without parallel in the Old Testament, seems to reflect his exacting obedience and fervent prayer life, a harbinger of the friendship that new covenant believers enjoy with God the Father through Jesus Christ (Jn 15:13-17). In the face of God's threat to withdraw his presence but dispatch an angel for their journeys (33:2-3), Moses pleads for the Lord to reinstate his earlier pledged presence (23:21) with these "your people" and "your inheritance" (33:12-13; 34:8-9). Moses' stubborn insistence on God's presence is directly linked to his call to lead them: He cannot fathom carrying out his ordained mission without the presence of God among his people (33:12).

God is pleased with Moses' request and reverses his threat of withdrawal (33:14, 17). Moses recognizes that it is God's presence among them that is the distinguishing mark of the people of God (33:15-16). Moses' yearning for deeper intimacy with his friend is satisfied as the glory and goodness of the Lord, merciful and unapproachably holy, passes by Moses as he is shielded in the cleft of the rock (33:18-23; 34:5-7).[7] This exposure to God's partially concealed glory causes Moses' face to be radiant, inspiring fear from Aaron and the people (34:29-32). To prevent the people from seeing the fading glory, Moses would put a veil over his face when he emerged from speaking to the Lord in the tent of meeting (34:33-35; cf. 2 Cor 3:12-18).

Skillful organizer of the tabernacle project (Ex 35:4-40:38)
Construction of the tabernacle where God's presence would be mediated to Israel was a national project. Moses, in strict accordance with the Lord's instructions, administers the project through selected delegation and extensive mobilization. Skilled craftsmen, Bezalel and Oholiab, are chosen to oversee the fashioning of the major articles from gold, silver, bronze, stones, wood and fabrics

---

[7] The uniform testimony of Scripture is that no one can see God directly, without refraction, and live (cf. Gen 16:13; 32:30; Ex 24:9-11; 33:20, 23; Num 12:8; Jdg 6:22-23; 13:21-22; Ezek 1:26-28; Jn 1:18; 5:37; 6:46; 14:9; 1 Tim 1:17; 6:16; 1 Jn 4:12).

(35:30-36:2; cf. 31:1-11). Moses wisely summons the people to a voluntary participation that results in "willing" offerings motivated from heart obedience (35:5, 21, 22, 26, 29; 36:2; cf. 25:1-7). Three characteristics of the project are: (1) generosity: "more than enough" is gathered from the willing givers (36:5-7); (2) faithfulness: everything is carried out "just as the Lord commanded Moses" (39:32, 42-43); and (3) skill: talents are consecrated to the service of God as Bezalel and Oholiab impart their craftsmanship to others (35:34; 36:1-2). The construction is completed and the tabernacle set up less than two months before leaving Sinai (40:1-2; Num 10:11). The obedience of Moses to God's specifications is the keynote of the record of completion (40:19, 21, 23, 25, 27, 29, 32). God's glory now fills the tabernacle, a voucher to Moses' fidelity as leader, and will remain with the nation for nearly one thousand years (40:34-35).[8] The consecrated nation now strides forward into history with the pillar of fire (night) and pillar of cloud (day) guiding them toward the land of promise (40:36-38; cf. 13:21-22).

Guardian of holiness (Lev 10:1-7)

After the solemn ordination and installation of Aaron and his sons as priests (Lev 8:1-9:24), all under Moses' supervision, Nadab and Abihu "offered unauthorized fire before the Lord, contrary to his command" (10:1).[9] The punishment is severe: Nadab and Abihu are immediately consumed by God's blazing holiness (10:2). Moses recognizes their sin as a horrific violation of God's character and expresses no remorse for the death of his nephews. While he permits the family of Aaron to mourn their loss (10:6-7), he interprets the event as a failure to reverence the holy God whom they approach as priests (10:3).

Dealing with doubts and complaints (Num 10:11-12:16)

The first stage of the journey from Sinai to Kadesh commences with a nation trusting in the Lord and united under his appointed leader (Num 9:23; 10:33-36). Moses has just led the nation in celebration of the Passover, the one-year anniversary since leaving Egypt (Num 9:1-5). How is it that this expectant faith so soon degenerates into doubts and complaints (Num 11-12), which serve as a prelude to open rebellion (Num 13-14)? Three incidents of murmuring are recorded. First, at Taberah or "burning," God's fiery judgment against complaints over physical hardship is only stemmed through Moses' prayerful intervention (11:1-3). Second, at Kibroth-Hattaavah, "graves of craving," wailing over the lack of variety in diet is accompanied by provision of quail and then swift judgment. Moses responds to the peoples' complaint with one of his own: the load of responsibility is more than he can bear (11:10-15). God patiently meets his servant's

---

[8] The shekinah glory finally departs from the corrupted temple on the eve of the Babylonian destruction of the southern kingdom (586 B.C.), leading to exile from the land of promise (Ezek 8:1-11:23).

[9] The author does not explain the nature of the "unauthorized fire" (אֵשׁ זָרָה) offered by Aaron's sons, only that it was contrary to the divine command. One plausible interpretation is that these priests took the burning coals from a place other than the altar of burnt offering as specified in Lev 16:12. Or, perhaps, they went even further and made an illicit attempt to enter the Holy of Holies in order to usurp Aaron's exclusive privilege for themselves. See John E. Hartley, *Leviticus*, WBC (Dallas, TX: Word, 1992): 132-133.

need by providing seventy leaders, endued with the Spirit, to help shoulder the burden (11:16-17). He feels no threat to his leadership when Spirit-given insight and utterance is granted to elders, including two outside the camp, a powerful lesson for the yet myopic Joshua (11:24-29). Third, at Hazeroth, an assault against Moses comes from unexpected quarters—Miriam, Moses' sister and a leading prophetess (Ex 15:20), and Aaron, Moses' brother and high priest. The attack on his Cushite wife (12:1) is only a pretext for jealousy over Moses' prophetic gifts and unparalleled intimacy with the Lord (12:2, 6-8). This rebellion is more than a popular uprising inspired by low-ranking malcontents, but an alliance of priest and prophet casting aspersion on the role of Moses as principal leader of the nation. The humble Moses will leave his defense with God (12:3; cf. 11:26-29).[10] God vindicates his servant by word (12:4-9) and deed (12:10-15). Miriam is discredited by being made leprous, only to be cleansed through Moses' intercession.

Crisis intervention (Num 13:1-14:45)

We now come to a watershed event in the life of the new nation. Israel, encamped in the Desert of Paran, is poised for the northern thrust into Canaan. The covenant promises of God ensure a bright future and rich inheritance. Moses organizes a reconnaissance mission of twelve leaders to Canaan, a preparatory step for the military campaign ahead, designed to assess enemy strength and steel the nation's resolve (13:1-25). Upon their return from forty days of exploration, two conflicting viewpoints emerge from the same evidence (13:26-33). The majority report, while acknowledging the abundant produce of the land, fixes on the well-fortified cities and the powerful inhabitants. The minority report of Caleb, aided by Joshua (14:6-9), courageously reaffirms the original mission of conquest: "We should go up and take possession of the land, for we can certainly do it" (13:30). At this strategic juncture unbelief rears its ugly head. The voices of faith are silenced. The majority wins the day by inciting fear, which foments open rebellion (14:1-10a). Grumbling, yearning for Egypt, and personal attacks on Moses' authority are once again recurrent themes. The community, within sight of its promised inheritance, chooses to abandon the whole redemptive plan. Moses and Aaron fall prostrate in fearful expectation of the swift judgment of God (14:5). The voices of Joshua and Caleb, courageously pleading with the people to resist panic and to trust God, are drowned out by the wails of rebellion. The multitude threatens to stone them.

As in the golden calf incident, the Lord threatens to wipe out the nation and start over with Moses (14:10-12a; cf. Ex 32:9-10). As always, Moses intercedes for Israel. His central concern is God's reputation (14:13-19). As always, God responds to the fervent intercession of his friend. Though forgiven, the temporal

---

[10]The Hebrew word עָנָו, translated "meek" in the AV, is best rendered "humble," "dependent," or "needy" (before God). This is its frequent sense in the Old Testament poetical literature (Ps 22:26; 25:9; 37:11; 76:9; 147:6; 149:4). See *NIDOTTE*, 3: 454-463: "Moses was prepared to submit to this unprovoked and hurtful attack by leaving his vindication to God. This selfless, trustful, nonassertive attitude to life is thus characteristic of the virtue" (p. 456). The consensus view among commentators is that Num 12:3 is a later editorial insertion by one impressed with the magnanimity of Moses under pressure.

consequences of the community's choice remain. An entire adult generation, except "my servant Caleb" (and Joshua) who "has a different spirit and follows me wholeheartedly" (14:24), will die in the desert. The sarcastic wish of the people to die in the desert will materialize (Num 14:2, 28-29). Those directly implicated for spreading the bad report (14:36-38) are struck dead. Rather than humbly accept God's ordained punishment, the Israelites ignore Moses' warnings and act presumptuously by launching an attack on the southern frontier, the hill country of Judah. Lacking the divine presence, Israel is routed by the Amalekites at Hormah (14:39-45). The nation has still not learned to take God's word seriously. God's promises, always realized through faith, are postponed. While the present generation dies over the next forty years, the younger generation, chastened by the desert experiences, will conquer and subdue Canaan under Joshua's leadership.

Withstanding a frontal attack (Num 16:1-50)

Korah, a member of a Kohathite family with sacred duties in the Tabernacle (Num 3:27-32; 4:1-20) and several Reubenites led by Dathan and Abiram, followed by 250 community leaders, launch an attack on the authority of Moses and Aaron (16:1-3). These Levites are not content with their privileged roles in tabernacle service. Korah's desire is to share power and his opposition centers on the priesthood (16:10). Moses unmasks their motives in a direct confrontation and looks to the Lord for vindication (16:4-11). The band's charge that Moses has exceeded his authority (16:3) is thrown back at them (16:7). Moses reacts with anger at attacks on his integrity (16:15). What follows the next day is the first of a series of vindications of Aaron's priestly authority. Once again, due to Moses' intercession, the assembly is spared (16:22-24). The earth swallows up the rebels and fire consumes the 250 men offering incense (16:31-35). Eleazar the priest, now the oldest son of Aaron after the death of Nadab and Abihu (Ex 6:23; Lev 10:1-12), gathers the censers of the victims and hammers them into a new bronze cover for the great altar of burnt offering (16:36-39; cf. Ex 38:2). This cover serves as a visual reminder of the Aaronic family's sole right to serve as priest (16:40). Shockingly, one day later Israel's addictive grumbling once again erupts (16:41). The pattern repeats: God threatens to destroy the nation; Moses' steps in as advocate; and retributive judgment (14,700 die) is limited only by Aaron's offering incense for atonement (16:46-50).

Severity toward the leader's sin (Numbers 20:2-13)

The event is strikingly similar to the Meribah incident of Exod 17:1-7. The difference is that in the earlier incident Moses strikes the rock at the Lord's command (Ex 17:6), whereas here the striking of the rock constitutes an act of defiance. Quarreling breaks out over lack of water (cf. Ex 16:3; Num 11:4-6), Moses and Aaron fall prostrate, and the glory of the Lord appears (20:2-6). Moses is commanded to "take the staff" and "speak to the rock" in order to produce water (20:7-8). Moses angrily responds before the assembly, "must we bring you water out of this rock?" He then strikes the rock twice with the staff causing water to gush out (20:9-11). His words indicate he is arrogating himself as the source of provision (cf. Ps 106:33). The Lord rebukes Moses for unbelief and for dishonoring him before the people (20:12a; cf. 20:24; 27:14; Deut 32:51).[11] The penalty is severe and irrevocable: he is barred from the privilege of bringing Israel to the promised land (20:12b).

Why such a severe penalty for a momentary failure, one that is out of character for God's faithful servant and intercessor? This is the man who has persevered through forty wilderness years and endured Israel's intolerable conduct (Acts 13:18), buoyed by the hope of entering the land of promise. Three times Moses bitterly laments this deprivation (Deut 1:37; 3:23-27; 4:21-24). From a human perspective the punishment seems to far outweigh the crime. But Moses is in an exalted position of influence. Along with the opportunity to lead comes grave responsibility, particularly when God's reputation (honor) is at stake. Moses' failure to sanctify him moves God to vindicate his own holiness before the people (20:12-13). Moses will die on Mount Nebo, overlooking Jericho, with Israel poised to seize its inheritance under his successor (Deut 34:1-8).

Discipline of a defiled community (Num 25:1-18)

Neither military attack (Num 21:21-35) nor pagan sorcery (Num 22-24) could harm Israel. The allurement of idolatrous Moabite culture on Israel's moral character, however, proved disastrous. Some of the men began to indulge in sexual immorality with Moabite women as part of the fertility cult of Baal (25:1-3a). As in the golden calf incident, national apostasy provokes God's anger. Judgment comes in the form of a plague with 24,000 victims (25:9). God commands that the leaders and common people implicated in this act of treason be summarily executed (25:4). Moses immediately mobilizes Israel's tribal leaders to implement the judgment (25:5). When one man defiantly brings a Midianite woman into his tent, thus defiling the camp, Phinehas, son of Eleazar the high priest, executes them both on the spot (25:6-8). His act of zeal "made atonement for the Israelites," halting the plague (25:13). God commends Phinehas' zeal and pledges an everlasting covenant of peace with him and his descendants (25:10-13), a confirmation of his earlier priestly covenant with Aaron (Ex 29:9; 1 Chron 6:3-4). Phinehas' zealous defense of God's honor (25:11) contrasts with the irreverence of his uncles Nadab and Abihu (Lev 10:1-3). Though not mentioned in the narrative, the figure of Balaam casts its dark shadow over this event (Num 31:15-16; 2 Pet 2:15; Jude 11; Rev 2:14). Courage to intervene in times of moral crisis marks Moses out as a worthy guardian of Israel's sacred calling to be a "holy nation" (Ex 19:6).

Preserving relational unity (Num 32:1-42)

As a united Israel prepares for the conquest of Canaan, two tribes, Reuben and Gad, are desirous of the excellent grazing land of Gilead for their herds. They lodge a request for the Transjordan for their inheritance (32:1-5). The request is

---

[11] Gordon J. Wenham, *Numbers*, TOTC (Downers Grove, IL: Inter-Varsity, 1981): 150, notes the disobedience of Moses to God's specific directions. He is instructed to take the staff, gather the people together, and speak to the rock (20:8); but in this instance he took the staff, gathered the people together, spoke to them instead of to the rock, and struck the rock (20:9-11). Here Moses departs from his uniform practice of precise obedience to the Lord's command with tragic personal consequences.

not wholly selfish, as they willingly relinquish any inheritance claims to Canaan (32:19). Yet Transjordan is outside the boundaries of the promised land (Num 34), so the request indicates a disturbing indifference to the covenant. Moses fears a repetition of the spy episode, where the nation was discouraged from claiming God's promise of the land (32:6-9). With such a devastating precedent, Moses' angry reaction and strict warning (32:14-15) are justified.

The Transjordan tribes respond with a pledge to wholeheartedly support the military campaign into Canaan, leaving their wives, children, and flocks behind in fortified cities, "until every Israelite has received his inheritance" (32:18). Satisfied with these conditions, Moses leaves the reckoning with God: "be sure that your sin will find you out" (32:23). There is no ambiguity in the terms of the agreement, affirmed by both parties (32:25-32). Moses, though barred himself from entering Canaan, will not allow divided loyalties among the tribes, as in the disastrous spy incident, to grow so that the flames of faith are quenched and the new generation's rightful inheritance squandered.

Preparing a successor (Num 27:12-23; Deut 31:1-34:12)

Moses' unique role as mediator of the Torah has no proper succession, as is the case with the Aaronic priesthood. Nevertheless, as his death draws near Moses prepares the nation for his faithful attendant, Joshua, to assume the role of national leader. Moses, like Aaron, has been denied permission to enter the land for dishonoring the Lord at Meribah (Num 20:12). Moses is told to ascend the Aharim mountain range, from which he can view Canaan at a distance, and after which he will be gathered to his people (27:12-14).

Rather than retreating into self-pity, Moses humbly submits to God's will and focuses on the future. His forward perspective expresses itself in prayer to God for a successor, a leader, and a shepherd for Israel (27:15-17). Joshua, Moses' proven assistant, is God's choice (27:18). Joshua' style of leadership, though, will not be a duplicate of his mentor's. He is to receive some of Moses' authority, but is to ascertain God's will from Eleazar, the high priest, by means of the Urim and Thummim (27:18-21; cf. Ex 28:30). Moses' direct communication with God "face to face," as both priest and prophet, would not be repeated with Joshua (Num 12:6-8; Deut 34:10-12). Through the laying on of hands by Moses, Joshua is commissioned before the high priest and the whole assembly (27:22-23).

Formal succession is recorded in the closing chapters of Deuteronomy (31-34) as a national event organized by Moses to ensure Israel's continuing faithfulness to the covenant under their new leader. Moses, now 120 years old, bids Joshua to be courageous in prosecuting the campaign of conquest (Deut 31:1-8). The law is recorded and deposited as a witness against Israel's coming apostasy (31:9-29). Moses recites a Song of Testimony both for and against Israel as they enter Canaan (32:1-43). With Joshua by his side, Moses reminds the people that the Lord and his word are their very life (32:44-47). In his final words of blessing on Israel's tribes, Moses extols the majesty of God and anticipates a bright future in the land (33:26-29). Moses, servant of the Lord (34:5), unequaled prophet (34:10-12), and intimate friend of God (34:10), dies on Mount Nebo while viewing the inheritance from a distance (34:1-4).

Leadership profile of Moses

1. **Forbearance and intercession**: *Moses' responses to the appalling lapses of Israel in the golden calf incident and the spy incident disclose his magnitude of character. His selfless love for and loyalty to his people transcend his exasperation with their "stiff-necked" condition. His intercession is their salvation. His undeterred pursuit of God's presence among his people is born of the conviction that without it he cannot lead them. They are the people upon whom God has staked his reputation and Moses will not let his heavenly friend forget it. Holy Scripture commemorates Moses along with Samuel as the greatest of Israel's intercessors (Ps 99:6; Jer 15:1).*

2. **Jealous for God's honor and Israel's good**: *Moses the leader combines in an unusual mixture the passion of a judge with the gentleness of a shepherd. He is jealous for Israel to fulfill her sacred calling as God's people in the world (Ex 19:6). When her identity is threatened, as in the golden calf idolatry, the spy report, and the Moabite seduction, he reacts with fierce anger. But his righteous exasperation is always met by intercession for them as their unfailing advocate. The glory of God and the welfare of the nation erase all pursuits of status and power. He is indifferent to an offer from no less than God himself to be the founder of a new nation. He bears the complaints of the people, the envy of his siblings, and the slander of his fellow Levites. His selflessness empowers him to delegate to others, to rejoice when the Spirit anoints a wider leadership, and to prepare a successor. He leads them in Passover, mediates the law, organizes the tabernacle, and ensures a covenant-based succession of leadership. Unparalleled gifting and elevation (Deut 34:10-12) have no intoxicating effect on this most humble of men (Num 12:3).*

3. **Higher level of accountability**: *Exacting obedience is required of those placed as leaders over God's people. Leadership is stewardship and the higher the level of the former, the greater is the accountability of the latter. In one unguarded moment Moses fails to reverence his Lord before the nation. His punishment is severe. His lifelong dream of entering the land promised on oath to his forefathers is shattered and no amount of appeal can reverse God's decision. A deep sense of privilege and responsibility must characterize the Moses-like leader.*

4. **Preparation of one's successor**: *Though Moses yearns for Canaan and laments his loss of opportunity to lead the people to their intended destination, he bravely bows to God's purpose and appoints his successor. Moses expresses no concern for preserving his place in history or securing a personal legacy. His concerns are for Joshua's success, Israel's prosperity in the land, and, above all, the Lord's honor. He dies gazing across at the promised land awaiting a greater fulfillment to come (Heb 11:39-40).*

Chapter 5.
Joshua: Courageous successor to a legend

Preliminary questions to consider:
1. *What kinds of experiences help to shape a future leader who is then prepared to step in and provide a smooth succession?*
2. *How does a leader combine strategic planning with prayerful dependence on God's guidance?*
3. *What steps can a leader take to build unity among those entrusted to his/her care?*
4. *What is the chief concern of a shepherd-leader (Num 27:17)? How is that concern communicated and regularly renewed?*

Apprentice under Moses

Joshua, the son of Nun, was from the tribe of Ephraim (Num 13:8). After the conquest Joshua received the town of Timnath Serah in the hill country of Ephraim (Josh 19:49-50), where he died at the age of 110 and was buried (Josh 24:29-30).[1] His ancestral lineage is recorded in 1 Chronicles 7:20-27.

Joshua is introduced as the military leader who defeated the Amalekites at Rephidim as Moses pleaded with the Lord with uplifted hands (Ex 17:8-13). His military prowess, even at this early stage, earned Moses' respect. By the time of the Sinai theophany Joshua is serving as Moses' aide.[2] He accompanies his mentor up the mountain except for the final ascent to God's presence (Ex 24:13). Joshua heard the commotion of the idolatrous revelry around the golden calf (Ex 32:17). He would not leave the tent of meeting outside the camp when Moses entered to speak with God, unlike the people who remained watching at a distance (Ex 33:11).[3] His attempt to prevent two men from prophesying in the Spirit is rebuked by Moses as a myopia born of envy (Num 11:28-29). These early experiences under Moses must have been formative for the young Joshua: God was to be honored above all and his good gifts multiplied not hoarded.

Man of faith and courage (Num 13:1-14:39)

Hoshea, his original name, represents the tribe of Ephraim as one of the twelve spies sent to reconnoiter the land of Canaan (13:8). Upon their return he and

---

[1] Joshua's life can be dated approximately 1500-1390 B.C.

[2] The Hebrew verb (שָׁרַת) behind the substantival participle (Ex 24:13; 33:11; Num 11:28) means to serve, minister, assist in the broadest sense of the term. Joshua was a servant-apprentice for many years before his exaltation to national leader. A different expression, literally "the one standing before you (to attend or serve)" (הָעֹמֵד לְפָנֶיךָ), is used in Deuteronomy 1:38 (cf. Deut 10:8; 18:7; 1 Sam 16:21, 22; 1 Kg 12:8).

[3] He may have served as guard or watchman of the tent against irreverent intruders. See Durham, *Exodus*, 443.

Caleb stand firm against the fears of the majority. They challenge the people to trust in the Lord who will surely give them the abundant land he has promised (14:6-9). For his faith he is awarded by Moses with the new name, Joshua, "the Lord saves" (13:16). The two men are nearly stoned for their steadfastness to the mission (14:10a), but in the aftermath become the only two spies shielded from judgment (14:38). They are also the only individuals of the present generation who will survive the desert years and enter Canaan (14:30; cf. Num 26:65). Both are remembered as men who followed the Lord wholeheartedly (Num 32:12; Deut 1:34-40).

Successor to an unparalleled leader (Num 27:12-23; Deut 31:1-34:12)

Moses accepted, though with protestations (Deut 1:37; 3:23-27; 4:21-24), the Lord's judgment on him for striking the rock at Meribah. He began to prepare his successor to lead the nation in the campaign of conquest. Moses prays for the divine appointment of a leader with a shepherd's heart (Num 27:15-17).[4] Joshua, empowered by the Spirit of God (27:18) and invested with some of the authority of Moses (27:20),[5] is God's choice to lead the nation. He is commissioned by Moses before Eleazar the high priest and the entire community (27:22-23). Joshua will thus serve without priestly prerogative in an exclusively civil role (Num 34:17). He will depend upon the high priest's Urim and Thummim for knowledge of God's will (27:21).

To replace one of Moses' stature, Joshua needs assurance both from his mentor and from God. Moses tells Joshua to remember the defeat of the Moabite kings Sihon and Og as a harbinger of coming victories and to be strong and courageous (Deut 3:21, 28). At the time of formal succession Moses delivers his valedictory address (Deut 31-33) of promise and warning to the nation and its future leader. Joshua and the people are summoned to be strong and courageous, fortified by the assurance of the Lord's continual presence (31:1-8). Joshua joins Moses at the

---

[4] The metaphor of the "shepherd" (רָעָה) for a leader who watches over the flock of the people of God is frequent in the Old Testament, and forms the background to its New Testament usage. God or Yahweh is the true shepherd who tenderly cares for his people (Gen 48:15; 49:24; Ps 23:1; 28:9; 80:1; Eccles 12:11; Isa 40:11; Jer 31:10; Ezek 34:12, 16; Mic 7:14). Leaders who share the Lord's love for the flock and lead them to obey the covenant are his faithful shepherd-leaders (Jer 3:15; 23:4; Mic 5:5; cf. Acts 20:28; Eph 4:11; 1 Pet 5:2), preeminently Moses (Isa 63:11), Joshua (Num 27:17), David (2 Sam 5:2; 7:7; Ps 78:71-72), Jeremiah (Jer 17:16) and the Davidic Messiah (Ezek 34:23; Mic 5:4; Zech 13:7; cf. Mt 2:6; 26:31; Jn 10:2, 11, 14, 16; Heb 13:20; 1 Pet 2:25; 5:4; Rev 7:1). False shepherds are those who lead the people of God away from their covenant allegiance (Isa 56:11; Jer 2:8; 10:21; 12:10; 22:22; 23:1-2; 25:34-36; 50:6; Ezek 34:1-10; Zech 10:3; 11:3, 5, 8; cf. Jn 10:12-13; Jude 12). Israel is often compared to sheep who go astray because there is no worthy shepherd (Num 27:17; 1 Kg 22:17; 2 Chr 18:16; Isa 13:14; 53:6; Jer 50:6; Ezek 34:5-6; Zech 10:2; cf. Mt 9:36; Mk 6:34).

[5] The Hebrew term הוֹד, rendered "authority" (NIV), has the meaning of power, splendor, or majesty that inspires the awe or, in this case, respect of those to whom it is displayed. The term can be used in the Old Testament of God's majesty (Isa 30:30; Hab 3:3; Ps 8:1; 96:6), the splendor of kings David and Solomon (Ps 21:5; 45:3; 1 Chron 29:25), and the majesty of Messiah the Branch (Zech 6:13). Some of the magnificent leadership qualities and divinely authenticated power/authority that had attended Moses would now fall upon Joshua in order to compel Israel's obedience and ensure a fruitful succession. See *NIDOTTE*, 1: 1016-1017; *BDB*, 217.

Tent of Meeting for his commissioning (31:14), where the Lord promises his presence as the guarantee of his success in conquering the land (31:23). Leadership passes to Joshua with the death of Moses. He is endowed with the Spirit of wisdom (34:9). He is confident in God's promised presence with him and secure in his role of military strategist and statesmen. Joshua will not be able, nor will he attempt, to duplicate the priestly and prophetic roles of his predecessor (Ex 33:11a; Deut 34:10-12).

Careful planner for the success of the mission (Joshua 1:1-5:12)

Joshua begins his tenure as national leader with an attentive ear to the Lord's reaffirmation of his purpose for and presence with him. The mission is confirmed (1:1-4), success promised (1:5), courage enjoined (1:6-7), and the instruction manual, the written book of the law, provided (1:8). The fact that God says "be strong and courageous" three times (1:6, 7, 9) to one who already possessed a resume of courage underscores the daunting scope of the task before him and the vacuum Joshua felt without Moses's strong presence. "As I was with Moses, so I will be with you; I will never leave you nor forsake you" (1:5b) would have special meaning for one who had studied under him whose singular passion was the divine presence (Ex 33:12-18). Joshua orders the tribal officers to prepare their people for the crossing of Jericho (1:10-11). He reminds the Transjordan tribes of their vows to take their place as full participants in helping their brothers conquer Canaan proper (1:12-15).

A clear mission must be pursued with thorough preparation. Joshua sends two spies on the reconnaissance of the fortified city-state of Jericho (2:1). He receives in their report the psychological profile he is seeking, namely, an enveloping fear at the reputation of Israel as a people supported by a mighty Lord (2:9-11, 24). At critical junctures before (Josh 3-5), during (Josh 8:30-35), and after (Josh 24) the military campaign, the faithful shepherd (Num 27:17) calls his flock to renew their covenant obligations. Though a bloody war of expulsion will ensue, Israel is a spiritual not militaristic people. She is reminded in a fourfold way of her identity as a nation covenanted with Yahweh to extend his kingdom upon the earth (4:24). First, the ark of the covenant, the symbol of God's dwelling place among them, is carried by the priests in advance of the army (3:3-4). Second, a twelve stone memorial representing each tribe is erected at Gilgal to signify to succeeding generations the miraculous crossing of the Jordan (4:19-24). Third, the new generation of males undergoes circumcision, the sign of the covenant (5:1-9). Fourth, the nation celebrates Passover to commemorate their redemption from bondage in Egypt, the first such celebration in forty years (5:10; cf. Num 9:1-5). A redeemed, specially marked out, united people will follow their Lord into battle. They revere Joshua as the one exalted by the Lord to lead them (4:14).

Initial triumphs and failures (Joshua 5:13-9:27)

When God calls a person to a great task he assures that one of his gracious enabling for its accomplishment. As with the call of Moses to lead Israel out of Egypt (Ex 3:1-7), so the Lord appears to Joshua in veiled form as the "commander of the army of the Lord" (5:13-14) to strengthen him for the imminent campaign.

41

Both are theophanies and in both cases the leader must remove his sandals before a holy God (5:15; cf. Ex 3:5).

The bizarre method of attacking the strong, well-fortified city of Jericho (6:1-5) could not possibly have been derived by human ingenuity. Joshua's obedience is exacting: the people make an orderly procession around the city once a day for six days, then seven times on the final day, led by an armed guard, seven priests with rams' horns, followed by the ark-bearing priests, and the rear guard of warriors (6:6-13). With precision the apparently meaningless and monotonous march routine continues for six days. On the seventh day after the seven encirclements, trumpet blast, and triumphant shout comes a final command by Joshua. The walls of the city collapse by faith (Heb 11:30). Everything in the city is "devoted" to the Lord (6:17-18) and must be utterly destroyed, save Rahab's family (6:22-23) and the precious items set apart for the treasury (6:19). The devoted item under ban meant a total surrender to God's service or required its total destruction (Lev 27:28-29). When a person, animal, city, or property was assigned to destruction it is because it impeded God's redemptive purposes and/or was injurious to his covenant people (Deut 7:2-6; 13:12-18).[6] The spreading fame of Joshua results from God's presence with him (6:27; cf. 3:7; 4:14).

Unnoticed in the triumphant attack on Jericho was the unfaithfulness of one man, Achan, who confiscated for his own use some of the "devoted things" of Jericho (7:1). As before, Joshua sends men to reconnoiter the next place of attack. The spies report optimistically that two or three thousand troops would be sufficient to capture Ai. Joshua acquiesces in the overconfident estimate and proceeds to attack Ai. Thirty six men are killed and the attack force flees in defeat (7:2-5). Israel is shocked and terrified (7:5b). The psychological impact of the defeat threatens to abort the entire campaign. Joshua had learned what to do in a desperate situation from his mentor, Moses. He falls on his face before God in prayer and pleads not only for the nation, but also for the honor of God's name (7:6-9; cf. Ex 32:11-13; Num 14:13-19). The Lord's demands are forthright: stand up (7:10); consecrate the people (7:13); present yourselves (7:14); destroy the offender (7:15). Joshua leads the nation in determining, by lots, the guilty person and in carrying out capital punishment by stoning (7:19-26). The attack on Ai resumes, this time with 30,000 troops (8:1-3). Joshua's javelin is the outward symbol of victory and another sign accrediting his leadership (8:18, 26). The ban on the Canaanite people, not their livestock and plunder, is carried out with ruthless obedience (8:26-29).

Before his death Moses commanded the nation that after crossing the Jordan a covenant reaffirmation, reciting the blessings and curses of the law, must take place between Mt. Gerizim and Mt. Ebal (Deut 11:26-32; 27:1-8). These symbolic peaks, the former of blessing and the latter of curse, are situated at Shechem, twenty miles north of Ai. Here in the very center of the land Joshua and the nation reaffirm their commitment to the covenant. Sacrifices are offered on the stone altar, the nation gathers in the presence of God, and the blessings and curses of the law are read to the entire assembly (8:30-35). Through altar, sacrifice, and word, with the ark at the center, in the very heart of Canaan, Joshua the shepherd

---

[6] See "חָרַם," in *TWOT*, I: 324-325; *BDB*, 356.

(Num 27:17) reaffirms the covenant so that euphoria over initial military successes will not desensitize the nation to its true identity.

After the successful central campaign by Israel the various kings of the Amorite city-states began to form coalitions to defend themselves against further Israelite penetration (9:1-2). The Gibeonites, a Canaanite people living in four cities just south of Ai and Jericho (9:17), wisely recognize the futility of resisting Israel militarily. They form a delegation and approach the camp of Israel, pretending to be travelers from a distant country. Taking moldy bread, cracked wineskins, worn out sacks, sandals and clothing, they give the appearance of having been on a long journey across the desert. The award-winning acting performance succeeds. Without seeking divine guidance, Joshua agrees to a peace treaty that is ratified by an oath in God's name (9:14-15). Three days later Joshua realizes he has been deceived. He and the tribal leaders are roundly criticized for the hasty agreement (9:18). Still, a treaty solemnly confirmed by oath cannot be broken (9:19; cf. Lev 19:12; Num 30:2). Unable to alter the agreement, Joshua decrees that the Gibeonites be reduced to slave status, serving as woodcutters and water carriers (9:26-27).

Military commander and spiritual warrior (Joshua 10:1-12:24)

The king of Jerusalem, Adoni-Zedek, shocked by the Gibeonites' treaty with Israel, now senses the direct threat. As a natural countermeasure he and four other kings of south-central Palestine form a coalition and attack the traitor Gibeon, a leading royal city with a fine army (10:1-5). Having received an emergency call from the besieged Gibeonites, Joshua launches a surprise night attack on the southern armies from his camp at Gilgal. Again we are reminded of the unwise oath, binding Joshua to protect the Gibeonites. Still, with the formation of alliances Joshua is able to concentrate his attacks and gain a wider and quicker subjugation over the land. The attack is wholly successful, with the routed armies cut down as they flee south (10:6-15). Victory is attributed throughout to divine intervention— this is the Lord's victory (10:8, 10, 11, 12, 14, 19, 25, 42). Two miraculous occurrences ensue: the Lord hurls hailstones upon the retreating armies (10:11) and, in answer to Joshua's prayer, suspends the earth's movement to extend the daylight hours so that the attack can be effectively consummated (10:12-14).

The conquest of southern Canaan proceeds with the execution of the five kings (10:16-27). Joshua, rather than engage in time-consuming sieges and occupations, chooses to make lightning-like raids on the key city-states, breaking their military might and preventing further coalitions. Following Makkedah (10:28) he attacks Libnah, Lachish, Gezer, Eglon, Hebron, and Debir (10:29-39). The area that comes under Joshua's control is a wide area to the far southern reaches of Canaan (10:40-42). The record states that in each city the native population is utterly exterminated (10:28, 30, 32, 33, 35, 37, 39). This extermination method is not a cruel massacre; it is the divine command of Yahweh that Joshua fulfills (10:40). Victory is attributed to God's power (10:30, 32, 42). Joshua and the army return to Gilgal (10:43).

The northern campaign largely parallels the progress and outcome of the southern campaign. The king of Hazor, head of the northern city-states (11:10), organizes a broad coalition of kings. Their united armies are powerful and numerous, with many horses and chariots (11:1-5). Joshua enters the battle after a word of confirmation from the Lord (11:6; cf. 10:8). At the waters of Merom a decisive battle takes place, the enemy routed and pursued until its forces are totally destroyed (11:7-8). Hazor, the main city, is captured, then the lesser royal cities are attacked and plundered (11:10-15). One unique aspect of the northern battles is the large number of horses and chariots employed. At God's command the horses are hamstrung and the chariots burned (11:6, 9). This was to prevent Israel from amassing military weapons and a large chariot force, which would weaken their sense of dependence on God (cf. Deut 17:16; Ps 20:7; Isa 31:1). The total extermination of the native population is carried out (11:8, 11, 14). Joshua's obedience to the command of the Lord is exact (11:9, 12, 15, 23). He even removes the feared Anakites (11:21-22) and shares the reward with his friend, Caleb, to whom he later allocates Hebron (14:13-14). Victory is credited to the divine favor (11:6, 8, 20). Just as Moses conquered Moab (12:6), so Joshua conquered the lands west of the Jordan (12:7-8).

Administrator of the tribal allotment (Joshua 13:1-21:45)
The work of nation building remains for Joshua, now over 90 years old (13:1). Moses had commanded Joshua to allot each tribe their fair proportional land area following the conquest (Num 26:52-56). Joshua and Eleazar, the high priest, with the assistance of appointed tribal representatives, are to allocate the inheritance of each tribe (Num 34:13-29). Now Joshua will administer the peace by carefully assigning the Transjordan tribes (13:8-33) and then the tribes in Canaan proper (14:1-19:48) their respective lands. Israel was either unwilling or unable to successfully expel the native peoples, a fact repeatedly noted in the narrative (13:13; 15:63; 16:10; 17:12-16; 19:47). Caleb, Joshua's kindred spirit, is given special attention because he demonstrates the kind of tenacious, energetic faith needed to wholly drive out the Canaanites and secure the land: "The Lord helping me, I will drive them out just as he said" (14:12).

After Judah and the two tribes of Joseph, Ephraim and Manasseh, receive their allotment (15:1-17:18), the time is ripe for the unifying of the tribes around a central place of worship (18:1-10). Joshua chooses Shiloh in the central and relatively secure area of Ephraim. Shiloh was also close to the important cities of Bethel and Shechem, sacred in the memory of the nation. The Tent of Meeting and the ark are brought from Gilgal (14:6) and placed there (18:1). For the next three hundred years, until the time of Samuel (1 Sam 4:3), Shiloh will serve as the political and religious capital of Israel, where all twelve tribes on both sides of the Jordan will assemble at the annual feasts. Joshua is systematic and judicious in his method. A team consisting of three men from each tribe surveys the remaining areas of Canaan. The descriptive survey is recorded and deposited with Joshua at Shiloh. Seven distinct areas are then allocated to the remaining tribes by the method of casting lots (18:3-10). Joshua's question, "How long will you wait before you begin to take possession of the land that the Lord, the God of your fathers, has given you?" (18:3), indicates hesitancy, even resistance, on the part of the remaining tribes to exercise faith and claim their rightful inheritance. Last of all, Joshua receives the city of Timnath Serah in the hill country of Ephraim (19:49-50). With characteristic humility he seeks no inheritance for himself until the entire nation has been properly and fairly assigned their portion.

Keeper of the Covenant (Joshua 22:1-24:33)

The promises of God to provide a land of rest (Gen 15:18-21) have been abundantly realized (Josh 21:43-45). Now the question arises, will Israel faithfully live out her covenant obligations in the land she has conquered? Entrance, victory, conquest and possession are no guarantee of continuing preservation in the land.

The two and one-half eastern tribes have upheld their promise to join the military campaign in support of their brothers, and now they are ready to return home. Joshua reminds them of their spiritual obligations: to keep the law (integrity); to love the Lord (loyalty); to walk in his ways (purity); to obey his commands (obedience); to hold fast to him (faithfulness); and to serve him wholeheartedly (dedication) (22:5). After commending them for their courageous support of the campaign, he sends them home with his blessing (22:6-7). However, on their return to Gilead they construct a large altar at the Jordan. The western tribes interpret this as a special sacrificial altar set up in opposition to the central altar at Shiloh. The western tribes immediately mobilize for war, recognizing any rival altar as a breach of the covenant. First, though, Phinehas and ten tribal leaders are sent to mediate the dispute (22:13-14). The charge against the Transjordan tribes is that they have broken the covenant, in rebellion against the Lord as at Peor (22:15-18; cf. Num 25:1-3). The Transjordan tribes successfully persuade the leaders of their covenant loyalty (22:21-29). Far from being a rival altar where sacrifices will be offered, the Geliloth altar was built as a memorial or "witness" (22:27, 28, 34) to future generations. Phinehas and the elders, satisfied at the pure intentions of their brothers, return to Shiloh with the encouraging report. The assembled tribes rejoice at the announcement and war is averted (22:30-34). The unity is grounded in theological confession: "A witness between us that the Lord is God" (22:34).

Toward the end of his life Joshua summons the entire nation before him twice, beginning with the national leaders (23:1-2; 24:1). A courageous and loyal servant in his youth, Joshua demonstrates the same unwavering commitment to the Lord in his final days. He is concerned that the gains of Israel be preserved, so he reminds the nation on two separate occasions in national assembly of its covenant responsibilities. In the first address, probably at the central sanctuary in Shiloh, he reminds the nation of God's faithfulness in bringing them into the land (23:1-5), their duty to obey the word of God (23:6), the danger of association with the surrounding peoples (23:7-13), and the consequences of future covenant violation (23:14-16). The theme is separation from the influences of paganism and consecration to the Lord God (23:6-8).

Joshua's final act is to formally renew the covenant with the entire nation assembled at Shechem (cf. Josh 8:30-35), where Abraham first built an altar to the Lord after receiving the promise of the land (Gen 12:6-7). The reenactment in Joshua 24 is an adapted form of a Middle Eastern suzerainty treaty between a ruler and his vassals:[7]

---

[7] K. A. Kitchen, *Ancient Orient and the Old Testament* (London: Tyndale, 1966): 90-102.

1. Covenant preamble (24:1-2a): identifies two parties, God and Israel.
2. Historical prologue (24:2b-13): reviews the blessings offered by the great King. From the call of Abraham right through Israel's brief history to the conquest of Canaan, Yahweh has been a gracious provider and powerful protector.
3. Stipulations of the covenant (24:14-24): to serve the Lord means reverence and faithfulness (v. 14), decisive commitment (v. 15), exclusive loyalty (vv. 16-18), holiness (v. 19), submission (v. 23), and obedience (v. 24). The term "serve" is repeated twelve times in the space of eleven verses.
4. Covenant terms recorded (24:25-26a): in the book of the law of God.
5. Stone of witness (24:26b-27): the seventh stone memorial in the land (4:20; 7:26; 8:29; 8:31; 10:27; 22:10). Stones are solid, lasting, and visible, so provide a fitting visual symbol of covenant privilege and responsibility (cf. Gen 28:18-22).

The record of Joshua concludes with his death at the age of 110 and burial at Timnath Serah. A new generation is coming on the scene. The destiny of the nation will be inextricably linked to the character of its leadership, as is always the case. The generation that was born in Egypt and grew up in the desert remained faithful under the shepherding of Joshua and of the elders he mentored (24:31). With the death of Joshua and Eleazar (24:28-33) the final ties to the age of Moses and Aaron, those with direct experience of the Lord's miraculous works, have been severed. How will the new generation do? What will be the quality of the leaders that follow Joshua? The period of the judges will answer these questions.

Leadership profile of Joshua

1. *Humility to follow and courage to lead: Joshua was blessed with the inestimable privilege of serving as Moses' aide during the forty years from Sinai to the entrance into Canaan. He observed firsthand Moses' singular pursuit of God's presence, his boiling anger at the reveling idolaters, resilience under constant harassment, and powerful intercession. These formative experiences never left Joshua. God does not clone leaders, he develops them. The desert years of service were not wasted. When the time of succession arrived Joshua stepped forth as his own man, supported by the promises of a faithful Lord and steeled by the exhortation to be courageous.*
2. *Strategy and prayer: As a military commander Joshua combined strategic thinking with prayerful dependence on God's guidance. The fortified city of Jericho was reconnoitered, but then defeated by the silly methods of God's choosing. The entire campaign of conquest was carefully organized. From Gilgal Joshua could establish a supply line from Transjordan and attack the central highlands. By pushing into the heartland Joshua's army dissected the country into two parts, cutting in half the enemy's strength. Before proceeding, however, he turned his attention to covenant renewal at Shechem. The southern thrust broke the southern Amorite coalition with surprising rapidity. But the decisive battle of Gibeon turned on a long day in which Joshua prayed, "the sun stood still" (10:13), and the Lord fought for Israel. The northern thrust*

targeted the mighty fortification of Hazor whose army of chariots and horses fell because the Lord handed them over to Joshua. Careful planning and courageous implementation were conditioned by prayerful reliance.

3. *Judicious administrator*: Joshua's mission was more than demolition. With the conquest of Canaan he turned his attention to building a unified nation. Few leaders combine the ability to both pioneer and to nurture. He was well served in both by the tribal leaders and clan heads. He refused to exploit the military triumphs for personal gain and took his own inheritance only after first ensuring his brothers received theirs.

4. *Shepherd of the Lord's flock*: Moses' prayer that his successor be a worthy shepherd of a wayward flock was answered (Num 27:17). Joshua's overriding concern was the spiritual health of the nation, so he renewed Israel in its covenant obligations before (Gilgal), during (Shechem), and after (Shiloh and Shechem) its military campaigns. His final acts were national conventions for spiritual remembrance and renewal. Joshua made his choice to follow the Lord (24:15b). His choice emboldened the people to make the same commitment (24:18b).

Chapter 6.
Deborah: A woman for the times

Preliminary question to consider:
How does one incorporate in a truly biblical philosophy of leadership the singularly gifted women leaders whom God has used in extending his kingdom?

A nation in trouble

A new generation arose, severed from the age of Moses and Aaron, Joshua and Eleazar, ignorant of the Lord and unfaithful to his covenant (Jdg 2:10). Incomplete obedience in expelling the Canaanites (1:27-36), spiritual harlotry to the seductive Baal fertility cult (2:12-13, 17), and intermarriage with the heathen (3:5) spelled disaster for Israel spiritually, socially, and politically. Covenant violation, then, was the root cause of national disintegration (2:20). Israel's history over the next three hundred years (11:26) becomes a monotonous, repetitive cycle.[1] It began with spiritual rebellion, the tribes forsaking Yahweh for the Baals and Ashtoreths of the Canaanite pantheon. God's anger brought punishment in the form of bondage and oppression from the surrounding peoples. When the heavy hand of oppression could no longer be tolerated, the Israelites cried out to the Lord for deliverance, who raised up judges to save them. Soon, however, the nation returned to the pit from which it had been dug, and after a brief respite, the vicious cycle began all over again. These cycles, however, were not merely repetitive; each time the apostasy was greater and the downward trend more severe (2:19). In Judges there are seven major cycles (3:7-11; 3:12-31; 4:1-5:31; 6:1-8:32; 8:33-10:5; 10:6-12:7; 13:1-16:31), indicating these are representative events of the whole period, with twelve judges, six major and six minor. These judges were leaders without dynastic succession or national position, raised up to confront a specific crisis.

Prophetess and judge (Jdg 4:1-5)

In the early period of the judges oppression came from either outside of Israel, from Mesopotamia (Jdg 3:8) and Moab (3:12), or on its perimeter from the Philistines (3:31). This time trouble arises from Canaanite forces within Israel proper. The military drama that follows has five central characters: (1) Jabin, a

---

[1] The entire period of the judges, from Othniel to Samson, can be dated 1375 B.C.-1055 B.C. (Jdg 11:26). The three judges discussed here can be given the following approximate dates: (1) Deborah: preceding 20 years of oppression, 1229-1209 B.C., followed by 40 years of peace, 1209-1169 (Jdg 4:3; 5:31); (2) Gideon: preceding 7 years of oppression, 1169-1162 B.C., followed by 40 years of peace, 1162-1122 (Jdg 6:1; 8:28); (3) Samson: preceding 40 years of oppression, 1115-1075 B.C., followed by twenty years of peace, 1075-1055 (Jdg 13:1; 15:20; 16:31).

Canaanite king reigning in Hazor who oppresses Israel for twenty years; (2) Sisera, commander of Jabin's army situated at Harosheth, at the Kishon river on the southern flank of Jabin's kingdom; (3) Deborah, judge and prophetess of Israel; (4) Barak, the leading warrior from the northern tribe of Naphtali, the tribe along with Zebulun most directly affected by Jabin's oppression; and (5) Jael, the wife of Heber the Kenite.

Israel had earlier defeated Hazor, the head of the northern federation, and killed its king, Jabin (Josh 11:1-15). The Canaanites have now regrouped, consolidated their position, and rebuilt the city. "Jabin" appears to be, then, a dynastic title rather than a personal name (cf. Josh 11:1; Ps 83:9). Due to covenant violation the Lord uses Jabin with his large chariot force to oppress the northern tribes of Israel for twenty years (4:3). In answer to the desperate pleas of the Israelites for relief, the Lord raises up a deliverer, the woman Deborah, who was settling Israel's legal disputes from her home near Bethel in the hill country of Ephraim (4:4-5).

The only judge who is a woman is also the only judge who is identified as a prophet(ess). Deborah is one of a significant line of prophetesses that span the history of redemption in both the Old and New Testaments: Miriam, the sister of Moses, who sang a song of praise for the deliverance at the Red Sea (Ex 15:20-21); Huldah who declared the word of delayed judgment to the boy king Josiah upon the discovery of the book of the law in the temple (2 Kg 22:14-20); the unnamed wife of Isaiah who bore him the son whose name presaged an Assyrian invasion (Isa 8:3-4); the aged widow Anna who spoke of the baby Jesus and his connection to the anticipated redemption of Jerusalem (Lk 2:36-38); the four unmarried daughters of Philip the evangelist who prophesied at Caesarea, perhaps of Paul's coming dangers (Acts 21:9); and the women of Corinth with the gift of prophecy (1 Cor 11:5).[2] The prophecy of Joel (2:28-29), cited by Peter at Pentecost as at least initially fulfilled on that day, anticipates a time when God's Spirit-inspired prophetic gifts will be given to his servants irrespective of gender (Acts 2:17-18). Deborah's prophetic gift is even more striking since from Moses to Samuel the direct prophetic word of the Lord largely ceased. Even Joshua was guided by written revelation (Josh 1:8; 23:6; 24:26) and by the priestly Urim and Thummim (Num 27:21). During the ensuing three hundred year period of the judges only Deborah (4:4) and an unnamed prophet (6:8-10) speak directly for God.

Mobilizer of Israel's forces (Jdg 4:6-16)

Leadership always involves taking the initiative. It is Deborah who summons Barak, a military leader from the tribe of Naphtali, and instructs him to recruit 10,000 warriors from Naphtali and Zebulun. They are to proceed to Mount Tabor where, it is promised, the Lord will lure Sisera the Canaanite general to his defeat (4:6-7). Even with the prophetic word of promised victory, Barak insists on

---

[2] There is also the (false) prophetess Noadiah, who along with some (false) prophets sought to intimidate Nehemiah in his rebuilding of the Jerusalem wall (Neh 6:14), and the false prophetess Jezebel, who was promoting religious syncretism in Thyatira (Rev 2:20-23).

Deborah's accompanying him: "If you go with me, I will go; but if you don't go with me, I won't go" (4:8). The timidity of the warrior is matched by the courage of the prophetess. She accompanies him, yet with a rebuke: "Because of the way you are going about this, the honor will not be yours, for the Lord will hand Sisera over to a woman" (4:9). Deborah's words presume that deliverance through a woman was both unexpected and would prove dishonorable to Barak, who was leaning on a woman for strength. Later when Abimelech is mortally injured by a millstone dropped on his head by a woman, he calls on his armor-bearer to run him through with the sword lest his epitaph read "a woman killed him" (Jdg 9:54; cf. 2 Sam 11:21). Such was the machismo of ancient middle-eastern culture. The death of Sisera at the hands of Jael will fulfill Deborah's prophesy (4:21) and prove that God is not bound to cultural norms or societal expectations, in this case related to gender, to accomplish his redemptive purposes. He secures the person of courage, Deborah the prophetess or Jael the humble wife of the Kenite, as his instrument of deliverance.

Three times it is noted that Deborah went with Barak to the battle (4:9-10). As a prelude to Jael's later appearance, the settlement of Heber the Kenite near Kedesh is mentioned (4:11). Hobab was the son of Reuel (or Jethro), the priest of Midian and Moses' father in law (Ex 2:15-18; 3:1). Moses had requested that Hobab accompany the nation on its journey to Canaan (Num 10:29-32). Hobab's descendants, the Kenites, had originally settled in the area of southern Judah (Jdg 1:16). Heber, though, left his kinsmen and settled near Kedesh in the area of Naphtali. Here the Kenites were in friendly relations with Jabin and the Canaanites (4:17). Sisera gathered up his chariot force and moved to confront Barak's hastily assembled army at Mount Tabor from the west. Deborah issued the command for Barak to attack and repeated the promise of the Lord's deliverance (4:14; cf. 4:6-7). Barak annihilated Sisera's army when it was forced to abandon the chariots and flee on foot (4:15-16). In the song of triumph Deborah refers to the flooding of the little river Kishon which swept away the enemy troops (5:21). The swelling river had turned the Jezreel valley into mire that clogged the wheels of the chariots. Throughout the narrative the victory is ascribed not to Barak or even Deborah, but to the Lord (4:7, 9, 14, 15, 23).

Honor to the woman (Jdg 4:17-24)
Sisera, who had abandoned his chariot, fled to the home of Heber the Kenite, hoping to find protection due to their friendly relations. Jael, sympathetic to the plight of the Israelites, lured the exhausted commander into her tent by providing shelter and food. When he fell asleep she murdered him by driving a tent peg through his temple. This was the crowning act of Israel's successful overthrow of her oppressors (cf. 5:24-30). The reader of the narrative might wonder why so much material, both in the historical narrative and in the song of praise, is devoted to Jael's murder of Sisera? The answer is found in 4:9: Jael was God's instrument designed to bring all the honor of victory to himself, rather than to Barak, by using a simple woman to destroy a mighty commander. This fits with the theme of Judges: God is the exclusive deliverer of Israel and delights to use weak (two

women, Gideon) and flawed (Jephthah, Samson) people to accomplish his purposes. Though Jael's act was a treacherous betrayal, one that brazenly disregarded the rules of oriental hospitality, she acted on behalf of the covenant nation and her act is thus commended in Israel's poetic annals. Just as God used heathen nations to chastise his people, so he can use even the heinous acts of individuals to further his redemptive program (cf. Mk 14:21; Acts 2:23; 4:27-28).

Song of Deborah (Jdg 5:1-31)

Deborah and Barak celebrated the Lord's deliverance of Israel from the oppressive hand of the Canaanites in a poetic masterpiece that has challenged the most skilled of translators and exegetes due to its archaic language, metrical patterns, and rhetorical features.[3] The author combines the passion of the prophet with the precise articulation of the poet. Deborah, the leader of her generation who mobilized the willing princes of Israel for battle (5:2, 9), was the poet of praise. The song of triumph parallels the order of the narrative that precedes it.

1. Praise (5:1-5): The terrifying presence of the Lord evokes awe.
2. Oppression (5:6-11): Normal life in Israel was disrupted, travel was dangerous, military strength decimated, and idolatry rampant.
3. Mobilization (5:12-18): The involvement of the tribes was limited to six: Ephraim, Benjamin, Manasseh, Zebulun, Issachar, Naphtali; whereas Reuben, Gilead, Dan and Asher are rebuked for their failure to join in.
4. Encounter (5:19-23): Victory is ascribed to the Lord.
5. Commendation (5:24-30): Jael's act of felling Sisera is praised. A woman's hand brings a tragic end to the expectations of Sisera's mother. The enemy is also a human being with aspirations.
6. Supplication (5:31): An imprecation on Israel's enemies is combined with a prayer for the nation's blessing. The supplication is grounded in an appreciation of God's character rather than in nationalistic ambitions: The Lord's enemies must perish, but those who love him will increase in strength.

Leadership profile of Deborah

Deborah was the recognized leader of her generation. She performed multiple roles to the blessing of her nation: discerning judge, courageous prophetess, military mobilizer, and accomplished poet. Above all, she was a person upon whom the divine favor rested. She was God's choice to bring deliverance at a time when the nation was demoralized by its northern oppressors (Jdg 4:3; 5:6-11). God's appointed leader was a woman in an age of male supremacy and dominance (Jdg 4:9; 9:54). At this point the interpreter could be tempted to draw either too much or too little from the gender of the leader. One might argue that Deborah became a leader by default, since the leading warrior of the day was too timid to act on his own (4:8-9a). On the other hand, here was a willing and capable person that God was not at all embarrassed to exalt over all of her countrymen

---

[3] Daniel I. Block, *Judges, Ruth* (Nashville, TN: Broadman, 1999): 211-219, provides a fine summary of the lyrical brilliance of the song and defends the view that Deborah is the primary, if not the exclusive, author.

and countrywomen to accomplish a great deliverance. God neither chose Deborah because she was a woman nor passed her by for the same reason. Though it would be unwise to adopt an entire theology of women in leadership from the singular case of Deborah, the record of this remarkable woman should cause one to pause before constructing strict parameters which limit an individual from exercising God-given gifts based on gender. As in ancient Israel so in the contemporary church, one will soon discover that the sovereign Lord delights to shatter such boxes and to do the unexpected.

Chapter 7.
Gideon: Divine power in human weakness

Preliminary questions to consider:
1. *Why does God delight to use weak and insecure people to accomplish his purposes?*
2. *What can leaders use as a stabilizing anchor when in the course of their mission they face innumerable obstacles to its accomplishment?*
3. *What can undermine the legacy of a leader, and prevent a good work from bearing lasting fruit?*

Context in crisis (Jdg 6:1-10)

The fourth cycle begins with Israel forsaking the Lord (6:1). Divine chastisement comes in the form of various desert peoples from the east swarming over the land, ravaging it and destroying Israel's crops. The Midianites, descendants of Abraham's son Midian through Keturah (Gen 25:1-4), were nomadic desert peoples scattered across many areas around the perimeter of Canaan (cf. Gen 36:35; Ex 3:1; Num 22:4; 25:1, 6; Joshua 13:21; 1 Kg 11:18). In league with the Amalekites and other eastern peoples, their vast numbers and livestock reduced the grazing lands of Canaan to nothing and brought destitution to the Israelite settlers (6:2-5; cf. 7:12). The people cried out to God after seven years of oppression (6:6). The Lord responds by sending an unnamed prophet to rebuke the nation for spiritual adultery (6:7-10). Before providing relief, God demands Israel's full acknowledgment of blame for the underlying cause of her plight.

Call of the "mighty warrior" (Jdg 6:11-24)

The call comes to Gideon, son of Joash, a resident of the town of Ophrah in Manasseh (6:11, 15), from the "angel of the Lord."[1] To a humble villager nervously threshing wheat in a secluded winepress, the title "mighty warrior" appears humorous. Yet Gideon's account is the story of a great God using a weak instrument

---

[1] The "angel of the Lord" in the book of Judges serves as God's spokesman, at times conveying such an exalted role that this interpreter is drawn to see this messenger as a veiled appearance of the Lord God himself (theophany). The angel speaks in the first person singular to remind Israel of her redemption and to rebuke her for covenant violation (Jdg 2:1-4). The angel issues the divine call to Gideon (6:11-12) and consumes the meat and unleavened bread with the fire signifying God's acceptance of Gideon's offering (6:20-21; cf. Lev 9:24). Gideon interprets the fire as the symbol of God's direct presence and expects to die from such exposure (6:22; cf. Lev 10:2), just as Jacob understood the wrestler at Peniel (Gen 32:30). The angel of the Lord announces Samson's birth and Nazirite identity (13:3-5), appears to his parents as a "man of God" (13:6, 8), announces his wonderful name to Manoah (13:18), then ascends to heaven in the flame from Manoah's altar (13:19-20). Manoah, like Gideon (and Jacob), fears death from exposure to the divine presence (13:22). If not a theophany, the angel is at the least the commissioned representative of Yahweh who mediates his word of redemption and judgment on special occasions (cf. Gen 16:7-14; 19:1, 16, 24; 31:11, 13; Ex 3:1-6).

to deliver an errant people. Attention is focused on the divine promises and Gideon's reluctance:

1. Gideon's skepticism (6:12-13): To the promise, "The Lord is with you," Gideon replies sarcastically, "Why has all this happened to us?" Gideon is unable to see any purpose in the present miserable plight of his people.
2. Gideon's inadequacy (6:14-15): Like Moses, Gideon raises the excuses of unsuitability and inability. He is poor, fearful, from a humble clan, and the youngest in his family. Clearly God has set his sights on a weak vessel to show his strength (cf. 1 Sam 16:7).
3. Gideon's timidity of faith (6:16-18): A weak faith demands signs since it is unable to humbly embrace the naked word of promise. God meets Gideon at his point of need; there is no rebuke or criticism.

Gideon voluntarily offers a young goat and unleavened bread, an act of faith in a time of famine. The angel touches the offerings and fire consumes them, proving their divine acceptance (6:19-22). At that point Gideon recognizes the divine character of the angel and expects to die due to exposure to God's holiness. The Lord's tender reassurance to the insecure Gideon is "Peace, do not fear" (6:23). Gideon, as an act of worship, constructs an altar to Jehovah-Shalom, "the Lord is peace" (6:24).

First test of faith (Jdg 6:25-32)

Gideon's faith is immediately tested. The Lord commands him to tear down his father's Baal altar, replace it with one dedicated to the Lord, and offer a bull for a burnt offering (6:25-26). To obey required a great deal of courage. Gideon would have been aware of the severe reaction of his neighbors, even demanding his life for this act of desecration (6:30). His fearful obedience takes place under the brief cover of night (6:27). Gideon's father, Joash, has already become convinced of the spiritual bankruptcy of Baalism, which is corrupting the Manassehite clans. He mocks the idol and defends his son (6:31). The present crisis has forced Joash to question his own values. Gideon is renamed Jerub-Baal, literally "let Baal contend" (6:32), an appropriate title for a mighty warrior battling false gods more than Midianites. Religious reform precedes military action.

Confirmation of the call (Jdg 6:33-40)

Like the other judges, Gideon's preparation was completed by the empowerment of the Spirit of God (6:34).[2] Cautious by nature, Gideon seeks one final confirmation of God's guidance before launching out. God once again graciously accommodates himself to the request of his servant (cf. 6:17-22). As

---

[2] The ministry of the Spirit of God is to provide special empowerment to the judges for their limited missions of liberating Israel from foreign oppression. The Spirit calls Othniel to war against the Mesopotamians (Jdg 3:10), gives Gideon courage to mobilize four tribes and lead them against the eastern peoples (6:34), employs Jephthah to advance against the Ammonites (13:25), stirs up Samson from his youth to battle the Philistines (13:25), and is the source of Samson's incredible physical strength (14:6, 19; 15:14).

proposed by Gideon, the dew accumulates first on the wool fleece, with the ground dry, while the process is reversed the second time (6:36-40). Gideon's flickering flame of faith, nearly quenched by feelings of inadequacy, is strengthened by a theophany (6:11, 22), accepted offerings (6:21), and a fleece. He begins to mobilize his fellow Manassehites, along with tribesmen north of the Jezreel valley in Asher, Naphtali, and Zebulun (6:35).

Preparations for battle (Jdg 7:1-15)

By a divinely guided process of elimination, the numerical strength of Gideon's army is reduced from 32,000 to 10,000 to 300 (7:1-8). The vast Midianite coalition numbers 135,000 (7:12; 8:10). The entire episode focuses on manifesting God's power in a humanly impossible situation "in order that Israel may not boast against me that her own strength has saved her" (7:2). First, those controlled by fear are told to return home (7:3). Then, the Lord commands Gideon to bring the men down to the water for a further test (7:5). Of the 10,000 remaining, only those who bring the water to their mouths with cupped hands and lap from them, rather than those who kneel down and lap the water with their tongues like a dog, can join in the campaign. The significance of the test seems to be that those who lap with cupped hands remain on their feet and thus are keeping watch for the enemy, so demonstrating cautionary wisdom. Both the fearful and the foolish have now been eliminated. Gideon's army has been reduced to a paltry 300 men (7:6-8).

The consistently cautious nature of Gideon, wavering at the commencement of the battle, receives further encouragement (7:9-15). Scouting the enemy camp from a secluded place, he and his servant Purah overhear a Midianite warrior relating a dream he had to his friend: a loaf of barley bread tumbled into the Midianite camp, struck and overturned the tent (7:13). Gideon understands the symbolism and with renewed courage offers worship to God and prepares to attack (7:15).

The battle belongs not to the strong (Jdg 7:16-8:21)

The narrator views the battle as God's triumph, not Gideon's (7:2, 7, 14, 15, 22). The eastern peoples amass in the valley of Jezreel near the hill of Moreh. Gideon's band encamps just to the south at the spring of Harod (7:1, 8-12). The tiny band of 300 is divided into three groups of one hundred each, armed with trumpets, jars, and torches (7:16). A more unlikely fighting unit could hardly be imagined! Gideon commands his band to imitate their leader: "Do exactly as I do" (7:17). When the Israelites blow their trumpets, smash their jars, raise their torches, and shout, the unsuspecting Midianites become completely disoriented, gripped by fear and panic, and turn on each other before fleeing north. Tribesmen from Naphtali, Asher, Manasseh, and finally Ephraim join the battle, seize the Jordan valley, and capture two Midianite leaders, Oreb and Zeeb. The proud Ephraimites sharply criticize Gideon for summoning them after the other tribes (8:1). He placates their wrath by praising their accomplishments (8:2-3). Gideon cruelly punishes the towns of Succoth and Peniel for refusing him aid (8:13-17). Such capricious revenge reveals character flaws that portend greater troubles ahead. He personally carries out the execution of the captured kings, Zebah and

Zalmunnah. The once fearful Gideon fulfills their proverb that courage is the true measure of a man (8:21).

Flawed legacy (Jdg 8:22-32)

Following such an outstanding victory Gideon demonstrates a strange combination of God-honoring humility and God-dishonoring idolatry. Even though the campaign was designed from first to last to demonstrate divine enabling, the hero-worshipping multitudes immediately ascribe glory to the human instrument and seek to make Gideon their king. Gideon stoutly refuses: "I will not rule over you, nor will my son rule over you. The Lord will rule over you" (8:23). Despite his humility, a subtle materialism combined with public pressure brings about spiritual chaos in Gideon's life, his family, and the nation. He is more attracted to the Midianite plunder than the prestige. Receiving gold rings amounting to about forty-three pounds (1700 shekels), Gideon fashions a golden ephod, which becomes an object of worship. Earlier he built an altar to the Lord at Ophrah (6:24); now he deposits there an idolatrous image. The ephod "became a snare to Gideon and his family" (8:27). Judges 9 records the tragic consequences of Gideon's polygamy (8:29-31, 35).

Leadership profile of Gideon

1. *Divine power in human weakness: A fearful Gideon is threshing wheat in a secluded winepress when he receives his commissioning as a "mighty warrior." But in the end the transformation of Gideon from fearful wheat thresher to bold commander makes that initial title seem appropriate. Did the angel address him as "mighty warrior" with a proleptic meaning, that is, in terms of what God would one day make of the man? The routing of a Midianite army of 135,000 by 300 Israelite soldiers led by an obscure son of a wheat farmer, acting in faith (Heb 11:32), magnifies the greatness of his Lord.*
2. *Reaffirmation of the call: The reluctant leader, whose excuses cannot deflect God's purposes for him, needs assurance before stepping forth in obedience. A terrifying theophany, offerings of meat and bread consumed by fire from a rock, a wool fleece first wet and then dry, and the dream of a Midianite warrior all serve to confirm that, yes, he was the person of God's choosing for such a time as this. Recollection of the unmistakable call of God has been the stabilizing anchor of many leaders who in the course of their work must face down fears within and adversaries without.*
3. *Personal flaws that undermine one's legacy: Gideon succeeded at the specific task of judging Israel during a time of Midianite expansion. Gideon's triumph over Midian is remembered in Israel's history as a great deliverance (Ps 83:11-12; Isa 9:4; 10:26; cf. Heb 11:32). However, his potential positive legacy for the reform of the nation, so anticipated in the courageous assault on the Baal altar in Ophrah, failed to materialize. He died and was buried in his hometown of Ophrah, where he both built an altar to the Lord and deposited a golden idol.*

Chapter 8.
Samson: Potential squandered by character flaws

Preliminary questions to consider:
1. *What is the necessary link between divine gifting and the actual fulfillment of one's God-given potential?*
2. *What are several areas of self-management that are crucial for leaders, if they are to effectively guide others?*
3. *How should one assess leaders with major character flaws, in terms of their calling and mission?*

Special identity and godly heritage (Jdg 13:1-25)

The seventh cycle begins with forty years of oppression from the Philistines who inhabited the coastal areas west of Judah and south of Dan (13:1). The deliverer's coming is announced before his birth. Born into the godly family of Manoah, Samson has every advantage, unlike the illegitimate and ostracized Jephthah (Jdg 11:1-3). His birth is announced by the "angel of the Lord" (13:3). This special child is to be a Nazirite, set apart to God from birth, and forbidden to cut his hair or drink anything fermented (Num 6:1-21). Until then Manoah's unnamed wife has suffered, like Sarai (Gen 16:1) and Rebekah (Gen 25:21), the tragedy of childlessness. Three times in this chapter Samson's Nazirite identity is emphasized (13:4-5, 7, 14). Though Samson is divinely conscripted for life, the Nazirite vow was normally a voluntary oath of commitment by a layperson to the Lord's service for a limited period, under the regulation of the priests (Num 6:10, 16-17, 19-20). A purpose beyond just physical deliverance is set for Samson's life. Manoah next inquires of the angel's name, being told it is "beyond understanding" (13:18 [NIV]).[1] When the angel ascends in the flame from the altar of sacrifice, Manoah suddenly realizes he has been standing face to face with deity (13:21-22). Like Jacob (Gen 32:30), Moses (Ex 3:6; 33:18-23), and Gideon (Jdg 6:22-23), Manoah fears immediate death from direct exposure to God's glory. Manoah's wife reassures her husband that the acceptance of the burnt offering indicates the Lord's good intentions to fulfill his promise of a son (13:23). A son is born to the couple and they name him Samson, related to the Hebrew word for "sun" (13:24).[2]

---

[1] The Hebrew adjective פֶּלִאי is from the verb root פלא ("to be marvelous, wonderful, extraordinary"), which is used to describe the mighty redemptive acts of God (Ex 15:11; Isa 25:1; Ps 77:12, 15; 78:12), the Lord's incomparable majesty (Ps 89:6), or even the identity of the Messiah as a "wonder of a counselor" (Isa 9:6). The adjectival form occurs elsewhere only in Psalm 139:6 to express the incomprehensible wonder of God's penetrating omniscience of the Psalmist's every thought and action. Accordingly, the answer of the angel may well point to this being a theophany (or preincarnate Christophany). See *NIDOTTE*, 3: 615-617.

[2] The name (lit. "little sun") may be intended to symbolize (the sun's) strength or brightness. It is unlikely (contra Block, *Judges*, 416-418) that the godly Jewish parents of Samson were simply following the common near eastern practice of naming their child in memory of the sun god, Shemesh.

In light of Samson's subsequent moral failures and tragic ending, it is well to the recall the spiritual privileges he enjoyed. First, he is born to godly parents who obey the angel's instructions, fear God's holiness, and seek divine guidance for his upbringing (13:8, 12). Second, his specially foretold birth coupled with dedication to God as a Nazirite sets him apart as the person of God's choice for his generation (13:5, 7). Third, his childhood is blessed by the Lord (13:24). Fourth, the Spirit of God moves Samson from his early years (13:25).

Physical exploits and character flaws (Jdg 14:1-20)
Being attracted to one of the Philistine women, Samson asks his parents to arrange the marriage (14:1-2). He operates on the basis of unrestrained impulse: "I have seen . . . now get her for me." Samson's parents recognize his request as a violation of the law, which forbade intermarriage with the heathen (14:3; cf. Ex 34:16; Deut 7:3-4). Though clearly outside the revealed will of God, the text states that this relationship is "from the Lord, who was seeking an occasion to confront the Philistines" (14:4). It is not necessary to justify this desire of Samson or many of his later actions. God's permissive will takes into account even the sinful actions of people to further his purposes (Gen 45:8; 50:20; Ex 9:16; Ps 76:10; Acts 2:23; 4:28).

Samson is able to persuade his parents to accompany him to Timnah and finalize the marriage. Samson has supernatural physical strength. Approaching Timnah he encounters a lion, which he tears apart with his bare hands by the power of the Spirit (14:5-6). Disturbing character flaws are disclosed in this narrative. Samson evidences a scheming sort of humor. On his return to Timnah for the wedding ceremony, he comes upon the carcass of the lion in which is a swarm of bees and honey. He scoops out some of the honey and eats it. Since bees avoid anything with decomposition, perhaps birds and decay had ravaged the carcass leaving only the skeletal remains. At the seven day wedding feast Samson speaks a riddle based on the incident, promising thirty sets of clothes to anyone who can solve it. An importunate wife coaxes her husband to reveal the riddle to her and she relays its meaning to his attendants (14:15-17). Samson pays his debt at their expense by slaying thirty Philistines at Ashkelon and stripping off their belongings. Did Samson design the entire scheme to move against the Philistines? His unbridled anger (14:19), rather than righteous indignation, has motivated his action. In this incident Samson violates two of the Nazirite prescriptions, namely, contacting a dead corpse (14:9) and drinking fermented drink at the wedding feast (14:12, 17).

Deliverer from Philistine oppression (Jdg 15:1-16:3)
God's purposes for Samson to relieve Israel of Philistine oppression are noted at his birth (13:5) and his marriage (14:4). In carrying out his mission Samson combines an impetuous character with dependence on the Spirit. For some reason Samson was away from his wife following the wedding feast until the time of the wheat harvest. The bride's father, perhaps angered at Samson's lack of love for his daughter, secures her another husband (14:20; 15:2). Samson is enraged and, as a method of getting even, he catches three hundred foxes, ties them together by

their tails in pairs, and fastens a torch to each end. Seeing their vineyards and olive groves destroyed by fire, the Philistines burn to death Samson's wife and her father (15:6b; cf. 14:15). Samson acts not as a consecrated instrument of divine wrath, but as one bent on personal vengeance—"I have a right to get even" (15:3)— and viciously slaughters many of them (15:7-8).

The Philistines organize a large force and pursue Samson to Lehi in Judah. Philistine oppression has reduced Judah to desperate conditions. Three thousand men from Judah approach Samson: "Don't you realize that the Philistines are rulers over us? What have you done to us?" (15:11a). Samson is clearly not an organizing force within Israel; his is a one-man campaign of destruction. His principle of conduct is lex talionis: "I merely did to them what they did to me" (15:11b). Allowing the men of Judah to bind him, Samson is brought to the Philistines and, seizing the opportunity, breaks the fetters by the Spirit (15:14). He finds a fresh jawbone of a donkey and single-handedly slays a thousand Philistines. Scripture neither conceals the failures of its heroes nor omits the merits of its weaker characters. The lustful, angry, vengeful, impulsive Samson is also capable of exercising faith in God's power. He prays in the posture of the Lord's servant and, ascribing the victory to God, pleads for water to drink. God rewards his faith by opening a spring in Lehi to refresh his servant (15:18-19).

Probably a representative event, singled out as an example of his physical prowess yet moral weakness, Samson is surrounded by the Philistines at Gaza during a one night stay with a prostitute (16:1-3). His attraction to the young women of Philistia has already ended in tragedy once (14:1-3; 15:6) and will ultimately bring about his downfall. Rising at night, Samson with arrogant delight removes the gates of the city from their posts and carries them to Hebron some forty miles away (16:3).

Tragic downfall (Jdg 16:4-22)

Abraham, Judah, David, Solomon and here Samson represent the vulnerability of believing men to sexual temptation. Samson's impulsive attraction to Canaanite women (14:1-2; 16:1-2) reveals a poverty of theocratic values (14:3). Late in life he falls in love with Delilah, a woman from his native area, the valley of Sorek (16:4). Probably a Philistine, she is offered by the rulers of the Philistines eleven hundred shekels of silver if she can uncover "the secret of his great strength" (16:5). Samson, again demonstrating his irrepressible sense of humor, playfully deceives Delilah three times. He pretends he can be subdued by being bound by seven fresh thongs (16:7), or new, unused ropes (16:11), or if his hair is woven into seven braids (16:13). Each time, however, when Delilah announces that Philistines are upon him Samson's power remains unabated. But Delilah perseveres due to the monetary rewards offered. Her incessant nagging finally wears Samson down. He foolishly reveals that his strength lies in his Nazirite identity represented by his uncut hair (16:17). Samson is utterly without moral discernment, for he is willing to reveal everything to a woman whose purposes are demonstrably destructive.

There was no magical power in the hair; rather his lifelong dedication to God as a Nazirite, his being set apart from birth for God's will, mediated the supernatural powers to carry out God's purposes. The unshaven head was one of the principal expressions of his spiritual calling (13:4-5, 7, 14). Samson's revelation to Delilah—an arrogant rejection of his Nazirite identity—brings tragic consequences. While asleep on Delilah's lap, his head is shaven and his strength departs. The sad commentary follows: "But he did not know that the Lord had left him" (16:20). The Philistines easily overpower Samson, gouge out his eyes, and reduce him to slave status as a grinder in the prison in Gaza (16:21).

Recovery of a lost identity (Jdg 16:23-31)

Samson becomes an object of ridicule to the Philistines. When a huge assembly of Philistines gathers at the temple of Dagon, the Philistine fertility god, Samson is cruelly paraded before them for their amusement. The blind, humiliated slave with multiple moral failures, however, is still the Lord's servant. In a suicide mission he positions himself against the supporting pillars of the temple. Samson entreats his God to remember him so that he can avenge himself against his enemies (16:28). To his final breath revenge is Samson's core value. With the requirement of his Nazirite vow again respected (16:22), and in answer to his prayer, God strengthens Samson to topple the pillars of the temple causing its total collapse. This brings about his own death and many thousands of assembled worshippers (16:29-30). Yet even his enemies allow him to have a decent burial (16:31).

Leadership profile of Samson

1. *Sacred purposes left unfulfilled: Three main prohibitions governed the Nazirite lifestyle with respect to diet, appearance, and association: (1) no eating of grapes or drinking of the fruit of the vine; (2) no cutting of the hair or the beard; and (3) no contact with dead bodies even at the funeral of one's family member (Num 6:1-8). Samson's adult life fails to fulfill the promises of his youth as he egregiously violates all three regulations of the Nazirite. Pious parents, a happy youth, early impulses of the Spirit, and a special identity do not guarantee spiritual success in later life. No lasting redemptive fruit survives his demolition activities.*

2. *Discipline over oneself: Samson was a man of incredible physical strength and mighty exploits under the Spirit's power. He tore apart a lion with his bare hands, struck down thirty Philistines at once, tore from his arms the bindings of two fresh ropes, killed a thousand men with the jawbone of a donkey, and carried the city gates of Gaza nearly forty miles to Hebron. Motivated by revenge (15:3, 7, 11; 16:28), consumed with anger (14:19), and controlled by lust (14:1-2; 16:1, 4), Samson moved through life on the impulses of the moment. He was a man who could conquer others, but could not master himself. As a result his military triumphs were temporary, while his spiritual defeats were lasting. He brought about the deaths of his wife and family as well as his own humiliation and death.*

3. *Usefulness of imperfect vessels: It is important to remember that Samson was still the Lord's chosen servant who, in terms of his calling to attack the oppressing Philistines (13:5; 14:4), fulfilled his mission. His physical powers came from the Spirit (13:25; 14:6, 19; 15:14). Although a flawed man, Samson's exploits are preserved in the historical record as acts of faith (15:18-19; 16:28; Heb 11:32).*

Chapter 9.
Samuel: Leader at the Crossroads

Preliminary questions to consider:
1. *What formative influences significantly shape the character of a future leader?*
2. *Why and in what cases is it necessary for a leader to defend one's integrity when it is under attack?*
3. *In times of crisis what is it that distinguishes a godly leader from an impetuous one?*

Pivotal period for the nation

The life of Samuel is a key turning point in the history of Israel. Chronologically, he belongs to the period of the judges. His early ministry spanned the latter days of Samson. He is properly seen as the last judge (1 Sam 7:15-17) and the first of the prophets (1 Sam 3:7, 20-21; 4:1a; cf. Acts 3:24; 13:20). Samuel's life brings Israel from the dark age of disunity (Jdg 21:25), foreign oppression (1 Sam 4:1-11), priestly corruption (1 Sam 2:12-17), and a prophetic vacuum (3:1) to the age of renewal where unity under godly rule, expansion of Israel's borders, a consecrated priesthood, and abundant prophetic expression become its outstanding features. Samuel, for this reason, is one of Israel's greatest leaders.

Heritage of a godly mother (1 Sam 1:1-2:10)

Samuel's father was from the hill country of Ephraim (1:1). He had two wives which, as in all the cases of polygamy in the Old Testament, produced family strife. Hannah, though greatly loved by Elkanah (1:5, 8), suffered the deep social stigma of barrenness. Peninnah, his other wife, bore a number of children. As with Hagar and Sarah (Gen 16) or Leah and Rachel (Gen 30:1-24), the two women became rivals caught up in a spiral of pettiness and jealousy. Hannah's life became unbearable, the painful reality especially felt during the annual family pilgrimages to Shiloh for the sacrificial feasts (1 Sam 1:7-8).

Desperation drove Hannah to earnest prayer. Provoked by her rival, swallowed up by bitterness, discouraged, weeping, unable to eat, Hannah poured out her burdens to the Lord. "Remember me" is the prayer of helplessness (1:11), the same prayer which the blind, humiliated Samson prayed at the temple of Dagon (Jdg 16:28), or the thief hanging on the cross uttered to the Son of God hanging next to him (Lk 23:42). Hannah also made a sincere vow: if the Lord would open her womb, she would give her son as a lifelong Nazirite to the Lord. The Nazirite was required to abstain from fermented drink, leave the hair untouched by a razor, and avoid ceremonial defilement (Num 6:1-6). Though initially misinterpreted by Eli as the babbling of a drunken woman, the high priest finally offered his blessing (1:17). Hannah found comfort in prayer, her appetite returned, and her spirit was no longer downcast (1:7-8, 18). "Lord, remember me" (1:11) found its response in "the Lord remembered Hannah" (1:19). The barren woman bore a son, whose very name embodies the heart of biblical prayer, Samuel, "heard of God" (1:20).

Vows to God once uttered must be carried out (Num 30:2; Deut 23:21-23; Eccles 5:4-5). As the Lord "made good his word" (1:23), so Hannah fulfilled her vow by dedicating her son to tabernacle service after the period of weaning, probably two to three years. At the dedication Hannah offered a bull as a votive offering, with its accompanying libation and grain offerings (1:24; cf. Num 15:8-12). Hannah's dedication was personal and permanent: "So now I give him to the Lord. For his whole life he will be given over to the Lord" (1:28). Certainly Hannah felt the pain of separation. After the dedication she only saw her son once a year, when she ascended to Shiloh for the Feast of Tabernacles (2:19). Despite the sacrifice involved, her only recorded words show gratitude and the joy of commitment (2:1). Hannah's act of dedication issues not in a lament of separation, but a prayer of praise (2:1-10). Her theme is the common biblical motif of God's exaltation of the humble and humiliation of the proud (Isa 57:15; 66:1-2; Mt 5:3-5; Lk 18:13-14; 1 Pet 5:5-7). God is a holy rock (2:2), an all-knowing discerner (2:3), a sovereign director (2:6-7), sustainer (2:9), and judge (2:10). The qualities of Hannah, namely, passion, devotion, sacrifice, integrity, faithfulness and dependence will have a formative influence on her son.

Protection in a corrupt environment (1 Sam 2:11-36)

The boy Samuel's life centered on "ministering before the Lord" (2:11, 18) in the tabernacle under Eli, the high priest. He must have felt the pain of separation from family, but also experienced the joy of service. Each year would bring a joyous reunion with his mother, who presented to her son a small robe at the time of the annual sacrifice (2:19). It was a visible symbol both of his mother's affection and his own unique consecration to serve the Lord. The annual pilgrimage to Shiloh, then, was the watershed event throughout Hannah's life. It marked the seasons of bitterness (1:7-8), dedication (1:10-11), renewed hope (1:19-20), separation (1:24-28), and reunion (2:19). Eli's prayer that God would honor Hannah's commitment (1:17) was answered. The loneliness of missing Samuel must have been somewhat relieved by the birth of three more sons and two daughters (2:20-21). Samuel grew up in the blessing of God (2:21) and, like Jesus, "grew in stature and in favor with the Lord and with people" (2:26; cf. Lk 2:52).

It is remarkable that Hannah's (and perhaps Eli's) godly influence on Samuel was enough to counteract the corrupt environment the young boy faced in the central sanctuary in Shiloh. Eli's sons were "sons of Belial," that is, wicked men who had no regard for the Lord (2:12; cf. Deut 13:13). In levitical legislation the priests were allowed to receive specified parts of the congregational offerings (Lev 7:28-38). These priests, however, began to disregard the limits of that provision, treating the Lord's offering with contempt (2:17). The sin of Eli's sons was fourfold. First, rather than the designated breast and right thigh of the fellowship offering, they took the portion they desired (2:13-14; cf. Lev 7:34; 10:13-14). Second, they took the meat before it had been properly offered to God (2:14-15a; cf. Lev 7:30-31). Third, rather than accepting the portion as the voluntary act of the worshipper, it was taken by force (2:16; cf. Deut 18:1-5). Fourth, boiling is the designated form of cooking the priestly portion, but Eli's sons, in confiscating the sacrifice early, desired to roast it, which was unlawful (2:15; cf. Num 6:19-20). Their sin was compounded by sexual immorality with the servant women at the tabernacle (2:22). Cultic prostitution, an integral part of Canaanite religion, was having an influence on Israel at its very religious center (cf. Deut 23:17-18). Moreover, Eli's sons refused their father's warnings and despised the peoples' report (2:23-25).

Severe judgment is announced on the house of Eli by an unnamed "man of God." Eli is reminded of his priestly calling, the privileges and responsibilities of his sacred office (2:27-28). The severity of the prophet's words is directed at Eli's handling of his sons, Hophni and Phinehas. Although Eli rebuked his sons for their blasphemy (2:22-25), it was too little and too late. Later when Samuel repeats the prophecy against Eli he condemns the priest for failing to restrain his sons (3:13, 18). Both as father and as high priest Eli has failed to honor the Lord (2:30b). No words are spoken to Hophni and Phinehas, only to Eli. Judgment will come in the form of cutting off Eli's house from the priesthood and raising up in its place a "faithful priest" to perform the will of God (2:31-36). The specific judgments announced here reach fulfillment in the following years: the death of Hophni and Phinehas (4:11); massacre of Eli's priestly descendants at Nob by Saul (22:18-19); removal of Abiathar from the priestly office (1 Kg 2:26-27); and installation of Zadok as a faithful high priest (1 Kg 2:35; 1 Chron 29:22b). Eli's actions will affect the destiny of future generations (cf. Ex 20:5-6; 34:6-7). Derelict leaders drag many others down with them.[1]

Unmistakable call to listen (1 Sam 3:1-21)

The silence of those dark days (3:1) is broken by God's prophetic word to Samuel. The voice of God comes to Samuel in the early morning hours. Samuel thinks the aged Eli is calling him. The Lord is persistent, his call repeated three times. Finally, Eli perceives the significance and Samuel is instructed to reply, "speak, for your servant is listening" (3:9). This begins the new intimate relationship and prophetic role of Samuel to the Lord of Israel (3:7). The voice of God must be heard by a willing, sensitive heart, which then fosters increasing familiarity and keener perception. The revelation to Samuel concerns the judgment on Eli's family line for his failure to restrain his sons (3:11-14). Though initially hesitant to declare such a harsh pronouncement to his beloved priest-mentor, Samuel, as a true prophet, declares fully God's word to Eli. From this time forth the prophetic gift is renewed. Samuel's attestation as a prophet becomes known throughout Israel (3:19-21).[2]

---

[1] God would not revoke the eternal priesthood of Aaron (1 Sam 2:27-30), but he did alter which Aaronic family would fulfill the priestly role. Though Eli, of the family of Aaron's second son Ithamar, was for some unknown reason high priest in Samuel's day, God transferred the high priesthood back to the line of Eleazar, Aaron's eldest son, in the person of Zadok during Solomon's reign (1 Kg 2:26-27, 35). Thus Eli's line continued to the time of Solomon (1 Sam 14:3; 22:20). Subsequently Zadok's line is promised an eternal succession, like Aaron's (1 Sam 2:35-36; cf. Ex 29:9; Num 25:13). In the messianic kingdom Zadok's sons will minister before the Lord (Ezek 44:15-16; 48:11).

[2] From Moses to Samuel the direct prophetic word of the Lord largely ceased. Even Joshua was guided by written revelation (Josh 1:8; 23:6; 24:26) and the priestly Urim and Thummim (Num 27:21). During the ensuing period of the judges only Deborah the prophetess (Jdg 4:4) and an unnamed prophet (Jdg 6:8) speak directly for God.

Prophet to a nation in decline (1 Sam 4:1-7:1)

The Philistines constituted the greatest military threat to Israel from Samuel's time onward. Israel encounters the Philistine armies at Aphek as these coastal people seek to extend their domain northward. Humiliated by defeat,[3] the nation asks itself the right question: "Why did the Lord bring defeat upon us today before the Philistines?" (4:3). The probe, however, proves superficial as they conclude that the underlying cause is ritual rather than spiritual. Influenced by pagan conceptions and encouraged by a corrupt priesthood (4:3b-4), Israel improperly substitutes the symbol for the substance to manipulate God into supporting their cause. The results are disastrous: Israel is defeated, 30,000 soldiers slain, Hophni and Phinehas killed as prophesied (2:34; 3:12-14), and the ark of God captured. Eli, hearing the news, fell backward, broke his neck and died. It is to his credit that his final concern is for the ark of God rather than his degenerate sons (4:13, 18), a reversal of his earlier priorities (2:29-30). The pregnant wife of Phinehas, hearing the news of the death of her husband and father-in-law, went into immediate labor and gave birth to a son, Ichabod, "no glory." This son's birth signifies the meaning of the capture of the ark: God's glorious presence departed from Israel (4:21). God allowed the ark to be captured to symbolize what had already taken place: His presence was withdrawn from the nation due to unfaithfulness to the covenant.

The narrator traces the movements of the ark and its effect on those in proximity to it. It is taken from its sanctuary in Shiloh (Josh 18:1) to Aphek/Ebenezer where it is captured (1 Sam 4:3, 11). In Philistine territory the ark moves from Ashdod (5:1-7), to Gath (5:8-9), and to Ekron (5:10-6:11). In Ashdod the ark is placed before the image of Dagon, the Philistine god of fertility. Dagon's image is first found prostrate before the ark, and after being set upright is later found with its hands and feet broken off, lying on the threshold of the temple. Still, the Philistines do not stop to reevaluate their belief system, but consecrate the threshold where the hands and feet of Dagon came to rest. Wherever the ark travels the people break out with tumors, accompanied by a plague of rats (5:6, 9, 12; 6:5).

The Philistine rulers, at the advice of the religious officials, decide to return the ark to Israel accompanied by "guilt offerings" of five gold tumors and five gold rats, one for each of the major Philistine cities (cf. Josh 13:3). The Philistines conveniently combined their knowledge of Israel's guilt offerings (6:3, 8) with their own brand of sympathetic magic, which involved the removal sickness through physical models of their affliction (6:4-5). After seven months in captivity (6:1) the ark is returned to Israel via Beth Shemesh (6:12-20), before finally settling in Kiriath Jearim (6:21-7:2). The ark is carried on a cart led by cows that have never been yoked or trained to pull a cart. Its return to Beth Shemesh confirms the Philistines' suspicion that the ark is the direct cause of the plague (6:9). At Beth Shemesh, a border town in Judah, the ark comes to rest in the field of Joshua (6:13-18). However, seventy men are put to death for looking into the ark (6:19-20). The ark represented God's holy presence and careful instructions had been

---

[3] The destruction of Shiloh probably occurred around this time (Jer 7:12, 14; 26:6, 9; Ps 78:60).

given for its handling and transportation (Num 4:4-6, 15-20). Only the high priest could enter the most holy place once a year with the blood of atonement. There was no excuse for such a flagrant violation of the law, for Beth Shemesh was a special city designated for priests and Levites (Josh 21:16). The covenant people suffer even greater temporal judgment—physical death—for this violation than the Philistines do for their manipulative actions—tumors and rats. The people of Beth Shemesh, terrified at the holy presence of God (6:20), transfer the ark to Kiriath Jearim where it remains for the next twenty years (7:2).

Reformer, intercessor, and judge (1 Sam 7:2-17)
    Into this period of military weakness and moral decadence steps Samuel, already revered throughout Israel as a prophet (1 Sam 3:19-4:1). Samuel is a multi-task leader if ever there was one. First, he is a reformer (7:2-4). Through Samuel's preaching Israel again begins to seek the Lord. Spiritual hunger replaces apathy. Yet Samuel will not settle for sentimental measures. He demands total separation from and removal of the Baal and Ashtoreth idols and renewed commitment to serve "the Lord only." Both negative and positive responses are required: "rid yourselves . . . commit yourselves" (7:3).
    Second, he performs a priestly prayer ministry on behalf of the nation assembled at Mizpah (7:5-14). Samuel's preaching and prayer are met by repentance and confession (7:6). The Lord responds to their leader's prayers by enabling Israel to defeat the Philistines at Mizpah and to break free of their control during Samuel's lifetime (7:10-14). Visible symbols mark the central events: water for confession (7:6); sacrificial lamb for intercession (7:9);[4] and Ebenezer, "stone of help," for the place of deliverance (7:12). The pattern is established: intercession, confession and repentance, removal of idols, and deliverance from enemies. "He cried out to the Lord on Israel's behalf, and the Lord answered him" could be the motto of Samuel's ministry (7:9b). Samuel's intercession will continue throughout his lifetime (8:6; 12:19, 23). He stands beside Moses as one of the great intercessors in Israel's history (Ps 99:6; Jer 15:1).
    Third, Samuel makes regular circular itineraries in order to settle legal disputes as judge (Bethel, Gilgal, Mizpah, Ramah) (7:15-17). His life can be viewed as a conclusion to the period of the judges, the initiation of the period of the prophets (3:1, 19-21), and the inauguration of the period of the monarchy (Chs 8-12). Samuel was God's crossroads man whose name deserves to stand alongside those of Moses, Joshua, and David in the annals of Israel. With the central shrine at Shiloh destroyed, the ark in captivity, the priesthood decimated, and the Philistines threatening, it is the leadership of Samuel that renews national morale and safeguards the national identity.

---

[4] Samuel's father was from a Kohathite clan of the tribe of Levi, but was not from the Aaronic line (1 Chron 6:22-26; cf. Josh 21:20-21). The sacrifice of a lamb as a burnt offering is credited to Samuel's initiative (7:9-10), but must have been carried out by the Aaronic high priest (cf. 9:12-13; 10:8). Alternatively, this sacrifice was an exceptional act of national significance, which Samuel was allowed to perform.

Prophetic misgivings about the monarchy (1 Sam 8:1-22)

Like Eli, Samuel proved unable to pass on his values to his sons who, in attempting to assume their father's office, sought personal gain. Unlike Samuel, who throughout his life walked in integrity (12:3-5), his sons perverted justice through bribery (8:3). With the priesthood decimated and the potential successors to Samuel corrupt, the elders of Israel voice concern over the nation's future and request the appointment of a central monarch (8:5). However, the underlying motivation behind this natural request is a desire to have a king "such as all the other nations have" (8:5, 20). Framed in this way, the petition constitutes a denial of theocratic principles (cf. Jdg 8:22-23). Conformity to oriental patterns of government mean more to the elders than preservation of their distinct identity as a people under Yahweh's rule. This was a rejection of the Lord as king (8:6-8; 12:12).

The Lord accedes to their request (8:22), while warning them through Samuel (8:9) of the financial, political, and military consequences of such a decision (8:10-18). With the appointment of a king will come centralized power, governmental bureaucracy, and the heavy burden on average citizens to support those structures: military drafts (8:11), weapons buildup (8:12), servitude (8:13), land confiscation (8:14), heavy taxation (8:15), and loss of personal freedom (8:16-17). But the nation has made up its mind (8:19-20). Under pressure of military attack from the surrounding nations, and lacking confidence in God's ability to protect them, the people are willing to sacrifice personal liberties for national security. The monarchy would reflect theocratic values to the degree the individual king obeyed the covenant and set the moral tone of the nation. In its brightest moments, especially under David, the human kingdom would be a harbinger of the coming kingdom of God (cf. Gen 49:10; Num 24:17; 2 Sam 7:11-16). But Samuel's ambivalence toward the monarchy reflects the tension between God's permissive will in granting the nation its request (8:7, 9, 22; 9:16-17; 10:24; 12:13) and Israel's moral responsibility in rejecting God's theocratic rule and evading their covenantal obligations (8:7; 10:19; 12:12, 17, 19-20).

Complex relationship with the first king (1 Sam 9:1-11:15)

Saul, a Benjamite from Gibeah, is sent by his father with a servant in search of donkeys who have wandered away (9:1-5). Samuel, the man of God (9:6), prophet or seer (9:9), is well known to the servant who counsels Saul to seek his advice about the whereabouts of the lost donkeys. The prophet, whose ministry is attested by its truthfulness (9:6), is approachable, for the two men draw near with only a small gift and regarding a small matter. Samuel is performing priestly duties as he presides over the sacrificial meal at the local altar or "high place" (9:12-14).

The Lord reveals to Samuel that Saul is his choice as leader over Israel (9:16). Samuel turns Saul's attention to more important matters, assuring him that the donkeys have been found, and instructs him to join in the sacrificial meal. From a humble mission to recover his father's donkeys and an unplanned encounter with the prophet, Saul is shocked by Samuel's revelation concerning the kingship (9:20-21). Samuel exalts Saul before everyone, offering him the leg or thigh of the peace offering normally reserved for the priest (9:24; cf. Lev 7:32-35). In a private ceremony Samuel anoints Saul as leader over the Lord's people, his inheritance

(10:1), as he later does with David (16:13). Samuel announces three signs to authenticate this initial act of appointment: (1) Two men at Zelzah will announce the return of the lost donkeys (10:2); (2) Three men approaching Bethel will offer him two loaves of bread (10:3-4); (3) Saul will join the procession of prophets near Gibeah, his hometown (10:26), in Spirit-inspired prophesying (10:5-7). Only one command is given, namely, for Saul to wait at Gilgal seven days, beginning at some unspecified future time they have agreed upon, until Samuel's coming to offer sacrifice (10:8). Saul will fail this singular test of obedience (13:7-14). Although the signs are fulfilled (10:9), the command is disobeyed. The charismatic gifts here provide enabling for ministry, but not permanent transformation of character (10:6). In an extremely short space of time the new king is both authenticated and discredited (13:13-14).

Samuel gathers the nation to Mizpah, as he had earlier (7:5-13), and publicly confirms the appointment of Saul as king. The method is lot-casting with Saul gradually singled out as the chosen (10:20-24). The prophet Samuel again castigates the nation for their demand for a king, yet accommodates their request (10:17-19; cf. 8:6-9). The nation, in turning from the direct rule of God, has heaped unrealistic expectations on a human instrument. All the desire of Israel is turned to Saul (9:20). They exalt him as a great deliverer, unparalleled and unequaled (10:24). At least a share of responsibility for Saul's later degeneration lies in the subterranean attitudes that created the demand for a king in the first place. The earlier stated regulations of the kingship (8:10-18) are recorded and deposited in the central sanctuary (10:25). This was to clarify that Israel's kingship was not to be patterned after the heathen nations, but was to be a mutually responsible, although accommodating arrangement. The monarch was to be a steward subject to the Mosaic law, for the Lord was still to be the great king over Israel (Deut 17:14-20).

Saul's kingship formally begins with an inauguration ceremony at Gilgal (11:14-15). This town, located northeast of Jericho near the Jordan river, had special significance in Israel's history. When Israel crossed the Jordan and entered Canaan it was at Gilgal that the entire nation camped, erected memorial stones, and resumed the covenant ceremonies of circumcision and Passover (Josh 4:19-5:12). Gilgal became the base camp from which the nation carried out the covenantal duty to conquer and subdue the promised land (Josh 10:6-7, 15, 43). It is appropriate, then, that Samuel chooses Gilgal, as the place to formally inaugurate the monarchy.

Samuel uses the inauguration ceremony as an opportunity to renew the covenant and to once again remind the nation that the kingship in no way alters their fundamental obligations to the Lord. His extended declaration is a passionate appeal for the nation to remember its unique identity as it enters the perilous practice of monarchical rule. First, Samuel defends his integrity as their leader (12:1-5). His testimony is a valid, accredited presentation by one who is publicly acknowledged to be above reproach in all his past dealings with the people. Second, he reminds the nation of the Lord's righteous acts on their behalf throughout their history. The Lord has been a faithful ruler, protector, and provider, but they have repeatedly forgotten his goodness and shifted their attention to the prevailing culture

(12:6-12). Still, the nation can have their king, though blessing or cursing remains dependent on their response to the obligations of the covenant (12:13-15). Third, with a visible demonstration of God's power, in answer to the intercession of Samuel (12:16-19), in sending thunder and rain in the dry, harvest season, the people openly confess their sin in seeking a human king. Fourth, Samuel reassures the nation that even under the monarchical arrangement blessing can be theirs if they reject worthless idols and remain true to the Lord (12:20-22). His role will be to pray for them and teach them in truth (12:23). The peoples' moral duty can be summarized in one complex command: "fear . . . serve. . . consider" (12:24). Yet, in a haunting admonition that portends future events, the kingdom will be swept away if they persist in evil (12:25).

Courage to rebuke and remove (1 Sam 13:1-14:48)
Throughout Saul's reign the chief threat to Israel was the Philistines, due to their large chariot force (13:5) and monopoly on the production of iron (13:19-22). Saul had scaled down his armed forces to 3,000 select men (13:2; cf.11:8), possibly indicating a false sense of security after his great victory over the Ammonites (11:1-11). Responding to the attack on Geba by Jonathan, Saul's oldest son, the Philistines assembled a vast army and chariot force at Micmash to assault Israel. This produced a chain reaction of fear and panic in the Hebrew camp, some hiding in caves, others fleeing to Transjordan (13:5-7a). Meanwhile, Saul was waiting for Samuel at Gilgal as previously instructed (10:8). Why Samuel required Saul to wait seven days is uncertain, though it may have been a designed test of faith to develop the young king's character. When the seventh day arrived with no sign of the prophet, coupled with the increasing defection of his terrified soldiers (13:2, 8, 15), Saul hastily took the sacrificial animals and offered burnt offerings (13:9). At that point Samuel appears (in the late hours of the seventh day?) and rebukes Saul for his foolish action (13:11-14). At first glance the harsh rejection of Saul for a single impetuous act seems unfair, similar to the punishment of Moses for striking the rock (Num 20:8-12). The principle seems to be that of strict accountability, particularly for one appointed as national leader, at the inauguration of a new era.

How are we to interpret the behavior of Saul? First, his action was a clear abrogation of Samuel's earlier instruction: he would come seven days from a specified future time to make the sacrificial offerings (10:8). Saul assumed this priestly prerogative for himself without hesitation. Second, Saul was snared by the fear of man and was moved by the pressures of the immediate. Saul cites the threat of the enemy and the scattering of his soldiers as justification for his actions (13:11-12). Third, Saul took things into his own hands, acted hastily, and then rationalized his action by claiming to have underlying spiritual motivation. He claimed to be seeking God's favor (13:12). Later in the Amalekite campaign he will justify his disobedience on the same grounds (15:15, 21).

Samuel administers the Lord's rebuke. Saul is summarily rejected as king (13:13-14). Unlike David (2 Sam 7:11-16), he will never produce a lasting dynasty. And like the faithful priest who will be raised up to replace the discredited Eli (2:30-36), the Lord will raise up "a man after his own heart" (13:14) to serve as leader over Israel in Saul's place. The desperate plight of Israel serves as a background to the battle of Micmash recorded in Chapter 14: the troops are decimated by panic to only 600 (13:15); the prophet Samuel departs; and Philistine raiding parties begin to plunder the land (13:16-18). The vastly outnumbered Israelite army is forced to fight with primitive, outclassed weaponry (bows, arrows, slingshots) because of the Philistine monopoly on the production of iron implements (13:19-22). A demoralized army led by a rejected king faces the powerful chariotry of the Philistines, to whom Israel is like the odious stench of spoiled manna (13:4).

Jonathan becomes the hero of the present crisis. His launches a surprise attack on the Philistines (14:1-14). While only a small-scale assault on a minor Philistine outpost by a single warrior and his armor-bearer, Jonathan's courageous act of faith has huge effects on the demoralized camp of Israel. Like David against Goliath, Jonathan's surprise move is bolstered by confidence in God's power to save "whether by many or few" (14:6). Jonathan's act of faith in slaying twenty Philistines inspires his fellow Hebrews and sends shock waves through the enemy camp. The confident Philistines fall into a panic, while the scattering, fear-stricken Israelites rally in pursuit (14:15-23).

Saul once again shows his characteristic tendency to make rash decisions when under pressure. With Jonathan leading the way, the Israelite army successfully pursues the fleeing Philistines. Saul, however, undertakes a series of foolish actions. First, rather than caring for the welfare of his troops, he utters an oath that the soldiers must not eat until the Philistines have been annihilated (14:24). He has turned the campaign into a matter of personal revenge "on my enemies," in place of fulfilling his covenantal duties to defeat the enemies of the Lord. Jonathan recognizes the total disregard his father has for his servants, but only after he unknowingly breaks the irrevocable oath by eating honey (14:28-30). Second, Saul's impulsive restriction is responsible for the actions of his soldiers when, in their famished condition, they slaughter enemy plunder and consume some of the meat with blood still in it, a serious violation of the law (14:31-33; cf. Lev 17:10-12). Third, the desperate king, aware of what has happened, tries to gain forgiveness by offering sacrifice and erecting an altar (14:34-35). This is only a temporary delay, however, in his single-minded focus on destroying the Philistines for personal advantage (14:36). Saul, at the reminder of the priest, does seek God's guidance, but God's voice is silent (14:37), either because the oath has been broken, or more likely because Saul has caused the men to commit a "high-handed" sin for which there is no sacrificial provision (cf. Num 15:30-31). Like Samson, the Lord has left Saul and he does not recognize it (14:37; cf. 28:6; Jdg 16:20b). Fourth, when Jonathan's act of violating the king's oath is discovered, Saul vows that his own son must die (14:44). This not only discredits Saul before his warriors, who applaud the exemplary leadership of Jonathan and rescue him from Saul's hand, but also reveals the depths to which Saul has fallen (14:45). His willingness to kill his own son for a foolish vow reveals a deepening fear of dethronement. This fear will eventually grow into a full-scale paranoia, producing a murderous assault on any and all suspected rivals.

Partaker of the Lord's grief (1 Sam 15:1-35)

Having left for Gibeah following the first announcement of Saul's rejection, Samuel emerges with a fresh prophetic word for the king (15:1; cf. 13:15). Through Samuel the Lord issues a clear command to Saul to execute judgment on the Amalekites. The total destruction of a people, including women, children, and animals (15:3), raises moral problems that cannot be easily answered. Other Old Testament passages bear the same character (Num 31; Deut 13:12-18; Joshua 6:17-18). Two things should be noted. First, the present campaign is a judgment on Amalek for its cruel treatment of Israel in history. The unprovoked Amalekites attacked vulnerable and peace-seeking Israel on her journey to Moab (Ex 17:8; Num 14:45; Deut 25:17-19). Second, this is no pursuit of personal vengeance, but a holy war grounded in religious principles. God is punishing those who sought to curse his covenant people (Gen 12:3).

Saul, after mustering his army and warning the friendly Kenites (15:6), carries out God's command, but only in part. He spares King Agag and the best of the cattle and property. The harsh denunciation of Saul and the severity of the punishment can only be understood in light of the Old Testament principle of "things wholly devoted to God." The term "devoted things" (15:3, 8, 9, 15, 18, 20, 21) refers to persons, animals, cities, or property that are assigned to destruction because they impede God's redemptive purposes and/or are injurious to his covenant people (cf. Deut 7:2-6; 13:12-18). The Canaanites and their cities are repeatedly placed under the ban (cf. Num 21:2-3; Joshua 6:21; 8:26; 10:28; 11:11; Deut 7:26). Achan's sin lay in violating this principle (Joshua 6:17; 7:12-13). Saul's sin was compounded by the excuse of having spared the best of the herd to sacrifice to the Lord (15:9, 15, 21). Giving to the Lord, by destruction, only the weak and despised, while preserving the best for oneself, was a reversal of biblical priorities and a direct affront to God's character.

Samuel announces God's assessment of Saul's act of partial obedience as being tantamount to wholesale rebellion. He refuses to mitigate the prophetic word of judgment for the pathetic appeals of the king. Samuel is bound by the unchanging character of God (15:29). As earlier (cf. 13:11-12), Saul attempts to rationalize his actions by claiming spiritual motives. He feigns obedience before the prophet: "I have carried out the Lord's instructions. But I did obey the Lord" (15:13, 20). He attempts to evade responsibility by laying the blame on others: "The soldiers brought them . . . but we totally destroyed the rest" (15:15). Pride and desire for prestige has begun to capture Saul's heart. He builds a monument to himself at Carmel (15:12). Samuel recalls nostalgically a time when Saul was once small in his own eyes (15:17). Saul forgets a basic principle that runs throughout the Old Testament: obedience is more important than ritual (15:22-23; cf. Ps 40:6-8; 51:16-17; Prov 21:3; Isa 1:1-17; Jer 7:21-23; Hos 6:6; Amos 5:21-27; Micah 6:6-8). True sacrifice was always meant to be an expression of faith, repentance and devotion, never a substitute for them.

Though Saul's kingdom has been declared invalid (13:13-14), Samuel now announces with finality the personal rejection of Saul as king (15:23b, 26-29). This rejection comes from the grieving heart of God (15:11, 35) to a mourning prophet (15:35; 16:1). What is meant by God's grieving that he made Saul king, since he earlier indicated Saul was his choice (9:15-16; 10:1)? The Hebrew word for "grieve" in 15:11, 35 is the same term rendered "change his mind" in 15:29 (NIV).[5] Thus the Lord who grieves that he made Saul king is also "the Glory of Israel" who neither lies nor changes his mind like a human being.[6] This biblical antinomy combines two truths in perfect tension. First, God is immutable and perfect in his purposes. He never regrets a past decision or feels remorse due to errors in judgment or unpredictable exigencies which later arise. That is why the finality of Saul's rejection, being God's sovereign will, cannot be revoked. Second, God is a person who has emotions, feels grief, and experiences empathy. He loves obedience and is pained by rejection. When the Lord "changes his mind" it involves a change in attitude, not purpose, toward a person who has changed his attitude toward him. God's sovereign will takes into account all that has and will take place. His emotive personality, within that framework, adjusts itself to the human situation.

Although Saul sought to reverse his destiny (15:24, 30-31), the opportunity was denied. Saul's subsequent behavior proves that more than the act of disobedience itself, it was the consequences of disobedience that worried him, namely, humiliation, loss of national confidence, and withdrawal of Samuel's support. Samuel demands that Agag be brought forth, pronounces condemnation, and puts him to death (15:32-33). The prophet then separates from the king he has anointed and now has been compelled to reject. Each one returns to his home (15:34). Never again will the prophetic word be given to this discredited monarch. Samuel continued to mourn for the one who grieved God's heart (15:35; 16:1).

Herald of a new beginning (1 Sam 16:1-13)

Samuel is told to stop mourning for Saul, to arise, go to Bethlehem, and anoint one of the seven sons of Jesse as his successor. Samuel voices concern over Saul's reprisal should the king hear of the prophet's anointing a successor (16:2a). He actually fears for his life from a king he had anointed and mentored, but who has betrayed his charge to covenant faithfulness. The Lord indicates the occasion for the anointing will be a sacrifice, which should allay Saul's suspicions. The elders at Bethlehem, frightened by the prophet's appearance in their little town, wondering about a pronouncement of judgment, are instructed to ceremonially prepare themselves for a special sacrifice (16:5). The seventh son of Jesse is chosen (16:12). Samuel anoints David confidentially among a small circle of witnesses

---

[5] The niphal form of the verb נחם can be rendered, depending on the context, "to be sorry, grieve, show compassion, relent, change one's mind." When God grieves or relents it is according to his sovereign purpose, while taking into account man's response (or lack thereof) to his overtures of grace (Gen 6:6; Ex 32:14; Jdg 2:18; 1 Sam 15:11, 35; Jer 18:8, 10; 26:3, 13, 19; Amos 7:3, 6; Jonah 3:10). These texts are in a healthy tension with those texts which stress the immutability of God's character and purposes (Num 23:19; 1 Sam 15:29; Ps 110:4; Jer 4:28; cf. Mal 3:6). See *TDOT*, IX: 342-347.

[6] The Hebrew verb שׁוּב is the normal Old Testament term for human repentance, that is, to volitionally turn away from evil (2 Kg 17:13; Jer 18:8; 26:3; Ezek 14:6; Jonah 3:10) and to turn toward (or return to) God (2 Chr 30:6; Isa 44:22; Jer 3:12, 14, 22; 4:1; 31:18; Hos 14:1; Joel 2:12-13). The niphal form of נחם is used of human repentance in a few instances (Job 42:6; Jer 8:6; 31:19). See *NIDOTTE*, 4: 55-59.

in the obscure town of Bethlehem and returns as always to Ramah (16:13). Early in his years as a fugitive David flees to Samuel at Ramah (1 Sam 19:18). Saul attempts to seize David there, but both he and his men are arrested by the Spirit and begin to prophesy in Samuel's presence (19:19-24). In this final ministry scene Samuel stands as the leader of a company of prophets who were probably trained under his tutelage (19:20). During David's fugitive years Samuel died and was buried in Ramah. He was mourned by the entire nation (1 Sam 25:1a; 28:3).

Leadership profile of Samuel

1.   **Unwavering commitment to his calling**: *Before he was conceived he was the yearning of a mother's heart. After his birth Hannah dedicated him to be a consecrated vessel to the Lord for life (1:11, 28). Hannah's prayers for her boy proved effectual. In all the vicissitudes of his ministry—the unhealthy environment of his boyhood, the struggles with his people over their demand for a king, the anointing, rebuke and then discrediting of the first king—Samuel remained steadfast in his call to be prophet, advocate and judge of his people. God's calling him by name during his youth continued to ring in his ears and the servant never stopped listening. Though revered (3:19-21) and later mourned by an entire nation (25:1a), never once did Samuel exploit the opportunity for personal gain. His was a long journey on the path of undistracted obedience. God's agenda ruled over and ruled out personal ambition. There are no blemishes, save his reprobate sons, on the record of this prophet of God.*

2.   **Spokesman for truth**: *When Samuel defended his integrity before the assembled nation at Gilgal, the universal response was an affirmative. What king, elders and people received from their prophet was the truth, the whole truth and nothing else. He pronounced judgment on Eli's house, demanded the removal of idols and implored genuine repentance at Mizpah, unmasked the ulterior motives behind Israel's demand for a king and warned of the consequences, confronted a disobedient monarch, and anointed his successor at the peril of his own life. He spoke the undiluted word of the Lord both in comfort and in confrontation. Samuel was the didactic leader: "I will teach you the way that is good and right" (12:23b).*

3.   **Prayer and worship**: *When the Philistines threatened at Mizpah Samuel interceded and offered a burnt offering (7:5, 6, 8-10). When the people demanded a king like the other nations Samuel paused and prayed before responding (8:6). Saul first encounters Samuel in Zuph as the latter presided over a communal sacrificial meal (9:12-13). He commanded Saul to wait in Gilgal for him to initiate the sacrificial offerings (10:8). In his farewell address at Gilgal he prayed and the Lord thundered (12:16-18). He promised to pray for the nation, for to neglect intercession would be to sin against the Lord (12:23a). The nation drew strength from Samuel's prayers (7:8; 12:19). Samuel's influence with people drew from the springs of his interior life.*

Chapter 10.
David: Man after God's Heart

Preliminary questions to consider:

1. *How does a leader conquer fear in crisis situations?*
2. *What regular practice can help a leader maintain a vibrant hope in the midst of otherwise disheartening circumstances?*
3. *What governing conviction will preserve a leader from falling into the common traps of becoming defensive or controlling?*
4. *How does the Bible define repentance and what are the signs of a truly repentant heart?*
5. *Why do so many leaders deemed 'successful' in terms of vocational accomplishment fail in their marriage and family life?*
6. *Whose agenda is the mandate of the servant-leader?*

Man after God's heart (1 Sam 16:1-13)

Samuel pronounces Saul's rule a failure and predicts the rise of a new leader who will be "a man after his own heart" (1 Sam 13:14).[1] The vibrant phrase describes one who will share God's heart for leading the people to obey the covenant and will view the kingship as a stewardship of the Lord's people who are his inheritance (9:16; 10:1). As a covenantal steward David will be a better man than Saul (15:28).

Samuel follows the Lord's instructions to proceed to Bethlehem and anoint one of the seven sons of Jesse as the next king (16:1-4). The elders at Bethlehem are frightened by the prophet's appearance in their little town, expecting a pronouncement of judgment. Samuel instructs them to ceremonially prepare themselves for a special sacrifice (16:5). Perhaps Samuel is again looking for an impressive young man of kingly stature like Saul (9:2), but the Lord says the heart qualities will determine the selection (16:7; cf. 13:14). The Lord chooses David, perhaps in part because he has evidenced a thirsting heart for God's presence (cf. Ps 27:4; 42:1-2). The seventh son of Jesse, still a young boy tending his father's sheep, and the least likely candidate from a human standpoint, is selected (16:12; cf. Ps 78:70-72). David is anointed confidentially among a small circle of witnesses in the obscure town of Bethlehem, which keeps the event away from the attention of the paranoid Saul. David's empowerment by the Spirit, symbolized by the

---

[1] The Hebrew text reads literally, a man "according to his heart" (כִּלְבָבוֹ). The same expression occurs in 1 Sam 14:7 where the armor-bearer affirms his commitment to Jonathan in his determination to attack the Philistine outpost. God chose David because he recognized that the shepherd boy possessed a heart wholly committed to honoring him (1 Sam 16:7). Jeremiah, using an equivalent phrase, looks forward to a day when God will raise up true shepherd-leaders "after my own heart," who will lead the people with knowledge and understanding (Jer 3:15).

anointing oil, comes from that day forward (16:13). This is the first of three anointings. Later he is anointed king over Judah at Hebron (2 Sam 2:4), and finally ruler over the entire nation (2 Sam 5:3). Thus David enters a long training period before the promises would find fulfillment.[2]

Spirit-inspired musician (1 Sam 16:14-23)

After Saul lost connection with God (14:37), he began to be tormented by "an evil spirit from the Lord" (16:14). This evil spirit would continue to trouble Saul for the remainder of his life (16:23; 18:10; 19:9). The demonic influence on Saul became the means to David's selection to serve in the court of Saul. David's qualities come to the attention of one of Saul's advisers: skilled harpist; brave warrior; eloquent, fine looking, and, above all, "the Lord is with him" (16:18). It is the harpist's skillful playing that soothes the spirit of Saul and even causes the evil spirit to depart for a time (16:15-16, 23; cf. 19:9-10). David's skills as a musician and warrior are the very gifts that end up making Saul dependent on him, both for emotional stability and for political security.

A brave warrior steps forth (1 Sam 17:1-58)

As Saul was attested in the Ammonite campaign following his anointing (1 Sam 11), so David's anointing is attested by his military confrontation with a Philistine giant. Goliath, possibly a descendant of the gigantic sons of Anak (Num 13:33; Josh 11:22), defied the troops of Israel. Goliath's challenge was that of "trial by ordeal" where a selected warrior from each side would step forth to battle in representation of their nation. The outcome was attributed to the gods and the loser would become the subject of the victor (17:8-9). The Philistines, however, later refused to honor Goliath's proposal (17:51-53). Saul and Israel were terrified (17:1, 24). Apart from faith in God, there was nothing to inspire courage or motivate David's bold action. He was young, inexperienced in warfare, mocked by his brothers (17:28-30), and initially rejected by King Saul (17:33). David was motivated wholly by a desire to preserve Israel's honor and the honor of her covenant Lord (17:26). He appeals to his experiences as a shepherd, expressing confidence in the Lord's protection (17:34-37). Armed with only a sling and five stones, not dressed in Saul's armor but with familiar weapons, he goes forth to battle (17:38-40).

The Philistine uses vile insults, cursing David by his idols (17:43). David replies nobly that the Lord Almighty will reveal his knowledge and supply the victory (17:45-47). The contrast in attitude, belief, and word is striking. The common biblical polemics of God supporting the weak and humiliating the strong and the vindication of faith over human, carnal means of warfare are central to the encounter (17:47). The conflict is over almost as soon as it begins. David is on target with his first sling, the Philistine collapses, and his head is cut off with his own sword as the young shepherd's military trophy. As with Jonathan's courageous act earlier (14:14-15), David's success fills the enemy camp with terror and inspires

---

[2] The total preparation period is twenty-two years: first anointing in 1025 B.C.; second anointing 1010; third anointing 1003.

Israel's troops to action and a great triumph over the Philistines (17:51b-52). Saul inquires as to the young man's family, whose identity becomes nationally acclaimed, David, the son of Jesse of Bethlehem (17:55-58).[3]

Target of undeserved hostility (1 Sam 18:1-19:24)

With the stunning victory over Goliath, David is made a permanent member of the royal court, serving as Saul's personal musician (18:2). Saul grows increasingly fearful of David. A folk song extolling David's superior spoils in war stirs up the king's envy (18:7-9). David's ability as a warrior captivates the imagination of the nation, and his popularity is rapidly rising (18:16, 30). David is successful in all he does because the hand of the Lord is with him (18:14). Saul, from whom the Spirit had departed (16:14; 18:12), feels increasingly threatened by David's presence. An evil spirit begins to operate, at least externally, on Saul's personality. On at least three occasions he tries to murder David by hurling his javelin at the harpist (18:10-11; 19:9-10). David's maneuverability probably saved his life. This method, proving unsuccessful, Saul employs a subtler means of seeking to destroy David by sending him to the front lines of battle. Saul offers his daughter Michal in marriage to David in return for 100 Philistine foreskins, another action springing from a desire for personal vengeance (18:25; cf. 14:24). However, David is successful and Saul is forced to surrender his daughter to David. He feels unworthy to be the king's son-in-law (18:18, 23). Though now a member of the royal family, the king's most capable warrior, the loyal friend of his eldest son, and the Spirit-filled musician who soothes his troubled spirit, David for the next fifteen years will be a fugitive, seeking to escape Saul's murderous pursuit. Later developments prove that all of Saul's fears were unfounded (24:6; 26:23-24), his paranoia fueled by the imaginary speculations of a disoriented mind. After David's third escape from Saul's javelin (19:9-10), he flees to Samuel at Ramah (19:18). Until Saul's death there is to be no reconciliation between the two men: "Saul became still more afraid of him, and he remained his enemy the rest of his days" (18:29).

With the help of Michal his wife, David manages to escape an ambush and flees to the home of Samuel. Perhaps he was seeking assurance in this period of danger. Saul, in finding David's whereabouts, sends three parties of men to capture his perceived enemy. On each occasion the Spirit of God descends upon each group causing them to prophesy and turn from their intended purpose (19:18-21). Finally, Saul, exasperated by their failure, leaves for Ramah himself. Yet the Spirit of prophecy arrests him as well. Saul strips off his robes and falls prostrate for the rest of the night (19:22-24; cf. 10:9-13).[4]

---

[3] How is it that Saul had to inquire about David's identity when David was already serving in the court of Saul as a royal musician (16:14-23) and David earlier asked Saul's permission to engage Goliath as Israel's representative (17:32-39)? The solution seems to be that Saul was not inquiring so much about David, as about his family background and social standing: "find out whose son this young man is" (17:56). Although introduced earlier as the son of Jesse (16:18), David was not a permanent resident of the king's court until after the victory over Goliath (18:2).

[4] How are we to interpret such behavior? Some see the influence of Canaanite religious expression on Saul, producing an ecstatic babbling. Leon Wood, *The Holy Spirit in the Old Testament* (Zondervan:

Affectionate friend (1 Sam 18:1-4; 20:1-42)

A deep friendship, characterized by reciprocal loyalty, emerges between Jonathan and David. Jonathan's love for David reveals a spirit of humility and sense of security, for David could easily have been considered a threat to his own rise to the throne. Yet the heir apparent is unmoved by his father's hatred and jealousy, though Saul later appeals to Jonathan to betray David to protect his own interests (20:30-31). The covenant of loyalty between David and Jonathan (18:3; cf. 20:8, 16-17, 42; 23:18) is ratified by Jonathan's giving to David his robe, tunic, sword, bow, and belt (18:4). These gifts signify a transfer of authority to David from one who is the rightful heir to the throne. Jonathan later expresses clear knowledge of David's future accession as monarch in his father's place (20:12-15; cf. 13:13-14; 15:27-29).

Though Saul attempts to drive a wedge between his son Jonathan and his rival David, by appealing to the former's interests, his hatred only serves to draw them closer together. Jonathan, at first unconvinced of his father's hatred of David (20:1-15), agrees to test David's claim at the Festival of the New Moon (20:16-23). Jonathan apparently still believed his father's oath that he made earlier (19:6). Whatever doubts remained, Jonathan was awakened to his father's true intentions when Saul exploded over David's absence at the banquet table. Saul hurls his javelin at his own son whom he accuses of betrayal (20:33). Grieved and angered by his father's unjustified hatred of David, Jonathan secretly alerts David of Saul's intentions as they earlier arranged, and David flees. For the next fifteen years David will live the life of a fugitive, hunted like a criminal, in a desperate attempt to preserve his life (20:3). Jonathan, godly son of an evil king, would be true to his pledge of loyalty to David (18:3; 20:8). When Jonathan is killed years later, David remembers his covenant with his descendants (20:15, 42) and deals graciously with his son Mephibosheth (2 Sam 9; 21:7).

Unwitting complicity in the death of the priestly family (1 Sam 21:1-22:23)

Parting from Jonathan, David flees to Nob, located between Anathoth and Jerusalem (Isa 10:30, 32), where the high priest Ahimelech now lived. David's flight first to the prophet (19:18), now to the high priest, reveals his theocratic values. Following the Philistine destruction of Shiloh (1 Sam 4:2-3; Jer 7:12), the tabernacle, priests, and vessels were relocated to Nob, although the ark was for some reason left in Kiriath Jearim (1 Sam 7:1-2; 2 Sam 6:2-3). David had on previous occasions sought Ahimelech for divine guidance (22:15). David's visit is again for the purpose of seeking the Lord's guidance by means of the Urim and

---

Grand Rapids, 1976): 114-115, however, argues that the company at Ramah was a young group of prophets being trained under Samuel's tutelage. The "prophesying" in these instances involved "praising" God (cf. 1 Chron 25:1-3). The Spirit of God miraculously moved upon Saul and his emissaries, changing their posture from murderous envy toward David to one of praise to God. One difficulty with this view is that it doesn't explain why "an evil spirit from the Lord" (19:9; cf. 16:14; 18:10) moved upon Saul in the first place to exacerbate his malicious disposition toward David. It may be that "from the Lord" should be understood in the permissive sense, though its mediate causation was demonic. Wood interprets Saul's disrobing and stupor as exhaustion resulting from such extremes of emotional change (p. 117).

Thummim (22:10). Nevertheless, David lies to conceal the real purpose of his visit, claiming to be on a special mission for the king (21:2). This deception (cf. 20:6) may be intended to protect Ahimelech from a later charge of collusion with the king's enemy (which was unsuccessful), or because David feared Ahimelech's loyalty to the king. Though David originally suspects that Doeg the Edomite had overheard and would conspire against Ahimelech, he fails to voice his suspicions and later assumes full responsibility for the massacre (21:7; 22:9, 22). Though reserved only for the priests in the holy place (Lev 24:9), Ahimelech allows David and his men to eat the showbread on the condition that they are ceremonially clean (21:4-5). David also receives the sword of Goliath, which he originally retrieved (17:54), but apparently later dedicated to the Lord (21:8-9).

David's journey took him next to Gath in Philistia (21:10-15), the cave of Adullam (22:1-2), Mizpah in Moab (22:3-4), and the forest of Hereth in Judah (22:5). It seems strange that David would seek asylum among the Philistines, even more so that he first goes to Gath, the hometown of Goliath (17:4), bearing the slain champion's sword. Still, David is forced to feign insanity before King Achish when his identity is discovered. At the cave of Adullam David gathers 400 desperate or discontented people around him; these outcasts ultimately became a mighty force (2 Sam 23:8-39). People were gradually defecting from Saul, and David's force soon grew to 600 (23:13). Gad the prophet (22:5) and Abiathar the priest (22:20-23) become key members of the rebel contingent. David's long trip to Moab is to provide protection for his parents from the vengeful Saul. The king of Moab was probably supportive of David's rivalry to Saul's kingdom, with which he had fought (14:47). The prophet Gad begins a long career as David's spiritual adviser.

Saul's fear of David has grown to intense levels. Doeg the Edomite became the means of Nob's destruction, when he both informed the king of Ahimelech's kindness to David, and executed his decree of death. Doeg exploited the eavesdropping for his own political advancement. The officers of the king refuse to attack the Lord's priests (22:17). That Saul would use a pagan herdsman against the anointed priests reveals the depths of his degradation. The honest admission of Ahimelech, who truthfully denies any knowledge of David's intentions, though he pleads David's loyalty to Saul, is rejected. Doeg slays eighty-five priests, then puts the inhabitants of Nob to the sword. Though Saul had earlier refused to carry out God's ban against the Amalekites (15:7-9), he cruelly applies the ban to the priestly city and spares no one (22:19). Abiathar, son of Ahimelech, manages to escape and finds refuge in the camp of David (22:20-23).

Awaiting God's timing and method for elevation (1 Sam 23:1-24:22; 26:1-25)

David desperately attempts to escape Saul's grasp by moving from one place to another: Keilah (23:1-12); "from place to place" (23:13); Horesh in the Desert of Ziph (23:14-23); Desert of Maon (23:24-28); En Gedi (23:29). David remained a loyal warrior of Israel and went to Keilah to save the city from a Philistine attack. As we have seen, it is David's pattern to seek divine guidance for his movements and actions (22:10, 15; 23:2, 4, 6, 9). But David's position was precarious in Israel, for at both Keilah and Horesh the inhabitants are willing to curry political favor by delivering him to Saul (23:11-12, 19-20). This explains why David on more than one occasion must seek political asylum in Philistine territory (21:10-15; 27:1-4). While in Horesh Jonathan helps his friend David "find strength in God" (23:16; cf. 30:6). Jonathan repeats his earlier assurances that David will one day be king with words of characteristic humility: "I will be second to you" (23:17; cf. 20:14, 42). The son of Saul willingly abdicates his right to the throne and accepts a role subordinate to David without any sign of resentment. This is the last recorded meeting between these two kindred spirits who confirm their covenant loyalty to one another (23:18). In the Desert of Maon Saul closes in on David (23:26). The Philistines, however, aware of Saul's preoccupation with David, exploit the situation and attack central Palestine. Saul is forced to break off his pursuit and defend against the raids, and so David manages to escape to En Gedi near the Dead Sea (23:27-29).

David and his men are hidden deep in the cave of En Gedi when Saul enters "to cover his feet" (24:3), a euphemism for "to have a bowel movement." His men interpret this as a divinely provided opportunity to strike down their pursuer (24:4). But David refuses, secretly cutting off a corner of Saul's robe. Saul leaves and David follows, beginning an exchange of words at some distance. David affirms his innocence and rebukes Saul for a baseless paranoia (24:8-15). David is moved by deep respect for the Lord's anointed one (24:6). He leaves his destiny in God's hands: "And may the Lord avenge the wrongs you have done to me, but my hand will not touch you" (24:12). Unlike Abraham (Gen 16), David not only embraces God's promises, but also leaves the timing and method of their fulfillment to divine sovereignty. Saul weeps, confesses David's righteousness, admits the validity of David's royal claims, and seeks an oath of protection from vengeance (24:16-21). Though David gives the oath, the two men part without true reconciliation. David is keenly aware of the instability of Saul, partly under demonic influence, and withdraws to an inaccessible stronghold (24:22).

The Ziphites again inform Saul of David's location, now at Jeshimon (26:1), and once again Saul launches a search and destroy mission. The pattern repeats itself. An opportunity arises for David to kill Saul, as he sleeps in the camp. David's men interpret the opportunity as providential (26:8). David refuses to touch the Lord's anointed (26:9-11). Like the piece of robe earlier, David secretly takes an item of proof, this time the spear and water jug at Saul's head. From a distance David and Saul have an emotional verbal exchange, which stresses David's innocence and Saul's unfounded suspicions. They depart, partially and only temporarily reconciled. Earlier David had compared himself to a wild dog that roamed the streets of Palestine as a despised scavenger in search of food (24:14). In both incidents he likens himself to a flea (24:14; 26:20), hardly visible, hardly worth pursuing. Here he compares himself to a "partridge in the mountains" being hunted (26:20). David returns the spear to Saul (26:22). The spear, which had been stuck in the ground near the head of Saul, was his sign of authority. By returning the spear David again indicates he will wait for God's timing to ascend the throne.

Protected from himself by a noble intercessor (1 Sam 25:1-44)

Carmel, a town seven miles south of Hebron (Josh 15:55), is where Saul built a monument to himself, and where he was rejected as king (15:12, 26). Here lived a wealthy couple, Nabal and Abigail. He was a landowner and sheep shearer, with many hired servants. The character of husband and wife are contrasted: he is harsh and inhospitable; she is intelligent, sensitive, and beautiful.

In the Desert of Maon David's men had dealt graciously with Nabal's shepherds, stealing nothing and even providing protection (25:15-16). David's men ask for provisions, seeking the treatment customarily accorded oriental guests. They greet Nabal cordially and make their request with politeness, making no threats or unreasonable demands. Nabal has no sense of gratitude for David's kind treatment of his shepherds. His ethic is "what's in it for me," and since David is a helpless fugitive he harshly denies the request. The insulted David vows in anger to destroy Nabal and his household (25:12-13). Nabal's servants report to Abigal their master's foolishness. Apparently they previously have had to seek Abigail's help in solving difficulties with their master. They have lost all respect for him, calling him a "son of Belial" (25:17), but revere the prudent Abigail.

The mediator Abigail stands between her foolish husband and the angry David. She makes an emotional plea for mercy. She never seeks to justify her husband's actions, calling him foolish and wicked (25:25). Her appeal is to David's mercy and to the divine purposes: he is to become king, inherit a lasting dynasty (25:28), and realize God's faithfulness to his promises (25:29-31). David later recognizes that Abigail has not only saved her husband, but prevented him from acting like Saul (25:33). Samuel (13:14; 15:28), Jonathan (20:13-15; 23:17-18), Saul (24:20-21; cf. 26:25), and now Abigail have predicted David's rise to the throne.

David praises the Lord and Abigail. Her mediation has brought him to see the folly of revenge and of establishing a reputation for bloodshed. In his dealing with Nabal, David temporarily forgot what he so nobly exemplified in his dealing with Saul: God will fulfill his purposes in his own time and way (25:28-31). The peace gifts are accepted and his wrath is propitiated. David learns a lesson he will later draw upon (2 Sam 16:5-14): all perspective is lost when a person is controlled by anger. The sudden death of Nabal at hearing the news of David's intended action is interpreted by David as divine judgment on Nabal and vindication of his own integrity (25:36-39). Abigail is summoned to be David's wife (25:40), in one sense a fine substitute for Michal, Saul's daughter, whom the king gave to another man (25:44; cf. 18:27). David eventually had eight wives who bore him many sons (1 Chron 3:1-9).

Drawing inner strength in dark days (1 Sam 27:1-28:2; 29:1-30:31)

Having moved from place to place, often barely escaping the grasp of Saul (23:26-27), David realized he would soon be apprehended if he remained in Judah. For the second time he flees to Philistia, encountering King Achish of Gath, before whom he had feigned insanity (21:10-15). Achish provides David refuge for two reasons. First, David is Saul's rival and a mighty warrior whom he can employ in his attacks on Israel (28:1-2). Second, David has become a complete outcast and so should not have divided loyalties. David asks for and is given Ziklag for himself and his men, with their families, to reside in. This provided David freedom from constant surveillance so he could launch attacks on various southern Canaanite peoples who were enemies both of the Philistines and of his own people. He accomplished three purposes. First, he won the confidence of Achish by protecting the southern borders of Philistia. Second, he eliminated some of the historical threats to Israel, such as the Amalekites. Third, David acquired knowledge of the Palestinian landscape and of military maneuvers, which would serve him well as future commander of Israel's forces.

Although King Achish had unquestioned confidence in David's loyalty to him (28:1-2), his military commanders, many of whom had front line battle experience against David, questioned his true intentions. They feared that David might turn into an adversary (29:4) in the battle of Aphek. The commanders' assessment was probably accurate. In light of his actions in twice sparing Saul's life, surely David would have used the present opportunity to once again demonstrate his loyalty to Saul. Achish bows to the pressure of his military commanders. David has no choice but to submit to the decision and return to Ziklag, perhaps relieved that he has been delivered from a troubling dilemma.

While the Philistines continue their march northward to Aphek, David and his men return south to Ziklag (29:6-7), only to find their city burned, homes destroyed, and families taken captive by Amalekite raiders. With David and his men away, the Amalekites sought revenge on the defenseless city for David's earlier raids against them (27:8-9). If Saul had effectively carried out the Lord's command concerning the Amalekites, this would never have happened (15:1-21). Faced with potential mutiny, David "found strength in the Lord his God" (30:6; cf. 23:16). Unlike the vengeful Saul (14:24), David seeks the Lord's will before pursuing the attackers (30:8). "Inquiring of the Lord" was now the pattern of David's life (22:10, 15; 23:9-12), not like Saul who inquired only as a last gasp attempt to secure divine help in crises (14:36-37; 28:6). Led by an Egyptian slave to the unsuspecting camp, David and his men annihilate the Amalekites while they are enjoying an extravagant victory celebration (30:16). The captives are recovered and a vast plunder taken. David then demonstrates wisdom and forbearance in managing the recovered goods. He stands against "the evil men and troublemakers" among his followers (30:22) and commands that all Israelites will share equally in the plunder, both those who joined the campaign and those who were unable to participate due to exhaustion or other duties (30:23-25). Credit is given to the Lord for the recovery (30:23). This is in keeping with Old Testament legislation for assigning the plunder of enemy towns: the Lord is the benefactor, the nation is the recipient, and the campaign is one of righteous judgment not selfish exploitation (Num 31:25-54). Further, David sends portions of the plunder to his friends among "the elders of Judah" (30:26-30). This accomplishes two purposes. First, it is an expression of thanks to those who have given him and his men protection and provision during their years of flight. Second, it reaffirms to these leaders that David remains a loyal Israelite in case some had begun to question his patriotism during his sixteen months exile in Philistia.

Saul and the spirit medium (1 Sam 28:1-25)

Meanwhile, Saul once again finds himself facing a large, formidable Philistine army (28:4; cf. 17:1-3; 23:27-28). And once again Saul is paralyzed by fear, his characteristic response in such situations (28:5; cf. 15:24; 17:11). He senses the need for divine guidance, but no answer is given whether by dreams, Urim, or the prophets (28:6).[5] The Lord had broken communion with Saul (14:37; 16:14). The priestly ephod, to which the Urim and Thummim were attached, was with Abiathar in David's camp (22:20-23; 23:6; 30:7). Samuel was dead (25:1; 28:3) and the prophet Gad served as counselor to David (22:5).

Although Saul had prohibited sorcery and necromancy from Israel (28:3), he now disguises himself and secretly seeks out a medium in Endor for guidance. Saul shows his brazen disregard for God's word in this time of crisis, for consulting the spirits of dead people is uniformly forbidden in Scripture (Lev 19:31; 20:6, 27; Deut 18:10-11). Clearly the woman had a reputation as a necromancer, who could consult the dead for purposes of determining the future. Saul desperately missed his former communication with Samuel (15:35), and asks the woman to "bring up" Samuel (28:11). How are we to interpret this incident? The natural sense of the text is that Samuel actually appeared (28:12, 14, 15, 16), that is, God by a special sovereign intervention, caused the spirit of Samuel to appear.[6] As to the actual powers of the woman, she is called one who possesses a "familiar spirit" (28:7). This term, used sixteen times in the Old Testament, refers either to the person who practices as a medium (28:3, 7, 9; cf. Lev 19:31; 20:6; 2 Kg 21:6) or to the spiritual existence such a medium would contact in this practice (28:8; cf. Lev 20:27; Deut 18:11; Isa 8:19; 29:4).[7] The story of the rich man and Lazarus (Lk 16:19-31) indicates that dead people are totally unable to return to earth for any reason. By an act of God Samuel appeared, which act is not wholly without precedent, for Moses and Elijah appeared with Christ at his transfiguration, although "in glory" (Mt 17:3; Lk 9:30-31). The story, then, serves to condemn the practice of consulting mediums and to confirm the reality of a future state after death.

---

[5] 1 Samuel 28:6 records that Saul "inquired (שָׁאַל) of the Lord, but the Lord did not answer." The Chronicler comments that Saul "did <u>not</u> inquire (דָּרַשׁ) of the Lord" (1 Chron 10:14). There is formal inconsistency here without substantive contradiction. Saul technically inquired (שָׁאַל), presumably through priestly mediation, for divine guidance, but did not seek from the heart (דָּרַשׁ) God's direction. Rather he sought out a medium contrary to God's revealed will.

[6] Various views have been put forth, from a deliberate imposture practiced upon Saul, to demonic powers imitating Samuel's physical form, to psychological impressionism or clairvoyance or telepathy, to an actual appearance of Samuel. Several factors in the account lend strong support to the last interpretation. First, the reaction of the woman was shock, indicating something far beyond her normal powers (28:12). Second, Saul's reaction was similar as he fell prostrate to the ground assured that this was the prophet himself (28:14). Third, the woman recognized that Saul was hiding under that disguise, which she failed to recognize before, and that God himself had made Samuel appear in order to give information to the king (28:12). Fourth, the message of Samuel was clearly from God, condemning Saul for consulting a medium and accurately predicting his downfall, in accordance with Samuel's earlier prophecy (28:16-19; cf. 15:28). Fifth, the medium of Endor's behavior following Samuel's disappearance was out of character: she was "greatly shaken," and then showed sympathy and offered Saul food (28:21-25). This is not the expected behavior of a professional necromancer, who would remain in control of the situation and then demand a considerable fee for her services.

[7] "אוֹב," in *NIDOTTE*, 1: 303-304.

Death of Saul, his sons, and his officers on Mt. Gilboa (1 Sam 31:1-13)
Complete disaster fell upon Saul. His army was annihilated, his three sons including Jonathan died in battle, and when wounded critically by the enemy archers Saul and his armor bearer took their own lives. Saul committed suicide lest the Philistines take him alive and cruelly torture him, like they did the fallen Samson (Jdg 16:21-22).[8] Jonathan, faithful friend of David, also remained the loyal son of Saul, battling by his father's side to the end. With Israel's leader slain and army scattered, the Philistines occupied her towns (31:7). Saul's corpse was recovered by the enemy, his head cut off, his armor placed in the temple of Ashtoreth as a war trophy, and his body fastened to the wall of Beth Shan as a display of utter humiliation (31:8-10). An intelligent, meek, attractive, gifted, divinely chosen and anointed monarch is now a defeated, humiliated, headless, mutilated corpse! A brighter beginning followed by such a tragic ending could hardly be imagined. The men of Jabesh-Gilead, whom Saul courageously rescued from an Ammonite siege years earlier (1 Sam 11:1-11), arose and reclaimed Saul's body and the bodies of his sons. Returning to Jabesh they cremated them and buried the bones (31:11-13). Cremation, though a sign of shame in the Old Testament (Lev 20:14; 21:9), was carried out here to prevent further abuse of the bodies. A seven-day fast of mourning followed (2 Sam 1:11-12). David later removed the remains of Saul from Jabesh to the family burial grounds in Zela in Benjamin (2 Sam 21:12-14).

****

Excursus on Saul: Tragic downfall of a leader
The forty-year reign of Saul as king of Israel is perhaps the most egregious case of failed leadership in all of Scripture. How could a kingship that began with so much promise descend so rapidly and end with such tragic consequences? The lessons are manifold:

1. **A clear call, impressive talents, and initial humility are gifts to be constantly nurtured and never neglected or taken for granted.**
    Saul had it all. He was the son of a noble Benjamite family, of impressive physical stature (9:1-2). His first task finds him the obedient, submissive son in search of his father's donkeys (9:3ff.). Saul is cautious in approaching Samuel (9:7) and later reluctant to report to his uncle the words Samuel spoke about his elevation (10:15-16). He was initially humble in his self-assessment (9:21) and avoided the spotlight (10:22). Clearly at this point Saul is not seeking prestige for himself. Saul is anointed by Samuel, filled with the Spirit, and given the gift of prophesying (9:16; 10:1, 6, 9-11). God touches Saul's heart (10:9) and he is "changed into a different person" (10:6). He is surrounded by gifted and godly men (10:26). When troublemakers despise him he is forgiving and non-retaliatory (10:27; 11:12-13). Saul is righteously

---

[8] The Amalekite's report of Saul's death recorded in 2 Samuel 1:1-16 differs from this account and presents a harmonistic problem. The Amalekite's claim that he was the instrument of Saul's death was probably a fabrication designed to exploit the situation for personal advantage.

angry by the Spirit at the Ammonites' threats against the citizens of Jabesh Gilead (11:6). He proves to be a skilled military leader against the Ammonites, ascribing the victory to the Lord (11:13). In terms of call, character, and conduct Saul appears to be a worthy monarch who will serve the nation well.[9]

The narrative leaves no doubt that Saul was the divine choice to be the first king of Israel. The Lord reveals to Samuel when Saul arrives at Ramah that this is the man who will lead and deliver Israel (9:15-17). The private anointing follows as Saul is made prince over the Lord's inheritance (10:1). Three signs confirm his appointment (10:2-8). The Spirit of prophecy provides a new heart for the task (10:6-11). At the public ratification ceremony at Mizpah Samuel identifies Saul as "the man the Lord has chosen" (10:24). Saul passes the military test against the Ammonites with requisite skill (11:8, 11). The formal inauguration ceremony at Gilgal reaffirms Saul's kingship with sacrifices and celebration (11:14-15). Samuel places the new arrangement on a theocratic foundation even as he grants their request: "Now here is the king you have chosen, the one you asked for; see, the Lord has set a king over you" (12:13).

2. **Strict obedience to the word of the Lord and, upon failure, sincere repentance without rationalization alone ensure God's ongoing presence and authentication for leadership.**

The turning point comes when Saul rashly offers sacrifices at Gilgal (13:8-14) as he refuses to wait for Samuel (cf. 10:8). He is moved by the fear of man (13:7-8), adopts a superstitious attitude toward God's favor, and rationalizes his actions (13:11-12). Samuel announces the rejection of the kingdom of Saul (13:13-14); from then on Saul is trying to hold on to something that is no longer his.

Saul utters a rash oath involving his soldiers in the heat of battle, causing them to violate the law (14:24, 31-32). He is personally vengeful (14:24), superstitious in approaching God (14:33-37), and loses connection with God (14:37). He is proudly insistent on his foolish oath, even to taking Jonathan's life (14:44). Saul is rapidly descending to egocentrism.

The third major failure of Saul is his partial obedience where he spares some of the "devoted things" in the Amalekite campaign. His values are reprobate, for he surrenders to the Lord only the weak and despised things (15:9). He rationalizes his disobedience by feigning spiritual motives (15:13, 15, 20-21) and places the blame on others (15:15). No longer small in his own eyes (15:17), Saul erects a monument in his own honor (15:12). He evidences a false repentance, showing concern only to escape the consequences and to preserve his prestige rather than painfully face the root cause of the violation (15:24-25, 30). True repentance, namely, the ruthlessly honest and

---

[9] Even in these early chapters, however, there may be subtle indications of a defective character: the stray donkeys perhaps symbolize the wandering, rebellious nature of Saul (9:3); his ignorance of the widely respected Samuel, the man of God (9:6), implies apathy or even disregard toward the covenant; the surprise at Saul's prophesying by those who knew him previously (10:11-12; cf. 19:24) indicates such spirituality is out of character for him.

painful heart-felt admission of guilt, is wholly missing. Samuel rebukes Saul for rebellion and arrogance and announces his irrevocable rejection as king (15:23-26). No amount of pathetic pleading can reverse his fortunes (15:27-31).

3. **Position without power, status without the Spirit, formal authority without personal credibility characterize the lost leader whose capacity for personal ruin and corporate malfeasance is unimaginable.**

    Samuel's departure (15:35) signals the beginning of Saul's rapid descent into delusion. Even the prophet himself fears for his life when commanded to anoint Saul's successor (16:2a). Tormented by an evil spirit, Saul finds relief only in David's harp playing (16:14-16, 23). Even as the Spirit comes on David (16:13), he has departed from Saul (16:14). Saul and the Israelites are terrified at the threats from Goliath (17:11, 24), a studied contrast with David's courage (17:32-37). Jealousy becomes murderous paranoia as Saul pursues David across the countryside seeking to eliminate his rival. All attempts to kill David end in failure for several reasons: David's maneuverability when the spear is hurled; Jonathan's loyalty against Saul's pressures to betrayal; David's triumph over the Philistines; Michal's deception of her father; and the Spirit of prophecy that arrests Saul and his men.

    Ultimately Saul's pursuit of David fails because of God's protection: "The Lord was with David but had left Saul" (18:12). The downward spiral of Saul into irrational, destructive behavior is appalling. He hurls his spear at his own son when Jonathan pleads David's innocence (20:32-33). The vicious massacre of the priestly family at Nob is a bold, defiant action against God's anointed servants, eighty-five men who wore the linen ephod (22:17-18). Saul's officials refuse to move against the priests, so an Edomite becomes the deadly instrument of Saul. He is willing to destroy an entire town, Keilah, in order to eliminate David (23:10). The witch of Endor incident underscores Saul's complete alienation from the Lord as he turns to a medium, which earlier he outlawed (28:3, 9), to bring him a word from the prophet who had anointed him (28:6-7).

    Saul comes to his end by taking his own life on Mount Gilboa. Forty years earlier a young man, attractive and gifted, began what seemed a promising career. Though Samuel warned the nation about placing trust in human leadership (12:13-15, 20-25), the Israelites heaped upon the young monarch unrealistic expectations. This, combined with the failure of Saul to handle early success, refusal to trust God in times of crisis, partial obedience and rationalized disobedience, and tragic loss of touch with both God and reality, accounts for the ruin of the first king of Israel.

****

Loyal subject and friend (2 Sam 1:1-27)

While David is executing vengeance on the Amalekites for their plunder of Ziklag (1 Sam 30), Saul and his sons are losing their lives in battle with the Philistines on Mount Gilboa (1 Sam 31). On the third day after David's return to

Ziklag, an Amalekite brings a report of Saul's death. This Amalekite could have been a mercenary soldier in Saul's army, or simply a scavenger plundering the battlefield who happened to be the first to come upon the body of Saul. It is ironic that it is an Amalekite who strips the fallen monarch of his crown (1:10), the people whom Saul had spared in the act of disobedience that cost him the kingship (1 Sam 15:1-23). The Amalekite's claim that he was the instrument of Saul's death contradicts 1 Samuel 31:4 and may well be a fabrication designed to exploit the situation for personal advantage. Whether or not the story is true, the Amalekite miscalculated David's response and it cost him his life. Rather than rejoicing in the death of his long time nemesis, David's respect for God's anointed remains firm and he orders the Amalekite's execution for striking down the Lord's anointed (1:16; cf. 1 Sam 24:6; 26:9, 16, 23). David must have accepted the Amalekite's account as true.

Even as the Amalekite expected a reward for slaying the rival of David, so one would expect a joyous celebration in David's camp. Instead there follows a lament, emotive and genuine, revealing a heart too noble to harbor revenge. This "lament of the bow" (1:17) was probably taught to David's men while they practiced the bow, Israel's most common weapon (2 Sam 22:35). Saul is praised as a mighty leader, a warrior to emulate, not an enemy to curse. David, then, will inaugurate his reign with a policy of reconciliation not recrimination. The civil war that follows is due to the aggressive attempt by Abner and Ishbosheth to seize power in the immediate interim (2:8-4:12). "How the mighty have fallen" is the refrain and theme of the lament (1:19, 25, 27). The eulogy is both for his dearest friend and for his bitterest enemy.

The time for elevation (2 Sam 2:1-7)

With Saul's death it is expected that David would return from Philistia to his homeland to assume the kingship. He had been set apart from his brothers and anointed by Samuel (1 Sam 16:1-13), and repeatedly assured of his future exaltation, even by Saul and Jonathan (20:13-16; 23:17-18; 24:20-21; 26:25). Fifteen years as a fugitive was enough to bear. Further, he was popular among the leaders of his own tribe (1 Sam 18:7; 21:11; 29:5) and would be able to quickly organize a new army and political base (30:26-31). Yet David remains committed to God's timing before making a move: David "inquired of the Lord" by means of the Urim and Thummim in the breastplate of the high priest, Abiathar (2:1). At the word of the Lord David ascends to Hebron and is anointed king over his native province of Judah (2:4). This was approximately fifteen years after the first private anointing (1025-1010 B.C.), David being now 30 years old (1 Sam 16:13; 2 Sam 5:4). Another seven years and six months (2:11) will pass before David assumes his full rights as national monarch (1003). God is molding his servant in the long periods of waiting and struggling, between the promise and its fulfillment. David begins his reign with an act of kindness, commending the people of Jabesh Gilead for their courage in reclaiming Saul's body and giving it a proper burial (2:4-7).

Defusing a potentially explosive crisis (2 Sam 2:8-4:12)

Abner, commander of Saul's army and a cousin of Saul (1 Sam 14:50-51), had vested interests in seeing a dynastic succession established. The surviving son of Saul, Ishbosheth, who was timid and unassertive (3:11; 4:1), proved an easy pawn for the ambitious commander. A skirmish at Gibeon (2:8-32) is the beginning of a long period of increasing hostilities between David's house and Saul's house (3:1). Abner initiates the conflict, hoping to check David's sphere of influence north of Judah, and to solidify the Benjamites' commitment to Ishbosheth. Representative combat is agreed upon and the two commanders, Abner and Joab, send twelve warriors each to the battle. The conflict soon spreads beyond the initial combatants. Asahel, Joab's younger brother, is determined to pursue Abner. The latter desires to avoid a blood feud with Joab and pleads with Asahel to turn aside. When Asahel is unwilling, Abner is forced to strike and kill the young man. The battle is called off after a peace initiative from Abner (2:26-28).

Abner, in his conflict with Joab and David's men at Gibeon, and in his own dealings with the house of Saul (3:6-11), comes to realize the futility of opposing David. He also realizes David's kingdom springs from the divine oath (3:9-10). Abner defects to David at Hebron (3:12). His peace initiative is to his credit and is a sincere offer of reconciliation. David accepts Abner's offer with no trace of bitterness. Joab, however, interprets Abner's move as a conspiracy designed to lure David into a dangerous agreement (3:24-25). Abner requests a formal agreement, probably as protection from later reprisals for his loyalty to the house of Saul, which loyalty David would respect. The covenant is ratified by the return of Michal to David whom Saul had given to another man (3:13-16; cf. 1 Sam 25:44). Abner similarly rallied the Benjamites to David, the last remnant of support for Ishbosheth (3:19).

Treachery then arises within the king's own ranks, the first of many ruthless actions taken by Joab, David's military commander (3:22-39). Luring Abner back to Hebron without David's knowledge, Joab treacherously murders Abner. His act is wholly without justification, as David himself laments (3:28-29, 37-39). Although Joab gained revenge for his brother Asahel's death (3:27, 30), Abner had pleaded for the young man to turn aside and only killed him in self-defense in the heat of battle (2:18-23). Further, Hebron was a city of refuge (Josh 21:13) where the avenger was forbidden to enter and slay the accused without a trial (Num 35:22-25). Perhaps Joab's real motive is to eliminate a potential rival, Abner, who has gained impressive support from the northern tribes. David is either unwilling or unable (3:39) to bring Joab to justice for his deed. Since Abner had gained the allegiance of the Benjamites and other northern tribes (2:8-9; 3:6, 19), his wanton murder holds dangerous political implications for David. The young king wisely issues a personal and official declaration of innocence, condemning Joab's treachery and affirming Abner's integrity (3:28). Joab is cursed (3:29), a period of mourning is held (3:30-35), and Abner is openly declared to be a fallen prince (3:38). David's lament expresses the genuine sorrow of a man who sees a human life unjustly taken. His consistent attitude throughout the struggles with the house of Saul is a desire to initiate his rule with amnesty, reconciliation, and renewal. His vision is focused on the future not the past. Thankfully, David's peace initiatives are successful, the entire nation recognizing his sincerity of grief and innocence of involvement in the Abner affair (3:36-37). A potentially disruptive event becomes the means of extending David's support in Israel.

With Abner dead and support for David growing, Ishbosheth loses all courage. Two of his military leaders, hoping to salvage something for themselves out of the crumbling regime, assassinate Ishbosheth and bring his head to David at Hebron (4:5-8). Like the Amalekite youth (1:2-16), they expect to be rewarded for eliminating David's rival, and like the same youth their miscalculation costs them their lives. David has the two men executed for their disloyalty. David knew that political assassination would only breed more of the same if left unpunished. Because of his respect for the office of kingship, David publicly exposes the bodies of the murderers (4:12; cf. Deut 21:22-23) and grants Ishbosheth, like Abner, a burial with full military honors.

Sowing seeds of family discord (2 Sam 3:1-5)

The theme of this entire section (1:1-5:5) is in 3:1: "David grew stronger and stronger, while the house of Saul grew weaker and weaker." To emphasize David's strength, the six sons born in Hebron are listed. David took four additional wives during the Hebron years to add to his earlier wives, Abigail of Carmel and Ahinoam of Jezreel (1 Sam 25:42-43). His first wife, Michal (1 Sam 18:26-28; 2 Sam 3:13-16), and later wife, Bathsheba (2 Sam 11:27), bring the total to eight. The Old Testament records eighteen sons of David and one daughter (Tamar). Absalom, who later rebelled against his father, was the son of a foreign princess (3:3). The narrator lets the ensuing record serve as the indirect censure of David's polygamy, a practice that contradicts the original design of marriage (Gen 2:18-25) and one which Moses warned against (Deut 17:17). David had other wives and concubines who bore him many children (2 Sam 5:13-16; 1 Chron 3:5-9).

Experiencing God's faithfulness to his promises (2 Sam 5:1-5)

Fifteen years of struggle with Saul followed by seven and one-half years of conflict with the former king's supporters come to an end with David's public anointing as king over all Israel. This is the long-awaited fulfillment of God's promise (1 Sam 15:28; 16:1). Elders throughout the land assemble at Hebron for the national event (5:1, 3). The elders confess their common heritage with David (5:1), his key military role in Saul's army (5:2a), and his divine appointment (5:2b). He is to be their shepherd and prince (5:2), that is, spiritual leader and civil ruler.[10] The compact (5:3) was a mutual commitment of submission to the kingship under the theocratic principles expounded by Samuel in his valedictory address (1 Sam 12). Within five years of this third anointing (cf. 1 Sam 16:13; 2 Sam 2:4) David

---

[10] Like Moses (Isa 63:11) and Joshua (Num 27:17), David shares the Lord's love for the flock of his covenant people and leads them to obey the law as a faithful shepherd (2 Sam 5:2; 7:7; Ps 78:71-72). He prefigures the Davidic Messiah who is the preeminent Shepherd of the people of God (Ezek 34:23; Mic 5:4; Zech 13:7; cf. Mt 2:6; 26:31; Jn 10:2, 11, 14, 16; Heb 13:20; 1 Pet 2:25; 5:4; Rev 7:17). He is also the ruler (נָגִיד) chosen by God to lead the nation as mediator of the theocratic rule of God over the covenant nation (2 Sam 5:2; cf. 1 Sam 13:14; 2 Sam 7:8; 1 Chron 28:4; 2 Chron 6:5-6).

will unite the nation, restore its confidence, and expand its borders. It is not until after Solomon's death that another serious foreign threat will occur.

Centralization and consolidation of power (2 Sam 5:6-25)

David inaugurates his rule with several strategic moves. First, he establishes a new capital in a central location (5:6-16). Second, he deals once and for all with the perennial Philistine threat which plagued Saul's reign from beginning to end (5:17-25). Third, he brings the ark to Jerusalem, the very symbol of God's presence and theocratic rule over his people (6:1-23). Building a nation from within enables the king to then expand its influence without. The consolidation of power advances in the stages of organization, centralization, and expansion. The reigns of David and Solomon are the golden age of Israel's history.

A number of factors made Jerusalem a proper choice for the new capital. First, in sacred history it was a place of divine encounter. Here Melchizedek, priest of God Most High, came forth to bless Abraham (Gen 14:18-20); thus it was a capital that would recall the theocratic character of the kingdom. Second, its location was on the border between Judah and Benjamin, though controlled by neither, and so would enable him to rule without giving political advantage to either his native Judahites or to the northern tribes who until now had been loyal to Saul. Third, its status was neutral, being a city still controlled by Jebusites (Josh 15:63; 18:28), despite temporary occupations of the city by Israelites (Jdg 1:8-9). The Jebusites were a Canaanite people who had inhabited this general area since the time of Moses (Gen 10:16; Num 13:29; Joshua 11:3; 15:8; 18:16). Finally, Jerusalem was a fortress, surrounded on three sides by deep valleys, making it easy to defend. The Jebusites could boast that even "the blind and lame" could thwart an assault (5:6).

David, with Joab in command (1 Chron 11:6), captured Jerusalem, "the fortress of Zion, the City of David" (5:7). David seems to have known of a secret tunnel, which provided access to the city, a part of the water supply system (5:8). This became the means of gaining entrance to the fortress city, and the method used to subdue it militarily. David then fortified the city by building up the supporting terraces, the Millo (5:9). David's success in establishing a new capital at Jerusalem brought both international recognition, seen in the Phoenician king Hiram's offer to donate cedar, carpenters, and stonemasons for the construction of the royal palace (5:11-12), and personal wealth and prestige, seen in the large harem he acquired (5:13-16). The harem was an act of disobedience to the covenant (Deut 17:17) and was later emulated by Solomon (1 Kg 11:1-13). David's adoption of the conventional moral standards of oriental kings set an example for Solomon that would lead to his son's downfall and the disruption of the monarchy itself (1 Kg 11-12).

Chronologically, the Philistine encounter (5:17-25) probably should be placed after the anointing at Hebron (5:3, 17), but before the capture of Jerusalem. With David assuming leadership over a now united national government, the Philistines sensed a threat to their newly occupied domain in the northern highlands (1 Sam 31:7). They approached Jerusalem twice, from the southwest through the valley of Rephaim. Both times David "inquired of the Lord" (5:19, 23), as had become his habit (1 Sam 22:20; 23:2; 2 Sam 2:1). Both times the Lord gave victory, first by "breaking out" against the Philistines (5:20), and then by sending the heavenly host to terrify the enemy with a loud marching sound in the tops of the balsam trees (5:23-24). Such a triumph brought welcome relief to the northern tribal peoples and helped bring the entire nation, north and south, under David's reign. In every way David "became more and more powerful, because he knew the Lord God Almighty was with him" (5:10).

Celebrating God's presence among his people (2 Sam 6:1-23)[11]

David wanted to reunite Israel not only politically, but religiously as well. Even as a monarchy Israel was to preserve its character as a community centered on the worship of the Lord. The ark of the covenant was the earthly throne and dwelling place of Yahweh among his people (6:2; cf. Ex 25:22). Since its removal from the central sanctuary at Shiloh (1 Sam 4:3-5) and its subsequent return from captivity in Philistia (1 Sam 4:11-6:20), the ark had resided in Kiriath Jearim (here called by its variant name, Baalah of Judah [6:2; Joshua 15:9]) in the house of Abinadab (1 Sam 6:21-7:1).

In transporting the ark to Jerusalem David fails to follow biblical instruction, which required the sons of Kohath to carry it and prohibited a cart or other vehicle being used (Ex 25:14-16; Num 4:5-6, 15). The account in 1 Chronicles (15:11-15) specifically relates the judgment on Uzzah to this failure to follow the Mosaic regulations for moving the ark. David followed the method of the Philistines (1 Sam 6:7-12). Perhaps he thought that the Mosaic regulations applied only when the entire nation was in formal tribal procession. The ark was transported on the new cart with David and all Israel celebrating with festive music, when at the rocky threshing floor of Nacon the ark began to totter. Uzzah reached out to steady the ark and touched it. God's wrath immediately killed Uzzah, his act condemned as one of irreverence (6:7). The Kohathites had been warned that to touch the holy things would mean instant death (Num 4:15). Like the judgment on the people of Beth Shemesh who looked into the ark (1 Sam 6:19-20), God was graphically reminding his people that he is the holy, sovereign Lord, to be worshipped and glorified. He is not a limited, finite being encased in a material dwelling, nor a capricious deity manipulated by human means for personal advantage.

David responds with anger and fear, assigning the ark to a Levite, Obed-Edom, for three months (6:10-11; 1 Chron 15:18-24), before proceeding again toward Jerusalem. He then moves with caution, six steps followed by sacrifice and praise (6:12-15). David's act of wearing the linen ephod (6:14; cf. 1 Sam 2:18) and dancing before the Lord (cf. Ex 15:20; 1 Sam 18:6-7), though a humble, joyous expression of praise, was despised by Michal as an inappropriate act for a king (6:16, 20). Three times referred to as "the daughter of Saul" (6:16, 20, 23), Michal reflects the values of her father who saw the kingship more as a source of position than a privileged stewardship. David made the procession of the ark to Jerusalem an occasion of national praise and worship (6:17-19; cf. 1 Chron 15:1-

---

[11] The parallel account in 1 Chronicles 13:1-14; 15:1-16:6 is fuller and supplies many details left out in 2 Samuel.

16:6), at which time Psalms 96, 105, 106 were composed and recited. He defended his honor in the face of his wife's sarcastic denunciations, vowing to humble himself rather than seek an isolated, artificial prestige (6:21-22). He is willing to be humiliated in order to worship his Lord passionately. Michal's subsequent barrenness is related to her bitterness toward David (6:23) and is a further judgment on the house of Saul.

Eternal covenant with the house of David (2 Sam 7:1-28)

The Davidic covenant is the continuation of the covenant theme beginning with the protoevangelium (Gen 3:15), focused then on Shem (Gen 9:26-27), Abraham (Gen 12:2-3; 13:16; 15:5), Isaac (Gen 26:23-24), Jacob (Gen 28:13-15), Judah (Gen 49:8-11), and now David (cf. Ps 89:34-37). Later the prophets point to a greater Davidic ruler who will sit on David's throne as perfect king and final redeemer (Isa 9:6-7; 11:1-16; Jer 23:5-6; 30:8-9; 33:14-16; Ezek 34:23-24; 37:24-25).

The occasion for God's revelation is David's concern for the honor of Yahweh. While he was living in a beautiful cedar palace (5:11-12), the ark was dwelling in a humble tent. Through Nathan God changed David's initial plans to construct a magnificent dwelling for the ark. The temple would become the architectural project of David's son, Solomon (7:12-13; cf. 1 Kg 5-8). Whereas David desires to build a "house" for the Lord, the Lord will build a "house" for David in the sense of a dynastic succession without end (7:11b). The biblical text provides three reasons why David's request was denied. First, historically God's presence among his sojourning people had never required an elaborate structure (7:6). Second, such an idea sprang from human imagination rather than divine revelation (7:7). Third, David's long career as a warrior involved in bloodshed disqualified him as the builder (1 Chron 22:8; 28:3). God's purposes for David supersede David's plans for God.

The unconditional covenant that follows (4 times: "The Lord/I will establish" [7:11, 12, 13, 16]), like the Abrahamic, includes posterity (7:12, 13, 16), a throne (7:13, 16), and a kingdom (7:13, 16). Though partially fulfilled in Solomon (7:12, 14, 15), the New Testament sees its ultimate realization in Jesus Christ (Mt 1:1; Lk 1:69; Acts 2:30; 13:23; Rom 1:2-3; 2 Tim 2:8; Rev 3:7; 22:16). The eternal, enduring character of the Davidic covenant is emphasized (7:13, 16). David's prayerful response is one of wonder and amazement at God's purposes:

1. Self-deprecation: Who am I? (7:18-21)
2. Adoration: How great you are! (7:22-24)
3. Supplication: And now, Lord God, do as you promised (7:25-29).

"Sovereign Lord," the repeated designation (7:18, 19, 20, 22, 28, 29),[12] fits perfectly the mood of David's prayer. The compound title first appears in the Hebrew Bible on the lips of Abram (Gen 15:2) after the Lord's sovereign pronouncement: "I am your shield, your very great reward" (15:1). Abram exalts

---

[12] The compound Hebrew designation behind the NIV rendering "Sovereign Lord," repeated in this passage seven times, is אֲדֹנָי יְהוִה.

the majesty of One who would make such a declaration, which becomes the preface to the promise of an innumerable seed (15:3-5), the justification of Abram by faith (15:6), and the pledge of the inheritance of Canaan (15:7). The parallel contexts of the employment of this relatively unusual divine appellation points toward the organic continuity of the Abrahamic and Davidic covenants: "Coming out of Abraham's experience with God was the promise of land for Israel; out of David's experience came the promise of a leader within that land."[13] David's prayer is that the Lord's name be magnified (7:23, 26). David refers to himself as "your servant" six times (7:20-21, 27, 29). He views his leadership as a gracious stewardship and he will aspire to fulfill his calling under divine enabling. He has come to the Lord with sincere, well-laid plans. But the Lord inverts David's requests and states his sovereign purposes not for his own house, but for David's.

Securing and expanding the borders (2 Sam 8:1-14; 10:1-19)
Under David the borders of Israel expanded and, including the tributary nations brought under his control, the nation realized for the first time, at least temporarily, her promised domain (Gen 15:18-21). The events of Chapter 8 (and possibly Chapter 10) occurred early in David's reign, before the revelation of Chapter 7 (7:1; 8:1; 10:1). These military triumphs extended in all four directions and subdued Israel's historical enemies: (1) to the west, the Philistines; (2) to the east, Moab and Ammon; (3) to the north, the Arameans; (4) to the south, the Amalekites and Edomites. All of the treaties, tributes, and expanding boundaries brought to Israel political security and sources of material abundance which would turn Israel from a divided, constricted tribal confederation to a united, growing prosperous nation.

Praise for deliverance (2 Sam 22:1-51)
This song of praise for God's deliverance is also preserved in Psalm 18 (cf. 22:1 and Ps 18 title). Perhaps it was composed shortly after David's victories over the surrounding nations (2 Sam 8:1-14). David retains his perspective in the midst of unparalleled success as a military leader by recalling the source of his triumphs:

1. Introduction: "the Lord is my rock" (22:1-4)
2. Rescue from danger: "He heard my voice . . . he reached down" (22:5-20)
3. Reward according to righteousness: "You are my lamp" (22:21-29)
4. Provider of triumphant power: "It is God who arms me with strength" (22:30-46)
5. Conclusion: "The Lord lives! Praise be to my rock" (22:47-51)

Though David is called "the lamp of Israel" (2 Sam 21:17; cf. 1 Kg 11:36; 15:4: Ps 132:17), a metaphor for the nation's life, hope and security,[14] David recognizes the true source of life and extols the Lord as his lamp who turns his darkness into light (22:29).

---

[13] Robert D. Bergen, *1, 2, Samuel* (Broadman and Holman, 1996): 343.
[14] "נֵר," in *NIDOTTE*, 3:159-160.

Delegation of administrative responsibilities (2 Sam 8:15-18; 1 Chron18:14-17)
With centralization in Jerusalem David developed a political and military organization with designated royal officers. He developed the skills of an effective administrator. The six main cabinet positions are listed:

1. Joab, commander of the army
2. Jehoshaphat, recorder; possibly a chief administrator of royal affairs, responsible for the royal records (cf. 2 Kg 18:18, 37)
3. Zadok and Abiathar, chief priests
4. Seraiah, secretary; duties included foreign and domestic correspondence and various administrative functions (cf. 2 Kg 12:10-12)
5. Benaiah, over the Kerethites and Pelethites who formed David's royal guard (cf. 2 Sam 23:22-23)
6. David's sons, the royal advisers[15]
7. Adoniram, later appointed to a new position, supervisor of forced labor (cf. 2 Sam 20:24)

Loyal to his oath (2 Sam 9:1-13; 16:1-4)
David brings Mephibosheth, Jonathan's son who was lame due to a childhood injury (4:4), to Jerusalem, restoring to him all of Saul's property, and committing his support to Saul's steward, Ziba. Although another reconciliatory gesture of David toward the house of Saul, David's main purpose is to fulfill his covenant of friendship with Jonathan (9:1, 7; cf. 1 Sam 20:13-17). Mephibosheth now had a young son (9:12), so this must be placed a number of years after David's capture of Jerusalem.

Ziba later approaches David as he is fleeing Jerusalem and claims that Mephibosheth had joined Absalom's revolt, generally considered to be an untruth. Without validating this assertion, David transfers Mephibosheth's property to Ziba (16:1-4). After David is restored he hears from Mephibosheth that Ziba's charges were unfounded and, facing conflicting testimony, orders the division of Saul's estate between the two men (19:24-30).

Tragic moral failure: adultery and murder (2 Sam 11:1-27)
We come to a watershed event in the life of David. He had accumulated many wives and concubines (3:2-5; 5:13-15), conforming to the practice of near eastern kings who assembled large harems. His moral failure in the Bathsheba-Uriah incident, then, is shocking, but not wholly unexpected. The man after God's heart (1 Sam 13:14) breaks four of the ten commandments, the sixth (murder), seventh (adultery), ninth (false witness), and tenth (coveting). The narrative focuses on David's covenant responsibilities and the moral judgment placed on his actions, which so egregiously violated a sacred stewardship: displeasing to the Lord (11:27), rebuked publicly by the prophet (12:7-12), and repented of by the perpetrator (12:13).

---

[15] The normal Hebrew term for priests (כֹּהֲנִים) is used in 2 Samuel 8:18, but is best understood in light of רָאשׁנִים, meaning "leading ones" or "chief officials" (NIV), in 1 Chronicles 18:17.

The context is the continuing Ammonite campaign, with 11:2-12:25 a parenthetical insertion into the narrative. Though the Ammonite-Aramean federation had been destroyed (10:19), Rabbah, the capital of Ammon, was still to be taken. During this spring siege David, for some unexplained reason, was still in Jerusalem and absent from the battlefront. His idleness became the occasion of his downfall. The pattern of sin is clear: "he saw . . . he inquired . . . he took her" (11:2-4). Pursuit was the deadly link between desire and deed. David's was a premeditated act of adultery for which there was no provision of atonement in the law, only the death penalty (Lev 20:10; 24:17). The text is silent on whether Bathsheba was a willing partner or was seized by force. Nathan's parable seems to imply that Uriah and Bathsheba enjoyed a warm, committed marriage relationship (12:3), although later incidents show Bathsheba was a woman lacking discretion (1 Kg 2:13-22). If she was intentionally bathing in full view of the royal palace, designed to lure the king into temptation, then her mourning at Uriah's death (11:26) is an artificial sorrow produced only for the occasion. Bathsheba was ceremonially clean at the time of the act (11:4), meaning her monthly menstruation period was over. This confirms, in the context, that she was impregnated not by her husband but by David (11:5).

Sin breeds sin. David became desperate as he received word secretly of Bathsheba's pregnancy. Summoning Uriah from the battlefield, David twice attempts to get him to return home and enjoy normal relations with his wife. This is to provide another explanation for the only proof of his act, namely, the pregnancy. Uriah, however, is a loyal soldier with a deep sense of duty. He refuses to enjoy the pleasures of home, while his fellow warriors are enduring the hardships of battle. There is no indication Uriah has any knowledge of his wife's affair. When the two cover-up attempts fail (11:6-13), David coldly calculates a way to eliminate Uriah (11:14-27). With Joab as his willing accomplice, David places Uriah in the front lines of the battle, near the most heavily defended part of the city. Uriah, as planned, is struck down. The king expresses no remorse at all (11:25). David can now not only explain the pregnancy, but even portray his act of taking Bathsheba into his harem as an act of kindness toward his faithful soldier, Uriah (11:27). David has thus lowered himself to the level of Saul, who similarly plotted against him out of desperation. This is the darkest moment of David's life. The pleasure was brief, the consequences lasting (Heb 11:25). The record closes with the divine assessment: "But the thing David had done displeased the Lord" (11:27b).

Prophetic rebuke and genuine repentance (2 Sam 12:1-25)
David spent many months tormented by a condemning conscience. He was distant from God and it took its toll on his mental and physical condition (Ps 32:3-4). Approximately one year after his sin (11:27; 12:15), God sent the prophet Nathan to openly rebuke the king and declare his judgment on his actions. Nathan captures the king's attention by a striking parable (12:1-6), contrasting a poor man and a rich man. The poor man is exploited by the rich man, unjustly robbed of his one precious ewe lamb to provide for the latter's guest. The rich man is unwilling to release one of his own numerous sheep or cattle, but is thoroughly

willing to plunder the sole possession of the poor man. Nathan is contrasting David with his vast harem, and Uriah with his one wife. David responds with anger, knowing as a shepherd how attached one could become to a little ewe lamb, and demands a fourfold restitution as required in Exodus 22:1.

Nathan moves from narrative to confrontation: "You are the man" (12:7). The prophet declares without dilution God's judgment on David's act. The king is made to feel the full force of what he has done (12:7-9). The consequences are threefold. First, "the sword will never depart from your house" (12:10), that is, his three sons, Amnon (13:28-29), Absalom (18:4), and Adonijah (1 Kg 2:25) are to meet violent deaths. Second, "out of your own household I am going to bring calamity upon you" (12:11a), that is, David is to become a fugitive again through his son Absalom's rebellion (15:1-15). Third, "one who is close to you will lie with your wives" (12:11b), also fulfilled by Absalom during his seizure of power (16:21-22).

Unlike Saul, who forced a reluctant confession only to gain Samuel's favor (1 Sam 15:24, 25, 30), David openly admits his sin, without any attempt at justification, and accepts its consequences. Nathan assures David of God's forgiveness, though the son born to Bathsheba will die as a consequence of his dishonoring the Lord (12:14). David fasts and prays for the child's recovery from illness, but then humbly accepts the Lord's discipline (12:15-23). A small, seemingly private act between two consenting individuals creates ever widening circles of loss and heartache. However, the forgiveness of God brings renewed peace, joy, and sanity to David's spirit (Ps 51:8-15). The king takes Bathsheba as his wife and she bears a son, Solomon or Jedidah, (12:24-25), who will one day inherit the throne (1 Kg 1:39).

The narrative of the Ammonite campaign resumes (from 11:1) after the interruption. The siege of Rabbah, led by Joab, is successful. With David's participation the capital is captured, plundered, and the Ammonites put to various forms of slave labor (12:26-31). Confession and judgment are followed by restoration and victory.

Family disintegration and political revolt (2 Sam 13:1-19:7)
Dynamic leadership traits were overshadowed in David's later life by colossal failure in the personal and family realms. David's own acts of adultery and murder are imitated by his sons: Amnon, David's oldest son, rapes his half-sister Tamar; in revenge Absalom murders his half-brother Amnon to defend the integrity of his sister. Amnon's 'love' for Tamar was infatuation, which produced fantasizing lust. It drove him to the point of sickness, and even when satisfied proved only temporary, quickly turning to disgust towards the object of his cruel exploitation (13:15). Tamar's virginity was stolen, eliminating any chances for normal courtship and marriage. Even more surprising is David's passivity. Although he was angered by Amnon's act (13:21), there is no record of him taking disciplinary action against his son. In fact, it was David's indulging attitude toward Amnon that brought Tamar into the compromising situation in the first place (13:6-7).

Absalom and Tamar were the products of David's marriage with Maacah, the daughter of Talmai, the king of Geshur (3:3; 13:1). From the time of Tamar's violation Absalom quietly planned the murder of Amnon (13:32). Surely the fact that Amnon was the eldest son and heir to the throne also motivated the politically ambitious schemer. Two years later the opportunity presented itself. At the festive sheep-shearing season Absalom urged David to send Amnon and his other brothers to join in the ceremonies. Even if David suspected sinister motives behind the request, he gave in (13:26-27). In both Amnon's deceit of Tamar and Absalom's deceit of Amnon, David's acquiescence to the desires of his sons provided the opportunity for their mischief. It underscores his insensitivity to the disintegrating family relationships and failure to discipline his children. Even after Absalom's murder of his eldest son, David "longed to go to Absalom" (13:39). With Amnon's elimination Absalom was now first in line to succeed David, since Kileab (3:3) must have died in childhood. Absalom spent the next three years in Geshur under the protection of his grandfather, Talmai (13:37-38).

Joab, despite his ruthlessness, was the loyal servant of David. He recognized the potential danger of the king's estrangement from his son and devised a plan to bring about reconciliation. Like Nathan the prophet (12:1-12), Joab uses a parable (14:4-11) and its application (14:12-17) to capture David's attention. Hiring a woman from Tekoa, she approaches the king about a story concerning her two sons. One murders the other and then becomes the object of the avenger of blood, which threatens to completely wipe out her deceased husband's family line. The king grants her request of protection for her surviving son from the avengers. As with Nathan, the woman of Tekoa turns to the application, which is a direct appeal for the king to restore his son Absalom from banishment for his murder of Amnon. In exempting the guilty son from blood revenge, David is logically exempting Absalom of the same for the murder of his brother. David immediately recognizes that Joab is behind this entire incident (14:19a), but agrees to restore Absalom from Geshur. Absalom is brought back to Jerusalem, but is not allowed to approach the king. For the next two years Absalom remains in practical isolation from his father, which proves politically unwise. His impressive appearance, particularly his rich head of hair, gains him a kingly reputation and a growing number of followers. During these two years Absalom is able to marshal political support, measure the pulse of the nation, and plan his future moves. Finally, at Joab's initiative, Absalom and David are physically reconciled, though there is no mention of repentance for the murder of Amnon (14:32-33). David once again proves to be the pampering father in the treatment of his son.

For the next four years (15:7), either dated from his initial return to Jerusalem (14:23) or from his restoration to the royal court (14:33), Absalom carefully prepared to move against the throne of his father. Absalom gathered a small military contingent around himself (15:1) and began to ingratiate himself with those who felt betrayed by the legal system (15:2-4). He deceitfully endorsed the grievances of dissatisfied people without inquiring into their legitimacy. Absalom's pandering to special interests gradually "stole the hearts of the men of Israel" (15:5-6). Under the pretext of fulfilling a vow, Absalom returns to his birthplace of Hebron (15:7-8; cf. 3:3). David once again fails to perceive the danger, having lost all objectivity with respect to his own children (15:9; cf. 8:18b; 13:6-7, 24-27; 1 Kg 1:6). In Hebron Absalom is proclaimed king (15:10-11) and also gains the valuable support of the wise counselor Ahithophel who served as adviser to David (15:12). Ahithophel, grandfather of Bathsheba (2 Sam 11:3; 23:34), may have harbored resentment toward David for his actions toward Bathsheba and Uriah. David later laments being betrayed by a close friend and trusted counselor (Ps 41:9; 55:12-14).

David returns to the life of a fugitive, this time fleeing the murderous pursuit not of his father-in-law but of his favorite son (15:13-18). The attitude of David throughout the ordeal is one of commitment to the divine disposition: "let him (the Lord) do to me whatever seems good to him" (15:26). He withdraws from Jerusalem because to remain would be to expose the city to bloodshed (15:14). He leaves with sorrow and in a posture of penitence (15:23, 30). At Bahurim David is cursed and pelted with stones by one Shimei, a member of Saul's clan (16:5-14). The king shows remarkable restraint, perhaps remembering the lesson learned in his encounter with Nabal where Abigail spared him the shame of needless retaliation (1 Sam 25:32-34).[16]

Near Mahanaim in Gilead at an area known as "the forest of Ephraim" (18:6) David's army in three divisions faces the massive army of Absalom. The enemy forces, despite their superior numbers, were no match for the seasoned troops of David. 20,000 of his troops are killed and Absalom loses his own life when his head gets caught in an oak tree. Joab, who had earlier sought Absalom's restoration to Jerusalem (14:1, 19-21), does not hesitate to strike Absalom despite the king's command to deal gently with his son (18:5). Absalom is buried under a large pile of rocks to mock the monument that he, like Saul (1 Sam 15:12), had erected to himself (18:17-18).

Two messengers bring the "good news" of David's victory over Absalom. David's concern from start to finish is Absalom's welfare. His repeated question, "Is the young man Absalom safe?" (18:29, 32), is taken by Joab as callous indifference to the loyal troops who have risked their lives for his sake and his preference for a treacherous betrayer. David is overcome with grief and only Joab's sharp rebuke brings David out of his uncontrollable sobbing (19:5-8). Joab's reaction is justified, for he senses a mass defection of the troops unless the king steps forward to affirm them. David's response to Absalom's death is consistent with his indulging, sentimental attitude toward his sons that we have seen throughout (18:33; 19:4; cf. 8:18b; 13:6-7, 24-27; 15:9; 1 Kg 1:6).

Favoritism sparks division (2 Sam 19:8-20:22)

The northern tribes of Israel were unanimous in their desire to restore David from exile beyond the Jordan (19:9-10). At this point David makes an unwise political move by appealing to his fellow tribesmen from Judah to take the initiative in restoring him. In addition, he promises Amasa, Absalom's commander, the leadership of the army in place of Joab, probably in retaliation for the latter's murder of Absalom. The result is that Joab treacherously murders another good man he considers a rival

---

[16] After David's restoration, Shimei approaches the king with a plea for forgiveness, which David grants on oath (19:16-23). In his farewell charge to Solomon, however, David implores Solomon to bring justice to Shimei for his earlier, unjustified cursing of God's anointed (1 Kg 2:8-9; fulfilled in 1 Kg 2:36-46).

(20:8-10; cf. 3:27). While David is successful in regaining the allegiance of the men of Judah (19:14), the men of Israel feel betrayed. Once again David has failed to reward those who have shown such loyalty to him. Tribal tensions provide one Sheba (20:1) an opportunity to exploit the situation for personal gain.

The troublemaker Sheba detects the injured feelings of the men of Israel. Being a Benjamite, he stokes the still simmering tribal jealousies over the transfer of authority from the house of Saul (Benjamin) to the house of David (Judah). He claims that David is guilty of favoritism toward his own disloyal tribe over the loyal tribes in the north. Sheba, like Absalom before and Adonijah after, enjoys temporary success as the men of Israel desert David to follow him (20:1-2). This time David acts quickly, unlike in Absalom's rebellion, to crush Sheba's uprising. Joab and the professional army pursue Sheba far north to Abel, a town known for its wisdom. Rather than see her city destroyed by the siege of Joab's forces, a wise woman organizes Sheba's capture and execution, delivering his head to Joab (20:15-22). The rebellion ends without wider repercussions.

Restoration of God's blessing and fellowship (2 Sam 21:1-14)

Three years of famine occurred as God's judgment for the violation by Saul of an earlier oath with the Gibeonites (21:1; cf. Josh 9:15-21). During the conquest of Canaan the Gibeonites had successfully deceived Joshua into a peace treaty by pretending to be foreign travelers. Oaths, once made, were to be kept (Num 30:1-2; Deut 23:21-23; Eccles 5:1-7). Saul's brutal action toward the Gibeonites is not mentioned elsewhere in the Old Testament. For restitution the Gibeonites demand that seven male descendants of Saul be delivered to them for execution, the number symbolizing completeness of vengeance. Though David spares Mephibosheth because of his covenant with Jonathan (21:7; cf. 1 Sam 20:14-17), he delivers to the Gibeonites' two sons and five grandsons of Saul who are promptly executed and exposed at Gibeah of Saul, the former king's residence. This action seems to be a clear violation of Deuteronomy 24:16, which forbids substitute restitution. This may be an example of the principle of priority, namely, the profaning of God's name by breaking an oath over a single piece of legislation. At any rate, God's judgment is removed, rain replacing famine (21:10), and answered prayer replacing silence (21:14b). David, as an act of respect for Saul's house, takes the bones of the exposed men and, along with the bones of Saul and Jonathan from Jabesh Gilead (1 Sam 31:11-13), gives them a proper burial in the tomb of Saul's father Kish at Zela in Benjamin (21:11-14).

Ruling in righteousness and fear (2 Sam 23:1-7)

In David's last poetic testimony, not his last will and testament which is recorded in 1 Kings 2:1-11, he declares the theocratic ideals for the kingship (23:3-4) and the certain fulfillment of the everlasting covenant (23:5; cf. 7:12-16). David's sweet song is given the status of a prophetic oracle (23:1) inspired by the Spirit of the Lord (23:2). Under David the nation is blessed by righteous rule and just punishment of evil people (23:6-7).

Loyal comrades in battle (2 Sam 23:8-39; cf. 1 Chron 11:10-47)

David was able to gather skillful, courageous and loyal men to his cause, always the mark of a great leader. His unparalleled acts of bravery won their respect and his loyalty to them won their affection. The gallery of David's mighty men lists 37 of his most valiant warriors. The parallel list in 1 Chronicles 11:10-47 includes 16 additional names (11:41b-47). These mighty men are arranged in several groups in order of honor: "the three mighty men," Josheb, Eleazar and Shammah; another group of three who courageously brought David water from a Philistine garrison (23:13-17), not including Abishai and Benaiah (23:18-23); and "the thirty" (23:24-39). When the three men return from retrieving the water, David pours it out as a libation offering to the Lord (23:16). He cannot bear to quench his thirst with the precious gift the men acquired "at the risk of their lives" (23:17). Such sacrificial affirmation could only inspire the deepest loyalty of those who fought by his side and knew him best.

Pride, judgment, and restoration (2 Sam 24:1-25; 1 Chron 21:1-22:1)

This time it is not a famine, but a plague, which once again must be atoned for before the nation can experience God's blessing (cf. 21:1 and 24:1; 21:14b and 24:25b). If sin is cherished in the heart, rather than repented of and forsaken, prayer is effectively blocked (Ps 66:18). This is a puzzling incident with a number of unexplained facts. In 2 Samuel 24:1 the Lord incites David to number Israel, whereas 1 Chronicles 21:1 attributes the action to Satan's instigation. The solution seems to lie in the mystery of providence. David's action is condemned as sinful (24:10), the enticement to which is never from God (Jas 1:13-15). Yet the biblical doctrine of providence places all events, good and evil, man's and Satan's, under God's sovereign control and management (Gen 50:19-20; Ex 4:21; 7:3; 9:12; 10:1, 20, 27; 11:10; 14:4; Joshua 11:20; 1 Kg 22:22-23; Job 1:2; 2:10; Ezek 3:20; 14:9; Acts 4:27-28).

David's action is the cause of God's judgment in the form of a plague that claims 70,000 lives. David is given a choice of three judgments. He chooses to be under the direct chastisement of God rather than once again fall into the hands of merciless enemies or a prolonged drought (24:14). David understands that true worship involves sacrifice, so he insists on paying Araunah for his threshing floor (24:24). Sacrificial offerings at the hastily built altar stem the plague and restore communion with God (24:18-25).

What was David's sin here, since taking a census of the nation's fighting men is not without precedent in Israel's history (Num 1, 26)? Probably it lay in David's motivation behind the census. Joab, not a man of sensitive nature, sensed something strange in David's behavior (24:3), and the king himself was conscience-stricken even before the prophetic rebuke came from Gad (24:10-11). Was David filled with pride, glorying in the vastness of his expanding kingdom and the strength of his armies, a pride which Samuel had earlier warned about (1 Sam 8:10-18)? Did military power, political security, and personal ambition steal away David's affections from the Lord? If so, the census became a visible expression of idolatry. God would not allow his covenantal steward to act like an oriental ruler whose sole concerns were personal prestige and military might.

Validating the right successor (1 Kg 1:1-2:11)

The third threat, following Absalom's and Sheba's, against David's rule comes again from one of his sons, Adonijah, the oldest surviving son (2 Sam 3:4). David's failure to manage his family is noted again: "His father had never interfered with him by asking, 'Why do you behave as you do'?" (1:6). Adonijah made his move while David was gravely ill, being around 70 years of age (2 Sam 5:4). Adonijah managed to gain the support of Joab and Abiathar the priest. Like Absalom, Adonijah attempted to gain control by quickly calling all of the royal officials to an inauguration ceremony at En Rogel accompanied by sacrificial offerings (1:9). But Nathan and Bathsheba also moved quickly to preserve the interests of Solomon, realizing that Adonijah's success would spell the elimination of all other potential claimants (1:12). The latter two appeal to David's oath, unrecorded elsewhere, where David swore the kingship to Solomon (1:13).

David acts with dispatch, despite his infirm condition, and convenes a public investiture ceremony for the young Solomon. Anointed by Zadok and Nathan, Solomon formally becomes king of Judah and Israel, attested by priest, prophet and king (1:32-40). While the cries of "Long live King Adonijah" ring out from En Rogel (1:25), the shouts of "Long live King Solomon" reverberate from Gihon (1:34). With David's support of Solomon now publicly attested, Adonijah realizes the hopelessness of his situation. Fleeing to the sacred tent, Adonijah takes hold of the horns of the altar (of burnt offering) and pleads for mercy (1:50-51; cf. Ex 21:13-14). Solomon grants to his half-brother clemency, provided that he relinquishes all claims to the throne (1:52-53). Later, however, Adonijah makes another attempt to gain power and, as Solomon warned, is summarily executed (2:13-25).

Like Moses (Deut 31:1-8), Joshua (Jos 23:1-16) and Samuel (1 Sam 12:1-25), David delivers his final testament, reminding his successor to be faithful to his covenant obligations so that his kingship might prosper (2:1-9). The covenant promises, initially stated to Abraham and certain of fulfillment (2 Sam 23:5), are individually and generationally realized through obedience to the Mosaic law. Justice for Joab's vengeful murders, Barzillai's kindness, and Shimei's cursings are committed to Solomon. David's forty-year reign comes to an end with this final charge (2:10-12). He is buried in Jerusalem, the City of David.

Leadership profile of David
1. *Faith, not fear, in crisis: King Saul and his army cower before the Philistine giant, Goliath, who blasphemes the Lord and defies his people. The shepherd boy steps forth, bolstered by faith, to defend the Lord's name and slay the giant. Throughout his flight from Saul, David seeks the Lord (1 Sam 21:1; 23:2, 4, 9-12; 24:12, 15; 26:9-11). Though only one step from death (1 Sam 20:3), David is helped by Jonathan to find strength in God (1 Sam 23:16). At the plunder of Ziklag and the near mutiny of his troops, David "found strength in the Lord his God" (1 Sam 30:6). He conquered his fears by exercising faith in a mighty God. "I sought the Lord, and he answered me; he delivered me from all my fears" (Ps 34:4).*

2. ***Praise and worship during times of adversity****: David composed many Psalms during his desperate years as a refugee (Ps 3, 7, 18, 34, 52, 54, 56, 57, 59, 63, 142 superscriptions). These Psalms record David's pleas for help (Ps 142:1-6) and praise for God's deliverance (142:7). David knew that the greatest treasure given Israel was her worship of the Lord. His Spirit-inspired music in Saul's court, unashamed dancing at the arrival of the ark to Jerusalem, and vision for the Lord's temple reveal a passion for worship. He offers sacrifices on an altar that he has purchased because true worship involves the sacrificial offering of oneself to God (2 Sam 24:24).*

3. ***Release of one's destiny to an all-wise and sovereign God****: David adamantly refuses to move against Saul, the Lord's anointed, though the 'providential opportunity' could easily have been justified both in the dark cave and in the sleeping camp. He shows a remarkable capacity to restrain the normal impulses to search out and destroy those that doubt or challenge his rule. He endures Shimei's cursing as from the Lord and recognizes the Lord sent Abigail to protect him from himself. After Saul's death, he inquires of the Lord before ascending to Hebron for the coronation (2 Sam 2:1). David begins his reign over all Israel with amnesty toward the house of Saul and laments Abner's unjust death. One of David's greatest traits is his covenant-keeping loyalty to friends and enemies, to Saul, Jonathan, Barzillai, and the Gibeonites. A leader who is wholly confident in a wise, loving, sovereign God is empowered to lead without paranoia, manipulation, or tight-fisted control.*

4. ***Repentance not rationalization in failure****: David's victories, over Goliath, Philistines, and the surrounding nations, were magnificent. Equally colossal were his moral failures. His adultery with Bathsheba was carefully planned and executed. His indirect murder of Uriah was cold and calculated. Both were highhanded sins for which there was no provision of atonement in the law. Psalms 32 and 51 supplement the narrative of 2 Samuel 12 to reveal a conscience-stricken leader who from his heart confesses, "I have sinned against the Lord" (12:13). No explanation, justification, or evasion accompanies David's repentance, only a plea for mercy (Ps 51:1-7). The word of forgiveness is immediate: "The Lord has taken away your sin" (12:13b). Augustine comments that David's fall should put upon their guard those who have not fallen, and save from despair those who have.[17] David acts quickly to atone for the violation of the Gibeonite oath and for the Satan-inspired military census, removing the divine judgments of famine and plague from the land.*

5. ***Career success and family ruin****: The worshipful shepherd, courageous warrior, Spirit-inspired musician, and skilled administrator failed as a husband and a father. The seeds of family discord were sown by polygamy and the acquisition of a large harem. He acted as the indulgent father toward his sons Amnon, Absalom, and Adonijah. The consequences were disastrous: rape, deceit, murder, political intrigue, rebellion, civil war, and three dead sons. He would be imitated by his son and successor Solomon with a disastrous*

---

[17] *On the Psalms* (51:3).

moral effect on the nation. The excesses of children cannot always be blamed on parental failure, but in David's case he experienced the principle that what one sows, one ends up reaping.

6. ***Faithfulness to God's covenantal purposes****: The reign of David becomes the standard of measure for other kings (1 Kg 9:4; 11:4, 6, 33, 38; 14:8; 15:3, 5, 11; 2 Kg 16:2; 18:3; 22:2). He is the exemplar of the theocratic ruler characterized by undivided devotion to the Lord and obedience to the covenant. David served the nation as steward of its covenantal identity, the man after God's heart. He set the ark, symbol of God's presence, at the center of national life. The covenant that God made with him promises an eternal kingdom, which finds fulfillment in the new covenant rule of Jesus the Messiah (2 Sam 7:11b-16; Mt 1:1). His final charge to Solomon is to walk in the ways of the Lord (1 Kg 2:1-4). "He shepherded them with integrity of heart; with skillful hands he led them" (Ps 78:72). More than just enjoying the longevity, wealth, and honor (1 Chron 29:28) accorded all monarchs, David is set apart as a leader who when he "had served God's purpose in his own generation, he fell asleep" (Acts 13:36).*

Chapter 11.
Solomon: Wisdom undermined by excess

Preliminary questions to consider:
1.   *What areas of self-management are especially critical for those in leadership positions?*
2.   *How is the compromise of one's integrity often a gradual and subtle process?*
3.   *What are the consequences of a task-driven leadership that overlooks the relational dimensions of the task?*

Favored but untested son (2 Sam 12:24-25)
After the death of the son born from their illicit union (2 Sam 12:19), David took Bathsheba as his wife and they bore a second son, Solomon, "man of peace" (12:24). The Lord indicated a special purpose for Solomon by instructing the prophet Gad to append a private name, Jedidah, "loved by the Lord" (12:25). He grew up in the royal palace in Jerusalem, witnessed the intrigues of his half-brothers Amnon and Absalom, and saw his father restored from exile. He never experienced the hardship that had forged his father into a godly leader.

Clemency for one's foe (1 Kg 1:1-2:12)
Adonijah, older half-brother of Solomon, attempted to usurp the throne with the support of Joab, the ruthless but until now loyal commander of David's army, and Abiathar the priest. On the other side supporting Solomon were Zadok the priest, Benaiah the cabinet officer, and Nathan the prophet (1:7-8). Through Bathsheba's intercession the king is made aware of the attempted coup of Adonijah and moves quickly to crown Solomon (1:15-27). The coronation takes place in Gihon near Adonijah's alternative ceremony in En Rogel. Benaiah prays for the expansion of Solomon's rule (1:36-37). Zadok anoints Solomon, which unlike a prophet's anointing, inaugurates a rule of dynastic succession (1:39). The infirm David worships on his bed and praises the Lord for the joy of seeing his son succeed him (1:47-48). Support for Adonijah crumbles and he seeks asylum by clinging to the horns of the altar of burnt offering (1:49-51). Here Solomon acts like a true son of David by granting clemency to his opponent, "if he shows himself to be a worthy man" (1:52-53; cf. 2 Sam 3:19-21, 31-39).

Grave responsibility (1 Kg 2:1-4)
David's final charge summons the new leader to courage and obedience. Both Solomon's success and his succession will depend on fidelity to the Mosaic covenant. He must set the pattern of faithfulness for future monarchs. A leader's faithfulness has the capacity to reverberate in expansive circles of blessing to future generations, and one's unfaithfulness possesses the same potential for ill.

Chapter 11. Solomon: Wisdom undermined by excess

Justice for those who threaten the kingdom (1 Kg 2:13-46)

Solomon deals firmly with those who make open attempts to gain power for themselves. Adonijah had been granted clemency conditioned on his quietly assuming civilian status (1:52-53). However, he again conspires against Solomon by requesting, through Bathsheba, Abishag for his wife. Abishag was the beautiful Shunammite girl who nursed David in his later years (1:3-4). Solomon immediately perceives the threat: "You might as well request the kingdom for him" (2:22). Though still a virgin, Abishag would be regarded as belonging to David's harem, and possession of the harem signified the right of succession to the throne (2 Sam 3:7; 12:8; 16:21-22). Solomon can no longer extend mercy and has Adonijah summarily executed (2:23-25).

Two other potential adversaries, Joab, who had supported Adonijah's conspiracy (1:7; 2:28), and Shimei also had to be dealt with. David had earlier committed the judgments of Joab and Shimei to Solomon (2:5-6, 8-9). Like Adonijah earlier (1:50-51), Joab sought refuge by taking hold of the horns of the altar of burnt offering (2:28-29). Yet the law granted the right of asylum only to one who had committed accidental homicide (Ex 21:14). Joab was guilty of the treacherous premeditated murders of Abner (2 Sam 3:27) and Amasa (2 Sam 20:10). Benaiah acts as Solomon's executioner on the spot. Such a just execution cleared the land of bloodguilt of the deaths of two innocent men (2:31-33). Finally, Shimei, who had cursed David (2 Sam 16:5-14) and was granted clemency (2 Sam 19:16-23), makes his final appearance in the biblical record, possibly as a representative of those in Israel still loyal to the house of Saul (2 Sam 16:5, 8, 11). Though confined to Jerusalem by Solomon under pain of death (2:36-38), Shimei three years later made a trip to Gath in search of runaway slaves (2:39-40). Once again Solomon orders the execution of the offender and for the third time Benaiah acts as the royal executioner (2:41-46). Abiathar the priest, however, is granted clemency due to his holy work in carrying the ark and for sharing in David's hardships (2:26-27; cf. 2 Sam 15:24). There is a decisive disposition of personal matters based on theocratic values, but none of the capricious brutality of the oriental ruler who without distinction eliminates all potential rivals. "The kingdom was now firmly established in Solomon's hands" (2:46b).

Unwise alliance and dangerous sanction (1 Kg 3:1-3)

Solomon's marriage to a daughter of Pharaoh (3:1) seals a political alliance with Egypt and reveals the extent to which Israel had gained international recognition. Pharaoh gave the town of Gezer, which the Egyptians had captured earlier, to his daughter as a dowry (1 Kg 9:16). This alliance may have been a shrewd commercial and political move by Solomon to protect Israel's southern border and open up trade routes along the Mediterranean. However, such treaties nurtured dependence on foreign powers rather than on the Lord for Israel's national security and economic prosperity. Marriages to pagan women led to the wholesale importation of idolatry into the royal palace and beyond (1 Kg 11:1-6).

Solomon also officially sanctioned worship at the "high places" (3:2-3), local altars on hills where pagan altars were often located. Such practice led to religious syncretism that contributed to the nation's downfall (2 Kg 17:9; 21:3; 23:5). The except-clauses in 3:2-3 indicate the divine disapproval.[1] Even at this early, and for the most part positive, stage of Solomon's reign he shows a proclivity for compromise and a shift away from the exacting standards of his father David.[2] A subtle and incremental erosion of covenant values has begun.

Pursuit of wisdom and discernment (1 Kg 3:4-15; 4:29-34)

At Gibeon, where the tabernacle and ancient bronze altar of burnt offering were located (1 Chron 21:29; 2 Chron 1:2-6), the Lord appeared to Solomon and made a striking offer: "Ask for whatever you want me to give you" (3:5). Solomon demonstrates humility as he ponders his greatest need—not wealth, fame, or revenge on his enemies (3:11), but a discerning heart to govern the nation and to distinguish right and wrong (3:7-9). Solomon recognizes his personal inadequacy as he enters the kingship around the age of 25. He calls himself "only a little child" (3:7) and "your servant" four times (3:6, 7, 8, 9). He feels the weight of the exalted task to which he has been appointed (3:8). His request shows his deep sense of accountability as a steward of the covenant.

The Lord was pleased with Solomon's priorities and granted him a "wise and discerning heart" (3:12).[3] God further granted to Solomon "what you have not asked for" (3:13), namely, riches and honor. But wisdom is not a spiritual reservoir that guarantees spiritual success; obedience alone would secure personal and national blessing (3:14). Wisdom sought and received is not the same as wisdom developed and applied. Due to wrong moral decisions in his later life Solomon failed to realize the promise of a long life (3:14b). Inaugurated in his early twenties, he would die forty years later (11:42-43). His kingship began appropriately with worship around the sacrificial altar of burnt offering (3:4, 15).

God made Solomon the wisest man in the world (3:12; 4:29-34). Only Jesus would possess a wisdom greater than that of Solomon (Lk 11:31; cf. Lk 12:27; Mt 12:42). Solomon's knowledge of botany and zoology brought him worldwide

---

[1] The adversative particle רַק (only, but, however, nevertheless) is followed by participial phrases in vv. 2, 3 to express a practice (sacrificing and/or burning incense at the high places) which contradicts or varies from that which precedes it (the divinely prescribed centralized worship at the Jerusalem temple and Solomon's initial obedience to the statutes of the covenant respectively). See *HALOT*, 3: 1286-1287; *BDB*, 956.

[2] The "high places" (בָּמוֹת) were originally Canaanite altars of worship normally located on places of natural elevation. Before the establishment of centralized worship in the Jerusalem temple the high places could be legitimate places of worship for Israelites as long as the Lord was exclusively honored (1 Sam 9:12; 1 Kg 3:4; 2 Chron 1:3). However, the religious practices of the Canaanites associated with the high places proved a seductive attraction to Israel and produced religious syncretism (2 Kg 17:9-13; 21:3-6). Josiah removed the provincial high places and their pagan priests (2 Kg 23:5-6), but it was too little, too late. The idolatry, which had seeped into the life of the nation during the long corrupt reign of Manasseh, would bring about the nation's ruin. See *TDOT*, II: 139-145; *NIDOTTE*, 1: 670.

[3] These are the same qualities attributed to and required of Joseph as Vizier of Egypt (Gen 41:33, 39). These two terms, חָכָם and נָבוֹן, appear together a number of times in the Old Testament (Deut 4:6; Prov 10:13; 14:33; 16:21; Hos 14:10). These are given to Solomon so that he might "administer justice" in Israel (1 Kg 3:11). The case of the two claimants to a dead child (1 Kg 3:16-28) evidences God's gift to Solomon of these two qualities: penetrating insight to see behind the two complaints (נָבוֹן); and practical wisdom to give a ruling that uncovers the truth (חָכָם).

fame (4:33-34). Solomon spoke 3,000 proverbs and many songs (4:32), a statement consistent with the traditional arguments supporting Solomon's authorship of Proverbs, Ecclesiastes, Song of Solomon, and Psalms 72, 127.

Wisdom applied (1 Kg 3:16-28)

A typical judicial case handled by Solomon demonstrates his deep discernment, which brought him widespread fame (3:28). Two prostitutes, each claiming a living child was theirs and a dead infant was the other's, brought their case to Solomon. The king determined who was the true mother by a severe test, ordering the child to be cut into two parts and each half given to the claimants. The true mother begged for the child's life while the impostor assented to the king's order. The nation grew in peace and prosperity under a ruler with wisdom to administer justice.

Administrative acumen and insensitivity (1 Kg 4:1-19)

Solomon continued and expanded the administrative posts established by David (2 Sam 8:16-18; 20:23-26). The cabinet of nine chief officials is listed in 4:1-6. Benaiah replaced Joab as commander of the army. Abiathar had been banished from the priesthood (2:26-27) and Azariah, the grandson of Zadok, was now high priest (4:2). Several new posts were added, namely, head of the district officers, personal adviser to the king, and keeper of the palace. Like every effective leader he surrounded himself with trustworthy and capable people and he delegated responsibility to them.

However, Solomon organized the land into twelve districts under a district governor with artificial boundaries unrelated to the twelve historical tribal allotments (4:7-19).[4] Various factors may have prevented Solomon from rigidly following the historical divisions: the need to incorporate newly occupied areas where the Canaanites had tenaciously held on;[5] the adjustments required from the conquest of foreign nations on the perimeter of the land; and the uneven agricultural productivity of the tribes so that new arrangements to support the royal estate had to be made. Each district was responsible for supplying the needs of the royal household for one month per year (4:7). Nevertheless, the new order eventually contributed to tribal friction and the breakup of the monarchy. Solomon's daughters were given to two of the governors and secured their loyalty (4:11, 15). Political and economic considerations, then, seem to be the driving forces behind the new organization of the land. C.-L. Seow observes that a number of the appointees are Judeans with old connections to the Davidic dynasty and that the emphasis in the list on the family ties rather than personal names of the officers suggests that Solomon appointed cronies who would loyally serve the interests of the royal

---

[4] Only five of the twelve tribal names appear in this listing: Ephraim (1 Kg 4:8), Naphtali (4:15), Asher (4:16), Issachar (4:17), and Benjamin (4:18). The first district, for example, is called "the hill country of Ephraim" (4:8), which included portions of the territory of Manasseh (Josh 17:14-18). The second district (4:9) includes both Shaalbim, originally assigned to the tribe of Dan (Josh 19:42; Jdg 1:35), and Beth Shemesh in the tribal territory of Naphtali (Josh 19:38; Jdg 1:33).
[5] In the fifth tax district (4:12) the three cities of Taanach, Megiddo, and Beth Shan had long been Canaanite strongholds beyond the tribal control of Manasseh (Josh 17:11-13).

estate.[6] "The irony in the passage should not be overlooked: Solomon is king over 'all Israel' (v. 1); yet, his officials in the cabinet and his appointees over the districts are not representative of all Israel. Solomon may have the gift of administrative wisdom, a genius for organization, but his record shows that he has a penchant for taking care of himself and his favorites first."[7]

Test of prosperity (1 Kg 4:20-28)

Financial prosperity and international recognition were the marks of Solomon's reign. The population increased (4:20), the borders expanded (4:21), and the nation experienced peace and prosperity (4:24-25). This was the golden age of Israel. The provisions gathered from the various districts and consumed by the royal court were massive. Samuel had warned about a royal household whose voracious appetite for goods and services would strain the resources of the nation (1 Sam 8:12b-18). Quotas were established for the district governors (4:27-28). What was a gracious gift of God, material wealth (3:13), was a test of character for the king. Solomon also amassed a large chariot force (4:26), similarly predicted by Samuel (1 Sam 8:11-12).

Harsh supervisor (1 Kg 5:1-18)

Because the borders of Israel were now secure, the land enjoying "rest on every side" (5:4), Solomon could concentrate his energies on strengthening the domestic economy and engaging in commercial enterprises. The project of first priority was the Lord's temple, originally the desire of David but committed to his son (5:5; 2 Sam 7:12-13). David, because of the bloodshed of his military campaigns, was forbidden to construct the temple (1 Chron 22:6-10; 28:2-3). Stone for the foundation and timber for its encasement were the two main materials needed. A formal agreement was signed between Solomon and Hiram, king of Tyre, who earlier had supplied cedar and stone for David's palace (2 Sam 5:11). The trade agreement between Israel and Tyre was mutually beneficial, the former supplying agricultural products in exchange for valuable building materials (5:8-12). However, Solomon temporarily conscripted Israelite laborers throughout the land (5:13-17), in addition to the forced labor of foreign workers under Adoniram's supervision that began late in David's reign (2 Sam 20:24; 1 Kg 9:15-23). Such conscription, which involved harsh labor and extended periods of separation from family, eventually led to discontent, tribal jealousies, and open rebellion (11:28; 12:1-19).

Builder of the temple (1 Kg 6:1-7:51)

Solomon was determined to construct the temple "for the name of the Lord my God" (5:5), as David had been instructed (2 Sam 7:13). The beginning of construction of the temple is dated in the month of Ziv (April-May) in the fourth year of Solomon's reign (6:1, 37). The temple was completed seven years and six

---

[6] Choon-Leong Seow, *The First and Second Books of Kings*, The New Interpreter's Bible (Nashville: Abingdon, 1999): III: 52.
[7] Ibid.

months later in the month of Bul (October-November), the eleventh year of his reign (6:38). The period of construction was April, 966 to October, 959 B.C. This is 480 years after Israel's exodus from Egypt (6:1).

The general layout of the temple was based on the tabernacle. Its overall size was 90 ft. x 30 ft. x 45 ft. (6:2), exactly twice the size of the tabernacle (Ex 26:15-30; 36:20-24). In front of the temple was the portico, measuring 30 ft. x 15 ft., with two large pillars, named Jakin and Boaz (6:3; 7:21). A structure with side rooms or chambers surrounded the temple proper (6:5-6, 8-10). The finishing work and the decoration were spectacular. The floor and walls were made of dressed stone covered with cedar and overlaid with gold (6:7, 15, 16, 17, 21, 22). Cherubim, palm trees, and flowers were carved on the doors and walls (6:29-35). The temple proper consisted of the outer chamber or Holy Place (6:17), and the inner sanctuary or Holy of Holies, measuring a cubicle of 30 feet (6:16, 20).

Emphasis is on the Holy of Holies which housed the "ark of the covenant of the Lord" (6:19). The ark of the temple was placed between two cherubim made of olive wood, overlaid with gold (6:23-28). The altar of incense is associated with this inner sanctuary (6:20, 22; cf. Heb 9:3-4), although it actually stood in the Holy Place before the curtain into the Holy of Holies. Instead of the single seven-armed golden candlestick of the tabernacle, there were now ten lampstands, five placed on each side of the Holy Place (7:49). There were also now ten golden tables of showbread, five on each side of the room (7:48; 1 Chron 28:16; 2 Chron 4:8, 19). The various temple furnishings are listed in 7:13-51. The golden articles, under Solomon's direct supervision, are listed in 7:48-50. An inner courtyard of stone and cedar (6:36) was the means of entrance to the temple, in which was placed the Sea of cast metal (7:23-26) and the bronze altar of burnt offering (8:64; 2 Chron 4:1). The "treasuries of the Lord's temple" were also stocked with valuable items dedicated by David, either tribute from vassal kings or booty taken in military campaigns (7:51).

That such an ornate, exquisite structure, so richly furnished, was completed within seven and one half years can be attributed to the preparations made by David (1 Chron 22:1-5) and the huge number of personnel that Solomon mobilized. Besides the vast number of conscripted laborers, wood cutters, stone masons, and carriers, there were the skilled craftsmen of Tyre to handle the detailed carving work (5:6, 18; 7:13-14).

Inserted in the middle of the temple description is the Lord's word to Solomon (6:11-13). The temple will be a place where the divine glory rests upon Israel only as long as there is faithfulness to the covenant (cf. 2:3-4; 3:14; 9:8). The prophets uniformly warned the nation that the temple and its sacrifices are no guarantee of security or a substitute for heart obedience (1 Sam 15:22; Hos 6:6; Jer 7:1-7).

Opulent enterprises (1 Kg 7:1-12)

Solomon took thirteen years, that is, nearly twice as long constructing his own personal palace than he did building the temple of the Lord (6:37-38; 7:1; 959-946 B.C.). The royal palace (150 ft. long, 75 ft. wide, 45 ft. high) was about twice the size of the temple (90 ft. x 30 ft. x 45 ft.) (6:2; 7:2). This contrasts with

David's uneasy conscience over living in a palace that dwarfed the tent in which the ark resided (2 Sam 7:1-2). Solomon is moving away from his father's theocratic values (cf. Hag 1:2-11). Several separate structures are mentioned here: Palace of the Forest of Lebanon (7:2); Hall of Justice (7:7); Solomon's dwelling place (7:8); palace for Pharaoh's daughter (7:8). Commentators are divided over whether these were separate structures in different locations, or simply various sections of the royal palace whose greater structure housed them all (7:1; 9:10). If the latter, then Solomon could administer the private, executive, and judicial functions of the kingship effectively from a central location.

Worship of a majestic Lord (1 Kg 8:1-9:9)

Following the completion of the temple in the 11th year and 8th month (6:38; 959 B.C.), Solomon waited eleven months until Ethanim, the 7th month (September-October), to formally dedicate the temple (8:1-2; 958 B.C.). Solomon summoned the elders, tribal heads, and clan chiefs to the celebration which was to precede the Feast of Tabernacles, celebrated the 14th-21st days of the 7th month (Lev 23:34). The Tent of Meeting, still preserved at Gibeon after the destruction of Shiloh (1 Kg 3:4; 1 Chron 21:29), and the ark of the covenant, which David had brought up to Jerusalem from the house of Obed-Edom (2 Sam 6), were brought to the temple with the sacred furnishings (8:3-4). Placing the ark in the Holy of Holies between the specially constructed cherubim, "the glory of the Lord filled his temple" (8:11) as it had filled the tabernacle in the wilderness (Ex 40:34-35). Standing before the whole assembly of Israel (8:14, 22, 55, 62), Solomon praised God and blessed the assembled nation. He emphasized that the temple's completion is a prophetic fulfillment of God's promises to David regarding his son (8:15-21; cf. 2 Sam 7:12-13): God "has fulfilled what he promised with his own mouth to my father David" (8:15).

In an eloquent expression of faith-commitment to the Lord and intercessory love for his people, Solomon kneels before the altar of burnt offering, spreading his hands to heaven (8:22, 54), and offers a prayer of dedication of the temple and nation to God. Though Solomon later wandered from the Lord (11:4-6), at the outset his theological understanding is strong and his grasp of the significance of the temple and its sacrificial system is impeccable. The temple is the localized focus of God's presence in Israel, an expression of her character as a covenant people, under obligation to walk in obedience or forfeit her covenant privileges. Solomon clearly voices a concern for the continuing faithfulness of Israel, realizing the temple itself is no guarantee of national blessing apart from such loyalty. His faith is personal and biblical, not liturgical or magical. The refrain is "When . . . hear from heaven and forgive." Solomon knows the weakness of his people and asks for divine mercy to meet repentance.

His view of God is lofty: the Lord alone is exalted, sovereign, faithful, and omnipresent, never contained in a physical dwelling (8:22-27). His view of man is realistic: prone to wrongdoing (8:31-32), subject to judgment and the curses on disobedience (8:33-40), inclined to war (8:44-45), sin and captivity (8:46-51). Solomon's concern is not nationalistic, but universal: "That all the peoples of the earth may know your name and fear you" (8:41-43, 60). Unfortunately his prayer is in the third person. He fails to pray for himself as he does for the nation. Rising from the altar, he closes with a final benediction and word of exhortation to the people: the Lord has kept his promises to us; now our hearts must be fully committed to him (8:54-61).

Because of the vast number of sacrifices offered (8:5), the courtyard was consecrated as an extended altar in addition to the altar of burnt offering (8:64). People from all over Israel gathered for fourteen days: seven days for the dedication festival and a further seven days for the Feast of Tabernacles (8:65). The next day (22nd day of 7th month) a final assembly was held, and on the 23rd day of the month everyone returned to their homes (2 Chron 7:8-10). Joy, unity, and the presence of God inhabited the community. Yet in a few years (958-930 B.C.: 28 yrs) the nation would be torn apart by a political revolt and corrupted by an alternative religious system (12:25-33).

The Lord appeared to Solomon a second time, as he had at Gibeon twenty years earlier (9:2, 10; cf. 3:4-5). This time the Lord reinforces the conditions to be met to secure his blessing: "If you walk . . . I will . . . but if you . . . I will." The imposing temple consecrated for "my name" (9:3, 7) will be destroyed and become an object of mockery if the nation abandons her covenant Lord (9:8-9).

Accumulation of wealth and debt (1 Kg 9:10-10:29)

Solomon's main two building projects, the temple and the royal palace, took 20 years (6:37, 38; 7:1: 966-946 B.C.). At the end of this period Solomon sought to repay Hiram of Tyre for the wood, gold, and labor he received by giving him twenty towns in Galilee. Hiram was unimpressed by the cities, and this method of payment proved unacceptable (9:10-14). The Chronicler records the sequel to this story: Hiram returned the cities to Solomon who rebuilt them (2 Chron 8:1-2). Perhaps these cities were intended to serve as a sort of collateral until Solomon could repay his debt. Either way, the record of Solomon's vast wealth and wisdom (9:15-10:29) is only part of the story. He ran into financial difficulty with the repayment of debts to Hiram and, combined with his conscripting slave laborers from Israel (5:13-18), produced a legacy of resentment that eventually brought national disruption. Much of the labor force behind the vast architectural projects, including the key fortifications of Hazor, Megiddo, and Gezer, came from foreign slaves, that is, subjugated peoples made into a permanent slave labor force (9:15-24).

The wealth of Solomon's kingdom was multiplied by its fleet of trading ships which were based at Ezion Geber, near Elath at the northern tip of the Gulf of Aqaba (9:26-28; 10:11-12, 22). These ships sailed to distant places such as Ophir (Somalia?), bringing back huge quantities of gold, silver, almugwood, ivory, and precious stones. Probably Solomon's fleet brought home slag and other metallic materials to be smelted and used in the construction projects. Solomon's fame spread worldwide as seen in the visit of the Queen of Sheba (s.w. Arabia) to Jerusalem (10:1-13). She was deeply impressed by his wealth and wisdom (10:7) and by his monotheistic faith (10:8-9). She brought vast quantities of gold, stones, and spices, and returned to her own country with "all she desired and asked for" (10:13). Finally, Solomon's wealth included a vast chariot force with 4000 stalls,

1400 chariots, and 12,000 horses (10:26-29; 4:26; 2 Chron 9:25). Though a sign of wealth, it was a violation of the law to accumulate such chariotry (Deut 17:16). Samuel had earlier warned the people about such ventures by their future monarch (1 Sam 8:11). This, along with his accumulation of foreign wives, brought about Solomon's spiritual demise.

Unequally yoked (1 Kg 11:1-13)

Although polygamy, like divorce (Deut 24:1-4), was accommodated in the Old Testament in the permissive will of God, it was never God's intended purpose for his people. Both the multiplicity of wives (Deut 17:17) and marriage to heathen women (Ex 34:16; Deut 7:3-4) were specifically forbidden. Scripture records graphically the tragic results of polygamy in the lives of Abraham (Gen 16:1-6), Jacob (Gen 30:16), David (2 Sam 13-19), and now Solomon. Many of Solomon's marriages were for the purpose of sealing political treaties with foreign kings, who gave their daughters in marriage to the other king (3:1). These wives brought with them pagan gods, shrines, and cultural practices steeped in idolatry. Solomon was unable to resist the pull of syncretism. The importation of idols became national policy (11:5-8; cf. Neh 13:26). His "heart" (five times in 11:2, 4, 9) turned away after foreign gods. God's judgment on Solomon is announced and later repeated by Ahijah the prophet (11:9-13, 29-39). As with Saul (1 Sam 15:27-28), the kingdom will be torn from Solomon's hands and given to a subordinate (11:11), in this case Jeroboam, an Ephraimite official (11:26). Nevertheless, for David's sake this will not take place in his lifetime and one tribe, Judah, will be preserved for his descendants (11:12-13). God would honor his eternal covenant with David (2 Sam 7), keeping his lamp always burning in Jerusalem (11:36; cf. 15:4; 2 Kg 8:19; 2 Chron 21:7; Ps 132:17).

Bitter fruit of apostasy (11:14-40)

God punished Solomon for his idolatry by raising up two foreign adversaries, Hadad the Edomite from the south (11:14-22) and Rezon of Damascus from the north (11:23-25). The security of Israel's borders, earlier established by David (2 Sam 8:3-4, 13-14), were being threatened even as internal division was developing. The disruption of the nation came through Jeroboam, an official in charge of the Ephraimite work crews that labored in Jerusalem (11:26-28). Jeroboam took advantage of the smoldering discontent he saw among the Ephraimites regarding Solomon's policy of conscripting labor from fellow Israelites (5:13-17; 12:4). His initial attempt to seize power failed and he had to escape to Egypt to save his life (11:40). His later return from Egyptian exile brought about not only political disruption, but the creation of an alternative sacrificial system at Bethel and Dan (12:26-33). Jeroboam thus became the archetypal evil king who "made Israel to sin" (21 times in Old Testament; cf. 12:30).

Untimely death (11:41-43)

Like David, Solomon reigned forty years (970-930 B.C.). He died in his early sixties and failed to realize the promise of a long life (3:14) due to his disobedience of the covenant. Solomon's great wealth and wisdom failed to translate into the one essential requirement of successful kingship: faithfulness to the covenant (2 Sam 7:12-15; 1 Kg 2:1-4; 3:3, 14; 6:12-13; 8:22-61; 9:1-9).

Leadership profile of Solomon

1. **Allurements of material wealth and sexual gratification**: *Money and sex are good gifts of God (1 Kg 3:13) to be enjoyed in the context of a sacrificial lifestyle and the covenant of marriage respectively. If the traditional view is correct in attributing Ecclesiastes and Song of Songs to Solomon, then the wise king understood at one point the inability of riches and pleasure to provide true happiness, and for a time experienced the beauty of monogamous love (Eccles 2:1-11; SS 2:16-3:5). The greatest test of the leader is his or her self-management. Solomon failed to realize that the flesh or fallen nature, if fed and nurtured, is never satisfied, but only grows hungrier. Material wealth and sexual pleasure occupied too much of Solomon's thoughts and energies and eventually displaced his affections for his God.*

2. **Wisdom undermined by compromise**: *Solomon was the son of favor, given incomparable wisdom, and yet gradually pulled from his spiritual moorings in an indulgent age. He began his reign well with a humble request for wisdom, one that was granted beyond measure. Solomon was a man with a vital experience of God's grace, seen in the appearings at Gibeon (3:4-5) and later in Jerusalem (9:1-2). His prayer at the temple dedication is a fervent expression of faith, repentance, and praise (8:22-61). However, the shift of a leader from a posture of servanthood to one of entitlement can be a subtle one. The incremental compromise of convictions began with small steps: one marriage alliance and the tolerance of high places. It continued as Solomon began to enjoy the perquisites and trappings of leadership. His failure to control his impulses to spend and consume is seen in the daily provisions required for the royal estate (4:20-28), the opulent character of the building enterprises (7:1-12), and the unprecedented wealth that was amassed (10:14-29) during his reign. Finally, his sense of covenantal stewardship all but disappeared at the end of his life as his affections fixed on foreign wives and his heart turned away from the Lord God. Solomon had been warned repeatedly that faithfulness to the covenant was the singular condition of God's continued blessing (2:1-4; 6:11-13; 9:1-9). The triad of wealth, wisdom, and honor was erased by the triad of pagan wives, idolatry, and foreign adversaries.*

3. **Projects and people**: *The leader who values projects over people, accomplishment at the expense of relationships, may achieve success, but at a prohibitive cost. Solomon organized his tax districts without regard to historical tribal boundaries. He conscripted Israelite laborers, in addition to the foreign slaves, and subjected them to harsh working conditions and extended periods away from their families. Solomon supported a large royal estate through heavy taxation, completed massive building projects through heavy debt to foreign nations and domestic labor, and built a powerful army by creating a military bureaucracy. His impressive accomplishments were a pyrrhic victory: within one year of his death the bitter resentment fueled by such policies tore apart the unified, prosperous nation of the Solomonic golden era.*

Chapter 12.
Daniel: Spiritual vitality in a secular setting

Preliminary questions to consider:
1. *How does the servant of God maintain a stable composure in an uncertain world full of political intrigue and social upheaval?*
2. *How can a leader who serves in a secular, even hostile, context engage and impact the culture, rather than being conformed to its values and norms?*
3. *Why is prayer so highly valued by the great leaders of Scripture? What does this tell us about their attitude toward the calling to serve the people of God?*

Beginning in exile (Dan 1:1-2)

Nothing is known of Daniel's background except that he was from a noble family in Judah (1:3). In 605 B.C. while Jehoiakim was king of Judah (609-598 B.C.) Nebuchadnezzar, recently crowned king of Babylon, invaded Judah and took Daniel and many others hostage to Babylon (2 Kg 24:1-2). Babylon was the ascendant power in the region since the fall of Ninevah, capital of Assyria, in 612 B.C. and the defeat of Egypt at the battle of Carchemish in 605 B.C. Daniel would spend the rest of his life in a foreign land, faithful to his Jewish identity, exalted to serve in high positions under three rulers of Babylon and one ruler of Medo-Persia:

Nebuchadnezzar	605-562 B.C. (Dan 1:1)
Nabonidus	556-539 B.C. (implied in Dan 5:7)
Belshazzar	553-539 B.C. (14 years co-regent) (Dan 5:1; 7:1; 8:1)
Cyrus the Great	539-530 B.C. (Dan 6:28; 10:1; cf. 5:31; 9:1: Darius)

Daniel was about sixteen years old when taken captive. He served until around 536 B.C. or a total of 69 years in Babylon and Persia (1:21; 10:1). He died, then, at approximately the age of eighty-five.

Testing of faith in the academy of Babylon (Dan 1:3-7)

To serve in the king's palace special young men from Israel were chosen. Their qualifications were physical, social, and intellectual (1:4a). Nebuchadnezzar designed a threefold method to reeducate the young moldable lads into obedient citizens of Babylon and her gods (1:4b-5). First, he would change their ways of thinking through educational indoctrination. The three-year training program involved instruction in language and literature, which included mastering the spoken lingua franca of Aramaic and the ancient literature of Babylon. Second, he would revise their way of living through dietary provisions. Third, he would transform their way of worship through a new identification with the gods of Babylon by changing their names, the oriental way of expressing one's desired character. The Jewish names were changed to Babylonian ones, an attempt by the king to change their identity from its basis of faith in Yahweh to a new allegiance to the Babylonian pantheon.

Daniel, "God is my judge" ------------ Belteshazzar, "Bel protect his life" (or Marduk, chief of pantheon)

Hananiah, "The Lord shows grace" -- Shadrach, "command of Aku" (moon god)

Mishael, "Who is what God is?" ----- Meschach, "Who is what Aku is?"

Azariah, "The Lord helps" ------------ Abednego, "servant of Nego" (god of wisdom)

Inner resolve, tact, and personal integrity (Dan 1:8-20)

Although young and pliable, Daniel's faith-grounded convictions proved steadfast. He "resolved" (lit. "set it upon his heart") not to partake of the meat or wine from the king's table because they were initially offered upon pagan altars (1:8). Although cooperative, positive, sensitive, and contributory throughout his years of service under four administrations, Daniel refused to engage even indirectly in the worship of idols. Eating food offered to idols contravened the teaching concerning clean and unclean foods in Leviticus 11 and Deuteronomy 14. Unclean animals were chosen and then slaughtered and prepared in a way contrary to the regulations of the law. Daniel and his friends demonstrated wisdom by requesting permission to abstain, first from the chief official and then from the guard (1:9-11), rather than simply insisting on their own diet and openly refusing the king's provisions. They also showed good judgment by offering an acceptable alternative, a diet of vegetables, rather than direct refusal. The test was permitted and vindicated the young men who demonstrated physical stamina beyond their peers. The four men distinguished themselves in wisdom, understanding, and insight (1:4, 17, 20). Daniel was at the top of the class because God granted to him supernatural insight, in addition to academic skill (1:17).

In summary, Daniel and his three friends were exiled (1:1-2), chosen according to the king's standards (1:3-7), tested according to God's standards (1:8-14), approved as superior in all respects (1:15-20), and appointed to serve the king as trusted advisors (1:19, 21).

Intercessor and herald of the triumph of God's kingdom (Dan 2:1-49; cf. 7:1-8:27)

In 604 B.C., the second year of Daniel's captivity, Nebuchadnezzar was troubled by a dream. In a strange yet characteristic fit of anger, he demands that the purported wise men of Babylon interpret his dream without hearing its contents. Though the astrologers protest the unreasonable demand, Nebuchadnezzar decrees their destruction unless they can declare both the dream and its meaning. Some suggest the king had forgotten the details of the dream. We are left with a royal decree to destroy all the 'clergy' of Babylon, including Daniel, and the utter human inadequacy to reverse the situation: "There is not a man on earth who can do what the king asks" (2:10).

Daniel becomes the means of saving the entire company of wise men, as he and his three comrades stand in the gap to intercede for God's intervention. His "wisdom and tact" in speaking to the commander of the guard and courage to approach the king himself buys them time to pray (2:14-16). Daniel's confession throughout is that the "God of heaven" alone is able to reveal such "mysteries," that is, the secret purposes of God that he discloses to his prophets.[1] The revelation of the mystery to Daniel in a night vision invokes an expression of praise, a sevenfold confession of God's wisdom and power (2:20-22). Daniel decries any attempt to make him into a god and confesses that the God of heaven alone has revealed the mystery (2:27-28; cf. 2:46-47). God's future purposes for Nebuchadnezzar, "things to come," not Daniel's wisdom, are behind the revelation of the mystery (2:29-30). The colossal statue that Nebuchadnezzar saw had four main parts made up of five materials:

1. Head—pure gold
2. Chest and arms—silver
3. Belly and thighs—bronze
4. Legs—iron; feet (ten toes)—iron and baked clay
5. A rock "cut out, but not by human hands" (2:34) strikes and smashes the feet, then successively the other parts of the statue until it is completely destroyed, leaving not a trace. The rock then grows into a huge mountain and fills the earth (2:35b).

Daniel not only discloses, but also interprets the dream (2:36-45), which concerns future developments in the historical process of successive Gentile kingdoms arising and being displaced (2:28, 29, 45). One plausible approach to the textual evidence is as follows:

1. Head of gold: Babylonian kingdom of Nebuchadnezzar (2:36-38)
2. Chest and arms of silver: somewhat inferior, less autocratic coalition of the Medes and Persians (2:39a)
3. Thighs and belly of bronze: universal kingdom of Alexander the Great (2:39b)
4. Legs of iron: Roman empire, powerful initially, but as the feet and toes are a mixture of iron and clay it becomes a divided, weakened kingdom (2:40-43). Iron and baked clay do not mix. The iron-clay mixture portends political divisions, vulnerable territories, and racial tensions that lead to gradual disintegration of the empire.
5. Stone which becomes a mountain: the eternal kingdom of God, eliminating forever the temporary, imperfect kingdoms of men (2:44-45). The emphasis is on the divine initiative in establishing the kingdom. It is a rock "cut out, but not by human hands" (2:34, 45). The "God of heaven" (2:44) establishes

---

[1] The Aramaic term רָז (or רָזָא / רָזָה [pl. רָזִין]) is the thematic term of this section of Daniel (2:18, 19, 27, 28, 29, 30, 47; cf. 4:9). It is a Persian loan word (*TWOT*, 2: 1071) that is translated in the LXX by μυστηριον. This is the background of the New Testament "mystery" (μυστηριον), which is a truth about the kingdom of God secreted away in the divine counsels until the time of full disclosure (cf. Mt 13:11; 1 Cor 4:1; Eph 3:3, 4, 9; Col 1:26-27).

this rule, unlike the other kingdoms which arise historically out of the previous kingdom's wreckage.

Nebuchadnezzar responds emotionally and reveals the characteristic worldview of an oriental animist. Daniel becomes an object of worship, as the king falls prostrate before him offering a sacrifice and incense, though Daniel is also distinguished from his God and Lord (2:46-47). Daniel, then, is venerated as God's visual representation on earth. Like Joseph, Daniel is exalted to a high position in the secular government, that is, vice regent over the province of Babylon and cabinet officer in charge of religious affairs (2:48). His three friends become provincial administrators under Daniel (2:49).

Undaunted faith of the provincial leaders (Dan 3:1-30)
Nebuchadnezzar constructs a huge gold-plated image and then summons all government officials (3:2-3) to its dedication. To fall down and worship before the image is an expression of loyalty to the king and the newly established empire. To refuse to comply means treason and is punishable by death. Three terms disclose the character of the king's decree: fall down (3:6, 7, 10, 15); worship (3:6, 7, 10, 12, 14, 15, 18); and serve (3:12, 14, 17, 18). Clearly the decree involves more than an expression of patriotic allegiance, but violation of the first two commandments (Ex 20:3-5).

The astrologers, probably jealous of their political office (3:12), openly accuse the Hebrew provincial leaders of treason. Shadrach, Meshach, and Abednego, fully aware of the angry king's absolute power and full intentions to carry out his threats to cast them into the furnace, utter one of the majestic faith-resolutions of Scripture: "The God we serve is able to save us . . . but even if he does not . . . we will not serve your gods or worship the image of gold you have set up" (3:17-18). They are committed to unqualified obedience to the Lord regardless of the consequences. Their faith in God's ability to deliver is coupled with resolve to leave the particular disposition of the present situation to his providence.

While many godly leaders in history have perished for refusal to compromise (Heb 11:35b-40), God here provided a miraculous deliverance. The furious king heated the furnace "seven times hotter than usual" (3:19) so that even the soldiers who bound the three perished. Able to see into the furnace, Nebuchadnezzar is shocked to see four figures, including one "like a son of the gods" (3:25). The further identification of this figure as an angel serves to link him with other Old Testament theophanies (3:28).[2] The deliverance is so complete that their appearance, smell, and clothing are unaffected (3:27). Nebuchadnezzar responds as before, proclaiming the greatness of the Hebrew's God, though he still does not confess the Lord as the universal and only God (3:28-29; cf. 2:46-49). He promotes the three to higher administrative positions (3:30). A pagan king praises

---

[2] One could compare here such texts as Gen 16:7-14; 19:1, 16, 24; 31:11, 13; Ex 3:1-6; Jdg 2:1-4; 6:11-12, 20-22; 13:3-5, 18, 22 where the angel is so identified with the Lord that we have either a veiled appearance of the Lord himself (possibly a preincarnate appearance of the Son of God) or, at the least, God's self-revelation through an authorized representative.

the faith of the three Hebrews: they trusted in the Lord, defied the king's command, and were willing to die rather than acquiesce (3:28). He then issues a fresh decree that anyone who slanders the God of the Hebrews will be dealt with in extreme measure (3:29). The first decree threatened to nationalize idolatry; the second decree guarantees freedom of worship. Providence has turned the astrologers' jealousy to the benefit of their enemies.

Declaring God's severity to the powerful (Dan 4:1-37)

The king relates in the first person a terrifying dream whose meaning escaped him. Unlike his earlier vision of the great statue, this time Nebuchadnezzar openly reveals its contents before demanding its interpretation (4:9). Again, Daniel, or Belteshazzar, is set apart from the other "wise men" as alone able to unlock its interpretation. Daniel is identified as one in whom "the spirit of the holy gods" resides (4:8, 9, 18).[3] Nebuchadnezzar's dream contemplates an enormous tree reaching to the heavens, beautiful, with abundant fruit, shelter for birds, and spreading branches. The "messenger" or "holy one" (4:13, 17) descends to announce the tree must be cut down, its leaves stripped, and its fruit scattered. However, the stump and roots are to be preserved, signifying its continuing life and later resurgence. The purpose of the vision is given in both its announcement and interpretation (4:17, 25). The king and the inhabitants of Babylon will recognize that the "Most High" (4:2, 17, 24, 25, 32, 34), "Heaven" (4:26), "the King of heaven" (4:37) is the sovereign ruler of human events, nations, and history.

Daniel, out of genuine respect for Nebuchadnezzar and out of full awareness of the dream's terrifying implications, carefully prefaces his interpretation to prepare the temperamental king (4:19). The tree is the king or, by extension, his kingdom which is going to be cut down. The luxuriant tree represents the vast extent of his present dominion. The temporary downfall of the king/kingdom, only to be revived and restored, is seen in the stump and roots which remain. The moral purpose of the dream is to humble the arrogant king to the point where he acknowledges God's sole lordship over the world (4:25-26). Daniel presses the application with penetrating clarity (4:27).

The interpretation is fulfilled just as Daniel announced. Nebuchadnezzar's spiritual pilgrimage takes him from self-worship (4:30) to a humiliating form of insanity where he acts like an animal in the fields, and finally to a gradual restoration of mental balance and sane reflection on his own pride and God's power and righteousness (4:34-37). Do the confessions of 4:1-3 and 4:34-37 which bracket the chapter constitute a genuine acknowledgment of and repentance before the true God? The great king issues a national confession that follows the humiliation. The confession provides the theme of Chapter 4, indeed the entire book of Daniel: the Most High God rules an eternal kingdom and possesses sovereign dominion over the temporary and limited kingdoms of mankind (4:3, 17, 25, 26, 32, 34-35).

---

[3] The expression "spirit of the holy gods" is the polytheistic king's way of describing Daniel's unparalleled, supernatural ability to unlock the interpretation of these mysterious dreams (cf. 5:11, 14). Pharaoh used an analogous phrase to account for Joseph's unequaled discernment and wisdom (Gen 41:38).

Apologist for God's honor (Dan 5:1-31)

A new administration is now in power. Nabonidus is king (556-539 B.C.), with his son Belshazzar as co-regent (553-539 B.C.). The scene is an evening of drunken revelry as Belshazzar calls his nobles and harem to a great banquet. The tone of the banquet is particularly blasphemous as Belshazzar brings out the sacred vessels plundered from the Jerusalem temple by Nebuchadnezzar in 586 B.C. (2 Kg 24:13; 25:14-15). He uses them for drinking vessels, while praising the material idols of Babylon.

A bizarre event disrupts the banquet and transforms the king from an arrogant blasphemer to a shuddering coward. The fingers of a human hand appear and write several words on the wall of the royal palace (5:5-6). Silence blankets the banquet hall. As before, the ineptness of the so-called "diviners" of Babylon is contrasted with the unique ability of Daniel to interpret the revelation (cf. 2:10-11; 4:6-7). Apparently Daniel has been a silent figure since the days of Nebuchadnezzar (d. 562 B.C.), for the queen mother (5:10: possibly the former king's wife or daughter) must relate the earlier deeds of Daniel to the ignorant Belshazzar. Daniel is described as one who has "the spirit of the gods" (5:11, 14; cf. 4:8, 9, 18), who possesses an extraordinary spirit (NIV: "keen mind"), knowledge, understanding, insight, and wisdom (5:12, 14).[4] Daniel is promised elevation to be third ruler of the kingdom, after Nabonidus and Belshazzar, if he can interpret the mysterious writing (5:7, 16).

Daniel, taking his life in his hands, boldly declares not only the interpretation, but also its full implications. He disdains the king's rewards, refusing to become a hireling by placing a monetary value on his services (5:17). Daniel reminds Belshazzar of Nebuchadnezzar's humbling experience, which brought about his restoration and the extension of his kingdom. Aware of this, however, Belshazzar has refused to be humbled and has brazenly defied God by desecrating the sacred vessels of the temple. The writing on the wall is a final declaration of judgment. No offer of extension or second chance to repent is given. Belshazzar has failed to "honor the God who holds in his hand your life and all your ways" (5:23).

Daniel both reads and interprets the enigmatic Aramaic inscription: *mene, mene, tekel, uparsin*, literally rendered, "numbered, numbered, weighed and divided" (5:25-28). Three weights or measures may also be intended here: *mene* = mina (50 shekels); *tekel* = shekel; *parsin* = half-shekel.[5] The meaning is the overthrow of Belshazzar's kingdom by the Medes and Persians. The three decreasing units of money may represent the gradually diminishing power of the three final Babylonian rulers, namely, Nebucchadnezzar, Nabonidus, and Belshazzar. As promised, in spite of the unfavorable contents of the inscription, Belshazzar makes Daniel the third ruler of Babylon (5:29). However, that very

---

[4] It is difficult to precisely distinguish the meaning of the five Aramaic terms that the queen mother (5:12) and King Belshazzar (5:14) use to describe Daniel. It may be that what we have here is semantic reinforcement by closely related terms to emphasize the God-given ability that Daniel possesses to "interpret dreams, explain riddles, and solve difficult problems" (5:12). For one attempt to individually define these five characteristics, see John E. Goldingay, *Daniel*, WBC (Dallas, TX: Word, 1989): 109-110.

[5] Goldingay, *Daniel*, 110-111.

night in 539 B.C. Belshazzar is assassinated and a new king, Darius the Mede, inaugurates the Medo-Persian empire (5:30-31).[6]

Worshipper of God in a totalitarian state (6:1-28)

The Persian empire was organized into 120 satrapies which were responsible to three administrators, one being Daniel, who reported directly to the king. Daniel once again proves his exceptional administrative acumen (6:4a) and moral integrity (6:4b-5). Motivated by jealousy, the administrators and satraps began plotting Daniel's downfall, but were frustrated in their search for personal flaws or deficiencies in the performance of his duties. Daniel could only be attacked on the grounds of his faith (6:5). The satraps, pretending loyalty to Darius and a deep concern for his honor, convinced the foolish king to establish a decree forbidding, on pain of death, any worship other than that directed toward the monarch for thirty days. By signing the decree "in accordance with the laws of the Medes and Persians," it became irrevocable (6:8-9, 15). Although the king was absolute in Babylon, the law was supreme in Persia.

Whereas the three comrades were judged for refusing to bow down to Nebuchadnezzar's golden image (3:12), this decree would have been easier for a Jew to obey: it simply involved abstaining from the worship of Yahweh for the limited time period. The satraps, however, calculated correctly that Daniel would continue "just as he had done before" his daily practice of worship, one centered on intercession and thanksgiving (6:10-11). Daniel refused to compromise his convictions, even temporarily, with full awareness of the consequences. The distressed Darius, unable to reverse the decree and now fully aware of the sinister motives of the satraps, could only hope for Daniel's miraculous deliverance (6:16). Daniel was cast into a den of lions ravenous with hunger because of being seldom fed (6:24). The immediate reward of faith was a den of hungry lions!

All credit is ascribed to God who provides a miraculous deliverance. Daniel's innocence (6:22) and trust in God (6:23) are extolled. Like the Chaldeans against the three (Dan 3:29), the false accusers bring about their own disaster as Darius feeds them to the hungry lions. Echoing Nebuchadnezzar's earlier decrees (4:1-3, 34-35), Darius extols the God of Daniel, and formally legalizes the worship of Yahweh in Persia (6:25-28).

Burdened prophet and intercessor (Dan 9:1-27)

The effect upon Daniel of his two extended visions of the future suffering of Israel (7:1-8:26) is exhaustion and illness (8:27). The prophet of God bears the burden of contemplating scenes of judgment that precede restoration. In the first

---

[6] Darius' identity is much disputed. Darius the Mede may refer to Gubaru (or Gobryas), governor of the newly conquered Babylonian territories who appears in the Nabonidus Chronicle and other Babylonian inscriptions. Another view is that Darius is another designation for the first ruler of the Medo-Persian empire, Cyrus the Great himself. Darius would be Cyrus' throne-name in Babylon. If the latter is the case, then 6:28 is appositional: "reign of Darius, that is, the reign of Cyrus the Persian." Stephen R. Miller, *Daniel*, NAC (Broadman and Holman, 1994): 171-177, provides a full discussion of the pros and cons of these alternatives and concludes that the identification of Darius with Cyrus the Great is the stronger view.

year of Darius the Mede (9:1; 539 B.C.), Daniel receives a still further vision of Israel's coming troubles. The context is his concern about the length of the desolation of Jerusalem. He recognizes that the seventy-year captivity predicted by Jeremiah (25:11-12; 29:10; cf. Zech 1:12; 7:5) is drawing to a close. Daniel sees the seventy years either as (1) 586-516 B.C. (from final captivity to completion of the second temple) or, more likely in light of the reference in 9:1 to the first year of Darius' (=Cyrus?) reign, as (2) 605-536 B.C. (from his own captivity to the beginning of work on the second temple following Cyrus' decree).

Daniel turns from reflection on Jeremiah's prophecy to prayer. His prayer moves from humiliation (9:3) to worship (9:4) to confession (9:5-14) and finally to supplication (9:15-19). Daniel places the blame for the present calamity of Jerusalem squarely on Israel's shoulders (cf. Ezra 9:5-15; Neh 1:4-11). Disobedience to the law has brought shame upon Israel. No excuses are offered. God's character is vindicated: his mercy is not lessened (9:9), nor his righteousness tainted (9:14), by the present state of judgment. The petition is a plea for God's mercy, not because it is deserved but for his name's sake (9:15, 18, 19). Daniel makes a plea for the vindication of God's name, for it is borne by Israel and attached to Jerusalem and its sanctuary.

Correspondent with Daniel's concern for the time extent of Israel's exile (9:2), and in answer to his prayer for his people's restoration (9:17-21a), God reveals a sweeping, detailed, though concise, panorama of Israel's future (9:21b-27). Gabriel the archangel serves as the Lord's prophetic messenger once again (9:21; cf. 8:16). Remarkably, he assures Daniel that his prayers have been answered because he is God's "highly esteemed" intercessor (9:23; cf. 10:11). God's program of judgment and redemption will unfold in a timetable of seventy weeks (9:24). From the decree to restore and rebuild Jerusalem (terminus a quo) until the coming of Messiah (terminus ad quem), sixty-nine (7 + 62) weeks will elapse (9:25), after which the Messiah will be cut off and the sanctuary destroyed (9:26). The final 70th week brings a ruler who breaks his covenant with Israel, abolishes sacrifice, and desolates the temple (9:27a). Then the end decreed for him will come (9:27b).

Spiritual warrior and heir of the kingdom (10:1-12:13)

Daniel is emotionally and physically affected by the contents of a further revelation regarding the future of his people (10:1-3). His concern is not merely with the schema of apocalyptic events, but with what they reveal of God's character and the appropriate response. He is burdened for his own people and emotionally involved with those who will become objects of God's mercies and judgments.

The vision is dated in the third year of Cyrus, 537-536 B.C. (10:1). Daniel sees "a man dressed in linen" (10:5-6), which forms both the prologue and sequel (12:7) to the vision. The prologue focuses upon Daniel's reaction to the revelation: he is overcome (10:7-9), revived (10:10-14), and strengthened (10:15-21). The bearer of the revelation is an angelic messenger (10:10-12), to be distinguished from the man in linen. The vision is given in answer to Daniel's prayerful concerns about Israel's restoration (10:12)

Two figures are introduced, namely, the prince of Persia (10:13, 20) and the prince of Greece (10:20). The princes appear to be demonic powers exercising some level of authority over these respective kingdoms. The messenger was hindered by these two princes until Michael, the archangel or chief prince (10:13, 21), brought help. Michael is assigned to protect Israel (10:21; 12:1). Angelic powers, then, are battling for Israel and will continue the struggle in the Persian and Greek periods (10:20-21), being opposed by anti-Israel demonic spirits. The intense struggle that Daniel sees explains his reactions and brings him to the point of bewilderment and utter exhaustion (10:9, 17). The prologue, then, not only introduces the content of the revelation, a struggle for control of Israel's destiny, but also emphasizes the humanness of the prophet Daniel and the sole ability of God's Spirit to interpret prophecy.

Daniel's vision extends to the end of human history with the emergence of a king who exalts himself and shows particular enmity toward the true God of Israel. His actions are arrogant and blasphemous, but very successful so that he gains multiplied riches and a vast kingdom under his domain (11:36-39). The arrogant king will be attacked by the king of the south and the king of the north. In this and subsequent military victories the arrogant king will extend his domain over Israel, Egypt, Nubia (Cush), and Libya, only Edom, Moab, and Ammon excepted (11:40-45). With headquarters in Jerusalem (11:41, "Beautiful Land;" 11:45, "beautiful holy mountain"), the king will make Israel, protected by Michael the great prince (10:13, 21), the central object of his fury, which brings upon Israel an unprecedented "time of distress" (12:1a). Many in Israel will experience deliverance (12:1b). There will take place the resurrection of the righteous and the wicked (12:2-3). Encouragement is given to those "written in the book," those who shine like the stars and lead others to righteousness. Whether they experience deliverance (12:1b) or are slain and experience resurrection (12:2), their reward is great (12:13b).

Daniel is to close up and seal (12:4, 9; cf. 8:26) the words of the book until "the time of the end," an often repeated phrase in Daniel (11:40; 12:4, 9; cf. 8:26; 11:35; 12:13). The sealing seems to stress the finality and certainty of the revelation, though its fulfillment is yet for the future. The book ends on a positive note with a final word of encouragement to Daniel to persevere until the end, mindful of the allotted inheritance he will receive (12:13). The reward of the righteous is the refrain of the epilogue (12:1b-3, 10, 12, 13).

Leadership profile of Daniel

1. *Confidence in the triumph of God's purposes in the world: The visions of Nebuchadnezzar that Daniel interprets declare the ultimate triumph of the kingdom of God over the empires of human history. The rock cut out of a mountain, but not by human hands, smashes the former kingdoms, but itself endures forever (2:34-35, 44-45). The enormous tree with abundant foliage, representing the Babylonian king, is cut down and replaced by an eternal kingdom (4:3, 17, 25, 26, 32, 34-37). Judgment comes on Belshazzar for his failure to acknowledge the Most High God who exalts and displaces the temporary kingdoms of people (5:21, 23). Darius is compelled to acknowledge the God of Daniel as the living God whose kingdom will never end (6:26). Daniel envisions a day when the Ancient of Days will enthrone the Son of*

man and his saints in an indestructible kingdom (7:9-10, 13-14, 18, 22, 26-27). The evil prince who at the end of time will seek to annihilate God's people will be destroyed, but not by human power (8:25; 11:45; 12:1-3). The gravitational center of Daniel's life is his confidence in a sovereign God who rules history and will accomplish his redemptive purposes.

2. ***Preserving one's identity and convictions in a secular context:*** *Daniel engages the culture in which he lives rather than isolating himself from it. He masters the language and literature of his adopted country. His name is changed to a Babylonian one. He serves with distinction for nearly seventy years in the upper echelons of secular, indeed idolatrous, governments. Yet he retains the cutting edge of his faith and so impacts the culture for God's glory. In the famous lion's den incident we see the array of qualities that enabled Daniel to balance faith and work in the secular world of his day. First, he was an exceptional administrator (6:3) who carried out his duties diligently and without a trace of corruption (6:4). Second, the regular practice of prayer was a first priority (6:10-11). Third, he could maintain calm in the midst of accusations, leaving his vindication to God (6:12-18). Fourth, he experienced and humbly acknowledged God's powerful intervention (6:22). Fifth, his trust in God was not shaken even under threats of death (6:23).*

3. ***Passionate prayer for the people of God:*** *The visions that predict the intense suffering, but final vindication, of the covenant people were a heavy burden for Daniel (7:15, 28; 8:15, 27; 10:2-3, 7, 10, 15-17; 12:8). He lived as an exile and yearned for Israel's redemption. His burden fueled intense prayer for the deliverance of his people (9:4-19) so that he became God's "highly esteemed" intercessor (9:23; 10:11). His prayers approximate two other great lovers of Israel who offer to sacrifice their very souls that God's people might be saved (Ex 32:11-14; Rom 9:1-3; 10:1).*

Chapter 13.
Nehemiah: Motivator and mobilizer

Preliminary questions to consider:
1. *How does a leader gain the confidence and support of the people he/she is seeking to mobilize for a unified mission?*
2. *What is the singular recourse of the leader whose work is beset by opposition without and dissension within?*
3. *Where does one focus their primary attention when seeking to lead the people of God in a great endeavor?*

Broken walls and a broken heart (Neh 1:1-11)

We first encounter Nehemiah, son of Hacaliah, resident in Susa as cupbearer to the king, Artaxerxes I, who ruled Persia 465-424 B.C. (1:1, 11b). The cupbearer was a position of great responsibility. One of the duties was to ensure the wine served in the royal court was not poisoned; thus only a person with impeccable character could have assumed this post.[1] Ancient Near eastern sources indicate the cupbearer included an advisory function: "Royal cupbearers in antiquity, in addition to their skill in selecting and serving wine and their duty in tasting it as a proof against poison, were also expected to be convivial and tactful companions to the king. Being much in his confidence, they could thus wield considerable influence by way of informal counsel and discussion."[2]

Nehemiah's brother Hanani came as part of an official delegation from Jerusalem and brought news of trouble and disgrace for the Jews in Judea (1:2-3). The background to the report is the record in Ezra 4:7-23 where an earlier attempt by the Jews to rebuild the walls of Jerusalem was halted under pressure from Rehum, the Persian officer over Judea. When he hears of the vulnerable position of the people because the walls are broken and the gates burned, Nehemiah weeps, mourns, fasts, and prays (1:4). His prayer begins with adoration and confession (1:5-7), then moves to recall God's promises to restore his repentant people from exile to "the place I have chosen as a dwelling for my name" (1:8-9; Deut 30:1-5). The prayer climaxes with supplication. As "your servant," Nehemiah asks the Lord to grant him favor with the king whom he will boldly approach about Judah's plight (1:10-11).

---

[1] The term translated "cupbearer" (מַשְׁקֶה) occurs in this sense twelve times in the Old Testament (Gen 40:1, 2, 5, 9, 13, 20, 21, 23; 41:9; 1 Kg 10:5; 2 Chr 9:4; Neh 1:11). Xenophon, the Athenian historian, records in his account of the life of Cyrus the Great the method of the ancient cupbearer: "Now, it is a well known fact that the kings' cupbearers, when they proffer the cup, draw off some of it with the ladle, pour it into their left hand, and swallow it down—so that, if they should put poison in, they may not profit by it" (*Cyropaedia*, I.iii.9).

[2] H. G. M. Williamson, *Ezra, Nehemiah*, WBC (Waco, TX: Word, 1985): 174.

Bold supplicant for his people (Neh 2:1-10)

Four months after the report Nehemiah approaches the king. Artaxerxes notices that his cupbearer is not wearing his normal cheerful countenance. Nehemiah explains the source of his sorrow and is given the chance to propose a solution. He answers deliberately and with prayer (2:4). The requests are ambitious and specific: (1) a leave of absence so he can go and rebuild Jerusalem (2:5); (2) letters of approval to the governors of Trans-Euphrates to guarantee safe-conduct (2:7); (3) a letter of requisition for timber for the building projects including wall, gates, and personal residence (2:8). Nehemiah's request was a delicate one, for it involved the refortification of the religious capital of a foreign people. The granting of the request was due to God's favor (2:8) and, no doubt, due to the king's implicit trust in his loyal official. The two major opponents of the mission are introduced, Sanballat the Horonite and Tobiah the Ammonite. They are disturbed when they accurately perceive that Nehemiah is coming "to promote the welfare of the Israelites" (2:10).

Situation surveyed and mission defined (Neh 2:11-18)

Nehemiah is cautious in surveying the state of the city. He waits three days and then makes a largely clandestine night walk around the southern hemisphere of Jerusalem. His survey confirms a bleak situation, broken down walls along with gates destroyed by fire. Rather than being a source of discouragement, the ruins move Nehemiah to act. The mission is set forth with clarity to the various groups of Jewish civic and religious leaders with a call to mobilize: "Let us rebuild the wall of Jerusalem, and we will no longer be in disgrace" (2:17). The positive response of the leaders to Nehemiah's exhortation is again attributed to God's favor (2:18; cf. 2:8). Sanballat and Tobiah, joined by Geshem the Arab, ridicule the plan and accuse Nehemiah of fomenting rebellion against the king. They sensed a threat to their political interests and were likely voicing anti-Semitic prejudices as well. Nehemiah resists the tactics of intimidation and issues a stern rebuke. For him the rebuilding project is a faith enterprise from start to finish: "The God of heaven will give us success" because "we his servants" are rebuilding the city of Israel's spiritual heritage (2:20).

Mobilization to a common task (Neh 3:1-32)

Nehemiah was able to gather widespread community support for the project. Forty key men, beginning with the high priest, reconstructed forty-five sections of the wall. The repair of the ten main gates is recorded, moving in a counter-clockwise circuit that begins and ends with the Sheep Gate on the north (3:1, 32). All sections of the Jewish community of Judah contributed: priests (3:1) as well as laymen, people from the outlying towns (3:7), and even women (3:12), although some aristocratic families refused such manual labor (3:5). Nehemiah's success in mobilizing such a working force originates in his passionate articulation of the mission, his skill as an organizer, and his manifest concern for the welfare of city and people.

Encountering organized opposition (Neh 4:1-23)

As the work gains momentum Sanballat and Tobiah seek to dishearten the laborers with ridicule. Their jeers emphasize the impractical nature, even futility, of the efforts. This is turned back by the prayers of their leader (4:4-5) and by perseverance in the task "with all their heart" (4:6). The fierce interchange continues as ridicule turns to an organized attempt to halt the project (4:7-8), a maneuver that had proved successful years earlier (Ezra 4:23). This time, however, a leader with an iron will is present. Nehemiah prays and then posts a guard, affirming God's enabling without underestimating the sinister resolve of the enemy (4:9).

At the half way point the energy of the builders begins to wane and, combined with threats of physical force, weakens their resolve (4:10-12). Nehemiah addresses the crisis as a defender, prophet, and pastor. He further fortifies the exposed places, exhorts all the workers to remember the greatness of their God, and reminds them that their fight is for their homes and families (4:13-14). Nehemiah organizes the builders into units protected by guards, bolsters their defense with a second protective shield of officers, arms the material carriers with weapons, announces a trumpet alarm system to unify their defenses at any point of attack, and arranges special protection for those working at night (4:15-22). Nehemiah does not command from a distance, but takes full part in the labor, guard duty, and supply of water at great personal sacrifice (4:23).[3]

Facing internal dissension with justice and compassion (Neh 5:1-19)

The struggle to complete the building project got worse before it got better. Added to the waning strength of the workers (4:10) and the threats of violence from the enemies (4:11), was an economic crisis that sparked strife between the various classes within the Israelite community in Judah. Famine had reduced people to the bare necessities of life, inflation was rampant, taxes were burdensome, and greedy landowners were exploiting the situation by exacting usury (5:3, 10-11). First, the landless poor were unable to feed their families. Second, middle class landowners were mortgaging their properties just to buy grain. Third, other landowners, already mortgaged, were reduced to selling their children as collateral which, if not paid on time, led to their virtual slavery (5:1-5).

Nehemiah responds with anger at the blatant injustices tearing the community apart (5:6). He successfully confronts the wealthy nobles and officials over their usurious practices toward their Jewish countrymen, practices which contravened the law of God and brought the reproach of the Gentiles (5:7-13; Ex 22:25-27;

---

[3] The biblical record is supplemented by Josephus' account of the fortitude of Nehemiah in the face of determined opposition from a coalition of Ammonites, Moabites, and Samaritans: "But none of these things could deter Nehemiah from being diligent about the work; he only set a number of men about him as a guard to his body, and so unweariedly persevered therein, and was insensible of any trouble, out of his desire to perfect this work. And thus he did attentively, and with great forecast, take care of his own safety; not that he feared death, but of this persuasion, that if he were dead, the walls for his citizens would never be raised. . . . He also went about the compass of the city by night, being never discouraged, neither about the work itself, nor about his own diet and sleep, for he made no use of those things for his pleasure, but of necessity" (*Antiquities of the Jews*, XI:V:8 [transl. William Whiston]).

Prov 28:8). Above all, Nehemiah models an exemplary sacrificial lifestyle, which brings him credibility as an agent of change. First, he purchases the freedom of many that have been sold as slaves to Gentile lords (5:8). Second, he lends money and grain without interest to needy families (5:10). Third, he forgoes collecting the taxes designated to supply the normal provisions of his governorship (5:14, 18b). Fourth, he does not abuse his authority by confiscating their produce in addition to their hard cash, as earlier governors and their assistants had done (5:15). Fifth, Nehemiah is a full participant in the manual labor of the building project, receiving no special exemption due to his office (5:16). Sixth, he shares his table with many officials and visitors who are contributing to the rebuilding effort (5:17-18a). That which sets Nehemiah's leadership apart from the customary paradigm is his piety: "But out of reverence for God I did not act like that" (5:15b). His unblemished record of seeking, at great personal cost, the welfare of the community silences the violators and wins the day (5:8b, 12). He wisely demands that the promises of the nobles to cease and desist from exploitative practices be confirmed by oath in a public ceremony officiated by priests (5:12-13).

Perseverance to complete the project (Neh 6:1-7:3)

Several final desperate attempts were made by the opponents of the project to block its completion. Through prayerful discernment Nehemiah detects their intentions and successfully resists them. First, the three enemies repeatedly attempt to lure Nehemiah away from Jerusalem. Nehemiah suspects their intention is to harm him so he refuses, citing his full engagement in the "great project" at hand (6:1-4). Second, Sanballat revives the treason charge (2:19) by writing a letter that Nehemiah is setting up a Jewish kingdom to challenge Artaxerxes' authority in the region. Nehemiah overcomes the intimidation tactics by defending the purely defensive nature of their project as loyal citizens of Medo-Persia (6:5-8). He prays for strength to persevere (6:9). The king of Persia's trust in his cupbearer must have remained firm, for there is no record that he was moved by such charges. Third, Nehemiah sees through the cunning attempt by a hireling priest-prophet, one Shemaiah, to frighten him to escape a supposed murder plot by fleeing into the temple. Cowardice that would cause him to violate the law and enter the temple proper reserved only for priests would, Shemaiah figured, discredit Nehemiah's leadership (6:10-13). Nehemiah prays for his God to protect him from all attempts at intimidation (6:14).

The project was brought to completion after 52 days. The walls and gates of Jerusalem, broken down and burned by the Babylonians nearly 150 years earlier (586-445 B.C.), were now rebuilt. The remarkable leadership of Nehemiah had unified a vulnerable, disgraced people (1:3), under multiple threats from within and without, to accomplish a historic work. The enemies of the project were disheartened, the people of God given a secure city in which to live and worship, and, above all, God was glorified (6:15-16). Nehemiah placed the city under the supervision of Hanani, not because he was his brother, but because he was a man of integrity and "feared God more than most men do" (7:2). He was not unaware of ongoing enemy activity (6:17-19) and so established measures for the security of the now walled city (7:3).

Partner in covenant renewal (Neh 8:1-11:2)

Six days after the completion of the walls (6:15) on Rosh Hashanah (8:2) Ezra the scribe, who had come to Jerusalem thirteen years before (Ezra 7:1-2, 8-10), assembled the community in the city square. As he and the scribes read from the book of the law of God, the people began to weep from a deep sense of gratitude for God's favor in establishing them once again in their holy city (8:1-9). Nehemiah supported the expositional preaching of Ezra and the Levites that compelled the people to renew their covenant obligations (8:8, 18). Their joint sponsorship of spiritual reformation became a catalyst for joyful celebration of the Lord's goodness while reminding the people to remember the less fortunate (8:10-12). The Feast of Tabernacles was celebrated with unprecedented joy (8:17-18). There is not a hint of rivalry between these two leaders, one civic and one religious, for both sought the welfare of the people above position or power.

Three days after the conclusion of Tabernacles (9:1) a community gathering heard leading Levites recite Israel's history around the themes of repentance for disobedience, confession of God's just judgment, supplication for relief, and obligation to obey the Mosaic covenant (9:1-36). The community then entered into a binding agreement (9:38; 10:28-29), affixed with the seals of civic and priestly leaders, to evidence concrete obedience to eight stipulations related to identity (no intermarriage with neighboring pagans), Sabbath keeping, and the support of the temple, Levites, and priests (10:30-39).

Nehemiah provided for the stability of the city by increasing its resident population to one tenth of the district, both by a system of lots and through voluntary relocation (11:1-2).[4]

Shepherd of a worshipping people (Neh12:27-47)

Time came for the dedication of the wall of Jerusalem and Nehemiah organized it as a national celebration to worship and praise God for his faithfulness. Two large choirs were formed, led by Ezra and Nehemiah respectively, and made a procession upon the city wall in opposite directions until they congregated in the temple precincts (12:31, 38, 40). The theme of their hymns was thanksgiving (12:27, 31, 40). Not just the structures of the wall, but the people as well, were consecrated for the occasion (12:30). The joyful celebration of God's goodness was the keynote of Nehemiah's administration (12:27, 43; cf. 8:9-10).

---

[4] Josephus provides an encomium of Nehemiah in light of the sacrifices he made to secure the physical and spiritual welfare of Jerusalem after the walls were completed: "But when Nehemiah saw that the city was thin of people, he exhorted the priests and the Levites, that they would leave the country, and remove themselves to the city, and there continue; and he built them houses at his own expense; and he commanded that part of the people who were employed in cultivating the land, to bring the tithes of their fruits to Jerusalem, that the priests and Levites having whereof they might live perpetually, might not leave the divine worship; who willingly hearkened to the constitutions of Nehemiah, by which means the city of Jerusalem came to be fuller of people than it was before. So when Nehemiah had done many other excellent things, and things worthy of commendation, in a glorious manner, he came to a great age, and then died. He was a man of a good and a righteous disposition, and very ambitious to make his own nation happy; and he hath left the walls of Jerusalem as an eternal monument for himself" (*Antiquities*, XI:V:8).

126

Reformer of community life (Neh 13:1-30)

Nehemiah's first term of twelve years as governor of Judah (5:14) ended with his recall to the service of the king of Persia (13:6). During the one year he was absent the post-exilic community of Judah broke the binding agreement they had pledged to and sealed (9:38; 10:29). Nehemiah returned to a sad state of affairs and took a series of decisive actions. First, Tobiah the Ammonite, with the assent of the high priest Eliashab, had defiled the temple precincts by securing for personal use a storeroom reserved for offerings and tithes (13:4-5; contra 13:1-3). Nehemiah removed Tobiah's goods, purified the room, and restocked it with grain offerings and incense (13:8-9). Second, Nehemiah learned that the tithes and offerings designated for the needs of the priests and Levites had either not been collected or, if collected, had been confiscated by others (13:10-11; contra 10:37-39; 12:44). Nehemiah rebuked the officials responsible for such neglect and reassigned trustworthy men both to receive and to distribute the tithes (13:12-13). Third, men from Judah were engaging in business transactions with Tyrian traders on the Sabbath (13:15-16; contra 10:31a). Nehemiah rebuked the nobles of Judah for allowing such desecration and took radical action to halt the merchandising (13:17-22). Fourth, Nehemiah became incensed, like Ezra many years before (Ezra 9:1-3), that intermarriage was taking place between men of Judah and women of the surrounding peoples. The children were growing up ignorant of Aramaic and, ostensibly, of their patriarchal heritage (13:23-24; contra 10:30). Nehemiah demands that they cease and desist from imitating Solomon's behavior, which brought such tragic consequences on the nation (13:25-27). Finally, even the priestly office was defiled with such intermarriage and had to be purified (13:28-30). Nehemiah was a civic leader with a reformer's agenda. He knew that the security of Jerusalem and her people depended more upon covenant fidelity than it did upon her newly fortified walls and gates.

Leadership profile of Nehemiah
1. *Sacrificial worker and mission mobilizer: From beginning to end Nehemiah's concern is the physical security and the spiritual welfare of the Jewish community of Jerusalem. It moves him to weep, pray, plan, work, and persevere. He mobilizes an entire community into sections to rebuild the city walls, aggressively defends the workers from threats of violence, and galvanizes the tiring workers to complete what they began. At every step he is a full participant in the project, from stone mason to night guard to water carrier. His personal sacrifices during the famine enable him to successfully confront the usurious nobles. Nehemiah's success as a mobilizer, his ability to win the confidence and move the will of so many people in one direction, lies in the selfless and sacrificial example that, with God's favor, transformed a community of disgrace into a community of joy.*
2. *Crisis an opportunity for prayer: Nehemiah's tireless efforts to organize, defend, and complete the project were undergirded by a prayer life so natural and spontaneous that it punctuates the narrative at every turn. He expresses his sense of dependence in his repeated request that God "remember" him with favor (1:8; 5:19; 13:14, 22, 30; cf. 2:8, 20; 4:14; 6:9, 14; 13:29). When*

the report comes of trouble in Judea, he prays. When the king probes his concerns, he prays. When his enemies try to intimidate him and the workers, he prays. When the community falls back into unfaithfulness to the covenant, he prays. Nehemiah needs God to be involved at every moment of crisis and seeks his wisdom in every solution.

3. ***Preeminence of personal and corporate purity****: To rebuild the broken walls and burned gates of the city is the immediate task at hand. Once God's people are secure in the holy city, Nehemiah turns his attention to their spiritual needs. He appoints the godly Hanani to govern the city, sponsors Ezra's reforms at covenant renewal, organizes the dedication ceremony around choir processionals of praise and thanksgiving, and moves quickly against members of the community who violate the Sabbath and intermarry with pagans. Nehemiah, "out of reverence for God" (5:15), became a different type of civic leader, one with the heart and manner of a caring shepherd.*

PART THREE

Jesus:
Equipper of Equippers

Chapter 14.
Kingdom harvest through sacrifice

Preliminary questions to consider:

1. *What are the two moments or phases of the kingdom of God in Jesus' teaching? How does a proper theology of the kingdom provide the proper framework for ministry with its triumphs and setbacks?*
2. *What was the pattern of Jesus' own ministry and of his training of the twelve? What implications does this pattern have for how we structure leadership training programs in the twenty-first century?*
3. *How would you define the mission that Jesus committed to his apostles? Is the contemporary church faithfully fulfilling the apostolic mission? If not, why not, and what is needed to recover it?*

After spending an entire night in prayer, Jesus chose twelve individuals to participate with him in the proclamation of the kingdom of God (Lk 6:12-16). Their appointment was to be with him to listen and to learn, to call people to repentance and submission to God's rule, and to engage in spiritual warfare against the counterfeit kingdom of Satan (Mk 3:13-15). The three years of public ministry, from his baptism until his death on the cross, was dedicated to training these people to be witnesses of the kingdom after his departure. He rested his legacy with a tiny group of individuals who as his "sent ones" would proclaim the kingdom to the nations, and enlist others as laborers in the harvest (Mt 9:37-38). His words and works recorded in the canonical Gospels reveal a leadership-training program designed to equip those who would in turn equip others. The material is vast and can be organized under any number of leading motifs. This writer has identified three central lessons that Jesus imparted with repetitive intentionality to equip the disciples as kingdom stewards. In the first place, Jesus communicated to them a theology of the kingdom of God that has two defining moments, an inaugural one and a consummative one. His perfect life and vicarious death inaugurates the rule of God over the hearts of those who respond to the person of Jesus with faith and repentance. A day is coming in the indeterminate future when he will return in glory to establish God's unchallenged reign over the universe. As a vision-caster Jesus gave his disciples the perspective of an advancing kingdom that, though small in its beginnings, will yield a great harvest among the nations. The harvest, however, will be reaped only through fearless proclamation in the midst of persecution. This interadvent age of an already-not yet kingdom will bring to its witnesses hardship, hostility, and in some cases physical death. Jesus trained leaders who could endure suffering because they expected lasting fruit to come from their labors and because they believed that beyond their sacrifices awaited a glorious kingdom.

Initial encounter, reflection, and a vision for the harvest (Jn 1:35-51; 4:27-38) The earliest disciples of Jesus were first attracted to the ministry of John the Baptist. Their hearts resonated with the desert prophet's demand for personal repentance (Jn 1:19-28; Mt 3:7-10). The recognition of their need for cleansing pulled them from Galilee south to the waters of the Jordan where John was baptizing. There they heard John speak of Jesus as the fulfillment of the Old Testament paschal lamb upon whom their sins could be placed (Jn 1:29, 36; Ex 12:3-7) and the Spirit-endowed Son of God prophesied by Isaiah (1:33-34; Isa 11:2; 61:1). The line of witness moved to Andrew and an unnamed apostle, probably John the son of Zebedee, who would relate his discovery to his brother James. Andrew in turn declared to his brother Peter that they had met the Messiah (Jn 1:35-42). Philip and his brother Nathaniel were found next (1:43-51). The initial exposure caused faith to germinate in their hearts that Jesus was the lamb of God (1:29, 35), Son of God (1:34), Messiah (1:41, 44), and King of Israel (1:49). These three sets of brothers are almost certainly the "disciples" who accompanied Jesus to a wedding in Cana (Jn 2:2, 11), observed his rage at the temple authorities in Jerusalem (2:12, 17), administered baptism with him in the Jordan (3:22; 4:1-2), and who listened in on his conversation with a Samaritan woman en route to Galilee (4:8, 27, 31, 33). This six to nine month period of reflection bridged initial exposure and confession with their later decision to abandon all to follow Jesus.[1]

From the outset Jesus communicated to his disciples his vision of kingdom harvest. Though the seed of the grain must ripen before it can be harvested, the villagers of Sychar were a people ready to be reaped for the kingdom of God (Jn 4:35). Whereas the disciples could see only the literal unripened grain fields and ignorant Samaritan schismatics, Jesus perceived the opportunity for kingdom advancement. Several observations about Jesus' harvest theology are in order. First, the Samaritan villagers were ready for reaping because of the sowing that had taken place in the past, probably from their reading of the Old Testament messianic prophecies (4:38; cf. 4:25). Second, the expectation of immediate reaping was spoken of a specific people in a particular place, rather than set forth as a universal principle in all settings. Third, the task of harvesting people for God's kingdom involves cooperative sowing and reaping, with both sower and reaper sharing in the joy of the harvest. The confession of the Samaritans that Jesus is indeed the Savior of the world (4:42) must have stunned the parochial disciples. They returned to their homes and vocations to reflect on what they had seen and heard.

[1] This **Early Judean** ministry is covered only in John's Gospel (2:13-4:42). The Synoptic Gospels move directly from the baptism/temptation to the ministry in Galilee based in Capernaum (Mt 4:12-13; Mk 1:14; Lk 4:14, 31). If we assume an A.D. 30 date for the crucifixion, these events took place Spring-Fall, A.D. 27 (nine months). Jesus' movements in this period were from Jerusalem to Judea and finally to Galilee via Samaria.

The kingdom of God and the analogy of fishing (Mt 4:17-22; Mk 1:14-20; Lk 4:14-15; 5:1-11)

Jesus began his ministry in Galilee with the proclamation: "The time has reached fulfillment, the kingdom of God has drawn near. Repent and believe in the good news" (Mk 1:15). The eschatological season anticipated by the Old Testament prophets has arrived. The promised kingdom of God is dawning. The precondition for entering God's kingdom is faith and repentance. As his ministry unfolds it will become clear that the kingdom Jesus introduces is in some sense present (Mt 12:28-29; Lk 17:20-21) and yet awaits a future consummation (Mt 6:10; Lk 19:11). In its present dimension the kingdom is expressed in God's authoritative rule over the life of the individual person who responds in faith and repentance to Jesus Messiah. The future dimension will involve the uprooting and replacement of the present social order as the whole world, human and subhuman, is placed under God's lordship. The kingdom proclamation of Jesus is aimed not at establishing a theocratic state for a renewed ethnic Israel, but advancing the lordship of God over the lives of those who enter by repentance and faith the new Israel which transcends ethnicity, race, gender, and age distinctions.[2] It will be a painstaking process of re-education for the disciples to grasp the meaning of the kingdom and to embrace the vision of kingdom harvest.

Jesus began to assemble a group of people in whom to pour his life and rest his legacy. Two sets of brothers were fishing on the Sea of Galilee. Andrew and Peter and then the sons of Zebedee heard his call, "Come, follow me, and I will make you fishers of men" (Mk 1:17). All have passed through the stages of initial exposure, germination of faith, and a careful reflection (above). Jesus' call was a relational and an educational one, that is, the four fishermen were commanded to trust and obey him. He then takes the responsibility to train them for their new vocation to fish for people. They abandoned home and career for a new gravitational center of life, Jesus, and a new vocation, to fish for (or harvest) human souls for the kingdom of God. Luke records the miraculous catch of fish when Peter, having labored all night in vain, let down the nets at the Lord's command. The large haul symbolized the unimaginable catch of people that will result for the kingdom fisherman who goes about the task under the direction of the Lord (Lk 5:4-7, 10). However, as will become clear, the lavish harvest (to switch back to the more common agricultural metaphor) will not come with mechanical submission to a command, but with tireless sowing, personal sacrifice, fearless confession, and the suffering and perhaps even death of the harvesters. The disciples have taken the first steps in that direction.

---

[2] A growing consensus of New Testament scholars across a broad theological spectrum interpret the New Testament doctrine of the kingdom as including both present rule and future realm. This already-not yet tension is born out of a modified eschatological dualism in which the resurrection of Christ ushered in the "last days." See George Eldon Ladd, *A Theology of the New Testament*, rev. ed. by Donald A. Hagner (Grand Rapids: Eerdmans, 1994): 54-67, 713 chart; *DJG*, 417-30; Leonhard Goppelt, *Theology of the New Testament*, transl. John E. Alsup (Grand Rapids: Eerdmans, 1981): 43-76; Herman Ridderbos, *The Coming of the Kingdom*, transl. H. de Jongste (Philadelphia: Presbyterian and Reformed, 1962): 3-60; George Eldon Ladd, *The Presence of the Future* (Grand Rapids: Eerdmans, 1974); G. R. Beasley-Murray, *Jesus and the Kingdom of God* (Grand Rapids: Eerdmans, 1986).

First tour of Galilee (Mt 4:23-25; Mk 1:35-39; Lk 4:42-44)

Growing numbers of people were coming to Jesus to be healed of their diseases or to be relieved of demonic oppression (Mk 1:27-28, 32-34). Jesus withdrew, refusing to allow the tyranny of the urgent to usurp what was of greater priority, the preaching of the good news of the kingdom to the villages of Galilee. After a time of solitary prayer he took the four disciples with him on a preaching tour of Galilee. Jesus' pattern of ministry would be one of thrust and withdrawal, that is, active engagement followed by periods of quiet prayer to the Father (Mk 1:40-44/ 1:45; 2:1-12/2:13; 3:1-6/3:7; 3:9-12/3:13; 3:31-35/4:1; 5:1-20/5:21). His authoritative preaching, authenticated by attendant miracles, accosted the whole personality with the demand for repentance. Jesus' kingdom theology was a call to submit to the lordship of God over one's entire life now, though its perfect fulfillment would come in a glorious realm of God's unchallenged supremacy in the future. Jesus' training program for the disciples from the outset integrated theological instruction, itinerant evangelism, and prayer. This was the first of three tours Jesus and his disciples would make around the 240 towns and villages of Galilee (cf. Lk 8:1; 9:6).

Call of the tax collector and a banquet with sinners (Mt 9:9-13; Mk 2:13-17; Lk 5:27-32)

Jesus continued to assemble his diverse team of core disciples. Levi, also called Matthew, was the customs and excise tax collector with an office situated at the border of the territories of Galilee and Trachonitis. He was attending to his duties when Jesus passed his way along the northern shore of Lake Galilee. Matthew's previous exposure to Jesus is unknown. Jesus' call of a tax collector to follow him must have stunned the four disciples. These civil servants of the Roman government had a reputation for harshness, even dishonesty, and were shunned by respectable Jewish society (Mt 5:46; Lk 19:8). Jesus' command to follow him, not a new set of legalistic prescriptions, was met by Matthew's willing abandonment of his lucrative career, present security and future prospects (Lk 5:28).

Matthew, as it were, immediately cast his kingdom net into familiar waters and invited his fellow tax collectors, and other friends regarded from the Pharisaic point of view as "sinners," to his home to dine with Jesus (Lk 5:29). Jesus showed no concern with contracting ritual defilement from contact with those considered untouchables by the religionists. The disciples were at a loss to answer the complaints of the Pharisees over their Lord's loose associations. Using the analogy of the physician whose concern is for the sick not the healthy, Jesus defended his actions. The "sick" are the "sinners" who recognize their depravity and seek inner cleansing from the one who has claimed authority to forgive sins (Mk 2:10-11). Jesus' mission was directed toward sinners who may enter God's kingdom by means of their repentance (Lk 5:32). The pejorative label that the Pharisees attached to him, "a friend of tax collectors and sinners" (Mt 11:19), was to Jesus a title of honor. The four kosher disciples must now learn to enjoy the company of a former servant of Rome, whose heart like theirs had been transformed by his encounter with Jesus.

Twelve pillars of the new Israel (Mk 3:13-19; Lk 6:12-16)

During the Early Galilean period of ministry[3] Jesus' popularity with the wider population grew and reached its peak when the crowds gathered to hear his "Sermon on the Mount" (Mk 3:7-12; Mt 7:28-29). The Sabbath controversies, however, caused the initial misgivings of the Pharisees to deepen into active opposition (Mk 2:23-3:6). As a result, Jesus began to concentrate his energies more and more away from the ambivalent multitudes to the training of his kingdom associates. A night of prayer preceded the momentous decision (Lk 6:12). He formally commissioned twelve men to be his "apostles," that is, "ones sent forth" to represent the dynamic rule he was inaugurating (Lk 6:13; cf. Mt 10:2). The appointment had a threefold purpose: (1) to be with him, that is, for fellowship and instruction; (2) to preach the dawning of the kingdom in Jesus Messiah; and (3) to cast out demons which authenticated their authoritative proclamation (Mk 3:14-15).

There are four New Testament lists of the apostles:

Mt 10:2-4	**Mk 3:16-19**	**Lk 6:14-16**	**Acts 1:13b**
Simon, Peter	Simon, Peter	Simon, Peter	Peter
Andrew, brother	Andrew		
James, of Zebedee	James, of Zebedee	James	
John, brother	John, brother	John	John
		Andrew	James
			Andrew
Philip	Philip	Philip	Philip
			Thomas
Bartholomew	Bartholomew	Bartholomew	Bartholomew
Thomas			
Matthew	Matthew	Matthew	Matthew
	Thomas	Thomas	
James, of Alphaues	James, of Alphaeus	James, of Alphaeus	James, of Alphaeus
Thaddaeus	Thaddaeus (Lebbaios)		
Simon the Zealot	Simon the Cananean	Simon the Zealot	Simon the Zealot
		Judas, of James	Judas, of James
Judas Iscariot	Judas Iscariot	Judas Iscariot	

[3] The **Early Galilean** period extends from Jesus' permanent move to Galilee until the choosing of the twelve (Mk 1:14-3:19; Lk 4:14-6:16). The nine month period is dated Winter-Fall A.D. 28 (nine months). The following are Jesus' movements: Cana; Nazareth; Capernaum; first tour of Galilee with the four disciples; return to Capernaum.

The following characteristics of the group must be noted:

1. "The twelve" (ten times in Mk; six times in Mt and Lk; four times in Jn; once each in Acts [6:2] and Paul [1 Cor 15:5]) is the technical designation. The apostles are the foundation-pillars of the new messianic community, replacing the twelve patriarchs of the tribes of Israel. Here is the beginning of the eschatological people of God, the new Israel, the church that Jesus will build (Mt 16:18; 18:17; cf. Eph 2:20; 1 Pet 2:9-10).
2. Peter, who will become the "rock" of the church (Mt 16:18), is always listed first. He assumes the role of spokesman for the group, the primus inter pares, "first among equals."
3. James and John, sons of Zebedee, are always listed together. Along with Peter they comprise a special group of three within the twelve (cf. Mk 5:37; 9:2; 14:33). Judged by their ambitious actions and fiery reactions (cf. Mk 9:38; 10:35-40; Lk 9:54), the ascription "sons of thunder" (Mk 3:17) was appropriate.
4. Judas Iscariot, the betrayer, is last in every list. He also was chosen in answer to prayer (Lk 6:12). Thus the betrayal of Jesus was an evil action for which Judas was responsible, but one ordained by God to fulfill salvation history (Mk 14:21).
5. Philip/Bartholomew and Thomas/Matthew are mentioned together in the Synoptic lists. Perhaps they comprise two more sets of brothers,[4] in addition to Peter/Andrew and James/John. Apparently Thaddaeus is the same person as Judas, of James.
6. The Synoptic lists are arranged in three groups of four each, perhaps divided into ministry teams along this line by Jesus himself.

In summary, Jesus deliberately set the apostles in a relational setting with all of its potential for tension, conflict, and personal growth. It was in some ways a most unusual collection of individuals. The one labeled the group's "rock" would emerge as a talkative reactionary. Two explosive brothers, labeled the "sons of thunder," would be pushed forward by an ambitious mother and incite the jealousy of the others. Simon had a political background as an anti-Roman zealot, while Matthew was at the opposite end of the spectrum as a former civil servant of Rome. All were Galileans, except Judas Iscariot. Family and sibling rivalries must have arisen at times. There were four sets of brothers. James and John were first cousins of Jesus. The loyalty of the twelve would be tested as Jesus' popularity waned and the wider group of followers evaporated. At Jesus' arrest the apostles would scatter, only to be reunited with reports of the appearances of the risen Lord. From a human perspective the chosen twelve seem unlikely to form a unified company. Here are the people in whom Jesus invested his life and upon whom he rested his legacy.

---

[4] Bartholomew may be another name for Nathaniel (Jn 1:45). Thomas is also called Didymus (Jn 11:16), which means "twin." Or perhaps James of Alphaeus is brother to Matthew (cf. Mk 2:14: Levi, of Alphaeus).

Dispelling doubts about the arrival of the kingdom[5] (Mt 11:2-19; Lk 7:18-35)

John the Baptist had been imprisoned in the fortress of Machaerus, east of the Dead Sea, for his condemnation of Herod Antipas' adultery with Herodias (Lk 3:19-20). While languishing in prison, John began to have doubts about Jesus' messianic identity. This is surprising in light of his earlier confession of Jesus as the lamb of God (Jn 1:29, 36). He sent his disciples to Jesus to ask: "Are you the one who was to come, or should we expect someone else?" (Mt 11:3). Surely the apostles, some of whom began their spiritual pilgrimage under John, must have entertained similar doubts when opposition from the religious leaders intensified. Jesus was not turning out to be the kind of Messiah—a political liberator and social reformer—that John and the people at large, including the apostles, had expected. Jesus pointed to the miracles that authenticated his authoritative claims and fulfilled biblical prophecy (Mt 11:4-5; cf. Isa 26:19; 29:18-19; 35:5-6; 61:1). He challenged John and his disciples to reexamine their suppositions about Messiah. Then he turned to the crowd and clarified John's role in salvation history. First, John is more than a prophet. He is the forerunner of Messiah prophesied in Malachi 3:1. Further, John is the Elijah-like figure of Malachi 4:5-6 sent to prepare the hearts of God's people for the arrival of the King (Mt 11:10). Second, John stands on the threshold of the kingdom. He is the last figure of the old era and thus, in terms of his place in the unfolding drama of redemption, is inferior in status to the citizens of the inaugurated kingdom (11:11). Third, in Jesus' ministry the kingdom of heaven "has been aggressively advancing and forceful people, that is, violent opponents, are attempting to halt its advance" (11:12).[6] In other words, John's disappointment sprang from the false expectation that all kingdom opposition would be swiftly rooted out. Advancement in the midst of intense opposition is the character of the kingdom in its inaugural stage.

The greater the debt, the greater the love (Lk 7:36-50)

Jesus gladly accepted invitations to meals whether the host was a tax collector (Mk 2:15), a leper (Mk 14:3), or, as in this case, a Pharisee named Simon. He could mix it up equally with social outcasts as well as religious sophisticates. The invitation may have been to an afternoon meal after the synagogue service on the Sabbath. A "sinful" woman, either a known prostitute or adulteress, courageously entered the Pharisees' house bringing with her a long-necked alabaster bottle full of ointment. She had probably heard Jesus teach and watch him heal and was drawn to his offer of the kingdom. Her repentance was expressed with tears of gratitude. She began to wet his feet with her falling tears, wipe them with her hair, kiss them, and apply the perfume, which was normally intended for the head. Her

---

[5] We have now moved to what is termed the **Middle Galilean** ministry. This period extends from the close of the Sermon on the Mount up to, but not including, the northern withdrawal (Mk 3:20-35; Lk 7:1-8:3; 8:19-21): late Fall A.D. 28-early Summer A.D. 29 (eight months).

[6] This paraphrase takes the verb βιαζεται as a deponent middle voice: "has been forcefully advancing." The subject and main verb of the second sentence, βιασται ἁρπαζουσιν, are taken in the negative sense: violent or rapacious people, such as the Pharisees and Herod Antipas, have been trying (conative present) to plunder it. See D. A. Carson, *Matthew*, EBC (Grand Rapids: Eerdmans, 1984): 266-268.

attention to the dusty feet of the Galilean traveler, remaining in the background without words only tears, revealed a penitent and devoted heart. Jesus silently accepted the woman's act of gratitude, but the Pharisee's logic was one of guilt by association—a true prophet, as the people are acclaiming him to be (Lk 7:16), would never allow such a thing!

Jesus related the parable of the two debtors, one of whom was forgiven an obligation of five hundred denarii and the other fifty denarii. Simon replied correctly when asked which of the two would love the master more: "I suppose the one who had the bigger debt canceled" (7:43). Love, Jesus said, is the active response of the forgiven one to grace bestowed. Simon was painfully aware of the implications that Jesus now applied to the present situation. Simon had performed the normal duties of hospitality, but this woman had offered to Jesus lavish service beyond all expectations. This woman, whose sins were great, loved more because she had felt the release of so great a burden on her soul. The one who has been forgiven little, because of the delusion of self-righteousness, is capable only of little love. The point is not that Simon needs only a small measure of forgiveness, but that he has failed to recognize the magnitude of his sin and thus underestimated his need for forgiveness. Jesus pronounced the woman forgiven and sent her away in peace, completing the chain of salvation that began with her pursuit and discovery of Jesus: trust—forgiveness—gratitude—love—peace. The other guests, probably including some disciples, were left to ponder: "Who is this who even forgives sins?" (7:49).

Second tour of Galilee (Lk 8:1-3)

For the second time Jesus toured Galilee, this time from town to town with the twelve apostles. This was a systematic campaign of evangelism in the countryside with the accent on the proclamation of the kingdom. Three prominent women were among the "many others" that accompanied them and helped provide financial support for the itinerant band. Mary Magdalene and the other women were living examples of the power of the kingdom at work to deliver from satanic oppression. Jesus imparted to the apostles a proper understanding of the kingdom of God, the mandate to proclaim it to unreached villages, and the thrilling experience of seeing lives transformed.

The Spirit, the kingdom and the strong man (Mt 12:22-37; Mk 3:20-30)

The successful extension of the kingdom brought with it determined resistance. Upon his return to Capernaum, Jesus met with fierce opposition both from his earthly family and from the Pharisees. His mother and brothers accused him of being out of his mind and sought to restrain him from further embarrassing them (Mk 3:20-21). When Jesus healed a dumb and blind demoniac, the Pharisees leveled a frontal assault against him: he casts out the demons by the power of Beelzebub, the prince of demons. They could not deny the miracle so they resorted to attributing it to satanic power. This perverse and stunning accusation became a favorite of the religious leaders (cf. Mt 9:34; 10:25; Jn 7:20; 8:48, 52; 10:20). Jesus made a rational defense by exposing the circular reasoning of his opponents. Their logic creates the patently absurd situation that Satan is working to defeat his own kingdom. The question that follows is an effective countercharge: "By whom do your sons cast them out?" The listening crowd must choose between him and the Pharisees as to which is carrying out the divine assault on Satan's dominion. Jesus posited that if, as is the case, it is by the Spirit of God that he is assaulting the hegemony of Satan, then God's kingdom has arrived (Mt 12:28).[7] Jesus has bound Satan, the strong man, so that he can "enter his house and plunder his goods." The goods refer to human beings subject to his binding influence. The apostles are participants with Jesus in an advancing kingdom, but its adversaries will not soon concede defeat (Mt 11:12). The binding of Satan is, as it were, with a long rope. Spiritual warfare is the means of rolling back the darkness and of breaking present demonic strongholds. The outcome of the war is certain, but the intervening battles will tax all the resources of the warriors-in-training.

True family of Jesus (Mt 12:46-50; Mk 3:31-35; Lk 8:19-21)

In Mark's Gospel the Beelzubub controversy interrupts the record of the visit of the family of Jesus to Capernaum. They were embarrassed over the reports of Jesus' growing popularity as a miracle worker. His mother and unbelieving brothers (Jn 7:3-5) came from Nazareth to compel him to desist from such maniacal behavior (Mk 3:20-21). When his family arrived, they were unable to enter Peter's house due to the pressing crowd. To the report that his family had arrived, Jesus returned a stunning question: "Who is my mother and my brothers?" (3:33). He then proceeded to answer his own question. His true family members are those who do the will of the Father. The character and makeup of the family of Jesus is wholly unrelated to racial lineage, religious affiliation, or even blood ties. Doing the will of the heavenly Father is what identifies and substantiates that one is a member of the family of Jesus, presently represented by the small group of disciples. Here is the fulfillment of the new covenant promise, "I will be their God and they will be my people" (Jer 31:33b). Familial intimacy is evidenced by submission to the divine purposes. The kingdom community is a supraracial family formed on the basis of heart allegiance to God's will.

Mysterious truths about the kingdom of God (Mt 13:1-53; Mk 4:1-34; Lk 8:4-15)

After the bitter interchange with the Pharisees, "that same day" Jesus went down to the shore of Lake Galilee and began to teach the large crowds that gathered (Mt 13:1). Thus the parables that follow, real life settings with extended metaphors designed to communicate spiritual truth, are linked to the controversy surrounding the healing of the demoniac (12:24). The disciples must have wondered, since the recognized religious leaders in Israel were vehemently denying Jesus' authority, can the kingdom of God really be dawning? The nine parables would provide great encouragement for them. Jesus articulated to the disciples, separate from the crowds, hermeneutical keys that unlocked the stories' details (13:36a; cf. 13:10-17, 34-35). They asked the Lord why he was addressing the crowd in parables (13:10). Jesus' reply magnified the distinction between his disciples and the crowd,

[7] The verb ἐφθασεν (from φθανω; cf Lk 11:20) is understood here as an effective or resultative aorist: "has [effectively] arrived." A similar sense is found in 1 Thessalonians 2:16.

"to you . . . but to them" (13:11). This distinction was grounded in the principle in v. 12, namely, that revelatory light is given in proportion to the heart response of the listener. The parabolic stories were designed to reveal knowledge of mysterious features[8] of the kingdom to the disciples, but to conceal such knowledge from the crowds, whose ambivalence had disqualified them from receiving further revelation (13:12-15). Like Asaph who narrated Israel's history in Psalm 78 and interpreted its enigmatic parts, so Jesus disclosed "things hidden" in earlier stages of revelation (13:34-35). The mysteries fill in the shadowy images of the kingdom sketched in the Old Testament. The disciples were privileged to see and hear what prophets and sages only longed to experience (13:16-17).

The disciples were expecting the kingdom to arrive in accordance with Daniel's apocalyptic imagery, one that would displace the present social order, destroy Satan's hegemony, and introduce the everlasting kingdom of the Ancient of Days (Dan 7:9-14). The parables, however, disclosed that the age to come is dawning in a totally unexpected, yet divinely planned manner. The kingdom first arrives in the form of internal rule over repentant hearts; only in the future will its advance over the entire socio-political order be realized. The following truths about the kingdom of God are disclosed in the nine parables:

Parable	Meaning
1. Sower and seeds (Mt 13:3-9, 18-23)	As the kingdom message is proclaimed there will be a variety of responses. However, some will hear, understand and receive, and in turn become its fruitful witnesses.
2. Seed's spontaneous growth (Mk 4:26-29)	The supernatural power at work in the sowing of the kingdom message ensures the reaping of a spiritual harvest. Even though its present character is veiled, the kingdom will one day produce a vast and visible kingdom community.
3. Weeds (tares) (Mt 13:24-30, 36-43)	The kingdom has arrived in provisional form and is making its advance in the world, but opposition remains until it is completely removed at the final judgment.
4. Mustard seed (Mt 13:31-32)	There is an organic unity between the small beginning of the kingdom in the present age and the full glory of the kingdom in the age to come.
5. Leaven (Mt 13:33)	The kingdom of God operates quietly with small beginnings, but will finally prevail and triumph over all opposition.

[8] The background of the New Testament term "mystery" (μυστήριον) is the Aramaic term רָז (or רָזָה / רָזָא [pl. רָזִין]), which in Daniel (2:18, 19, 27, 28, 29, 30, 47; cf. 4:9) refers to God's purposes for the future that he reveals according to his sovereign pleasure. In the New Testament era of prophetic fulfillment, "mystery" takes on the sense of a truth about the kingdom of God that, heretofore having been secreted away in the divine counsels, is disclosed to those with receptive hearts (Mt 13:11/Mk 4:11/Lk 8:10; cf. 1 Cor 4:1; Eph 3:3, 4, 9; Col 1:26-27). See *NIDNTT*, 3: 502-505.

6. Hidden treasure (Mt 13:44)	The kingdom is of incomparable worth. The rational response to its offer is to joyfully abandon all other attractions in order to promote its interests.
7. Hidden pearl (Mt 13:45-46)	Though the kingdom may at present seem trivial, it is worth sacrificing everything to gain.
8. Net (Mt 13:47-50)	The community created by the proclamation of the kingdom is in the present age a mixed one, composed of true believers and superficial professors. At the future judgment a thorough distinguishing of authentic believers from false disciples will take place.
9. Houseowner (13:52)	The promissory-prophetic revelation of the old covenant is fulfilled in the new covenant inaugurated by Jesus and is expounded by his kingdom disciple-teachers.

The comprehensive sense of the "mystery of the kingdom," then, is its initial arrival in a veiled manner that works secretly but powerfully in the hearts of people. One day, however, this provisional beginning will break out with apocalyptic power to bring the universe, human and subhuman, under the lordship of God. The kingdom theology of their Lord equipped the disciples to align themselves with God's purposes, free from both triumphalism on the one hand and marginalization on the other. They had committed themselves to the King who with authority was even now establishing his rule over repentant hearts. Though the community is small and the opposition is intense, the ultimate triumph of the kingdom is certain. The apostles will need to be reminded of these truths as the journey ahead gets steeper and more perilous.

Laborers needed for the harvest (Mt 9:35-38; Mk 6:6b)

Matthew records a summary statement of Jesus' Galilean ministry, which involved three major activities: preaching in the open air in the towns and villages; formal teaching in the synagogues on the Sabbath; healing of those with physical diseases. Jesus' missionary activity was driven by compassion for the ordinary people of the land who were like sheep without a shepherd to guide them. This was an indictment of the religious leaders who had proven to be false shepherds (cf. Jer 23:1-4; Ezek 34:1-10) and hirelings (Jn 10:12-13). Jesus shifted metaphors from sheep farming to the familiar symbol of the wheat field (cf. Jn 4:35-38; Mt 13:24-30). He instructed his disciples to pray for workers who will go out and reap a ready harvest. Jesus saw many among the faceless, harassed multitude ready to be reaped for the kingdom. The disciples were being trained to be instruments for kingdom advancement, and were to pray that the Lord who ensures the harvest will produce through them even more harvesters.

Commissioning the heralds of the kingdom (Mt 10:1-42; Mk 6:7-11; Lk 9:1-5) The call and training of the kingdom heralds has come in stages. Four fishermen abandoned their career and accompanied Jesus through Galilee (Mk 1:16-20, 39). A tax collector made the same decision (Mk 2:14). These and seven more were designated his "apostles" after a night of prayer (Mk 3:13-14). A second tour of Galilee followed (Lk 8:1). Jesus imparted to the disciples in stages the theology of the already-not yet kingdom (Mk 1:15; Mt 11:11-13; 12:28-29; 13:1-52; Mk 4:26-29). Now he formally commissioned them to proclaim his kingdom, first within Israel, but with a view to ultimately evangelizing the nations of the world. The gospel of the kingdom was, in Paul's words, "first for the Jew, then for the Gentile" (Rom 1:16). The stream of salvation history is a Jewish one that eventually overflows its banks and waters the Gentile world (Jn 4:21-24; Mk 7:24-30). The mission to the lost sheep of Israel (Mt 10:6) was designed to gather laborers who will harvest the Gentiles for the kingdom (10:18). The redemptive focus on a man, a family, and a nation was designed to reverberate into universal blessing (Gen 12:1-3). Jesus' manual of instruction (below) combined in perfect tension a belief in the vast potential for kingdom advancement, along with recognition that its promoters would be required to make tremendous sacrifices.

Particularized stage of the commission (Mt 10:1-16)
1. The apostles' initial sphere of ministry was not to Gentiles or even to Samaritans, but only to the Jewish villagers and townspeople who were like lost sheep (10:5-6).
2. Their message was the same as that of John (Mt 3:2) and of Jesus (Mt 4:17): "The kingdom of heaven has drawn near" (10:7).
3. Four representative miracles provided attestation of the arrival of the kingdom and demonstrated the delegated authority of the heralds (10:8a).
4. They were to serve without mercenary motives (10:8b). The apostles were to be unencumbered by material possessions and dependent on God to supply their needs through his people (Mt 10:9-10).
5. Confidence in God's sovereignty must govern their attitudes to those who were receptive and to those who were hostile to their message. The christological core of their message must be undiluted, for people's eternal destiny depends on their response to Jesus. The apostles were learning that the promotion of the kingdom is divisive and meets with violent opposition (10:11-15).
6. Their mental posture is described as "wise as serpents, innocent as doves" (10:16). Prudence and caution toward determined opponents was combined with pure motivation free from guile.[9] To be realistic without becoming cynical or suspicious would be the delicate balance.

To summarize, the apostles were sent forth with authority to boldly proclaim the arrival of the kingdom of God in Jesus Messiah. Their total dependence on

[9] W. D. Davies and Dale C. Allison, *A Critical and Exegetical Commentary on the Gospel according to Saint Matthew*, ICC, 3 vols. (Edinburgh: T & T Clark, 1991): 2: 180-181.

God and his people for food, shelter and clothing was a lifestyle that communicated the grace character of the message. Their preaching of repentance, accompanied by attesting signs, sifted the listeners' hearts, producing joyful receptivity or aggressive hostility. Next the Lord prepared the apostles for the persecution that the heralds of the kingdom would inevitably face.

Preparation for persecution (Mt 10:17-36)

1. The apostles will be arrested and brought before religious and secular authorities. This will provide opportunity to witness to Gentile magistrates. They should not be anxious because the "Spirit of your Father" will guide the testimony (10:17-20). Jesus indicated that the source of the initial persecution would be Jewish, but he anticipated an extended time of witness beyond Jewish parameters. Suffering becomes the context for worldwide extension of the kingdom.
2. Bitter division over the kingdom message and the king himself, his claims and demands, will take place even among family members (10:21-22a; expanded in 10:34-36). Kingdom proclamation demands total allegiance, one that transcends family bonds. The apostles and all kingdom heirs must show endurance to the end of life or to the end of the age, whichever comes first, to prove the reality of their confession (10:22b). Perseverance is the seal of one's true kingdom identity.
3. The witness to Jewish people and, by extension, to Gentiles will continue until the end of the age signaled by the glorious return of the Son of man to consummate his kingdom program (10:23; cf. Mt 24:30; 25:31; 26:64).
4. The heralds should not be surprised by how harshly they are treated, for they are in solidarity with the King who is being accorded the same. The blasphemous accusations leveled against the teacher, the master, and the head of the house (Mt 12:24), will surely produce even greater suffering ("how much more") for the student, the servant, and the member of the household (10:24-25).
5. Therefore, the apostles must continue their faithful proclamation regardless of the cost. This exhortation to fearless confession is supported by theological propositions. First, the truth will ultimately emerge and be vindicated. Thus it needs to be boldly declared now to provide an opportunity for those who do have ears to hear (10:26-27). Second, God is to be feared, not Satan or people, because he alone has authority to destroy soul and body in hell (10:28). Jesus implies that martyrdom is the price some of the kingdom heralds will pay for their allegiance to his kingdom. Third, the disciples can trust their temporal security and their eternal destiny to their loving heavenly Father whose providential care covers the tiniest details of life and thus those of the greatest magnitude (10:29-31). Fourth, public acknowledgment of Jesus is evidence of one's trust relationship with Jesus, one that will be vindicated at the final judgment (10:32-33).[10]

---

[10] Jesus reiterated these truths to his disciples about one year later in the **Early Perean** ministry (Lk 12:1-12).

In summary, at the center of the kingdom message is the demand of repentance that accosts the personality of the listener. A great distinguishing work is taking place and the apostles out of compassion for people and reverence for God must courageously fulfill the task of the herald. The eternal fate of people rests with their response to Jesus and his kingdom offer. Faithfulness to Jesus' mission will invite opposition, suffering, and perhaps even death. They can trust their Father with whatever consequences follow, for his final approbation will outweigh every kind and level of sacrifice.

Radical demands and incomparable rewards (Mt 10:37-42)

Jesus now shifted to more general language that encompasses both the apostles and all who would embrace the kingdom through their preaching.[11] Anyone who aspires to become Jesus' disciple must be informed they are taking on a life-absorbing commitment. First, the new allegiance to Jesus takes precedence even over the most intimate family ties (10:37). Second, sacrifice, self-denial, suffering, and even physical death—all symbolized by the cross—are the willing experiences of the worthy disciple (10:38). Third, the one who "finds his life," that is, determines to spare it from such hardships, will forfeit all reward; the one who "loses his life," that is, pours it forth as a sacrificial offering to promote the kingdom, will be abundantly rewarded (10:39).[12] The promise of reward is based on the continuity between Jesus, his disciples, and those who receive them as the king's emissaries (10:40-42). God delights to honor those who in turn honor his beloved Son (cf. Mt 3:17; 17:5).

Third tour of Galilee (Mt 11:1; Mk 6:12-13; Lk 9:6)

With a mandate to carry out and the manual to guide them, the disciples set out on a third tour of Galilee. They preached repentance and healed the sick. Jesus followed them and carried out the same ministry in the towns (Mt 11:1). After their tour the disciples returned, reported, and rested. Their training to be people of impact for the kingdom of God followed a familiar pattern: concentrated instruction regarding the kingdom of God (Mt 10:1-42); intense activity in itinerant evangelism (Mk 6:12-13); return and debriefing (Mk 6:30; Lk 9:10a); and withdrawal from the demands of the crowds for rest and further teaching (Mk 6:31-32; Lk 9:10b; Jn 6:1-3). They reported the results of the tour because they were accountable to Jesus as his authorized representatives. However, the cycle began again as the crowds, like sheep without a shepherd, discovered his location

[11] The language Jesus employed becomes increasingly general as the discourse in Matthew 10:1-42 proceeds. Imperatives in the second person plural, along with many second person plural pronouns, dominate through v. 31. The final three paragraphs (10:32-36, 37-39, 40-42) contain numerous relative clauses (10:32, 38), indefinite relative clauses in the subjunctive mood (10:33, 42), and substantival participial clauses (10:37, 39, 40, 41) which apply to all those who fulfill the stated conditions.
[12] Davies and Allison, *Matthew*, 2: 224. This must have been one of Jesus' favorite sayings, judged by its attestation in the Gospels (Mt 10:39; Mk 8:35/Mt 16:25/Lk 9:24; Lk 17:33; Jn 12:25). The saying was expressed in different ways, using different verb combinations (find/lose; save/lose; love and lose/hate and keep), but its basic sense (above) seems clear.

and thronged the hills north of Bethsaida to which Jesus and the disciples had withdrawn (Mk 6:33-34; cf. Mt 9:36).

Struggle to merge kingship and suffering (Mt 16:13-17:8; Mk 8:27-9:8; Lk 9:18-36; Jn 6:14-15, 60-71)

When evening approached, the disciples expressed concern that the crowds should be sent back to the villages so the people would not be stranded at night in a desolate place without food (Mk 6:35-36). The Lord tested them with a command: "you (pl.) give them something to eat" (6:37). When five loaves of bread and two fish were discovered in the lunch of a small boy, Andrew responded with incredulity: "What are they among so many?" (Jn 6:8-9). Jesus then proceeded to satisfy the physical needs of 5,000 men plus women and children by multiplying the loaves and fish and distributing the food, through the disciples, to the crowd (Mk 6:41). The disciples then gathered the leftover fragments that filled twelve baskets (6:43). The multitude began to declare Jesus as the eschatological "prophet who is to come into the world," clearly a messianic designation (Jn 6:14; cf. Deut 18:15-19). Jesus, however, knew that such acclaims were filled with socio-political notions. The people were looking for a conquering king who could rally Israel, drive out the Romans, and cleanse the priesthood. Jesus dismissed the crowds, sent the disciples ahead by boat to Capernaum, and withdrew to a mountain by himself (Jn 6:14-15). The disciples appear as confused onlookers overtaken by the events surrounding the miraculous feeding. They stand half way between an adoring multitude filled with messianic fervor and their reluctant Lord who recedes into the hills to pray.[13]

When Jesus and his disciples made their way back to Capernaum, he delivered an extended discourse in the synagogue in which he revealed the deeper meaning of the feeding of the 5000: "I am the bread of life. He who comes to me will never go hungry, and he who believes in me will never go thirsty" (Jn 6:35). His satisfaction of their physical hunger symbolized his ability to meet the deeper yearning of their hearts for cleansing and forgiveness. But when he spoke of their need to personally appropriate the benefits of his coming redemptive death, under the language of eating his flesh and drinking his blood, the listeners stumbled (Jn 6:53-60). Many of his "disciples," that is, loosely attached followers attracted by the miracles, "turned back and no longer followed him" (Jn 6:66). With the crowd of disciples evaporating away, Jesus put the apostles to the test: "You do not want to leave too, do you?" Peter stepped forward as the group's spokesman and made the first of two exalted confessions of Jesus' Messiahship: "We have come to believe and know that you are the Holy One of God" (6:69). As will become clear, the apostles' hearts were far ahead of their heads at this point. They have a settled assurance that he is the Anointed One of God, but possess no understanding of how suffering can fit into that identity.

After entering the final phase of the Galilean ministry, Jesus withdrew for a

---

[13] The **Middle Galilean** ministry is drawing to a close: late Fall A.D. 28-early Summer 29 (eight months). The feeding of the 5000 is a clear example of where John's Gospel complements and amplifies the Synoptics.

period beyond the borders of Israel and brought his disciples to the far northern city of Caesarea Philippi.[14] There for the second time in recent weeks Jesus probed the understanding and loyalty of his core followers. In light of the rumors and speculations about his identity circulating among the people of the land, he asks, "what about you (pl.), who do you say I am?" (Mt 16:15). Peter represented the others with his confession: "You are the Christ, the Son of the living God." Jesus immediately affirmed Peter's words as God-given revelation (16:17). The faith of the disciples germinated early in their journey with Jesus (cf. Jn 1:41, 45, 49), but their understanding of the nature of his Messiahship grew over a long process of exposure and reflection. Rather than celebrate this dawning of understanding, Jesus immediately turned the conversation toward his impending suffering, death, and resurrection. Peter was caught off guard by such dire predictions and sought to dissuade the Lord from such thinking. The one who moments before uttered a confession with divinely given insight now is rebuked for active opposition to the purposes of God and for unwitting alignment with Satan (16:23)! A mixture of insight and confusion filled the minds of the disciples. They forthrightly exalt Jesus as King-Messiah, but do not yet grasp that he is also the suffering Servant.

The focus on his death from this point forward dominates Jesus' dialogue with the disciples (cf. Mk 9:30-32; 10:32-45). But this is balanced by corresponding promises of glory and vindication. Beyond his death and the disciples' own sacrifices as heralds of the suffering Servant, the Son of man will return in glory to reward the faithful (Mt 16:27). What follows is an enigmatic prophecy: "Some who are standing here will not taste death before they see the Son of man coming in his kingdom" (16:28). This may be a reference to the transfiguration event that follows. However, the apocalyptic accent on a glorious appearing with the angels to vindicate his people (v. 27) points toward the second advent of the Son of man. At that time he will consummate the kingdom that is only now in its inaugural phase. The ones "who are standing here" is a prophetic foreview of the final generation of witnesses who stand in solidarity with the first witnesses, the apostles. The Lord anticipates a period of indefinite duration in which his witnesses will proclaim him the suffering Servant and coming King to all nations. Some will even live until the arrival of the King. The disciples, then, must understand that all of the sacrifices—loss of possessions, shame, physical hardship, suffering and even death—pale in comparison to the glorious kingdom that will be their inheritance.

The inner circle of three disciples was given a glimpse of this glory on the mountain when Jesus was transfigured so that "his face shone like the sun, and his clothes became as white as the light" (Mt 17:2). The apostles needed this self-disclosure from their Lord and the authenticating voice of the Father that urged them to pay heed to his beloved Son (17:5). They needed reassurance that the kingdom, one for which they were challenged to sacrifice everything, held a future

---

[14] The **Later Galilean** period of ministry begins with a series of withdrawals to Tyre and Sidon (n.w.), the Decapolis (s.e.), and Caesarea Philippi (n.e.). This period extends from Summer to Fall, A.D. 29 (to the Feast of Tabernacles [Jn 7:2]; four months). It is covered in Mt 15:21-17:13; Mk 7:24-9:13; Lk 9:18-36b.

beyond the darkening present. The religious authorities claimed he was demon possessed. His earthly family accused him of mania. The crowds were growing distant from the healer who preferred the loneliness of the hills to their company. Many of the more promising followers turned back when Jesus' graphic language of eating his flesh and drinking his blood offended them. To the apostles the Lord seemed too taken up with thoughts of suffering, betrayal, and death. When Peter tried to cheer him up he was shouted down. Jesus here made it clear that beyond the cross of shame—his and theirs (Mt 16:24)—will be a crown of glory. The Transfiguration scene, bracketed as it is by two Passion predictions (Mt 16:21; 17:9, 12), revealed that the One who will suffer is God's Son, possessor of kingdom authority and majestic deity.

Dependent faith and believing prayer (Mt 17:14-20; Mk 9:14-29; Lk 9:37-43a)

Jesus and the three disciples descended Mt. Hermon and approached the area of Caesarea Philippi. From the transfiguration glory on the mountain they returned to the tortured lives of ordinary people. As they entered the town, they observed the other nine disciples surrounded by a large crowd. The controversy surrounded the disciples' inability to exorcise a demon from a young boy who had since childhood been thrown into convulsions and robbed of his speech. The boy's desperate father pleaded for Jesus to take pity on the boy. He had requested the disciples to help, "but they could not" (Mk 9:18). At Jesus' authoritative command the demon departed and the boy was restored (9:25-27).

The disciples were delegated the authority of exorcism in their formal commission to proclaim the kingdom (Mt 10:1, 8). Until now they had experienced unbroken success in casting out demons. They were surprised at their failure in this instance. Had they begun to view their authority as some kind of magical property to be used apart from humble dependence on God's power? Jesus attributed their failure to lack of believing prayer. Some forms of demonic possession are so deeply rooted they can only be defeated through importunate prayer (Mk 9:29). Even a small faith directed to the mighty God could break the most tenacious demonic strongholds, symbolized by the mountains around Caesarea Philippi (Mt 17:20-21). The disciples must believe in the potentials for kingdom breakthrough in the darkest corridors of human depravity and satanic oppression. They must also remember that exorcism is a kingdom ministry performed through dependent prayer, not a mechanical ability they now possess in isolation from its source and purpose. Their proclivity to triumphalism will emerge again in a few weeks and will once again be met with a gentle rebuke (cf. Lk 10:17-20).

First things first (Mt 8:19-22; Lk 9:57-62)

Nearly two years had passed since the twelve disciples had abandoned their homes and careers to follow Jesus into an unknown future. The initial excitement had long worn off. Along with thrilling experiences of lives changed by Jesus' power, were times of bitter debate with the religious leaders and the frustrating ambivalence of the crowds. Now Jesus was determined to leave their beloved Galilee for Jerusalem, a city filled with long-robed Pharisees and Sadducees deeply hostile to their Master (Lk 9:51). As they traveled south through Samaria and Perea, Jesus invited others to follow him, just as he had called the four fishermen and the tax collector. One by one these would-be followers offered reasons why they could not make such a commitment. One man offered to follow "wherever you go," but turned back when Jesus spoke of a nomadic life with few earthly comforts, the absence of social prestige, and no offers of financial security (Lk 9:57-58). Crowds, miracles, and excitement were in this man's mind in the offer to follow Jesus. Along with those things, Jesus said, would come deprivation, loneliness, hostility, and no permanent home to retreat to and feel secure.

A second man heard the call to follow and replied, "Lord, first let me go and bury my father" (9:59). In light of his father's death the request for a delay seems like a reasonable one. Jesus' reply comes across as harsh and unloving: "Let the (spiritually) dead bury the (physically) dead, but you go and proclaim the kingdom of God" (9:60). However, the uncompromising demand of Jesus is what was needed in this man's case, even as the rich young ruler was told to sell all of his possessions or their grip on his heart would remain (Lk 18:22). Behind the term "first" Jesus detected one whose supreme priority was filial allegiance. To become a true disciple there must be a decisive transfer of loyalties so that the kingdom and its righteousness becomes one's "first" pursuit (Mt 6:33).

Another offered to follow, but only after he "first" return home and say good-by to his family (Lk 9:61). Jesus again detected behind this 'reasonable' request a division of loyalty, a lack of resolve, the pull of earthly ties over kingdom values. Just as it is impossible for the farmer who "puts his hand to the plow and looks back" to run a straight furrow, so the disciple must maintain an undivided focus on the mandate to proclaim and live out God's lordship through faith and repentance. Those who aspire to enter the Jesus way would have to do so through a gate that is small and narrow from the start (Mt 7:13-14). These terse interchanges, overheard by the twelve disciples, served as a reminder to them that, along with promises of future reward, the pursuit of the kingdom in the present age would be a hard one.

Seventy (two) missionaries[15] (Lk 10:1-24)

The twelve apostles were the foundational representatives of Jesus and had proclaimed the kingdom throughout the villages of Galilee on three separate tours. They had been instructed to pray for more laborers for the harvest (Mt 9:37-38). The Lord of the harvest now answered those prayers and expanded the laborers to seventy, which included the twelve (Lk 10:1a; cf. Lk 22:35). These seventy (or seventy-two) people correspond to the number of names in the table of nations in Genesis 10. The symbolism seems to be that Jesus is sending out missionaries of the kingdom that correspond to the number of (ethnic) nations on earth and are thus a harbinger of the coming universal proclamation of the gospel (Lk 24:47-

---

[15] This discourse and tour occurred in the **Later Judean** period of ministry: Fall A.D. 29, from the Feast of Tabernacles (Jn 7:2, 11; September) to the Feast of Dedication (Jn 10:22; December). It is covered in Jn 7:11-10:39; Lk 9:51-13:21. Jesus' movements are to Jerusalem (Jn 7-10), to Judea and Bethany, (Lk 10-13) and once again to Jerusalem (Jn 10:22-39).

49; Acts 1:8).[16] What is clear is that Jesus enlisted and authorized kingdom workers far beyond the initial twelve. Even these seventy, like the twelve earlier, were enjoined to pray for still more laborers for the harvest (Lk 10:1-2). The seventy missionaries went two by two through the villages of Perea and Judea to prepare for the Lord's follow-up visit.

The missionaries' practice of ministry corresponds to the earlier instructions given the twelve at their formal commissioning (Mt 10:5-16), except that they are no longer explicitly precluded from evangelizing Gentiles or Samaritans (Mt 10:5-6). The correspondence points toward normative principles designed to govern the manner in which his kingdom workers go about their task, even if the context of ministry is a particular one.

1. Simplicity of lifestyle (Lk 10:3-4; cf. Mt 10:9-10): Like lambs among wolves, they enter a mission fraught with danger. No money bag or extra pair of sandals means they will be dependent on God and his people for their basic needs. To refrain from salutations signifies the urgency of their message that must be delivered without distraction.

2. Authoritative message of blessing and judgment (Lk 10:5-15; cf. Mt 10:11-16): Their message is "the kingdom of God has drawn near," one authenticated by healing miracles (Lk 10:9, 11). A benediction of peace is to be pronounced on the receptive towns and homes, but a warning of strict judgment on those whose refusal of hospitality reveals their spiritual obduracy.

3. Missional solidarity (Lk 10:16; cf. Mt 10:40): The ground of their authority is the unbroken solidarity between the Father, Jesus, and his disciples. They are mediators of the kingdom mission committed to them by Jesus and to Jesus by the Father. Theirs is thus a derived authority. The disciples must maintain fidelity to the traditions passed on to them by their Lord. As they accurately proclaim revealed truth, the listeners possess a grave responsibility to hear with their hearts, not just their ears, for their eternal destiny depends on it.

Jesus followed the seventy disciples to the towns of Perea and Judea that they had visited in their teams of two. He then gathered them for a debriefing session regarding the results of the tour. The disciples exulted in their power to exorcise demons "in your name" (Lk 10:17). Jesus detected here the danger of misplaced priorities, arrogance in success, and a propensity for power encounter over truth encounter. His rebuke, however, is gentle. In the exorcisms, both his and theirs, Jesus saw the sacking of Satan's kingdom, one being displaced by the dawning of

---

[16] The UBS *Greek New Testament* committee sees the external and internal evidence of the readings "seventy" and "seventy two" in Luke 10:1 equally divided and thus has inserted δυο in square brackets (Bruce M. Metzger, *A Textual Commentary on the Greek New Testament*, 2nd ed. [United Bible Societies, 1994]: 126-127). The LXX of Genesis 10 includes seventy-two names and possibly helps account for the variant reading. An alternative view is that Jesus is viewed as the new Moses who appointed seventy elders to be administrative leaders and share his burdens (Exod 18:25-26; Num 11:14-25). However, it is Matthew's Gospel that is generally seen as expressing that typological connection rather than Luke.

the messianic rule (10:18; cf. Mt 12:28-29). He has delegated to them authority to dispel the enemy's destructive hold on human beings, symbolized by stinging scorpions and biting snakes. The Lord did not discourage their joy, but redirected and purified it. Their deepest level of satisfaction should spring not from the submission of evil spirits, but from the security they possess as God's beloved ones whose names are listed in the heavenly registry of the redeemed. Jesus' greatest joy comes from his relationship with the Father and the gracious work of the Father in securing the fellowship of believers with him in the inaugurated and soon to be consummated kingdom. Jesus wants his disciples to share this joy. He reminded them of the inestimable privilege of standing on the threshold of the long-awaited kingdom, though it comes in a form they did not expect, namely, God's reign operative in the lives of people mediated through the coming sacrifice of the suffering Servant (10:23-24).

Who are the true kingdom citizens? (Lk 13:22-30)

Jesus had now left Judea and was traveling with his disciples through the towns and villages of Perea on his way to Jerusalem (Lk 13:22; cf. Lk 9:51).[17] In recent days Jesus had spoken about judgment for those who fail to heed his call to repentance (Lk 13:1-9), as well as the incredible expansion of the kingdom which will follow its inconspicuous beginnings (Lk 13:18-21). The admonitory tones, however, filled the mind of an unnamed listener who brought forth the question: "Lord, are only a few people going to be saved?" (13:23). The listener must have witnessed the bitter clash of values between Jesus and the Pharisees (cf. Lk 13:10-17) and reasoned as follows: If the majority of the people in Israel, especially the religious leaders who are trained in the law, are refusing Jesus' offer of the kingdom, how few there must be who will ultimately be saved.

The Lord did not answer the question with theological abstraction, but confronted the listener with the urgency of the kingdom offer. "You strive to enter," he commanded, for the door of entrance is narrow and the opportunity for entrance is of limited duration. At the appointed time the door will be shut. Entrance is conditioned on a repentant and believing heart, not on Jewish lineage. The true kingdom citizens are those of the line of faith with Abraham, Isaac, and Jacob, not merely racial descendants of the patriarchs. Jesus anticipated people from the four corners of the earth streaming to join the messianic feast, one of his favorite metaphors for future kingdom blessing (13:29; cf. Lk 14:7-24; Mt 8:11; 25:1-10; 26:29). Surprising reversals of destiny will characterize God's final sifting of the human race. Those who are last now, ignorant Gentiles, will be first then; those who have the privilege of hearing the kingdom offer first, the people and leaders of Israel, will be last. The quantitative question has thus been given a qualitative answer. It is not a matter of how many will be saved, but who will be saved. Jesus had consistently made faith/repentance the sole condition for kingdom citizenship and not racial lineage or religious sophistry (Lk 4:25-27; 6:46-49; 7:9; 8:4-15;

---

[17] The **Early Perean** ministry is recorded in Lk 13:22-17:10; Jn 10:40-42; 11:1-54. Jesus' ministry during this period of perhaps six to eight weeks is during the Winter of A.D. 30. Jesus' movements are through Perea to Bethany to Jerusalem and then north to Ephraim.

10:25-37; 11:29-52). Over time and through painful experiences the ethno-centric disciples would come to understand and embrace this matter of utmost importance to their Lord, namely, that the kingdom is all about the heart (cf. Acts 10:34-35).

Banquet for the poor and afflicted (Lk 14:1-24)

Jesus often used provocation to press home his kingdom theology. Dining as a guest at the Sabbath meal in the home of a prominent Pharisee was not the diplomatic choice for a healing miracle. With the Pharisees "carefully watching him," Jesus instantaneously healed a man with dropsy (Lk 14:1-2). The Pharisees held their tongues. Were they afraid of being discredited as shepherds of the people for such callousness, one that valued legal technicalities of greater weight than the suffering of a fellow human being? He then upbraided his fellow guests for seeking to polish their image by scrambling for recognized seats of honor around the table. He criticized his host for limiting his guest list to rich friends who would return the favor. The parable of the lavish banquet was his way of contrasting kingdom values with those of Israel's elite religious class. Preparations were made and invitations sent out to the preferred guests (14:16-17). Those who were invited accepted the offer initially, but then, at the last minute, offered excuses why they could not attend, namely, concerns over material possessions, career, and family relationships. So the angry master sent his servant out again with fresh invitations for the poor, injured, blind, and lame. They were literally taken by the hand and brought in, not out of coercion but because they believed themselves unworthy to enjoy such a sumptuous feast (14:21-22). Then the servant was sent to compel all that were willing to join the banquet until all the seats were filled. The point of the parable lies in Jesus' concluding interpretive comment: "not one of those people who were invited will get a taste of my banquet" (14:24). The opportunity for the disenfranchised and distant ones was due to the forfeiture by the original invitees of their place at the banquet. The master wanted his house to be filled with guests (v. 23). All who will respond to God's gracious invitation to submit to his reign over their lives, forsaking all notions of self-righteousness and ethnic priority, may freely partake of redemptive blessing (cf. Lk 13:28-29). The original particularized mission to the lost sheep of Israel (Mt 10:5-6) is giving way to the universal summons of "whosoever will."

Heaven's joy over the sinner who repents (Lk 15:1-32)

To eat with someone meant, in the noble traditions of oriental hospitality, to accept them, to treat them with dignity, to relish in their company without preconditions. Jesus clearly enjoyed sitting down to a meal with "tax collectors and sinners" (cf. Lk 5:29-30; 7:34, 39; 11:37-38; 14:12-14). To the Pharisees and legal scholars that criticized such associations Jesus delivered three parables (Lk 15:1-2). First, a lost sheep (1 of 100) is earnestly sought and found. Its return to the fold becomes the source of great personal and communal rejoicing (15:3-6). Second, one of ten silver coins is lost. The woman lights a lamp, sweeps the house, and diligently searches for the coin "until she finds it." She invites her neighbors to celebrate with her the recovery of the lost coin (15:8-10). Third, a father distributes shares of his estate to his two sons. The younger son departs and squanders his portion on immoral living, so that he is reduced to the verge of starvation as a keeper of swine. For a Jewish son in a privileged family, this degraded condition is almost unimaginable. At his lowest point he comes to his senses and decides to return to his father. As he makes his way back, he plans his confession of guilt before God and his father. He will make a humble plea for forgiveness, not restored status. Seeing his silhouette in the distance, the father is moved by compassion, runs to, embraces (lit. "falls on his neck") and kisses his son. He celebrates the son's return with gifts of a robe, ring, shoes and a fatted calf. The eldest son protests that his own faithfulness has gone unrewarded, while "this son of yours" who squandered the inheritance is lavished with gifts! The father defends his action. It is fitting to celebrate, he replies, for "this brother of yours was dead and is alive again; he was lost and is found" (Lk 15:11-32).

Jesus provided the interpretation to the first two parables and left the listeners to figure out the meaning of the third. The parables of the lost sheep and the lost coin symbolize the joy that fills the heart of God when a sinner repents, that is, when a person alienated by sin is brought into the fellowship and rule of his kingdom (Lk 15:7, 10). The searching shepherd and housewife represent God the lover of souls who will do whatever it takes to find and bring back the lost. By analogy the prodigal son and the father represent the lost sinner and the forgiving God respectively. In all three parables the theme is the Heavenly Father's yearning love for lost people (15:7, 10, 20b-24, 32). The offer is not just restoration, but a summons to heartfelt repentance as the way to restoration (15:7, 10, 18-19, 21). Jesus would not compromise his call to repentance, faith and surrender by his association with sinners. But neither would he make oral traditions based upon the old covenant concept of ritual purity a precondition for genuine friendship and table fellowship. The first and last parables contain inferences that condemn the exclusive attitudes of the Pharisees: ninety-nine righteous persons who do not need to repent (15:7b); the older son who pouts over his father's treatment of his restored brother (15:28-30). The real prodigal sons alienated from their father, he implied, were the religious leaders. The real tragedy was that they saw no need to repent and return.

Rewards that dwarf the sacrifices[18] (Mt 19:16-30; Mk 10:17-31; Lk 18:18-30)

A young man approached Jesus and asked what he must do to inherit eternal life. He is identified as rich, young, and religious, probably a lay leader in the synagogue. The young man was at least concerned about vital issues, not casuistry over food laws and the Sabbath. However, his mind gravitated toward works and achievement rather than repentance and faith. Jesus kept the conversation on the same plane and demanded that he obey the law's commandments. For the one who can obey the law perfectly, Jesus implied, there is a hypothetical offer of

---

[18] The **Later Perean** ministry is recorded in Lk 17:11-19:28; Mt 19:1-20:34; Mk 10:1-52. This period of perhaps six to eight weeks is during the late Winter and early Spring of A.D. 30. Jesus' movements are from the border of Galilee and Samaria to Jerusalem via Perea and Jericho.

eternal life (Mt 19:17b).[19] The standard of complete obedience is set forth to confront the young man with the stark reality that he is a lawbreaker and must look elsewhere for eternal life. Only when he recognizes that the standard is unattainable and admits his spiritual bankruptcy will he turn from human merit to God's grace. Even when he proceeded to defend his piety from childhood, the man sensed something was missing: "What do I still lack?" (Mt 19:20). Jesus made the radical demand that he first sell all his possessions, give them to the poor, then come and follow him. What hindered the young man from following Jesus was a heart entangled with enjoyment, pursuit, and management of his abundant material possessions. He was able to concentrate his energies on the task of external piety, but could not extricate himself from the treasures that held a firm grip on his heart. Jesus' demand saddened rather than angered him, pointing to a divided heart yearning for but unable to find release. Apart from God's liberating grace, Jesus concluded, it is impossible for a rich person to be freed from the binding distractions that great wealth brings, just as it is impossible for a camel to pass through the hole of a sewing needle.

The disciples were astonished at this final assessment. Their surprise indicates they viewed material wealth as a sign of God's favor. One need only look at the aristocratic members of the Jewish Sanhedrin to see how piety and wealth complemented one another. The disciples asked, if the rich cannot be saved, who then can be saved (Lk 18:26; cf. 13:23)? Jesus replied that all people are potentially redeemable because salvation depends on the ability of God, not on the extremity of the human condition. Peter suddenly interjected into the conversation the great sacrifice he and the other disciples had made when they became his followers: "We have left all we had to follow you" (Lk 18:28). He wanted Jesus to acknowledge how different they were from this rich man who could not bear such loss. The Lord did not castigate them for such boasting, but gently corrected their shortsightedness. One can never outgive God. Both in the present life and in the life they will enjoy in the consummated kingdom, to be ushered in at the return of the Son of man (Mt 19:28), there will be incomparable rewards for those who have sacrificed possessions, family ties, comfort, and security in order to extend God's rule among people (Lk 18:29-30).

Mission of the Son of man (Lk 19:1-10)

Jesus was passing through Jericho on his way for the final time to Jerusalem. The wealthy chief officer of the tax district of Jericho, named Zacchaeus, wanted to see this Jesus who was attracting so much attention from the crowds. Being short, he climbed up the branches of the sycamore tree to get a glimpse. When Jesus reached the spot he looked up, called Zacchaeus by name, and invited himself to a meal at his home. Jesus perceived that the deep desire of Zacchaeus to meet him was more than superficial curiosity. Zacchaeus came down and gladly

---

[19] Paul quotes Leviticus 18:5 twice, the Old Testament text that makes the same hypothetical, but unattainable, offer of life through perfect obedience to the law (Rom 10:5; Gal 3:12). James underscores the law's demand for perfect, not relative, conformity to its demands. Anything less than total compliance renders one a lawbreaker (Jas 2:10-11).

welcomed him to his home. The religionists murmured about Jesus having table fellowship with a sinner like Zacchaeus, for tax collectors were viewed as extortionists and traitors. Zacchaeus, keenly aware of the criticisms, defended his integrity by citing his record of generosity toward the poor. He offered to make four-fold restitution for anyone he defrauded, even though the law required only double restitution (Ex 22:4, 7, 9). In this offer Jesus detected a repentant heart and pronounced Zacchaeus' salvation as a true son of Abraham, one justified like his forefather by faith (19:9; Gen 15:6). Jesus' necessary visit to the home of Zacchaeus was a particular act of obedience to his divinely appointed mission: "For The Son of man came to seek and to save that which was lost" (19:10).[20] Jesus was on a mission to search for and find those who are lost and bring them under God's saving rule. The murmurers could only see a civil servant of Rome, lax to Jewish traditions, greedy for gain, and friendly with the enemy. Jesus saw a lost human being who needed to hear of God's saving mercy.

Mountain-moving faith (Mt 21:18-22; Mk 11:12-14, 20-25)

On Monday morning of the final week of his earthly life Jesus and his disciples made their way from Bethany across the Mount of Olives toward Jerusalem. Jesus saw a fig tree, but was disappointed to find that, though its leaves signaled the promise of fruit, there were no figs. Jesus pronounced a curse upon the fig tree which, occurring the day before the cleansing of the temple, was clearly a symbolic condemnation of the religious leadership of Israel. These leaders pretended to be fruitful tenders of the fig tree of Israel, but were actually barren purveyors of spiritual death.[21]

The next morning as they retraced their steps the disciples saw the same fig tree, now withered from the roots. How could a leafy tree become utterly barren in twenty-four hours, they wondered? Their surprise was born out of failure to believe Jesus' authoritative command the day before. Rather than develop the theological meaning of the symbolism, Jesus used it as an opportunity to teach his disciples a lesson on the possibilities of faith. His following words are a command: "Have faith in God" (Mk 11:22).[22] As his life was drawing to a close, Jesus wanted the disciples to learn to exercise faith in God for themselves, rather than continuing to live vicariously through his faith. He specified several features of authentic faith. First, faith is unwavering trust in God's willingness and ability to do what is humanly impossible, like transporting a mountain from here to there (11:23). Second, faith is expressed in concrete prayers and in the confidence that God will do the very thing that is requested of him. Jesus viewed prayer not as a

---

[20] The visit to Zacchaeus' house was a divinely constrained one (lit. "it is necessary [δει] for me to stay in your house" [19:5]). The saving mission of Jesus is what compelled him to seek out Zacchaeus (19:10, causal γαρ).

[21] The fig tree and its figs are common symbols of Israel in the Old Testament (Jer 8:13; 24:1-8; 29:17; Hos 9:10, 16; Micah 7:1-6). The indictment is not of Israel racially, but of Israel theologically as represented in the religious establishment (cf. Lk 13:6-9).

[22] The words could also be translated, "you have the faithfulness of God" (ἐχετε can be either present indicative or present imperative, second person plural form). In this rendering Jesus gives prominence to the faithful character of God as the object of their faith.

subjective exercise to sanctify the attitudes of the one who prays (however much that may be true), but an objective transaction that links the request to its realization (11:24; cf. Jn 14:13-14; 15:7; 16:23). Third, the spirit of unforgiveness toward another person saps faith of its energy and short-circuits the power supply that connects the request to the answer (11:25). Jesus envisioned the kingdom being extended into the frontiers of darkness through the audacious faith of his disciples directed toward a mighty God.

Inter-advent age of tribulation and proclamation (Mt 24:1-35; Mk 13:1-37; Lk 21:5-36)

Tuesday of Passion week was a long day of controversy. The disciples had listened in as an assortment of religious and political alliances sought unsuccessfully to discredit Jesus. As they departed from the outer court of the temple, the disciples called attention to the magnificence of the temple complex (Mt 24:1-2). Jesus made the shocking prediction that the temple would soon be reduced to rubble. The disciples seem to have missed the gravity of Jesus' earlier lament over the coming desolation of Jerusalem (23:37-39). Upon their arrival at the Mount of Olives, the disciples probed him about his ominous prediction: "When will this happen, and what will be the sign of your coming and of the end of the age?" (24:3). The extended inquiry seems to indicate that the disciples envisaged the coming of the Son of man to occur at the same time as the desolation of the temple.[23]

Jesus answered the question in the extended Olivet discourse (Mt 24:4-25:46). The most natural way of interpreting Jesus' language, in this writer's view, is to see the near event, the destruction of Jerusalem, serving as a historical anticipation of the distant event, the return of the Son of man at the end of the age. This bifocal or bicameral approach, whereby the prophet views a distant event through the descriptive lens of a near event, is a common feature of Old Testament prophecy.[24] The discourse expresses a preterist-futurist polarity. First, the present interadvent age is previewed in Matthew 24:4-14. Second, the fall of Jerusalem is set forth in 24:15-28 with a double reference to the final stage of human history before the parousia. Third, the return of the Son of man in glory to consummate his kingdom is described in 24:29-31. It must be remembered that this is a private discourse given to Jesus' closest followers to instruct them on what to expect in the days ahead as they carry out their mission to be heralds of his kingdom.

1. Antecedent signs will take place to indicate the end is near but not yet (24:4-8). These are "the beginning of birth pains" (v. 8), an Old Testament expression for the period of travail or distress for God's people that precedes the arrival of the messianic kingdom (cf. Isa 13:8; 26:17; Jer 4:31; 6:24; Micah 4:9-10).

---

[23] In Mt 24:3 the question is framed in two parts, which might suggest a distinction between the (near) event of the temple's desolation and the (far) event of the parousia and end of time. However, in the Markan (13:4) and Lukan (21:7) parallels the two events are merged; the two questions thus concern the timing and antecedent sign of the singular composite event.

[24] G. B. Caird, *The Language and Imagery of the Bible* (London: Duckworth, 1980): 256-268.

These doctrinal, political, and natural disturbances will extend through the entire interadvent age and be accompanied by intense periods of persecution for the kingdom witnesses (24:9-14).

(i)   False Christs that deceive many (24:4-5)

(ii) Wars and rumors of wars; conflicts between nations (24:6-7a)

(iii) Famines, earthquakes (24:7b)

(iv) Many levels of persecution and adversity: arrest, martyrdom, betrayal by apostates, deception of many by false teachers, increase of wickedness, cold orthodoxy (24:9-12). The tribulations serve to sift true believers, whose faith is evidenced by perseverance, from false professors (24:13).

(v)   In the context of persecution the gospel of the kingdom is proclaimed to all the nations of the world (24:14).[25]

2.   Daniel's "abomination of desolation" (24:15; cf. Dan 8:13; 9:27; 11:31; 12:11) was initially fulfilled when Antiochus Epiphanes in 168 B.C. erected an altar to Zeus Olympius in the temple courtyard in place of the brazen altar of burnt offering (cf. 1 Maccab 1:45-54; 2 Maccab 6:2). However, the language of Matthew 24:16-20 and especially Luke 21:20-24 seem to describe the coming destruction of Jerusalem when it will be surrounded by armies and the inhabitants put to the sword.[26] A still further realization in the multi-stage fulfillment of Daniel's prophecy will take place in the "great tribulation" at the denouement of human history (24:21). This will be a time of unprecedented suffering for the people of God and of the deceptive work of the Antichrist (24:22-24). The "times of the Gentiles" (Lk 21:24) may refer to the entire period between the first and second advents of Christ in which the church fulfills her mission to proclaim the gospel to the nations. This period of proclamation will end at the return of the Son of man.

3.   After the sustained persecution of the interadvent age, including both preliminary and final tribulations (24:9, 22), the Son of man will return to earth in a glorious display of salvation and judgment (24:30). Like the flashing of lightning across the sky or the gathering of vultures around a carcass (24:27-28), the event will be clearly recognizable. Cosmic disturbances will signal his return (24:29). Those who have rejected the offer of the kingdom will mourn in despair over their judgment (24:30). Angels will be sent to the four corners of the earth to gather the elect for their places in the consummated kingdom (24:31).

4.   The heralds of the kingdom, then, must carry out their mission with urgency as they strain toward the final day of accountability. Though they should be sensitive to the antecedent signs that presage his return, believers must remember that the events of the end time could unfold very rapidly (24:32-35). God the Father alone knows the exact time of the Lord's return (24:36). In the midst of the normal activities of life, which continue unabated until the

---

[25] The redemptive mission to the Gentiles (τα ἐθνη) is a recurrent theme in Matthew's Gospel (1:1; 2:1-12; 3:9; 4:15-16; 8:11-12; 10:18; 12:18, 21; 21:43; 24:14; 28:19-20).

[26] The horror and savagery of the siege of Jerusalem is described in similar language in Josephus, *Wars of the Jews*, V: X: 1-5.

end, believers are to live responsibly, compassionately, courageously, and expectantly during the Lord's absence (24:37-44). The five parables that follow are a summons to vigilance and faithfulness in the intervening time of delay:

(i)   Absent master and entrusted servants (Mk 13:33-37): like servants who faithfully carry out their assigned tasks while the master is away, ready and not caught off guard when he returns.

(ii) Homeowner and thief (Mt 24:43-44): like the homeowner who keeps watch and thus prevents his house from being plundered by a thief.

(iii) Good and wicked servants (Mt 24:45-51): like the wise and faithful steward who is placed in charge of his master's household, carefully carries out his duties, and is entrusted with even greater stewardship at the master's return.

(iv) Ten virgins (Mt 25:1-13): like five wise bridesmaids who are prepared for delay, but also ready when the bridegroom suddenly summons them at midnight.

(v)   Talents (Mt 25:14-30): like the good and faithful servants who take the talents entrusted to them and invest and multiply them for the benefit of their master.

Eschatological sifting of the human race (Mt 25:31-46)

Jesus concluded the Olivet discourse by impressing upon the disciples the gravity of the commission to be heralds of the rule of God. The authoritative proclamation of the kingdom binds for judgment or releases for salvation the listeners according to their heart response (cf. Mt 16:19; 18:18). At the Son of man's glorious return to establish his reign over the universe, his first act is one of judgment. All the nations of the earth are gathered before him and individuals are separated into two groups. The sheep of the flock represent his beloved children who once were lost sheep, have been found by the good shepherd, and have gone out among wolves to testify of his grace (Mt 9:36; 10:16; 18:12-14; 26:31). The goats are a symbol of those outside the redeemed community who have refused to submit to God's lordship over their lives. The King first addresses the sheep on the right, then the goats on the left. He recalls the good works of the former, who are surprised at their mention ("When did we . . . ?"). The King views the good works as directed toward him because of his solidarity with "these brothers of mine" who were visited in prison, fed, given water, and clothed. The good works of the redeemed ones, then, are evidential of their faith and loyalty to the King and also instrumental in promoting the kingdom. Those on the left, conversely, are equally surprised at their rebuke ("When did we not . . .?"), which indicates a failure to recognize their need for repentance, the first condition of kingdom entrance. In the context of the discourse, the "least of these brothers of mine" (25:40, 45) must refer to Jesus' disciples who go forth to proclaim the kingdom at great personal sacrifice (cf. Mt 12:48-50; 23:8; 28:10). In prosecuting their mission they are imprisoned, become hungry and thirsty, become ill, and are at times without warm clothing. The good deeds done to Jesus' faithful brothers show that the benefactors are equally loyal to the elder Brother. There is a final separation of the sheep from the goats. The former ones are invited to inherit the kingdom, while the latter are banished to eternal punishment.

Arresting the attention of unbelievers (Jn 13:34-35; 15:18-16:4; 17:9-26)

On Thursday evening at the end of the Passover meal Jesus spoke to the gathered disciples of his coming suffering with the language of glorification (Jn 13:31-32; cf.12:23; 17:1). His impending sacrificial death would secure redemption. The disciples' transformed lives and courageous witness would glorify the Father and the Son. Before departing the upper room for Gethsemane, the Lord issued his followers the "new command" to love one another as he loved them. The newness rested not in the formal requirement, for to love one's neighbor was a fundamental ethical command in the Old Testament (Lev 19:18). The comparative clause, "as I have loved you," spells out the transcendent character of love under the new covenant. The unconditional love of Jesus demonstrated in the cross becomes the paradigm for how believers must treat one another. Not only is self-giving love the mark of the true disciple, it is also the visible means that will arrest the attention of unbelievers (13:35). Though the hostility of the world, a value system that leaves God out of its motive and purpose,[27] would remain unchanged, the sacrificial love of committed disciples would have the power to attract unbelieving people to Jesus and bring them under his lordship.

Such love, however, would be tested and refined in suffering. As in the Olivet discourse (Mt 24:9-14), so in the farewell discourse,[28] Jesus placed the interadvent witness of the disciples in the context of opposition (Jn 15:18-16:4). Because of their solidarity with Jesus the hatred of the world would fall upon them as it did upon him. This assumes the faithful proclamation by disciples of the redemption and judgment preached by Jesus during his earthly ministry. In spite of hostile circumstances, the Spirit of truth from the Father would empower their fearless confession of Jesus (15:26-27).

The farewell discourse concludes with the sad prediction of Jesus' imminent departure, followed by a benediction of peace for those who will face trouble in the world but draw strength from his resurrection victory (Jn 16:31-33). In his longest recorded intercessory prayer Jesus renewed his commitment to finish the work of redemption entrusted to him by the Father (17:1-5). He prayed for the protection of the tiny, vulnerable group of present disciples (17:6-19), and requested protection for the future generations of disciples "who will believe in me through their message" (17:20-25). Jesus was confident that the Spirit from the Father would protect, sanctify and empower the little band of disciples to fulfill his great

[27] The usage of κοσμος for the value system or world view that leaves God out and is under the controlling influence of Satan is frequent in John's writings (Jn 8:23; 9:39; 12:25, 31; 14:30; 16:11; 18:36; 1 Jn 2:15-17; 4:3-5; 5:4-5, 19).
[28] The second part of the discourse may not have been delivered in the upper room. One must note Jesus' exhortation, "Come now: let us leave" (Jn 14:31b). This is either (1) an expression of intent to leave the upper room shortly, but not actual departure, in which case the discourse and prayer of Jn 15-17 were given while still in the upper room (actual departure from the upper room recorded in Mt 26:30; Mk 14:26; Lk 22:39; Jn 18:1); or (2) it indicates actual departure from the upper room, in which case the discourse and prayer of Jn 15-17 are given as Jesus and his disciples walk from Jerusalem toward Gethsemane (Mt 26:30; Mk 14:26; Lk 22:39 are parallels to Jn 14:31b, while Jn 18:1 refers to departure from the city itself).

commission to proclaim the gospel to the nations.

The impact of the faith community upon the world (i.e. unbelieving humanity)[29] would depend upon its love-grounded unity (17:21-23). The nature of this oneness is disclosed in Jesus' prayer. First, this is no artificially contrived unity that compromises doctrinal purity, for the prayer for unity is preceded by the prayer for consecration: "Sanctify them by the truth; your word is truth" (17:17). Second, this is a relational unity that pursues oneness of motive, the honor of the Father and the Son, and oneness of mission, the building of God's kingdom community among the nations. This organic, relational unity, patterned after the oneness of Father and Son (17:21-22), would present a united voice of testimony to the world of lost humanity. Third, the attention of unbelievers (the world) would be arrested by a unity grounded in the transcendent love of Father and Son experienced among believers. Human beings without the knowledge of God would recognize Christ's disciples as a much-loved people (17:23; cf. 13:34-35). Conversely, a fractured community of faith with a voice divided due to intramural disputes over nonessential matters would discredit the witness and alienate rather than attract the attention of unbelieving people.

Testamentary Commission (Jn 20:19-23; Mt 28:16-20; Lk 24:44-53; Acts 1:3-12)

Three of the four canonical Gospels conclude with the testamentary charge Jesus delivered to his disciples. This "great commission," as it is often called, was spoken at three separate appearances of the risen Lord. Coming as it does in the aftermath of the easter event, the message of the kingdom entrusted to the disciples now takes on its full-orbed character, that is, the gospel of the crucified and risen Lord Jesus Christ (1 Cor 15:3-4). John's Gospel records the charge given after Jesus' appearance to the ten disciples in the upper room (Jn 20:19-23). Matthew's account relates the commission of the disciples on a mountain in Galilee (Mt 28:16-20). Luke-Acts contains the final words of Jesus before his ascension from the Mount of Olives (Lk 24:44-53; Acts 1:3-12). There is a solemn character to the redundancy. The risen Lord rested his legacy on the Spirit-energized obedience of the disciples to his final command. The provisions and parameters for its fulfillment are carefully detailed:

1. Missional continuity: The program of redemption was planned by the Father and carried out by his Son. The work of redemption accomplished by the Son is entrusted to disciples to proclaim to the nations. The Son is the great missionary of the Father and disciples in turn are his "sent ones" (Jn 20:21). The preparation, execution and proclamation stages of the redemptive program are in perfect solidarity, bound together by a driving passion to enter the world of lost humanity.

2. Internal empowerment: In his appearance to the ten disciples Jesus breathed on them and pronounced the reception of the Holy Spirit (Jn 20:22). This was an acted parable anticipatory of Pentecost when the Spirit would descend upon the Jerusalem believers (Lk 24:49; Acts 2:1-4). God the Father created

---

[29] The usage of κοσμος to refer to unbelieving human beings who were created by God, are now alienated from him, and are those for whom God sent his Son to redeem, is frequent in John's writings (Jn 1:10; 3:16, 17, 19; 7:7; 14:17, 19, 31; 15:18-19; 17:18, 21, 23; 1 Jn 2:2; 4:9, 14).

the universal church through his baptizing work with the Spirit (Acts 1:4-5; 11:15-17). The Spirit in turn empowers the church for its universal witness to the nations (Acts 1:8).

3. Royal authorization: The resurrection of Christ was the prequel to his exaltation to the right hand of the Father and his investiture as Lord and King (Acts 2:32-36; Php 2:9-11; cf. Dan 7:13-14; Ps 110:1). The exercise of universal authority both for salvation and judgment has been committed by the Father to the Son (Mt 28:18). The authorized ambassadors of the king go forth and proclaim forgiveness or retention of sins based on the response of the listeners (Jn 21:23).[30]

4. Comprehensive task: The central mandate is to disciple the nations, which incorporates both evangelism and teaching (Mt 28:19-20a).[31] Water baptism is the public verification of the personal response of faith to the gospel and incorporation into the community of faith subject to the lordship of the Triune God. Teaching new believers all the commands of Christ with a view to obedience will be the task of each generation of disciple-makers. The mandate, then, aims to bring new believers to submit every dimension of their lives to the lordship of Christ. Because the Lord Jesus Christ is invested with universal authority as Savior and Judge his teachings form the binding constitution for the transformed character and behavioral standards of the new covenant disciple.

5. Universal scope: All the peoples of the earth are viewed as potential disciples of the king. Jesus' constant concern for the non-Jewish peoples (Mt 4:15-16; 8:5-13; 10:18; 13:38; 24:14) now issues in a centrifugal mission to go, seek, find, and proclaim to "all the nations" that the suffering Servant is the exalted King (Mt 28:19; cf. Lk 24:47-48; Jn 20:21; Acts 1:8).

6. Benedictory presence: In the intervening period while he is physically absent, the Lord promises to mediate his presence to his disciples through the Holy Spirit (cf. Jn 14:16-18; 16:12-16). His continuing presence with the disciples encompasses "all the days until the consummation of the age" (Mt 28:20b). "Day by day and with each passing moment" the kingdom witnesses will draw strength from their constant Companion until time recedes into eternity and a tiny mustard seed becomes a mighty tree (Mt 13:31-32).

7. Anticipatory hope: Just before his ascension the apostles inquired if now, at last, he would usher the nation of Israel into her kingdom glory (Acts 1:6). The Lord neither corrected nor affirmed the implications of the question. They must, he countered, resist the temptation to speculate on the finer points of eschatology and leave the "times and seasons" to his sovereign disposition (1:7). Their task is to engage in ever-expanding concentric circles of witness

[30] The inferential conjunction οὖν (v. 19, "therefore") establishes the accomplishment of the mission (Mt 28:19-20a) as the logical and necessary consequence of Christ's investiture with universal authority (28:18).
[31] The main verb is the aorist imperative μαθητεύσατε. It is modified by three adverbial participles of attendant circumstance. The final two participles are in the present tense, thus durative in force, and fill out the ongoing activities included in the command to disciple the nations: baptizing (βαπτιζοντες) and teaching (διδασκοντες).

from their present neighborhood "to the ends of the earth" (1:8). The promise of his personal and visible return to earth was the angels' words that rang in their ears as he disappeared from their sight (1:11).

Leadership Profile of Jesus: Kingdom harvest through sacrifice

1. **Theology of the kingdom***: Though Jesus was not a trained rabbi with a polished academic resume, he communicated to his disciples a profound theology of the kingdom of God. The dynamic rule of God was now dawning in his earthly life, to be inaugurated at his death and resurrection, and to be consummated at his glorious return. Between the two advents the disciples will serve as the advance guard of the new messianic community comprised of all who submit to God's dynamic rule with faith and repentance. The kingdom will advance forcefully, but also with intense opposition. Satan is a defeated, but not yet vanquished foe. The kingdom heralds move forward through faith, prayerful dependence, fearless confession, and willingness to bear hardship, even at the cost of their physical lives. But the harvest is sure and the triumph of the kingdom certain. They go forth as brave warriors in a campaign whose victorious outcome is assured. Neither marginalized by setbacks nor triumphalistic over successes, the kingdom leaders imitate a Lord who is both suffering Servant and exalted King. All sacrifices, however, will become a distant memory when the kingdom assumes its glorious triumph at the return of the Son of man. Abundant rewards will be graciously distributed for even the smallest acts of faithful service like offering a drink of water to one who is thirsty. A proper understanding of the kingdom dignifies the toils of its heralds by investing them with eternal significance. To enter this saving rule and to promote it to others is worth sacrificing everything for.*

2. **Engagement-withdrawal pattern of training***: The training program of Jesus was not carried out in an antiseptic environment removed from the pains and prejudices of ordinary people. The four fishermen, then the tax collector, then the twelve, and finally the seventy all began their spiritual pilgrimage with evangelistic engagement. Three tours through the villages of Galilee and Perea introduced them to the unparalleled experience of seeing demon-scarred lives transformed by the power of God's rule. They encountered recalcitrant demons, ambivalent curiosity seekers, angry legalists, open-hearted pagans, broken-hearted prostitutes, desperate lepers, blind people, hemophiliacs, paralytics, and above all, sinners, lost sinners, that Jesus came to seek and to save (Lk 19:10). The Jesus Seminary combined active periods of evangelism with quiet periods of prayer to the Father. His students would learn to imitate him as he engaged in public ministry punctuated by regular periods of quiet withdrawal. Like their Lord they would be neither frenetic, unreflective activists nor distant, passive mystics. Courses in prayer, exegesis of the Old Testament, and worship were combined with field training in evangelism and spiritual warfare to provide a comprehensive development of their knowledge, character and practical skills.*

3. **Clarity of the mission***: In his testamentary commission Jesus articulated the mission of his disciples during the period of his physical absence: to disciple*

160

the nations by baptizing them in the name of the triune God and by teaching them to obey all of his commands. To borrow two other metaphors, one Jesus used at the beginning and one at the end of his ministry, disciples are called to fish for people (evangelism) and to feed the sheep who are enfolded in his flock (edification). Jesus would not tolerate mission drift. He was a vision caster, a resource provider, and a character and skill developer. His disciples must give due attention to both the evangelistic and pastoral dimensions of the mandate, for the spiritual quality of the kingdom communities would determine their effectiveness in impacting the world. A love-grounded unity among believers would capture the attention of unbelieving people and draw them into the community of the redeemed. Authentic kingdom leaders stay focused on the essentials, strive to maintain unity, and sound out a coherent message to a fractured world.

Chapter 15.
Kingdom righteousness through freedom

Preliminary questions to consider:
1. *What is at the heart (no pun intended) of Jesus' clash with the Pharisees?*
   How does Jesus understand and interpret the relationship of freedom and righteousness?
   What implications does Jesus' new covenant theology have for leadership training?
2. *What (rather, who) is the divine provision that enables a leader to embrace and live out Jesus' radical ethical demands?*
   How does the presence of the Paraclete condition the practice of discipling others?

Jesus and his apostles proclaimed the dawning of the kingdom of heaven in a context charged with religious and political ideologies. The Pharisees were the dominant religious party and had forged a faith-works synergism, one that stressed God's gracious election of Israel, as well as rigorous obedience to the teaching of the Mosaic law. The biblical teachings were supplemented by oral traditions that had grown over the four centuries since Malachi to massive proportions and, in practical effect, had achieved canonical status. The ordinary people of the land, especially in Galilee, were less rigorous in their adherence to rabbinical traditions, but fervent in their expectations of a Messiah who would free the nation from its Gentile oppressors and cleanse the temple from its corrupt priesthood. Thus the atmosphere was swirling with legalism, ethnocentrism, and socio-political activism. In this context Jesus carefully articulated, through action and word, distinctive kingdom values to his disciples. The righteousness demanded by the kingdom of God was a superior and different kind of righteousness than that taught by the Pharisees (Mt 5:20). The rule of God would accost the entire personality of an individual and community, searching the motives behind the actions. Jesus aimed at interior reconstruction rather than external conformity to a set of rules. He would equip his disciples to equip others by giving first priority to the heart as the governing force behind all kingdom activity. Such heart transformation would occur not by fencing in sinful human tendencies with extrabiblical standards. Rather, the renewal of the personality could take place only by first removing the binding shackles of tradition and restoring one's direct interface with the penetrating vitality of Holy Scripture. As the heart and the mind were invaded by the new covenant fulfillment of the ancient commands of Scripture, a real, not contrived, righteousness could spring forth. This, then, is the second great principle that Jesus both modeled and taught to his future kingdom leaders: Freedom in the new covenant is not the right to do as one pleases, but the Spirit-energized ability to live a life that pleases God because it reflects his character.

Fasting and feasting (Mt 9:14-17; Mk 2:18-22; Lk 5:33-39)

The disciples of John the Baptist were puzzled that Jesus and his disciples did not practice regular fasting. Others who observed the practice of voluntary fasting by both John's disciples and the Pharisees also asked why Jesus' disciples "go on eating and drinking" (Lk 5:33; cf. Lk 18:12). Jesus answered by setting forth three extended metaphors to explain what set his disciples apart from the others.

1. Bridegroom: The presence of the bridegroom bestows joy. The guests at the wedding feast celebrate with eating and drinking. Only when the bridegroom departs will mourning translate into fasting. It is appropriate for John's disciples to fast and mourn because his ministry demanded repentance in anticipation of the coming kingdom. In this analogy Jesus announced the messianic feast, an image of the dawning of the kingdom of God (cf. Mt 8:11; Lk 13:29; 14:15-24; Rev 19:7). He is the bridegroom now present with his betrothed people, a cause for joyous celebration, not mournful self-denial.

2. Old garment: A patch from a new garment cannot be used to repair a tear in an old garment. Not only will the new garment be ruined, the tear in the old garment will get worse, and the new patch will not match the old cloth. In every way the old is incompatible with the new. Jesus' parable contrasts the character of the law with that of the kingdom. The preparatory stage of salvation history (law) has run its course and has given way to the stage of fulfillment (inaugurated kingdom).

3. Old wineskins: If fermenting new wine is poured into brittle, worn out wineskins, they will burst and the wine will be spilled. New wine must be poured into new wineskins, if its contents are to be preserved and enjoyed. The parable means that new truth is to be accompanied by new forms for expressing that truth. Luke adds that one's acquired taste for old wine makes the new wine taste awful (Lk 5:39), that is, the tenacious defenders of old covenant traditions, the Pharisees, find Jesus' revolutionary offer of the kingdom distasteful.

In summary, Jesus echoes the prophecy of Jeremiah that God's "new covenant" is not like the covenant he made with Israel at Sinai (Jer 31:31-32). Its four "better promises"—internalization, intimacy, accessibility, and forgiveness—come to realization in the person and work of Jesus and culminate all the shadows of the old covenant (31:33-34; cf. Heb 8:6-13). The images of the wedding, the new cloth, and the new wine indicate the arrival of the kingdom that is marked by the presence of the king. Jesus does not satisfy the demands of the Pharisees who longed for the rejuvenation of the old order. Rather he fulfills the hopes of the prophets who, like Jeremiah, strained toward the arrival of something new and better. The new by its very character bursts the old, breaks out of its confines, and seeks a new shape to contain its dynamic life.

Lord of the Sabbath (Mt 12:1-14; Mk 2:23-3:6 Lk 6:1-11)

The hungry disciples began to pluck the heads of grain and eat them as they passed with Jesus through the fields in northern Galilee. The action itself was permitted in the Jewish law (Deut 23:25). However, the Pharisees quickly protested because the act was committed on the Sabbath. They interpreted the plucking as "reaping," one of thirty-nine categories of work forbidden on the Sabbath in rabbinical teaching.[1] The mindset of the Pharisees was to restrain sinful human behavior by fencing it in with an extensive array of regulations. The tragic result of the centuries' long process of scribal accretion was that the Old Testament precepts became obscured. Even the rabbis at times lamented that they had lost touch with Holy Scripture: "The rules about the Sabbath, Festal-offerings, and Sacrilege are as mountains hanging by a hair, for Scripture is scanty and the rules are many."[2]

Jesus turned to the Old Testament narrative to remind the Pharisees that when David and his men came to Nob the high priest Ahimelech fed the men with the consecrated bread which had just been replaced in the tabernacle by fresh hot loaves (1 Sam 21:1-6).[3] Though this was a technical infringement of the law, since the priests had exclusive right to eat the "bread of the Presence" (Ex 25:30; Lev 24:9), concern for the physical needs of the people superseded the letter of the law. Further, Jesus argued, the priests themselves formally violate the Sabbath command against work by performing their cultic duties in the temple on the seventh day (Mt 12:5). The Pharisees viewed themselves as holy defenders of God's law against a subversive Galilean rabbi whose disciples were treating the Sabbath command with contempt. Jesus, however, looked deeper and sought to recover the original intention of the Sabbath ordinance: "The Sabbath was made for man, not man for the Sabbath" (Mk 2:27). In other words, the original divine purposes for the Sabbath were rest for man's body and nurture of man's soul in undistracted worship of God. Just as mercy prevails over animal sacrifice (Mt 12:7, quot. Hos 6:6), so human need takes priority in the divine economy over technical compliance. Jesus ultimately appealed to his own authority as Lord of the Sabbath to support his interpretation (Mt 12:8; Mk 2:28; Lk 6:5). His final appeal unmasks the central issue at stake between him and his detractors: not only have they lost sight of the deeper intent of the law, they also have failed to recognize the one who possesses authority to properly interpret it.

The setting of a second conflict over the Sabbath was the Capernaum

---

[1] Mishnah, Shabbath 7.2; Jerusalem Talmud, Shabbath 7.2, 9c. See Davies and Allison, *Matthew*, 2: 306-307.

[2] Mishnah, Hagigah 1.8

[3] On Abiathar in Mk 2:26, who was actually the son of Ahimelech, the high priest mentioned in 1 Sam 21:1, see William L. Lane, *The Gospel according to Mark*, NICNT (Grand Rapids: Eerdmans, 1974): 115-16.

synagogue where Jesus and his disciples had come to worship. There was present in the service a man with a shriveled hand. The Pharisees initiated the controversy by asking Jesus if it was lawful to heal on the Sabbath (Mt 12:10). All three Synoptic accounts disclose that the questions were not honest inquiries, but attempts to bait Jesus into acting in such a way that they could accuse him of being a Sabbath breaker. Jesus turned their question back on them, but framed it as a moral rather than legal choice: "Which is lawful on the Sabbath: to do good or to do evil, to save life or to kill?" (Mk 3:4; Lk 6:9). The Pharisees remained silent. In their tradition aid could be offered on the Sabbath only if it involved an immediate threat to life.[4] Healing of a paralyzed hand could wait; a more urgent concern was the discrediting of their opponent. Jesus was angered by such callousness of heart (Mk 3:5a). He rebuked them for caring more for a sheep, which they would rescue on the Sabbath if it fell into a pit, than for a fellow human being in distress (Mt 12:11-12). Jesus commanded the man to stretch out his hand and it was completely restored. His opponents responded not with joyful amazement, but with murderous anger. Jesus, as Lord of the Sabbath, both rescued the individual from a debilitating handicap and freed the Sabbath from the shackles of legalism. The Sabbath was designed by the Creator to be a day of rest, worship, renewal, joy, and praise. Jesus did not disregard the Old Testament law itself (cf. Mt 5:17-20), but sought to recover its intended meaning, which had become obscured by rabbinical accretions.

Constitution for Kingdom Citizens (Mt 5:1-7:29; Lk 6:17-49)

After the formal appointment of the twelve apostles to kingdom ministry (Lk 6:12-16), Jesus now turned his attention to reeducating them in the transformational values of kingdom citizenship. The "Sermon on the Mount" was primarily directed to the disciples (Mt 5:2; Lk 6:20), though by the end of the two or three day period of teaching large crowds had gathered in the hills of northern Galilee to listen in (Lk 6:17-19; Mt 7:28-8:1). The address must be interpreted in light of Jesus' kingdom theology (Mt 4:17, 23): the already-not yet rule of God bears its force on the deepest recesses of the human heart and from this internal transformation springs a life of moral excellence and sacrificial service. Its radical demands seek to reshape the entire personality. Its standards reflect the very perfection of God himself (Mt 5:48) and thus can only be perfectly fulfilled when the kingdom reaches its fullness. Jesus' sermon assaults all those who have submitted to his lordship with the cold fact that they are lawbreakers whose wretchedness can only be healed by divine grace. Nevertheless, triumphant kingdom living becomes the definite, albeit provisional, experience of all whose broken and contrite hearts "hunger and thirst for righteousness" (5:6), a righteousness of internal alignment with the character of God rather than external conformity to a moral code (5:20).

1. **True Happiness** (Mt 5:3-12; Lk 6:20-26)

The truly blessed person is one whose interior life aligns with the character

---

[4] Mishnah, Yoma 8.6: "Whenever there is doubt whether life is in danger, this overrides the Sabbath."

of God.[5] The eight descriptive qualities focus on the heart, the controlling center of the personality, out of which springs pious conduct. The rewards confirm the state of blessedness and are bestowed as gifts of the present-future kingdom.[6] The language is declarative, but implicitly exhortational. These are the character attributes Jesus would have his disciples nurture. The eight qualities are listed with their dynamic equivalents and Old Testament precedents.

   (i) <u>Poor in spirit</u>: humility, lowliness, contriteness toward God, dependence (Isa 57:15; 66:2)

  (ii) <u>Mourn</u>: personal grieving for one's sins and that of one's generation (Ps 119:136; Isa 61:1-3; cf. James 5:1; 2 Cor 7:9-11)

 (iii) <u>Meek</u>: gentle consideration of others; freedom from malice and a vengeful spirit; not harsh or tyrannical (Ps 37:9, 11, 29)

 (iv) <u>Hunger and thirst for righteousness</u>: deep longing for personal ethical righteousness and the triumph of social justice (Ps 27:4, 7; 42:2; cf. Mt 5:20)

  (v) <u>Merciful</u>: forgiveness for the guilty; compassion on the needy and suffering (Ps 72:13; Hos 6:6; Mic 6:8; cf. Mt 6:12-15; 9:13; 12:7; 18:27, 33)

 (vi) <u>Pure in heart</u>: inner moral purity not just ceremonial cleanness; sincere and undivided focus on God and his kingdom (Ps 24:3-4; cf. Mt 6:33)

(vii) <u>Peacemaker</u>: mediator of vertical peace with God through proclamation of the Prince of peace (Isa 9:6-7; 52:7; cf. Rom 5:1); agent for horizontal reconciliation between people and by the removal of strife and bitterness (Ps 34:14; cf. Jas 3:17-18; Rom 14:19)

(viii) <u>Persecuted for righteousness'sake</u>: courageous stand for God's standards, both personally and corporately; enduring hostility because of identification with Jesus (Mt 5:11-12) with triumphant joy (cf. Acts 5:41-42)

In summary, Jesus exhorted his leaders-in-training to give first priority to their interior life. Three dimensions of kingdom living would intersect in their core being: integrity (selfward); willing submission to God's lordship (Godward); and compassion (manward). These attributes would transform them into the truly

---

[5] The adjective μακαριος (happy, blessed, fortunate) is applied elsewhere in the canonical Gospels to those who submit to the authority of King Jesus with faith and obedience, and thus align themselves with God's redemptive purposes (Mt 11:6; 13:16; 16:17; 24:46; Lk 1:45; 11:28; 12:37-38; 14:14-15; Jn 13:17; 20:29). This is consonant with the usage of μακαριος in the LXX (always for the Hebrew אַשְׁרֵי) to describe the pious or godly person who trusts in the Lord and comes under his loving care (Job 5:17; Ps 1:1; 2:12; 32:1-2; 34:8; 41:1; 84:4, 5, 12; 94:12; 106:3; 112:1; 119:1-2; 128:1; Prov 3:13; 8:32; Isa 30:18; 32:20; 56:2). Thus Jesus employs a term that denotes not subjective happiness or emotional well-being, but the blessed state of being that enfolds the person who is rightly related to God through his Son.

[6] After each descriptive statement is a causal ὅτι: the promise confirms rather than provides the ground for the blessedness. The final statements in 5:3, 10 are in the present tense and form an inclusio around the future tense verbs in 5:4-9. The benefits occur now provisionally, but in fullness when the kingdom is consummated.

blessed ones and bring inestimable rewards both now and in the future.[7]

2. **Visibile witness** (Mt 5:13-16)
   (i) Salt of the earth: Salt was used in the ancient world to flavor food, but above all as a preservative. The latter is the meaning of the metaphor here. To be a moral force in a corrupting world requires that one retain distinctive kingdom virtues (the eight listed above). To conform to the world's norms is to lose one's effectiveness. The challenge is to remain "salty" and make an impact.
   (ii) Light of the world: In order to illumine a dark world the disciples must display their moral character for all to see. "Good works" are the rays of the inner light of an illumined heart. Even as the oil lamps of elevated ancient towns would shed their glow over the surrounding area, kingdom citizens must display their virtue through visible acts of service. In this way the invisible majesty of God can be manifested for unbelievers to embrace.

3. **Transformative not conformative righteousness** (5:17-20)
   The Old Testament is a record of God's mighty acts and the interpretive word. All of its rich narrative typology and numerous prophetic predictions point toward Jesus. His kingdom proclamation is no innovative message springing from a fertile imagination, but the culmination of the former stage of God's progressive self-revelation. Jesus came to bring salvation history to its intended climax. Jesus in this sense "fulfills" rather than "abrogates" the Old Testament by ushering in its intended conclusion (5:17-18). Jesus positions himself as the authoritative interpreter of the Old Testament by establishing kingdom reward on the basis of obedience to his teachings (5:19). His kingdom demands an absolute righteousness, one that rules the entire personality and penetrates its deepest recesses. External conformity to the Decalogue, even precise concentration on the minute details of rabbinical case law, can only compel an outward show of piety. Jesus aims for heart transformation, without which no one can enter the kingdom of heaven (5:20). Jesus contrasts his approach to the law as its "fulfiller" with the misreading of the Old Testament the disciples have inherited from their religious teachers. With six antitheses ("You have heard that it was said . . . , but I tell you . . .") Jesus expounds the true direction in which the law points, namely, to a mind-transforming freedom that produces holiness in thought, motive, and action. Whether he intensifies the literal command to a deeper level (first two antitheses), replaces accommodating measures with more radical standards (next three antitheses), or corrects rabbinical distortion of the original text (sixth antithesis), Jesus makes his own interpretation the standard that possesses binding authority in the new covenant community.

---

[7] Luke's focus on one's physical condition (6:20-26) does not contradict Matthew's ethical emphasis. Poverty, hunger, sorrow and mistreatment bring blessing, not because they are meritorious conditions in themselves, but because, under kingdom authority, they nurture meekness, dependence, peaceableness, purity, and compassion. On the other hand, wealth, satiation, laughter, and social esteem (Luke's four woes) easily lead to arrogance, self-centeredness, and artificiality, which hinder and obstruct repentance and submission to the will of God.

(i) Murder and anger (5:21-26): Not only murder (sixth commandment), but anger, hostility, and bitterness is prohibited. Disciples must rid themselves of retaliatory bitterness toward others and quickly reconcile, if possible, with one who harbors anger toward them for just or unjust cause (cf. Mt 18:15-17).

(ii) Adultery and lust (5:27-30): Not only the physical act of adultery (seventh commandment), but also the lustful progression in one's heart that fantasizes over such an act is prohibited. To prevent sexual attraction from turning into controlling meditation Jesus uses a metaphor for radical spiritual surgery: the causes or means behind looking (eye), touching (hand), and pursuing (foot) must be brutally removed.

(iii) Divorce and adultery (5:31-32): God's standard for marriage in the new covenant is one man and one woman for life, as established in the original mandate (Gen 2:18-25). The Deuteronomic divorce code (Deut 24:1-4) was a temporary divine accommodation to human weakness. Marriage is a permanent, inviolate covenant of two people not to be broken.[8]

(iv) Oaths and truthfulness (5:33-37): The Old Testament permits oath-taking, but forbids carelessly uttered oaths or breaking one's vows (Ex 20:7; Lev 19:12; Num 30:2; Deut 5:11; 6:13). The rabbis used elaborate distinctions that created various degrees of binding authority depending on the name or place associated with a given oath.[9] Jesus demands that his disciples refrain from all oath-taking and let their speech be marked by uncomplicated, thorough and consistent truthfulness. Such unadorned veracity of speech is the true intent of the law.

(v) Retaliation and forbearance (5:38-42; Lk 6:29-30): The disciples will in the course of promoting the kingdom suffer personal injury and loss. They are to return to their persecutors generosity in exchange for ill-treatment. The lex talionis ("eye for eye, tooth for tooth" [Ex 21:24]) was meant to ensure that the punishment fit the crime; it is not to be the norm for one's response to adversarial treatment.

(vi) Love for one's enemies (5:43-47; Lk 6:27-28, 32-36): The maxim of loving one's neighbor and hating one's enemy, especially Gentiles and Samaritans, circulated in the Jewish communities, but was an ethno-centric distortion of the Old Testament love command (Lev 19:18).[10] The kingdom heir, Jesus says, is to show unconditional love toward all people, even those who mistreat you or fail to reciprocate your kindness. New covenant morality is distinctive and supracultural; it exceeds the conventional morality of tax collectors and pagans who preserve good

---

[8] The exception clause for marital unfaithfulness (πορνεια: Mt 5:32; 19:9) leading to divorce is found only in Matthew. Mark 10:11-12 places mutual responsibility on husband and wife for preserving the marriage bond (Mt 5:31-32/Lk 16:18 is directed toward the man). In the case of adultery, according to Matthew, divorce may be permitted but not mandated. Scholars disagree whether remarriage is then legitimated (for another possible exception, cf. 1 Cor 7:15).

[9] An entire tractate in the Mishnah, Shebuoth ("Oaths"), is devoted to this kind of casuistry.

[10] One approximate example of this is the Qumran prescription of loving those within the covenant community and hating outsiders (1QS 1:4, 10; II:4-10; 1QM IV:2; XV:10).

relations simply as a matter of common decency and for mutual benefit.

(vii) <u>Summative command</u>: "Be perfect, therefore,[11] as your heavenly Father is perfect" (5:48). Jesus demands that the disciples make God's perfection their standard for attitudinal and behavioral righteousness. The radical demands that accost the entire personality find their basis in the character of God. The standard is perfection, not maturity. The fact that such perfection can only be fully realized in the consummated kingdom does not discourage Jesus from setting the bar so that his disciples will strain toward majestic heights. This is a call for the kingdom citizens to bring every fiber of their being under the all-embracing rule of the God of perfection.

4. **An audience of one** (Mt 6:1-18)

Jesus identified the three "acts of righteousness" (6:1) commonly practiced by the pious in Israel: giving of alms (6:2-4), prayer (6:5-15), and fasting (6:16-18). He assumed that his disciples would regularly practice these disciplines, but from a different motivation than what lay behind the piety of the religious leaders ("When you give, pray, fast, do not . . . , but. . ." [6:2, 5, 16]). What Jesus condemned was self-serving religious devotion motivated by the desire to gain popular approval. Kingdom living must be directed to an audience of one, to please the Father rather than people. First, the one who calls attention to the giving is like an actor who plays a dramatic role and views the world as the stage of performance.[12] The disciple should give as the natural outflow of a generous heart without calling attention to one's deed.

Second, even prayer is hypocritical when it becomes extended oratory delivered in visible settings to impress the listeners with one's theological sophistry. What matters, Jesus said, is not one's posture or words, but the motive behind the prayers: to gain the ear of the heavenly Father, not to gain the attention of people. Pagan prayer is incantational babbling designed to extort personal benefit from the impersonal realm of the supernatural; biblical prayer is sincere communication of one's concerns to a loving, omniscient Father who knows our needs and is inclined to hear and answer. What is commonly termed the "Lord's prayer" could more accurately be labeled the "disciples' prayer." Jesus set forth this prayer not as a rigid formula to be recited, but as the manner in which kingdom citizens should approach the King (Mt 6:9-13).

(i) "Our Father in heaven:" God is the father of disciples, transcendent, sovereign, invisible, yet personal and approachable. Calling upon God as "Abba," the intimate term in Aramaic for one's father, was Jesus' most distinctive approach to prayer, one that stunned the disciples and transformed their understanding of God. The available evidence points

---

[11] The inferential conjunction οὖν gathers up the six preceding antitheses and makes the final command the necessary and logical principle that governs the exposition in its entirety.

[12] This is the original meaning of the Greek term ὑποκριτης (*NIDNTT*, 2: 468-470), which is rendered in the English versions "hypocrite," that is, one who pretends to be something other than what one in reality is. It is used often by Jesus to excoriate those who make pretensions to piety (Mt 6:2, 5, 16; 7:5; 15:7; 22:18; 23:13, 14, 15, 23, 25, 27, 29; 24:51).

toward Jesus as being the first to employ this intimate designation to address God (cf. Rom 8:15; Gal 4:6).[13]

(ii) "Hallowed be your name:" request that the God who is holy may be recognized and honored as such by all people.

(iii) "Your kingdom come:" petition that God's power might be extended now in bringing people to joyfully submit to his lordship; it also looks forward to the consummation of the kingdom when God's unrivaled sovereignty will be manifested over the created universe.

(iv) "Your will be done:" the same present-future manifestation of God's saving power as the previous request; the unrivaled sovereignty of God operative now over the heavenly beings to be extended over the people of the earth. The preeminent concern of this prayer is God's name, rule, and will. The disciple begins by aligning one's life concerns into conformity with God's revealed purposes. God the Father is the gravitational center of kingdom life. Now the believer turns to supplication for personal needs to a caring Father.

(v) "Give us today our daily bread:" the prayer is for one day's needs, not wants, recognizing that all good things, including the ability to work for one's livelihood, is a gift of God. The disciple is dependent on God's supply and content with the measure he gives.

(vi) "Forgive us our debts:" sin is viewed as a "debt" owed to God, placing us in need of his forgiveness. "As we have forgiven our debtors" is the accompanying posture of those who recognize the extent to which they have been forgiven by God and thus extend the same to others. For prayer to be effectual the disciples must constantly pursue mutual forgiveness and nurture a community of reconciliation (6:14-15).

(vii) "Lead us not into temptation, but deliver us from the evil one:" perhaps the permissive nuance, "let us not be brought into temptation by the devil" and/or "preserve us in the midst of testings that, under the influence of Satan, become means to enticement to sin."[14]

Third, as with trumpet-announced almsgiving and lengthy, ostentatious prayers, so the hypocrites fasted with grief-laden countenances to demonstrate their pious self-denial. The opposite of performance-oriented acts of piety is the natural, inconspicuous, devoted works of the kingdom citizen whose life-focus is the glory of God. Jesus would have his disciples engaged in acts of service, but always with the heart attuned to the only audience that matters, their Father in heaven.

5. **One's treasure is where the heart is** (Mt 6:19-34)

From a severe denunciation of contrived religious behavior, Jesus turns to the more seductive pull of material possessions. The pursuit of wealth can

---

[13] See *NIDNTT*, 1: 614-615.

[14] The term πειρασμος can refer to either a moral temptation (Mt 26:41; Lk 4:13; 1 Cor 10:13; 1 Tim 6:9) or a character test/trial (Lk 8:13; 22:28; Acts 20:19; Gal 4:14; Heb 3:8; Jas 1:2, 12; 1 Pet 1:6; 4:12; 2 Pet 2:9; Rev 3:10). In a number of instances the meaning may be a temptation that is also a test of character (e.g. Lk 4:13; 8:13; 1 Cor 10:13; Heb 3:8).

become an idol that replaces God (6:24). Anxiety over material needs can sap one's energy to promote the kingdom of God, one's first pursuit (6:33-34). Again, Jesus' laser-like focus is on what occupies the heart, the center of one's personality (6:21).[15] A "treasure" is an object of affection, what is deemed precious and of great worth. Treasures become the center of one's thoughts, desires, and dreams. Jesus compels his disciples to make the kingdom of God their singular pursuit rather than perishable, transitory material things. To pursue God's rule over one's life and to promote his rule among one's contemporaries has eternally lasting significance, like a treasure that can be laid up in heaven (6:19-21). Critical to one's spiritual health is controlling what passes through the eyegate (cf. Mt 5:28; 1 Jn 2:16; Prov 27:20; Eccles 4:8; Job 31:1). "The lamp of the body is the eye" (6:22). Jesus means that the window to the soul is the eye, allowing either the beatific vision of God and a panoply of virtue to enter and influence the mind, or permitting degrading scenes of compromise to darken and corrupt it (6:23). The metaphor serves as a warning against becoming fixated upon one's financial portfolio, which has the power to pull the heart away from God (6:24).

The antidote to such divided loyalty, and even the more subtle danger of worry, is trust in the care and concern of the Father (6:25).[16] Faith has the power to drive anxiety from the heart. Jesus cites two examples from the natural world: the birds of the air are abundantly fed without fretting and without storing up supplies for the future; the lilies of the field do not weave their clothing, but are gloriously arrayed (6:28-30). In the same way, disciples must rest in the loving heart of their Father who knows about and will provide for their needs. Such faith-induced freedom from anxiety is to be a mark that distinguishes believers from the pagans who spend their time and energy pursuing perishable riches (6:31-32). Kingdom citizenship, however, entails more than refraining from worry, but active pursuit of personal righteousness and the extension of God's rule in the world (6:33). To conclude,[17] worry is unnecessary and illogical, for worry borrows its strength from an indeterminate tomorrow which, if it arrives, will find its needs more than met by the God who has satisfied the needs of today (6:34).

6. **Critical discernment, not hypocritical judgment** (Mt 7:1-6; Lk 6:37-42)

A commitment to the exacting standards of righteousness demanded by the King brings with it the danger of adopting a censorious attitude toward

---

[15] The term customarily rendered "heart," καρδια," is pervasive in the record of Jesus' teaching preserved in the Synoptic Gospels: 16 times in Matthew; 8 times in Mark; and 13 times in Luke. It is Jesus' preferred term for the center of the human personality, the place where God addresses a person, and the place where a person can either respond with faith and repentance, or refuse those overtures of grace and become dull and darkened. The heart is the place of decision and destiny. See *NIDNTT*, 2:182-184.

[16] The inferential phrase δια τουτο (v. 25, "therefore") connects the prohibition of anxiety that follows with the commands of vv. 19-21 and warnings of vv. 22-24.

[17] The conjunction οὑν (v. 34, "therefore") introduces the summary conclusion of the entire paragraph (vv. 25-34), which in a sense reiterates the petition, "give us our bread for the coming day" (Mt 6:11).

those who fail to measure up to those standards. Jesus prohibits the disciple from standing in the place of God who is the sole lawgiver and judge (cf. Jas 4:11-12; Rom 14:4). The command here is not to suspend one's wise assessment of people and situations, which is enjoined in Scripture (cf. Mt 7:6, 15-20; Jn 7:24; 1 Cor 5:5; Gal 1:8-9; Phil 3:2; 1 Jn 4:1), but to cease and desist from hypocritical judgment. One must remove the "log" that impairs one's own vision before attempting to remove the "speck" from the eye of another. The precondition of being able to administer a timely reproof to a brother is to first judge oneself. The manner of judgment will be gentle and the purpose remedial, for how one treats others will be reciprocated, whether with harshness or generosity.

To eliminate all hypocritical judgment does not mean to throw caution to the wind. Disciples must exercise restraint in situations where incorrigible opponents seek to undermine their mission. There is thus a moral symmetry in Jesus' instruction that balances generous appraisal with critical discernment.[18] The metaphor he used is framed in a chiastic arrangement: dog, pigs, (pigs) trample, (dogs) tear to pieces (7:6). Dogs and pigs represent those who treat the precious gospel of the kingdom with utter contempt. Just as he enjoined the disciples to shake the dust off their feet as a symbol of judgment on an unwelcoming town (Mt 10:14), and to leave the blind guides well enough alone (Mt 15:14), so Jesus commands them to show thoughtful restraint in promoting the kingdom among those whose proven agenda is to obstruct its advance.

7. **Persistence in prayer** (Mt 7:7-11)

Prayer can guide the disciple through the confusing maze of situations and personalities encountered in the course of kingdom ministry. To strike the balance between generous forbearance and cautious discernment one must seek God's wisdom. The promise of answered prayer is given to the one who keeps on asking, seeking and knocking.[19] Jesus often put the accent on persistence when instructing his disciples in the art of prayer (Lk 11:5-13; 18:1-8). They must remember to whom their prayers are directed: not a stingy miser whose reluctance must be overcome, but a gracious Father who delights to provide his children with the "good things" that are beneficial to them (7:11). These provisions are, first and foremost, the attributes of kingdom citizenship expounded in the sermon—righteousness, truthfulness, purity, humility, love, freedom from anxiety. They are effectualized in the disciple's life by God's greatest gift, the Holy Spirit (Lk 11:13).

8. **Golden maxim** (7:12)

Rabbi Hillel framed "the golden rule" in a negative manner: "What is hateful to you, do not do to your neighbor: that is the whole Torah, while the rest is commentary thereon; go and learn it."[20] Jesus, however, stated it in

---

[18] The same tension is expressed in Jesus' later command to be "as shrewd as snakes and as innocent as doves" (Mt 10:16b; cf. Rom 16:19b; 1 Cor 14:20; Php 2:15-16).

[19] The three verbs in Mt 7:7 are all present imperatives and carry a durative or continual force; the three present participles in 7:8 have the same nuance.

[20] Babylonian Talmud, Shabbath 31a. Many other 'parallels' are cited in Davies and Allison, *Matthew*, 1: 686-687.

positive form, one that incorporates avoidance of offensive conduct with constructive action: "Do to others what you would have them do to you." Rather than a binding "rule," this is a simple ethical maxim that is both expansive and liberating. The rabbis dictated precise regulations for every possible occasional permutation. The Mishnah, Gemara, and Tosephta are the multi-layered traditions produced in the attempt to micromanage the complexities of life. The new covenant morality of Jesus is beautiful and profound in its simplicity. It brings the heart into ethical decision-making by making the personal welfare of others one's first priority.

9. **Definitive choice between two alternatives** (Mt 7:13-27; Lk 6:43-49)

Jesus brought his sermon to a conclusion by demanding, through a series of contrastive metaphors, that the listeners choose between two alternatives. The ambivalent multitudes have started to gather and need to hear, along with the disciples, that faith and obedience are inextricably linked in the kingdom of God. First, there are two gates to enter (narrow and wide), two roads that extend from the gates (narrow and broad), and two destinations at the end of the roads (life and destruction) (7:13-14). The crucial decision is which gate to enter, for the respective roads and destinations stretch out before the traveler after that choice is made. A narrow gate to life means that the restrictive path must be chosen from the outset. Jesus' kingdom theology knows nothing of two tiers or two categories of kingdom citizens, one of whom is obedient and rewarded, the other of whom is disobedient and unrewarded. Such a dichotomizing of faith and obedience has to be superimposed on dominical teaching in order to find support. Jesus sets forth an integrated pattern of progressive discipleship under his authoritative direction: decisive commitment to enter the already-not yet kingdom (narrow gate), perseverance in faith in the midst of persecution and adversity (narrow way), and final arrival as heir of the consummated kingdom (life). Kingdom citizens are obedient disciples and obedient disciples inherit the kingdom.

Second, Jesus warned the listeners against false prophets that will arise and attempt to pull the kingdom community away from Jesus' authoritative teaching. They will be like "wolves in sheep's clothing," that is, their innocuous appearance will provide no clue to their corrupt character. They will profess allegiance to the King and even prophesy, exorcise demons, and perform miracles in his name (7:22). However, the evidence to establish such claims, namely, obedience to the will of God, will be missing (7:21). Their words and actions will reveal the character of their heart just as fruit, good or bad, shows the health of the tree (Lk 6:45). Good trees do not produce good and bad fruit in alternative seasons. Disciples must, then, carefully assess the moral character of those who claim to speak for God. The precondition for entry into the kingdom of God is not impressive outward piety, fine-sounding confession, or dynamic miracle-producing ministry, but a vital relationship that produces obedience to the will of the Father. Jesus will banish from his kingdom those who possess the former without the latter.

Third, the two levels of response to his kingdom offer are compared to two builders, their materials, and the outcome of their work. The one who hears and obeys is like a wise builder who erects his house on a rock foundation so that it withstands surging floods and beating winds. The one who hears and does not obey is like a foolish builder who builds his house on the sand so that it collapses under the torrential rains (7:24-27). Again, the metaphor militates against a two-tier approach to kingdom citizenship: the wise builder does not choose solid materials now and flimsy materials later. "These words" (7:24, 26) are the authoritative declarations of King Jesus who inaugurates his kingdom over the hearts of those who prove the authenticity of their faith-repentance by obedience. Jesus made astounding claims in the first person, distinct from the Old Testament prophets who voiced "the word of the Lord," and certainly unlike the rabbis who cited other rabbis. The Sermon on the Mount stunned the listeners. This was not academic theology to be parsed, but truth to be obeyed (7:28-29).

Clean hands or pure hearts (Mt 15:1-20; Mk 7:1-23)

The setting was a private house in Capernaum, probably Peter's, where Jesus and his disciples were enjoying a meal together. A delegation of Pharisees from Jerusalem arrived and observed some of the disciples eating without washing their hands in the prescribed way. They immediately charged Jesus with allowing his disciples to "transgress the tradition of the elders" (Mt 15:2). The Pharisees had earlier clashed with Jesus over the issue of Sabbath observance (Jn 5:10, 16, 18; Mk 2:24; 3:2), and now precipitated conflict over another area of difference, hand washing before meals. Mark explains the Jewish customs for his Roman readers (Mk 7:3-4). The "tradition of the elders" refers to the massive body of rabbinical rulings passed down orally for several hundred years and later codified in the Mishnah.[21] An entire tractate of the Mishnah, Yadaim or "hands," is devoted to the area of hand washing before meals. One who violated the prescribed method for washing hands, as well as for the cleansing of eating and cooking utensils (Mk 7:4b), would contact ritual defilement, which would render them unfit members of the covenant community.[22]

Jesus shot back with a stinging rebuke for his accusers. They were guilty of replacing the clear teaching of Scripture with man-made doctrines (Mk 7:8). The Pharisees had elevated their traditions to the level of canonical status, which

---

[21] The body of oral teachings (παραδοσις) was commonly called the "tradition of the elders" (Mt 15:2) or the "traditions of the fathers" (Gal 1:14). Jesus employed the pejorative designations "tradition of people" (Mk 7:8; cf. Col 2:8) and "your tradition" (Mt 15:3, 6; Mk 7:9, 13) to distinguish it from the divine commands.

[22] In simple terms, the distinction in the Jewish law between cleanness (καθαρος / טָהוֹר) and uncleanness (κοινος / טָמֵא) relates to ritual or ceremonial purity. Those who are ritually pure have access to the benefits of life in the covenant community, at the center of which is atonement for sin through the sacrifices of the tabernacle (temple). Those who enter the category of unclean are denied such communal access until the prescribed means of restoration are fulfilled. Those Old Testament passages which give primacy to heart purity (e.g. Ps 24:3-4; 51:7-12; 73:1; Prov 20:9; 22:11) adumbrate a time when these provisional categories will be terminated. Jesus instituted the new covenant which abrogates the ceremonial regulations of the Torah and provides definitive heart cleansing (Mk 7:19b; Acts 10:9-16; 11:1-18; 15:7-11; Heb 9:6-14, 23-28). See Richard E. Averbeck, "Clean and Unclean," in *NIDOTTE*, 4: 477-486.

standards became the basis for judging the behavior of others. Isaiah's denunciation of the hypocritical leaders of his day for creating a lips-heart chasm (Isa 29:13) applied equally to them (Mt 15:6-9).

Jesus provided a concrete example of how the traditions had ended up nullifying the ethical force of the Old Testament law. The fifth command states: "Honor your father and your mother" (Ex 20:12). This is supplemented by a severe warning: "Anyone who curses his father or mother must be put to death" (Ex 21:17). Jesus interpreted this divine command as laying responsibility on children to care for parents in their old age. But the rabbinical traditions allowed a son to declare money set aside for parental support to be "Corban,"[23] that is, a gift devoted to God and placed in the temple treasury (Mk 7:11). It is unclear whether such a vow could later be annulled. What is clear, and Jesus' central point, is that the tradition negated the functional authority of the clear command of God. A pretentious claim to piety, giving money to support the temple ministry, would be the means to justify dishonoring one's parents (Mk 7:12-13). The Pharisees are nothing more than blind guides who lead the unsuspecting people of the land into a spiritual pit by such hypocrisy (Mt 15:14).

Jesus made this an object lesson for his disciples on the nature of uncleanness. That which enters from the outside, food, does not make a person unclean. Mark adds that Jesus in this statement "declared all foods clean" (7:19b). Jesus abrogated the old covenant category of ceremonial purity and replaced it with its new covenant fulfillment, purity of heart (Jer 31:33b; Ezek 36:26; cf. Rom 14:14-18; 1 Cor 10:31; 1 Tim 4:4; Tit 1:15). What defiles a person, rather, is the panoply of words and actions that spring from the heart (Mk 7:21-23).[24] It is the heart that is the place of consecration or defilement. What a person truly is—hidden character, motives, thoughts—determines what one says and does (cf. Mt 12:34-35). Thus the hearts and lips of his disciples must possess congruity. Only by stripping away the layers of oral tradition could Jesus help his disciples recover the unadulterated teaching of Scripture and bring their lives under its penetrating authority.

Summative commands of the law (Lk 10:25-37; Mt 22:34-40; Mk 12:28-34)

An expert in the interpretation of the Old Testament law approached Jesus with a question: "Teacher, what must I do to inherit eternal life?" (Lk 10:25). The question was not an honest inquiry after truth, but a test designed to discredit Jesus. In the mind of this scholar "doing" was the precondition for receiving eternal life. The Lord kept the conversation on the legalist's plane of thought in order to drive home the futility of such an approach to God. Jesus reminded him of the two summative commands of the law, to love God from one's entire being and to love one's neighbor to the extent one naturally loves oneself (Deut 6:5; Lev 19:18). Whoever fulfills these commands in their entirety, Jesus posited, will be granted eternal life (10:28). Jesus, and Paul later (cf. Rom 10:5; Gal 3:12), saw in Leviticus

[23] This is the transliteration of the Hebrew word for "offering" or "gift," קָרְבָּן (HALOT, 3: 136-137).
[24] Jesus' language stresses that it is the heart (καρδια: Mk 7:6, 19, 21) and that which is "from within" (ἐσωθεν: 7:21, 23), not that which is "from without" (ἐξωθεν: 7:15, 18), that determines the true condition of a person.

18:5 a hypothetical offer of life to the one who obeys the law perfectly. Unwilling to face the spiritual bankruptcy that such an unattainable standard exposes, the scholar sought to evade the implications of Jesus' counterquestion (10:26) and command (10:28). "Desiring to justify himself," he responded with a further question: "And who is my neighbor?" (10:29). The question was an attempt to quiet his conscience by stimulating a dispute over the meaning and range of the word "neighbor." If he could shift the conversation away from the applicational force of the law's command to one of theological disputation, he reckoned he would gain the upper hand over the uneducated Galilean.

Jesus reframed, by means of a parable (or perhaps an actual incident), the lawyer's question from "Who is my neighbor?" (10:29) to "To whom am I acting as a neighbor?" (10:36). The seventeen mile steep decline from Jerusalem (3000 ft. above sea level) to Jericho (1000 ft.) was a rugged and rocky road around cliffs that straddle wadis. Robbers, hidden in hollow places, attacked a traveler who was robbed, stripped, beaten, and abandoned. Two religious officials, a priest and a Levite, were returning to Jericho, perhaps after performing their duties in the Jerusalem temple, and came upon the "half dead" man. Each one "passed by on the other side." Such callous disregard was a clear violation of the law, which enjoined mercy toward those in need (Ex 23:4-5; Lev 19:34; Micah 6:8). Precise attention to carrying out the duties of their religious vocation had obscured the "weightier matters" of the law, namely, justice, mercy, and faithfulness (Mt 23:23). Finally, a despised Samaritan (cf. Jn 4:9; 8:48) came by, saw the helpless victim, and was moved with compassion. He went to him, bound up his wounds, pouring on oil and wine, took him to an inn on his own donkey, cared for him, paid two denarii for lodging, and pledged to repay whatever expenses were incurred to nurse the stranger back to health.

Now Jesus moved to the probing interpretive question and its direct application. The original passive question of interpretation, "Who is my neighbor?," is restructured into an active question of engagement: "Which of these three was a neighbor?" (10:36). Unable to evade any longer, the lawyer answered correctly: "the one who had mercy on him" (10:37a). The one who began the conversation with a precondition of "doing" to gain eternal life was told to "go and do likewise" (10:37b). To love one's neighbor as oneself meant to seek proactively the welfare of the person in need who crosses one's path. Did the light begin to dawn in the darkened mind of the Torah scholar that such a command was impossible to obey perfectly and that he must abandon every attempt at justifying himself before God? There is no recorded sequel.

A similar conversation took place between a legal scholar and Jesus on Tuesday of Passion week. The Pharisees put forth one of their own to ask Jesus: "Teacher, which is the greatest commandment in the law?" (Mt 22:36). This was another attempt by his adversaries to discredit Jesus, though the lawyer seemed to respect Jesus and have affinity with his answer. After reciting the Shema, Israel's confession of God's oneness (Deut 6:4), Jesus quoted the Old Testament commands to love God with the entire being and to love one's neighbor as oneself (Deut 6:5; Lev 19:18). "On these two commands," Jesus stated, "all the law and the prophets hang" (Mt 22:40; cf. Rom 13:8-10). In other words, these are the two essential commands that incorporate all other teaching into their framework to produce an integrated whole.[25] If one does not love God and one's neighbor, then, regardless of the precise fulfillment of its ceremonial requirements, the law is being violated. The lawyer registered his wholehearted agreement with Jesus' answer. He added that he understood and endorsed Jesus' implied elevation of the love ethic over animal sacrifices, a common Old Testament comparison (Deut 10:12; 1 Sam 15:22; Isa 1:11-18; 43:22-24; Hos 6:6; Amos 5:21-24; Micah 6:6-8; cf. Prov 15:8; 21:27; 28:9). Probably they could hear in the background the bleating of the sheep from their location in the outer court of the temple. Jesus returned the compliment: "You are not far from the kingdom of God," a kingdom that centers on the heart not on performance (Mk 12:34). Was this Pharisee, perhaps like Nicodemus and Joseph of Arimathea, able to break free from the suffocating traditions and surrender to Jesus' rule? Again, there is no recorded sequel.

The good portion (Lk 10:38-42; Jn 12:1-8)

Jesus and his disciples came to the home of his friends, Mary, Martha, and Lazarus, in the town of Bethany on the eastern slope of the Mt. of Olives just two miles from Jerusalem. This was their favorite place to lodge when they traveled to Jerusalem (cf. Jn 11:17-18; 12:1-2; Mt 21:17). The two sisters were quite different in temperament. Martha was the aggressive personality (cf. Jn 11:20, 21, 28; 12:2), while Mary was quiet and contemplative (Jn 12:3-8). In this instance Martha threw herself into the preparations for her thirteen guests as a model oriental hostess, while Mary "having sat at the Lord's feet, was listening to his word" (Lk 10:39). Martha became irritated at her sister for not pulling her share of the load, and even at Jesus for not reproving Mary: "Lord, don't you care that my sister has left me to do the work by myself? Tell her to help me" (10:40). Martha found herself in the place of issuing a command to her Lord. Jesus' gentle rebuke that followed must have stung, especially since it came from one who was to enjoy the lavish meal she was preparing. The Lord reproved Martha for being anxious and troubled about the many lesser, unnecessary things. He had come to Bethany more for the fellowship than the food. Mary, on the other hand, is commended for having chosen the "one thing needed," "the good portion," that is, to sit with Jesus and give heed to his word (10:41-42a). The truths gleaned from drawing close and listening would have greater lasting impact than the finest meal (10:42b). The priority was worship before work, listening before doing, relationship over service.

There is a happy sequel to this incident. Later when Jesus came to Bethany after the death of Lazarus, it was from Martha's lips that the astounding confession came: "I believe that you are the Messiah, the Son of God, who was to come into the world" (Jn 11:27). Her bold affirmation came before the miraculous restoration of her brother from death to life. A few weeks later, on Friday before Passion

---

[25] Davies and Allison (*Matthew*, III: 246-247) argue persuasively that the verb Matthew employs here, κρεμαννυμι (Mt 22:40, "hang" [NIV]), is the material equivalent of Paul's usage of the verbs πληροω (Gal 5:14; Rom 13:8) and ἀνακεφαλαιοω (Rom 13:9b). All three texts, drawing on Leviticus 19:18, conclude that love for God and neighbor are the essential commands that capture the intent of all of the law's commands and integrate them into a unified whole.

week, the Lord was once again in Bethany enjoying a meal with the two sisters in the home of Simon the leper. Mary anointed Jesus' feet with a pint of costly ointment and wiped the unguent with her hair. This was more than an act of humble devotion but signified, Jesus said, an anointing "for the day of my burial" (Jn 12:7).[26] Mary appears to have grasped what the disciples utterly failed to discern, namely, that the Lord was hastening to consummate his mission of redemption through his suffering. It is not that Mary lacked compassion for the poor, as Judas accused her, but that, in light of his soon departure, her opportunity for worship and intimacy was rapidly fading (12:8). The habit of quietly listening at Jesus' feet brought an understanding that surpassed the others. Her devotion had also begun to have a salutary effect upon Martha who should surely be remembered more for her bold confession (Jn 11:27) than for being a distracted hostess.

Prayer that prevails with God (Lk 11:1-13; Lk 18:1-14)

One day when Jesus was engaged in prayer the disciples interrupted him with a request: "Lord teach us to pray, just as John taught his disciples" (Lk 11:1). The request reveals the degree to which they were impressed by the Lord's manner of prayer to his Father. Behind the request was a yearning for such relational intimacy with God. He had earlier imparted to them a model prayer (Mt 6:9-13), which he repeated here in abbreviated form (11:2-4). The disciples' broad request (lit. "teach us to pray"), however, was not only a search for the methodology of prayer, but for its manner and motivation. The parable of the importunate friend provided the latter. An unexpected guest arrived at midnight and there was no bread to serve for a late meal. The host went to a friend's house to borrow three loaves of bread, but was refused because the latter would have to disturb his sleeping family. However, the friend eventually got up and gave him the bread because of the supplicant's "shamelessness"[27] to continue asking (Lk 11:8). The parable contains an implicit lesser to greater argument: if an earthly friend will extend help under pressure rather than from sympathy, how much more will the heavenly Father abundantly extend grace to his children who earnestly continue to seek his face. The interpretive words which follow confirm that persistence in asking and trust in a benevolent Father are the central points of the parable (11:9-13). The parable clearly does not mean that God is a reluctant giver who must be coaxed against his will to grant our wishes. Rather Jesus exhorted the disciples to persevere in asking even when the heavens are silent, though the request would appear to be in line with God's will and assured by his promises (cf. 1 Jn 5:14-15).

As his final trip to Jerusalem drew near, Jesus concentrated on preparing his disciples for his departure. The interadvent period of his absence would find them

---

[26] The NIV seems to accurately capture the sense of the Greek verb τηρεω ("keep"), which here means to devote (the ointment) for the very use Mary had in mind, that is, anointing for burial: "It was intended that she should save this perfume for the day of my burial" (Jn 12:7).

[27] The noun ἀναιδεια occurs only here in the New Testament. It is rendered in a variety of ways in the English versions: boldness (NIV); importunity (KJV); persistence (NASB). The Amplified Bible paraphrases it: "shameless persistence and insistence," which is an attempt to capture the audacious and obtrusive nature of the action described by this term.

engaged in promoting the kingdom to both responsive and resistant hearts. During those often difficult and lonely days the disciples would long for his return (Lk 17:22). The antidote to discouragement, of losing heart amidst the disappointments and persecutions, would be persistent prayer (Lk 18:1). A second parable illustrates the kind of prayer that would prevail with God. An unrighteous judge, moved by neither fear of God nor respect of persons, acted to vindicate a widow who tenaciously persisted in pushing her case to his court. She literally "beat him down",[28] that is, wore him out with her persistence (Lk 18:5). The limits of the analogy must be recognized: just as God is not a reluctant friend (Lk 11:5-8), neither is he an unjust judge. A lesser to greater argument is once again implicit in the parable: if an unrighteous judge, who neither fears God nor respects people, is moved by the tenacious demands of a helpless widow, how much more will a just and merciful God act to vindicate his elect who cry out to him day and night for justice (18:6-7). The setting of the prayer is a time of severe persecution and rapid decline of faith as the return of the Son of man draws near (Lk 18:8; cf. Mt 24:12-13). As they promote the kingdom in this hostile context, Jesus' disciples are to be bold and persistent in bringing their requests to God.

A Samaritan gives thanks (Lk 17:11-21)

The Lord was passing through Samaria and Galilee, probably to join the pilgrims from the north, on his way to Jerusalem for his final Passover (Lk 17:11). In a village, perhaps in Perea, ten lepers called out from a distance if the renowned healer might show mercy upon them. Their debilitating disease had made them social outcasts, banished from normal participation in community life (cf. Lev 13:45-46; Num 5:2-4; 2 Kg 7:3-4). All ten lepers were cleansed when they obeyed Jesus' command to go and present themselves to the priests. Earlier Jesus had healed a leper who then was required to go and perform the elaborate ritual for restoration to ceremonial purity (Lk 5:12-14; cf. Lev 14:1-32). This time, however, the lepers exercised faith to obey Jesus' word and were healed as they proceeded to the temple. Incredibly, only one of the healed lepers, a Samaritan, returned to offer thanks to his healer. Jesus asked the man incredulously, "Where are the other nine?" They also had been restored to the community, shame and ostracism removed, a painful debilitating condition healed, but turned no longer to Jesus after relief was provided. Jesus pointed out to his disciples that it was the one foreigner of the group, and a despised Samaritan at that (cf. Jn 4:9, 22; 8:48; Lk 9:52-55), who acknowledged God's good gift of wholeness and gave thanks.

This was by no means the first time that Jesus pointed out that spiritual insight bears no connection to racial lineage or religious background. He first taught his disciples about the spiritual harvest by engaging an immoral Samaritan woman in conversation, which led to her conversion and that of an entire Samaritan village (Jn 4:39-42). In the synagogue at Nazareth Jesus angered the Jewish listeners by reminding them that in the days of Elijah God providentially selected a Sidonian

---

[28] The verb ὑπωπιαζω originally took on the literal sense of "strike in the face" or "give a black eye." Its two occurrences in the New Testament are figurative extensions from this: to "wear down" (by persistence [Lk 18:5]) one's adversary and to "ruthlessly control" (by self-discipline [1 Cor 9:27]) one's physical body. See *TDNT*, VIII: 590-591.

widow and a Syrian general to show his favor (Lk 4:24-27). On two rare occasions did Jesus register astonishment at a remarkable display of faith, once of a Roman centurion (Mt 8:10) and once of a Syro-Phoenician woman (Mt 15:28). When asked by a legal scholar about the meaning of "neighbor," Jesus told a parable about a Samaritan who fulfilled the great command to love one's neighbor and two Jewish religious leaders who did not (Lk 10:30-37). At the final judgment, Jesus declared, the Queen of the South, who came to inquire of Solomon's wisdom, and the Ninevites, who repented at the preaching of Jonah, would rise up and condemn the wicked generation of Israelites who have rejected the one who is greater than Solomon and Jonah (Lk 11:29-32). In the case of the lepers it was the lone foreigner who possessed a heart of gratitude, and rendered that most fundamental expression of what it means to be in a right relationship with God, namely, the giving of thanks.

House of prayer for the nations (Jn 2:13-22; Mt 21:12-13; Mk 11:15-18; Lk 19:45-48)

On the first Passover of his public ministry Jesus had entered the outer court of the temple and confronted the moneychangers who had turned his Father's house into a market. This was Jesus' initial act of confrontation with the Jerusalem authorities (Jn 2:13-17). He asserted that the ultimate proof of his authority to restore the temple to its original purpose as a place of prayer is his resurrection. The disciples came to understand his usage of "temple" for his physical body only after he was raised from the dead (2:18-22). Three years later on Monday before his final Passover, Jesus once again entered the temple.[29] The first cleansing had failed to put an end to the deeply rooted and profitable business enterprise housed in the court of the Gentiles. Rather, it persisted and he was forced to confront it again. Jesus' second, culminative confrontation of the temple leaders, who permitted such activity, made them furious and sealed his destiny as one irreversibly opposed to the established customs of the entrenched powers. Four days later they would move to secure his death. At his trial the religious leaders would misuse his saying about the temple, taking it in a literal sense, in their charges against him (Mt 26:59-62).

The moneychangers were Jewish merchants who converted Greek and Roman currency into the required local currency for the worshippers to purchase what was needed for sacrifices including animals, wood, oil, wine and salt. Others sold pigeons for those too poor to purchase animals (Mt 21:12) and for use in other purification rites (Lk 2:24; cf. Lev 12:6-8; 14:22; 15:14, 29). There was rampant extortion in the exchange rates charged in the currency transactions, an opportunity afforded further by the requirement that the annual temple-tribute required of all Jews and proselytes had to be paid in exact half-shekels.[30] The temple court was

[29] John's Gospel refers to three Passovers during Jesus public ministry (2:13; 6:4; 11:55). If the unnamed feast of Jn 5:1 is a fourth Passover, then the earthly ministry extended over four years. We are inclined, however, to take this feast as Tabernacles. The two cleansings of the temple, then, can be dated April A.D. 27 and 30 respectively (assuming an A.D. 30 date for the crucifixion).
[30] The usurious practices of the moneychangers and the entire commercial enterprise in the Temple that Jesus confronted is graphically described in Alfred Edersheim, *The Life and Times of Jesus the Messiah*, 2 vols. (London: Longmans, Green, and Co., 1900): I: 367-376.

even being used as a convenient transit to ship goods from the city to the Mt. of Olives (Mk 11:16). The normally measured anger of Jesus boiled over into a holy rage as he went through the courts driving out merchants and shoppers alike, and overturning the tables of the moneychangers and pigeon hawkers. Jesus borrowed the language of two Old Testament prophets in condemning the officials for turning the house of prayer for the nations (Isa 56:7) into a den of robbers (Jer 7:11). Isaiah described the redemptive purpose for the temple: to mediate God's gracious presence to his people and thereby attract the surrounding nations to draw near to the God of Israel for prayer in its outer court (56:7-8). The centripetal missionary witness of Israel was designed to presage the centrifugal witness of the new Israel to all the nations of the earth (Mt 28:19-20). Jesus was moved with holy zeal (cf. Jn 2:17, quot. Ps 69:9) to recover the temple from those who had obscured its intended role to be a distinctive witness to the Gentiles of the holiness of Israel's God and the necessity of cleansing from sin. The provisional paschal sacrifices would soon find their fulfillment in a final efficacious sacrifice, the offering of the temple of his body. Ironically, the plot of the paranoid priestly authorities to kill Jesus (Mk 11:18) would precipitate the very event they feared, the dissolution of a system that had run its course.

Woeful effects of legalism (Mt 23:1-36; Mk 12:38-40; Lk 20:45-47; cf. Lk 11:37-54)

The long day of debate in the temple court, Tuesday of Passion week, ended with the religious authorities silenced but hardened in their resolve to kill Jesus (Mt 22:46; cf. Mk 11:18). The crowds had listened with delight as Jesus confounded the educated rabbis with his answers (Mk 12:37b). As his interrogators stalked away one by one, Jesus turned to his disciples and to the crowd and issued a blistering indictment of the hollow religion that filled the corridors of religious power in Israel. The censure crystallizes the essential points of difference between Jesus and the Pharisees. Here is a violent clash of worldviews, of governing values, motives and visions of the future. While the Pharisees created a faith-works synergism, Jesus stripped away every human pretension of placing God in one's debt. If the scribal schools originally expounded a covenantal nomism that made obedience to the law the willing response to God's gracious election, by the time of Jesus the nomistic portion had driven its covenantal partner into exile.

1. The Pharisees and legal scholars teach the law, but do not obey it (23:2-3; cf. Mt 7:1-5; Rom 2:1, 21-24). They view themselves as Moses' successors as they "sit" on the stone seat of the synagogue to teach.
2. They burden down others with their exacting demands, unlike Jesus whose burden is light and who gives rest (Mt 11:28-30). They fail to live up to their own standards while showing no compassion toward others who fall short (23:4).
3. The motivation behind their piety is to gain recognition: phylacteries, long fringes, places of honor at banquets, best seats in the synagogues, salutations in the market place, and the designation of Rabbi (23:5-7; Mk 12:38-39; Lk 20:46). Jesus would remove such hierarchical designations among his followers as Rabbi, Father, and Teacher. In his kingdom all are equal as

181

brothers, all accountable to one Master (23:8-10). In the kingdom of heaven servants who humble themselves rise above self-promoting lords (23:11-12).

4. The **seven woes** (Mt 23:13-36) are not a personal attack on individuals, but the prophetic condemnation (cf. Isa 5:8-23; Hab 2:6-20) of a system of theology that has displaced the interior life for an exterior righteousness, because it has replaced Holy Scripture with man-made traditions.

    (i) Obstinacy: They take others to hell with them by refusing to surrender allegiance to the King and by persuading others to follow their course (23:13).

    (ii) Misguided zeal: They are zealous to find converts who in turn exceed even their teachers in zeal for a Torah-centric way of righteousness (23:15; cf. Acts 21:20; Rom 10:2; Gal 4:17-18).

    (iii) Falsehood: They create arbitrary, self-serving distinctions to mitigate their oaths, separating life into free/secular (temple, altar) and bound/sacred (gold, gift) compartments (23:16-19). For Jesus all of life is to be lived in integrity before God. Since, then, every oath is binding, he would eliminate oath-taking altogether and replace it with the unadorned word of truth (23:20-22; cf. Mt 5:33-37).

    (iv) Misplaced priorities: They are meticulous in the matter of tithing even their garden spices, but neglect the weightier matters of the law: justice, mercy and faithfulness.[31] Scrupulousness is not condemned ("without neglecting the former"), only distorted priorities. They "strain out a gnat but swallow a camel," that is, fuss over trivialities but overlook the essential character qualities that Scripture so forcefully expounds (23:23-24).

    (v) Moral defilement: Great attention is given to maintaining ritual purity, while the heart is left unattended. Greed is masked behind a strict adherence to ceremonial regulations such as the proper washing of cups and dishes (23:25-26; cf. Mk 7:4).

    (vi) Deceptive appearance: In the month of Adar, just before Passover, tombs were washed with lime to alert pilgrims to steer clear and avoid ritual defilement through incidental contact with corpses (cf. Jn 11:55; 18:28). The Pharisees are "whitewashed tombs full of dead people's bones," that is, they give the appearance of piety due to scrupulous maintenance of ritual laws, but are inwardly full of corruption (23:27-28).

    (vii) Defiance: They pretend to honor the prophets and saints of old by building their tombs and decorating their graves. This only heightens the guilt of those who stand in continuity with their forefathers in persecuting those who call the nation and its leaders to repent (23:29-32). They remain defiant in their opposition to God's purposes by persecuting those sent by Jesus to proclaim the kingdom (23:33-36).[32]

[31] Old Testament ethics give prominence to these three qualities (that translate into action): justice (Deut 16:19-20; 1 Kg 3:11, 28; Prov 29:4, 7; Isa 42:3-4; Mic 6:8); mercy (Hos 6:6; Mic 6:8); and faithfulness (Num 12:7; 2 Sam 22:26; Prov 28:20; Hab 2:4).
[32] The Old Testament line of martyrdom runs from Abel (Gen 4:8) to Zechariah, son of Jehoiada (2 Chron 24:20-22). 2 Chronicles is the last book in the Hebrew canon.

To conclude, Jesus reserved the harshest language of his earthly ministry for the Pharisees and legal scholars. He called them hypocrites (23:13, 15, 23, 25, 27, 29), blind guides (23:16, 19, 24, 26), sons of hell (23:15), murderers (23:31), snakes and vipers (23:33; cf. Mt 3:7; 12:34). The seventh woe closes with a defiant, ironical imperative: "Fill up the measure of the sins of your fathers" (23:32). Jesus denounced those in positions of influence that should have been stewards of the covenant and good shepherds of God's flock, but squandered their stewardship and led the flock astray. Jesus' catalog of the vices of legalism provides a serious admonition to all leaders not to start down the path of assessing the conduct of others by extrabiblical criteria, for once one starts down that path it is almost impossible to stop.

Giving out of one's poverty (Mk 12:41-44; Lk 21:1-4)

Toward the end of the long day of debate Jesus stood near the temple treasury in the court of women with his disciples. They were observing the Jewish worshippers place their offerings in the thirteen trumpet-shaped receptacles. Jesus had urged his disciples to carefully guard their hearts from the allurement of material things (Mt 6:19-24). They were to trust their Father to provide their needs (Mt 6:25-34) and maintain a simple lifestyle and attitude of dependence on God as they engaged in kingdom ministry (Mt 10:8-10; Lk 10:3-4). They should not envy the rich person, for all the money in the world could not redeem the soul (Mt 16:26; Mk 8:36-37; Lk 9:25). His instruction about the dangers of covetousness had become a point of emphasis during the final months leading to his final trip to Jerusalem (Lk 12:13-34; 16:1-15; 18:18-30).

1. A stranger asked the Lord to intervene in an inheritance dispute. One brother felt he was being cheated in the settlement of the family estate. Jesus refused to interfere. He knew that behind the request lurked covetousness, not a sincere desire for justice. Jesus warned the sibling disputants against "thirsting for more,"[33] for a person's true worth is wholly unrelated to the extent of one's monetary portfolio (Lk 12:13-15). The warning was supported by a parable. A rich farmer whose land produced an abundant harvest "thought to himself" that he would expand his barns, store up the grain, acquire more goods, then "eat, drink and be merry" for many years out of the security of his vast wealth. There was no thought of God as the source of such blessing, no sense of stewardship, no concern for the less fortunate, only a determination to maximize his pleasure. He acted as if he was the captain of his soul. But God announced the untimely death of the rich fool and asked him: Who will consume the grain and goods that you have dedicated your energies to accumulate (12:20b)? Such is the tragedy of the person who spends one's life on things that do not outlast the grave, rather than laying up lasting treasures in heaven (Lk 12:13-21). Did the rich fool leave behind a family in discord,

---

[33] This is the literal meaning of the Greek term πλεονεξια, a sense beautifully captured in the German Bible by the term Habgier, and one which carries over into a number of its New Testament occurrences (e.g. Lk 12:15; Col 3:5; 1 Thess 2:5). See *TDNT*, VI: 266-273.

fighting over the spoils of the estate, that is, sons who became just like their father?

2. A few weeks later Jesus told his disciples another parable. A rich man called the manager of his estate to give an account when he received reports the manager was squandering the possessions entrusted to him. The manager felt too proud to beg and too weak to do manual labor, so he devised a scheme to secure his future if he should lose his job. He called in a number of his master's debtors and reduced the amount they owed. These tenant farmers made their livelihood out of the annual produce from their rented fields and were glad to relieve their heavy debts. They quickly wrote out promissory notes to the manager. The master commended the manager for his shrewdness. Though he had squandered part of the estate, and even engaged in what appears to be fraudulent business transactions, the manager secured his own future by ingratiating others who could be a source of help in the uncertain days ahead. Jesus was impressed that the "sons of this age" pursue their earthly interests more shrewdly[34] than the "sons of the light" pursue heavenly concerns (Lk 16:1-8). Now to the lesson of the parable: the sons of light should use material wealth to promote the kingdom. Those who are then brought under God's redemptive rule through such sacrificial giving will form a joyous welcoming party for the givers when they leave behind their earthly habitation and enter their eternal dwelling place (16:9). Money has the power not only to control the heart (Lk 18:22-25) and to divide family members (12:13); it also possesses the potential, if faithfully managed (16:10-12) and ruthlessly controlled (16:13), to promote God's interests in the world.

Now as they watched the worshippers drop their coins into the offering boxes, Jesus called his disciples attention to a poor widow (Mk 12:43). While the rich people threw in numerous coins "out of their abundance," this widow offered two lepta, the smallest coin in circulation in Palestine.[35] For her, however, this was a large sum of money: "She out of her poverty put in all she had to live on" (Lk 21:4). Whether this was her entire weekly or monthly allowance, the widow made deep personal sacrifices in order to support God's temple. Others offered large gifts, but had the abundance to retain much more. Jesus drove home that it is not the amount of the gift, but the degree of sacrifice represented by that amount which is central to the divine accounting. This lesson crystallized all Jesus had taught the disciples on many occasions about money. Here was a person whose heart was released from the binding control of materialism, a temptation to poor and rich alike, and was thus free to give joyfully as an expression of worship.

---

[34] The adverb φρονιμως and the comparative adjective φρονιμωτερος (Lk 16:8-9) are built on the adjective φρονιμος, which can mean either wise/prudent (Mt 7:24; 24:45; 25:2, 4, 8, 9) or, in this case, shrewd in the positive sense of exploiting a legitimate opportunity for noble use (Mt 10:16; cf. 1 Cor 4:10; 10:15; 2 Cor 11:19[all with sarcasm]).

[35] Mark (12:42) adds that two lepta (λεπτα) equaled one kodrantes (NIV: "penny" [κοδραντες]). One lepta was 1/128 denarii; one kodrantes was thus 1/64 denarii. A denarius was a normal day's wage for a laborer in the first century (Mt 20:2; cf. Mk 14:2). Two lepta were thus worth very little in terms of purchasing power.

Another Paraclete

Jesus sought to strip away the layers of scribal tradition and to restore the functional authority of Holy Scripture over those in training to be kingdom leaders. He showed little regard for the rabbis' scrupulous adherence to oral traditions that surrounded such practices as fasting, ritual washing, tithing, and keeping the Sabbath. Jesus' concern was that the disciples give first priority to the interior life out of which would then flow the willing obedience of a thankful heart. In this sense Jesus' ethical demands, encapsulated preeminently in the Sermon on the Mount, were far more penetrating than the most exacting standards of the rabbis, for they searched the motives, thoughts and intents of the heart behind the acts of service. Herein resides the dilemma of authentic kingdom living. How could the disciples fulfill such absolute ethics, for example, as freedom from lustful desires and love for one's sworn enemy (Mt 5:28, 44)?

In his farewell discourse, the Lord promised his disciples an unparalleled resource that would provide such enabling grace to fulfill, provisionally if not perfectly, his searching demands. His distinctive term for the Holy Spirit was Paraclete, literally, "the one called to be beside (them)" (Jn 14:16, 26; 15:26; 16:7; cf. 1 Jn 2:1).[36] All of the attempts to find a dynamic equivalent of this Greek term in the English translations (Comforter, Helper, Counselor, Advocate) have failed because of its deliberately ambiguous and thus comprehensive sense. It is best to simply transliterate the term and then pour into it the semantic content derived from each context. This is the person, the third person of the triune Godhead (Mt 28:19), who would provide every resource needed for the disciples to attain the kingdom quality of heart righteousness and to gather in the kingdom harvest of souls. He would be their counselor, comforter, strengthener, helper, teacher, and everything else that Jesus had been to them in his earthly ministry. The Spirit was "another Paraclete" to replace the one who had until now fulfilled that role (Jn 14:16). In fact, he would provide even more for them than Jesus had during his earthly state of humiliation, because he would mediate the presence of the now risen and exalted Lord (Jn 14:12-14; 16:7). It is helpful to summarize Jesus' doctrine of the Spirit recorded in the Gospels.

1. Regeneration: Jesus told the Pharisee Nicodemus that a new birth was required to enter the kingdom of God. Nicodemus could only think of physical procreation, but Jesus spoke of being reborn of the Spirit (Jn 3:5, 6, 8). To be born "of water and of the Spirit" (3:5) is a composite phrase drawn from Ezekiel 36:25-26 and means the cleansing, regenerative work accomplished by the Spirit of God in the heart of one who believes and repents (cf. Ezek 39:29; Joel 2:28). The flesh, that is, natural human life with its limitations and transience,[37] contains no potential for generating spiritual life, which is

---

[36] This is the transliteration of the Greek παρακλητος, used four times in John's Gospel to designate the Holy Spirit (14:16, 26; 15:26; 16:7), and one other time in the New Testament in its historical sense of a legal advocate or defense lawyer (1 Jn 2:1). See *NIDNTT*, I: 88-91.

[37] The Greek term σαρξ in the New Testament regularly takes on the meaning of human existence with its finiteness, limitations, weakness and transience, with no definite implication of sinful corruption (Jn 1:14; 3:6; 6:63; Rom 1:3; 6:19; 2 Cor 10:3; Gal 2:20b; 1 Pet 1:24).

the precondition for entrance to God's rule. The words of Jesus offer life in the spiritual realm to those who personally appropriate them (Jn 6:63). The Spirit of God creates new redemptive life and becomes like "streams of living water" that flow from within to satisfy the heart with deep assurance of forgiveness and a restored relationship with the Father (Jn 7:37-38; cf. 4:13-14).

2. Baptism with the Spirit: The settled residence of the Spirit in the hearts of believers would become a reality at the Pentecostal outpouring (Jn 7:39). This event is anticipated in the acted parable where Jesus breathed on the disciples and commanded them to receive the Spirit (Jn 20:22). John the Baptist spoke of the one who would come after him and baptize people "with the Holy Spirit and with fire" (Mt 3:11). The immediate context points toward two separate baptisms, one of regeneration for believers and one of judgment for unbelievers (3:12). The baptism of the Spirit, predicted by John, took place at Pentecost and not only brought regeneration to individual believers, but incorporated them into the new covenant community (Acts 1:4-5). Since that time when individuals or groups of individuals believe they are baptized with the Spirit of God and incorporated into the body of Christ (Acts 11:15-16; 1 Cor 12:13). God the Father or the Lord Jesus is the baptizer and the Holy Spirit is the (personal) element in or with whom believers are baptized.[38]

3. Help in verbal witness: One of the ministries of the Holy Spirit, Jesus promised, would be to provide wisdom and courage for witness in times of persecution (Mt 10:20; Mk 13:11; Lk 12:12). Jesus anticipated for his disciples, and succeeding generations of disciples, a worldwide witness to the nations that would transcend the present evangelistic tours within Israel (Mt 10:23; Mk 13:10). Witness would elicit persecution that would in turn provide further opportunity for witness. They need not be anxious in such circumstances, for the Holy Spirit would be their Paraclete, "the one beside them," to guide and strengthen their witness to the person and work of Jesus (Jn 15:26-27).

4. Mediation of the divine presence: The Spirit of God had certainly been present in special times during the old covenant era to provide enabling for God's servants to fulfill their divine calling (Ex 31:3; Num 11:29; Jdg 3:10; 15:14; 1 Sam 10:6; 16:13; 1 Kg 18:12; 2 Kg 2:16; Neh 9:30; Ps 51:11; Isa 48:16; Ezek 2:2; 3:14). During Jesus' earthly ministry the Spirit was "with" the disciples as they toured Israel and heralded God's rule. But now, in the new era to be formally inaugurated by his death and resurrection, Jesus promised the Paraclete would be "in" them (Jn 14:17).[39] The promise of the indwelling presence of God's Spirit in the hearts of believers is one of the foundational realities of the new covenant prophesied by Ezekiel (Ezek 11:19; 18:31; 36:26-27) and Jeremiah (Jer 24:7; 31:33). As an ever-present companion, the Spirit will represent Jesus who is ascending to the right hand of the Father. This is

---

[38] The preposition ἐν with the dative πνευματι is best taken consistently in a locative sense in these related texts: Mt 3:11; Acts 1:5; 11:16; 1 Cor 12:13.

[39] There is a clear distinction and progression of thought expressed in the change of preposition from "with you (pl.)" (παρ᾽ ὑμιν) to "in you (pl.)" (ἐν ὑμιν).

the sense of Jesus' promise: "I will not leave you as orphans; I will come to you (in the person of the Spirit)" (14:18). The Spirit will assure them of the abiding love of the Father and the Son (14:19-20; cf. 15:1-8). He will enable them to reciprocate that love by obeying his commands (14:15, 21; cf.15:9-17).

5. Revelation of authoritative truth: After his departure the "Spirit of truth" (Jn 14:17; 16:13), that is, the Spirit who is himself truthful and communicates truth,[40] will perform a critical ministry for the character of the new community. He will reveal authoritative truth that becomes the doctrinal foundation for the faith and life of those under God's rule. Jesus predicts several components of the Spirit's task. First, he will help the apostles remember the words that Jesus spoke when he was with them (14:26b). This was imperative since they possessed the common tendency to selective hearing (Jn 2:22). Second, the Spirit will enable them to understand and interpret the meaning of those words (14:26a), something they often lacked during his earthly ministry (Jn 12:16). Third, there are "many things" the apostles still needed to learn, but were at present unable to grasp (16:12). The Spirit of truth will guide them into new and deeper stages of truth about Jesus' person and work (16:13). It is the things that relate to Jesus, both present and future, that will be the essence of the revelatory corpus (16:14-15). There is perfect harmony in the process of the self-revelation of the triune Godhead: Father, Son, and Spirit share an exclusive body of knowledge and cooperate in communicating the portions essential to kingdom life to the apostles. This ensures the reliable transmission of the charter for faith and mission to the kingdom community.

6. Conviction of the world: As the apostles and succeeding generations of kingdom heralds fulfill their mission of discipling the nations, the Spirit will attend their verbal proclamation with the work of conviction. The Spirit will identify, like a prosecuting attorney, three areas of guilt people must face and repent of. First, he convicts people of their sin because[41] they have rejected Christ whose death is the sole means of removing that guilt (16:9). Second, he convicts people of their need for righteousness because Jesus has ascended to the Father and from his position as exalted Lord will justify all who believe (16:10). Third, the Spirit convicts people of the certainty of eschatological judgment because the prince of the world, Satan, and the entire world order were condemned at the cross. Therefore, final condemnation is certain and can be averted only by embracing Jesus' death and resurrection (16:11).

---

[40] We take the genitive τῆς ἀληθείας (Jn 14:17; 15:26; 16:13) in a dual sense that incorporates both the objective genitive and descriptive (adjectival) genitive categories. Truth (ἀληθεια) is what Jesus himself embodies (Jn 1:14, 17; 14:6) and what he came to earth to reveal (Jn 8:32, 45-46; 16:7; 17:17; 18:37); the Spirit communicates truth by calling to remembrance and illuminating the truth imparted by Jesus. Though an entirely different grammatical structure, the designation "Holy Spirit" similarly has a dual sense: the Spirit who is himself holy and communicates holiness to God's people.
[41] The causal ὅτι in each case (Jn 16:9, 10, 11) provides the ground or reason behind the Spirit's work of conviction.

Leadership Profile of Jesus: Kingdom righteousness through freedom

1. **The truth that sets one free**: *The Pharisees were, in one sense, moved by the sincere desire to preserve Israel's covenant identity in a pagan world. As a people subjected to foreign rulers and the wholesale importation of pagan practices, the Jews were in danger of losing touch with the Torah, their holy guidebook for faith and life. In order to apply the teaching of the law to contemporary settings and to prevent erosion of their distinctive values, the Pharisees supplemented Scripture with layer upon layer of traditional rulings. The Rabbis ruled on how and when one must fast, wash hands and kitchen utensils before meals, classify various kinds of activity permitted or forbidden on the Sabbath, articulate oaths that were binding or non-binding, avoid ritual defilement through contact with impious Israelites, Samaritans, and Gentiles, and on and on. Even the noble Pharisee, one who asked what he must do to inherit eternal life, and then resoundingly agreed that love for God and neighbor are the summative tasks of the law-keeper, even this young man could not shake his addiction to performance theology. Though he was not far from the kingdom of God (Mk 12:34), he was still some distance away. Unlike these religious sophisticates were the simple pious souls whose hearts had not been captured by rabbinical casuistry: the worshipful Mary, the grateful leper, and the generous widow. Jesus saw the binding traditions as an obstacle to true holiness because they obscured the teaching of Scripture and neglected the matters of the heart. The disciples must become leaders who would continually unmask their souls before the invasive searchlight of Scripture and cultivate a renewed mind, a clean conscience, and a pure heart.*

2. **New covenant promises and provisions**: *In his two great discourses, one in the hills of northern Galilee and one in the upper room, Jesus expounded the vital dimensions of life under God's rule. First, the Sermon on the Mount sets forth a transformative righteousness that grows from within, rather than is imposed from without, and produces a life of moral excellence. Second, the Upper Room Discourse describes a relationship between children and their Father characterized by prayerful intimacy, abiding love, willing obedience, and lasting fruit. The great resource that translates these promises into realities is the Paraclete, the Spirit of truth, who will both inspire the authoritative New Covenant (Testament) word (Jn 16:13) and permanently indwell the hearts of the kingdom citizens (Jn 14:17). With the coming of the new covenant, with its better promises and superior provisions (Jer 31:31-34; Ezek 36:25-27), the old preparatory method of conduct regulated by the law and of ministry performed by a sacerdotal class has run its course. Kingdom leaders go forth to model heart-hands integrity searched by the Spirit, and to proclaim truth revealed by the Spirit to the consciences of people convicted by the Spirit. Dependence on the Word and the Spirit, rather than reliance on traditions and structures, characterizes all authentic kingdom ministry.*

Chapter 16.
Kingdom greatness through servanthood

Preliminary questions to consider:
1. *Why is taking on the role of a servant, in imitation of the Lord, so difficult and yet so necessary for those who aspire to usefulness in the kingdom of God?*
   How does one nurture the attitude and foster the lifestyle of a willing servant who places the needs of others above oneself?
2. *How would you assess the models of leadership you have witnessed in contemporary Christian ministries?*
   In what concrete ways does a truly biblical philosophy of leadership differ from the secular views of leadership espoused in your own culture?

Formal leadership in the secular or religious world is always a moral test. To be placed in a position of influence over others often means the enjoyment of higher monetary remuneration, societal prestige, the admiration of one's peers, and the internal satisfaction of having achieved vocational success. The rewards of prominence are why leadership positions are eagerly pursued and jealously guarded. However, elevation brings with it heightened opportunities for the vices of greed, arrogance, and vanity to creep in and overtake one's soul. The disciples had grown to a settled assurance that King Jesus would one day establish his rule over the nations. They reminded him of the sacrifices they had made for him, and felt entitled to positions of prominence when he took his seat on the throne. They revealed by their repeated attempts at self-promotion, and intramural squabbling over who would be the greatest, that they had imbibed a healthy dose of the secular leadership theories of their day. Leadership in the kingdom of God, however, was unlike other models of leadership they had encountered. Here was a kingdom where hearts governed by a childlike dependence would rule, and where the ladder of success was achieved not by ascending but by descending its rungs. This is the third essential principle Jesus imparted to the disciples as leaders-in-training: greatness in God's kingdom consists in imitating the Son of man who came not to be served, but to serve.

A kingdom for little children (Mt 18:1-4; Mk 9:33-37; Lk 9:46-48)
     Jesus and his disciples had returned to Capernaum after their trip north to Caesarea Philippi (Mt 17:24). During their northern excursion Jesus had begun to talk openly about his coming death, something that completely escaped Peter and the others (Mt 16:21-23). He demanded of them the highest level of commitment as his followers (16:24-26), but also promised them unparalleled rewards and gave them a glimpse of his coming glorious vindication after suffering (16:27-17:9).

189

This is a period, only a few months before the cross, where Jesus faced the cynicism and shallow fickleness of the crowds (Mt 16:14), a disintegrating constituency (Jn 6:66), and the deepening hostility of the religious leadership (Mt 15:1-2; 16:1, 6, 12). In the fourth major discourse recorded in Matthew's Gospel (5:1-7:29; 10:5-42; 13:1-52; 18:1-35) Jesus set forth those attitudinal qualities that must govern the disciples' relationships with one another and with outsiders: humility, generosity, seriousness, purity, compassion, prayerful agreement, reconciliation and forgiveness. Jesus invited them as aspiring leaders to embrace servanthood not lordship. For these ambitious people who imagined themselves the vice regents of an advancing kingdom, this lesson was the most difficult test of all.

The discourse began in response to a question from the disciples: "Who is the greatest in the kingdom of heaven?" (Mt 18:1). The question was not an academic one. Piecing the Synoptic accounts together, it appears that Jesus detected their rivalry for elevated positions in the kingdom (Lk 9:46), challenged and silenced them (Mk 9:33-34), and then they blurted out their question. Jesus' priority—his coming Passion (Mt 16:21-23; 17:22-23)—and the disciples' priority—kingdom status—were completely at cross-purposes. Jesus' object lesson was a little child, perhaps Peter's if this took place in his house (cf. Mt 17:25). He summoned and stood the child in their midst and declared that one must humble oneself like a child both to enter the kingdom, as well as to attain greatness within it (Mt 18:2-4).[1] Obviously Jesus is not commending qualities that children often demonstrate such as naivety or playful foolishness. A child, however, has not yet mastered the adult arts of manipulation, self-aggrandizement, and political maneuvering. There is a trust, a simplicity of motive free from concern for social status, in a child that the disciples must study and imitate. To those with childlike hearts God reveals his hidden treasures of wisdom (Mt 11:25) and promotes to places of unexpected prominence (18:4).

How quickly the disciples forgot this lesson is seen a short time later when they stepped in to rebuke some people who were bringing their children to Jesus for his blessing (Mt 19:13). Jesus was angered by their protective attitudes and commanded his disciples to stop hindering the children from approaching him (Mk 10:14). His kingdom is comprised of those who receive his rule "like a little child," that is, with humility and trust (19:14). The dissembling of the multitude, the pride of the religious leaders, and even the ambition growing among his closest followers ran contrary to the kingdom values of faith and repentance. It will take much more than the object lesson of a child to drive the deeply rooted desire for exalted position in the kingdom from the hearts of the disciples, but at least the process has begun.

Extreme care for the "little ones" (Mt 18:5-14; Mk 9:38-50; Lk 9:49-50)

John informed Jesus that they encountered an individual outside their circle

---

[1] When Jesus refers to "the one who is great" (ὁ μειζων [18:4]), he is not necessarily defining the term 'greatness' in the sense of elevated status/position meant by the disciples when they discussed the one who is "great" (μειζων [18:1]). He means greatness in the sense of meeting the standards for divine approval.

who was exorcising demons in his name. Perhaps the disciples expected to be commended for commanding the man to stop (Mk 9:38). However, Jesus has just commanded them to welcome "little children" who are drawing near because to do so is to welcome him (Mk 9:37; Mt 18:5; Lk 9:48). The strange exorcist may well have been one who was moving toward Jesus with a childlike, faltering but growing, faith, though not yet given to a full commitment like the apostles.[2] Are not John and the others in danger of excluding a "little one" who bears his name and thus potentially causing offense, that is, irreparable damage to his spiritual development? The subsequent warning against causing offenses is issued, at least in part, as a response to this incident (Mt 18:6-7; Mk 9:42).

Jesus gave three reasons to support his command that the disciples stop hindering the exorcist (Mk 9:39-41).[3] First, such a person will no longer be negatively predisposed to Jesus (9:39b). At least this person recognized Jesus' authority and placed himself on the side of God's kingdom, against Satan. This recognition will lead to deeper understanding and must not be quenched. Second, "whoever is not against us is for us," that is, one cannot drive out Satan by proclaiming Jesus' name and at the same time be opposing Jesus' kingdom (9:40). There are two opposing forces, with no neutrality possible, and this individual has chosen to align himself with the forces of good against evil.[4] Third, all who serve the disciples of Jesus because they bear his name will be rewarded (9:41). Even small sacrifices, in this case supporting their kingdom mission by exorcising demons in Jesus' name, call forth God's approbation. The disciples must shed their myopic outlook and give special care for people who are moving toward Jesus but still have a distance to travel.

Jesus followed up his lesson of the child with a severe warning not to cause offense toward "these little ones who believe in me" (Mt 18:6-10). The "little ones" (18:6, 10) refers not only to literal children who desire to be near Jesus (18:2, 5), but also to all who humble themselves like a child (18:3-4; 19:14), believe in him, enter his reign, and bear his name. To cause grave spiritual harm to young, vulnerable believers (or even seekers) invites the severest judgment. It would be better if such a potential offender's life were taken from him, such as being drowned in the sea by being cast in with a heavy millstone hung around the neck, than for such an offense to occur. Such offenses that lead people into sin and away from God are inevitable in the fallen world, but those who aspire to kingdom leadership must take the most radical steps to avoid being the cause of another person's spiritual ruin (Mt 18:7-9).

In this context the metaphor of removing one's hand, feet and eye refers to the eradication of any attitudes or actions, especially pride, exclusivism, and sectarianism that would hinder people from entering Jesus' reign. Jesus used a series of expressions to warn of eternal punishment for those who cause such

---

[2] There is no suggestion that the strange exorcist was in any way exploiting the name of Jesus for personal gain like the false prophets in Mt 7:15, 21-23, or the seven sons of Sceva in Acts 19:13-16.
[3] Three statements, each introduced by a confirmatory γαρ, modify the present imperative: "stop hindering him."
[4] The converse saying, "He who is not with me is against me, and he who does not gather with me, scatters," (Mt 12:30; Lk 11:23), was spoken concerning those actively opposing Jesus' mission.

offenses: eternal fire (Mt 18:8); the Gehenna[5] of fire (18:9); Gehenna, the unquenchable fire (Mk 9:43, 45, 47); the place where "their worm does not die and the fire is not quenched" (9:48); salted with fire (9:49). However one processes this theologically, Jesus is holding his aspiring kingdom leaders up to the most searching standards regarding how their ministry will influence others, either toward or away from the rule of God. The disciples must maintain their role as moral preservatives, symbolized by salt, in a corrupting world where offenses are frequent (Mk 9:50). Not only overt actions but subtle attitudes such as despising or looking down on vulnerable believers can cause offense (Mt 18:10a). This final warning is given support: the Father has deep concern for these little ones by dispatching guardian angels to watch over them (18:10b). The Father is a shepherd who rejoices over the recovery of even one lost sheep (Mt 18:12-14). How can anyone who aspires to share the Shepherd's heart not guard their lips, hearts, hands, and feet from any fault that might cause another to stumble and fall?

Courage to rebuke and humility to forgive (Mt 18:15-35)
The loving unity of the kingdom community commends the gospel and has the power to favorably arrest the attention of unbelievers (Jn 13:34-35; 17:20-23). Conversely, a community spoiled either by the tolerance of moral impurity or by refusal to offer reconciliation to its fallen members who repent brings the kingdom message into disrepute and repels those who might otherwise embrace its liberating promises. Jesus had already addressed the case where "your brother has something against you" (Mt 5:23). In that instance the disciple should temporarily suspend the act of worship and quickly reconcile, if possible, with the estranged brother (5:24-26). Now Jesus addressed the other case where "your brother sins against you" (18:15a). Reconciliation grounded in repentance, in this case the other person's, is again the rule with a four-step process to be followed:

1. The initial step is private reproof "just between the two of you," with the redemptive purpose to win the offending brother over, that is, lead to repentance and effect his restoration (18:15). The offended brother takes the initiative in seeking truth-grounded reconciliation.
2. If the offending brother refuses, the offended brother is to take two or three others and expand the circle of confrontation, in line with the law of confirmation by two or three witnesses (18:16; Deut 19:15).
3. If the brother remains recalcitrant, the matter should be brought before the church[6] as a whole (18:17a). Each successive step is triggered by the offending brother's refusal to listen (18:16, 17a, 17b).

---

[5] Gehenna (Gk. γεενα) is the transliteration of the Hebrew for "valley of Hinnom," the valley south of Jerusalem where infants were sacrificed to pagan gods (2 Kg 16:3; 21:6; Jer 7:31), later desecrated by Josiah (2 Kg 23:10), and which became a trash dump (worms/smoldering fire). The expression came to denote the place of eternal punishment in Jewish intertestamental literature. See *EDNT*, 1: 239-240.
[6] The term rendered "church" in most English versions in both Mt 16:18 and 18:17 is εκκλησια, its only occurrences in the canonical Gospels. In Mt 16:18 the universal church is in view, while in Mt 18:17 the local congregation is specified.

4. The final stage is excommunication, that is, the severance of formal ties and community privileges: "treat him as you would a pagan or a tax collector" (18:17b). The binding and loosing in this context refers to the disciplinary expulsion and the restoration of the offending brother respectively (18:18; cf. 16:19). As two or more believers come to prayerful consent about the judicial matters raised in the confrontation, God will respond to preserve the purity of the community, which is the motivation behind all disciplinary measures (18:19). Jesus who is present in the gathered, unified prayer team will, as divine judge, ratify the decision of the offended brothers and move to preserve the purity of the community against unrepentant offenses (18:20; cf. 1 Cor 5:4-5). God's answer to the prayers of the brothers is due to his commitment to the mission of the community who bears his Son's name.[7]

Peter wondered whether there might be some limit to the amount of times a repentant brother should be offered forgiveness (18:21). The rabbinical approach was to forgive an offending brother up to three times; the fourth repeated offense relieved one of the responsibility to forgive.[8] Peter was more generous and suggested a limit of seven times. Jesus offered the number seventy-seven times, which means without limit (18:22). Lamech's principle of revenge (Gen 4:24) was transformed into a principle of forgiveness. In the kingdom community forgiveness is to have no bounds with respect to frequency or quantity. All disciples have been forgiven by God far more than they could ever forgive another person. This is the point of the subsequent parable of the unforgiving servant (18:23-35). A servant was relieved of a huge debt by his gracious king. That servant, however, showed appalling callousness toward a fellow servant who begged to be given time to pay back his much smaller debt. When the other servants protested to the king about the unforgiving servant's actions, the king condemned him and delivered him to the jailers until he could pay off his huge debt. Jesus made the lesson of the parable clear: the Father will severely judge those who, having experienced God's unlimited forgiveness, do not forgive from the heart their offending brothers (18:35). God's forgiveness of sins is the climactic promise of the new covenant (Jer 31:34b). The people over whom God reigns will model forgiveness in their relations with one another. Here we encounter once again the moral symmetry in Jesus' teaching. The need to confront and discipline offending members (18:15-20) must not degenerate into harsh measures that prevent restoration. Because the church is a redeemed community, it must also be a redemptive one.

Unprofitable servants (Lk 17:1-10)
During the Perean ministry Jesus reiterated some of the relational lessons he had earlier imparted to them in Galilee. First, they must guard themselves against causing the spiritual ruin of "little ones" (Lk 17:1-3a). In this context "little ones" are the poor, vulnerable members of society like Lazarus (Lk 16:19-31) who

---

[7] The promise of Jesus' presence among those who assemble in his name (18:20) supports (γαρ) the promise of the Father's response to their prayers (18:19).
[8] Babylonian Talmud, Yoma 86b-87a

responded enthusiastically to the offer of salvation. Second, one is to openly and honestly reprove one's offending brother, but always be prepared to offer forgiveness if he repents (17:3b-4). To put it together, one is to be without offense, and when confrontation is necessary, to be ever forgiving. Such an attitude of continual forgiveness without limit toward a repentant offender would require supernatural faith in God's enabling grace. Thus the request from the apostles is "increase our faith" (17:5). Such a request is met with a challenge to exercise the faith that is already theirs, for even a small faith in a great God can effect humanly impossible things such as uprooting and replanting a mulberry tree in the sea (17:6). Third, the spirit of forgiveness (17:3-4) and trust (17:5-6) must be accompanied by the attitude of a servant bound by a resolve to obey and overwhelmed with gratitude at the privilege of serving. Jesus used the analogy of a slave who returned to the master's home at night after a day of tending sheep and plowing in the field. Before he could rest and eat, the servant was required to prepare a meal for and wait on his master (17:7-9). In the slave-master relationship of the first century the slave did what the lord demanded without expecting reciprocation or thanks. There is a limit to every analogy. Jesus was not comparing service in the kingdom to slavish obedience to an insensitive Lord performed out of grudging disdain.

The application of the analogy to the disciples comes at the end: even when they have done everything that was commanded, they should confess: "We are unworthy[9] servants; we have only done our duty" (17:10). The disciples are being equipped as servants of the King. Their obedience will always be partial and imperfect. Still, the Lord chooses to dignify their service with lasting fruit (Jn 15:8, 16) and to reward their service with kingdom inheritance (Mt 19:27-30). Rewards are gifts of grace like the kingdom itself; they are never a quid pro quo type of mechanical repayment for meritorious service. The disciples must view themselves as entirely the products of grace and so serve, out of an overwhelming sense of gratitude, a servant-King who does the unthinkable, waits upon them (Lk 12:37b; 22:27) and washes their feet (Jn 13:4-5, 12-16).

The exaltation of the lowly (Lk 18:9-14)

The central point of the parable of the Pharisee and the tax collector is introduced before the story itself (Lk 18:1): rebuke for those who look with judgmental disdain on those who fail to measure up to their external standards of righteousness (18:9). In the story there are two people, two prayers, and two results. Both men engage in private prayer in the temple. The Pharisee's prayer was self-directed ("to himself"), self-confident ("standing up"), and self-congratulatory ("I thank you that I am not like the rest of people") (18:11). He recited his practice of fasting twice a week (cf. Lk 5:33), which was far more than the law's requirement of once a year (Lev 16:29). He reminded God of his practice of tithing one tenth

---

[9] The adjective ἀχρεῖος in Lk 17:10 means utterly unfit (to receive reward) or wholly without merit. The same term is used of the "worthless" servant who is cast into judgment for squandering his talent (Mt 25:30). The cognate verb, ἀχρειοομαι, refers to the universal condition of people apart from God's justifying grace, that is, they have "become worthless" (Rom 3:12).

of all he possessed, not just wine, grain, and olive oil as commanded in the law (Deut 14:22-23), but even garden herbs (cf. Lk 11:42). He singled out the tax collector ("or even as this tax collector") for special scorn. There is no request, only a rehearsal of his religious credentials.

The tax collector approached God with the posture of repentance. He recognized his unworthiness ("standing at a distance"), was deeply contrite before a holy God ("was not willing even to lift his eyes up to heaven"), and felt a mournful sorrow for his sin ("he was beating his breast" [cf. Jer 31:19; Ezek 21:12; Lk 23:48]) (18:13). He makes the humble plea for God to show mercy on a sinner. No excuses are offered and no comparisons are made with others. The tax collector looks into the recesses of his own heart, discovers sin, and feels the need for divine pardon. The Pharisee looks in the mirror and sees a paragon of virtue. Only the former sees himself as God does, a guilty sinner deserving judgment.

The outcome is that the tax collector who made no claim to righteousness went home having been declared righteous by God. The Pharisee who was persuaded of his own righteousness was condemned (18:14a). A principle of paradox embodies the contrastive outcomes: those who exalt themselves will be humbled, while those who humble themselves will be exalted (18:14b). Jesus imparted to the disciples this unbreakable law of the kingdom on a number of occasions (cf. Lk 14:11; Mt 18:4; 23:12). The biblical principle of humility before honor, service before status, suffering before glory, a cross before a crown is given special prominence in the new covenant community where all are brothers and the coming King is first a suffering Servant (Lk 1:48-49; Rom 8:17b; Php 2:5-11; Jas 4:10; 1 Pet 5:6; cf. 1 Sam 2:3-10; 2 Chr 7:14-15; Job 5:11; Prov 3:34; 25:6-7; Isa 57:15; 66:1-2).

Rewards disproportionate to the service (Mt 20:1-16)

Thoughts of reward and privilege to accompany their sacrifices continued to circulate in the minds of the disciples. At the end of a long conversation between Jesus and a rich man who could not leave his wealth behind, Peter blurted out: "We have left everything to follow you. What then will there be for us?" (Mt 19:27). Jesus affirmed that their sacrifices would be met by one hundredfold rewards both in the present provisional experience of his reign and in the consummated kingdom where the apostles will serve as vice regents (19:28-29). At the time of the final divine accounting, there will be stunning reversals: many who are first (now) will be last (then), and many who are last (now) will be first (then) (19:30). This saying is repeated, in reverse order, at the end of the parable of the laborers in the vineyard (Mt 20:16). The parable supports[10] the principle that Jesus has just declared, namely, that God's grace will prevail over all human priorities of wealth and status in the allocation of rewards in his kingdom.

Jesus now illustrated what "the kingdom of heaven is like" (20:1). A landowner hired laborers for his vineyard at different times of the twelve hour workday (6:00 a.m.-6:00 p.m.). He agreed to pay one denarius to those who came at 6:00 a.m.

---

[10] The explanatory γαρ (Mt 20:1) links the parable to the promise of rewards that precede it (Mt 19:28-30).

Later other workers were added, at 9 a.m., 12 p.m., 3 p.m. and 5 p.m., and in each case the landowner promised to pay "whatever is right." When evening came, at 6:00 p.m., the steward of the landowner paid all the laborers their wages. All received one denarius, from those who were hired last and worked one hour to those who were hired first and worked twelve hours. The early workers began to grumble that those who worked only one hour in the cool of the late afternoon received the same as those who labored all day in the scorching sun. With a series of rhetorical questions, the landowner defended his right to "do what I want with my own money" (20:15). The early workers were begrudging not the landowner's fairness to them (one denarius was the agreement), but his generosity to others. The parable supports the promise of Jesus that his servants will be rewarded far more than they deserve, and immeasurably more than all of their sacrifices merit (19:29). God will distribute his rewards not based on human notions of fairness, but according to his sovereign, and abundantly gracious, determination. Kingdom rewards, then, depend wholly on sovereign grace and in that grace surprising reversals will take place.

Son of man and Suffering Servant (Mt 20:20-28; Mk 10:35-45)

Jesus was making his way to Jerusalem for the final time in a circuitous fashion through Perea. For the third time[11] he openly predicted what awaited him in the holy city: arrest and trial before the high priest, condemnation to death, deliverance to the secular authorities where he will be mocked, scourged and crucified, and on the third day he will be raised from the dead (Mt 20:17-19; Mk 10:32-34; Lk 18:31-34). Even after three predictions of his coming Passion in unmistakable language, the disciples were utterly mystified: "Its meaning was hidden from them, and they did not know what he was talking about" (Lk 18:34b). What the disciples did remember, however, was his recent prediction of the return of the Son of man and his promise that they would share his glorious rule (Mt 19:28). The problem of selective hearing, then, was behind the request of the two sons of Zebedee (Mk 10:35). Urged on by their mother (Mt 20:20), they asked to be granted the most prominent positions in the coming kingdom (20:21). Apparently they had forgotten their Lord's earlier teaching that servanthood was central to kingdom elevation (Mt 18:1-4). Though James and John were among his first disciples, and part of an inner circle of privilege along with Peter, they have made little advancement in their understanding of the core kingdom value of deferential humility. Zebedee's wife was probably Jesus' aunt on his mother's side,[12] and thus was asking special favors for his two first cousins. Though they were misguided, there was also an element of faith behind this request, for they

---

[11] The first prediction took place in the **Later Galilean** period of ministry after Peter's confession near Caesarea Philippi (Mt 16:21; Mk 8:31; Lk 9:22). The second prediction of the Passion took place only a short time later as Jesus and his disciples were traveling through Galilee (Mt 17:22-23; Mk 9:30-32; Lk 9:43b-45). These two predictions can be dated approximately early autumn A.D. 29. Now the final prediction takes place in late winter A.D. 30, only a few weeks before his arrival in Jerusalem for the final Passover.

[12] Salome, sister of Mary the mother of Jesus, supported Jesus ministry and was one of four women at the cross (Mt 27:55-56; Mk 15:40; 16:1; Lk 8:2-3; Jn 19:25-27).

looked forward to a kingdom where they could function as vice regents under King Jesus.

Jesus challenged their presuppositions. They were thinking only of kingdom glory, not of the suffering that must precede its arrival. They envisaged the crown without the cross, which is compared to the "cup" that Jesus must drink (Mt 20:22). The cup is a biblical metaphor for God's holy wrath or retributive judgment (Ps 75:8; Isa 51:17, 21-22; Jer 25:15; Rev 14:10; 16:19) and signifies that Jesus would experience God's wrath in his propitiatory death on the cross (cf. Mt 26:39, 42; 27:46). To their overconfident assertion that they were able to drink the same cup, Jesus affirmed that they would indeed suffer because of their identification with him. James, in fact, would be the first of the apostles to make the ultimate sacrifice for his Christian witness (Acts 12:2). Though John would live to a ripe old age, he would be persecuted by the Sanhedrin in Jerusalem (Acts 4:1-22), along with the other apostles (Acts 5:17-42), and later be exiled to the penal settlement of Patmos "because of the word of God and the testimony of Jesus" (Rev 1:9). Suffering is a gift granted by God to all of his faithful witnesses (Php 1:29), but favored positions were determined not by Jesus but by the Father, the source of his derived messianic authority (Mt 20:23; cf. Mt 11:27; 24:36; 28:18).

When the other ten disciples learned of the preemptive move of James and John to seize the top positions in the cabinet, they became indignant (Mt 20:24).[13] The disciples had earlier argued among themselves who would be the greatest in the kingdom (Mk 9:33-34) and were told that the method of elevation in the kingdom of God is to take the place of the servant. Now the squabbling degenerated into jealous hostility and threatened to divide the company of the committed few. Jesus immediately called them together and reminded them that leadership in God's kingdom is completely different from the kind of leadership practiced in secular society. The latter is authoritarian and hierarchical. Gentile rulers, whether military, governmental, or civic, possess authority due to the positions they hold and demand compliance because of such vested power (Mt 20:25).[14] The possession and exercise of ruling authority is wholly unrelated to the moral character of the leader. The centurion who came to Jesus earlier spoke about the unquestioned obedience his soldiers rendered to him: "I tell this one 'Go,' and he goes; and that one, 'Come,' and he comes. I say to my servant, 'Do this,' and he does it" (Mt 8:9). In the kingdom of God, however, one climbs only by first descending. One

---

[13] The other New Testament occurrences of the verb used here for the disciples' indignation, ἀγανακτεω, confirm that it is a strong one: the anger, born out of envy, of the religious leaders at the shouts of acclamation by the crowd as Jesus entered Jerusalem on his triumphal entry (Mt 21:15); the anger of the disciples over Mary's perceived waste of costly perfume (Mt 26:8/Mk 14:4); the rage of the synagogue ruler when Jesus healed a crippled woman on the Sabbath (Lk 13:14). The verb (and its cognate noun ἀγανακτησις [2 Cor 7:11]) can also refer to holy anger, as with Jesus' indignation over the disciples' attempt to hinder little children from approaching him (Mk 10:14).

[14] The two statements in Mt 20:25 are parallel and use very broad generic language to describe leaders in the secular world of all kinds (οἱ ἀρχοντες, "rulers," and οἱ μεγαλοι, "great ones"). The two verbs are not to be precisely distinguished. Both verbs (κατακυριευω and κατεξουσιαζω) stress the authority to enforce the law or their will upon those in the domain of their rule. In Luke's record of the subsequent dispute during the Lord's supper (Lk 22:24-30), the uncompounded verbs, κυριευω and ἐξουσιαζω (22:25a), are used with the same meaning.

becomes a servant of others before one can be elevated by God to lead others (Mt 20:26-27). This indicates that there are favored positions of delegated authority even in the kingdom of heaven, but they are sovereignly granted, rather than pursued, to those who first qualify as servants. The servant in this context is one who seeks to promote the welfare of one's brother and to sublimate all personal agendas under the all-consuming ambition of promoting God's name and kingdom in the world.[15] This is the opposite of the self-aggrandizing action of James and John and of the ensuing jealousy that threatened to overtake the others.

Jesus pointed to his own sacrificial manner of life and to his coming substitutionary death as the concrete example of what it means to be a servant-leader (Mt 20:28; Mk 10:45).[16] He pointed the disciples to his motivation and to his action. First, as the Son of man his mission to the world is not to be served like secular officials, but to give of himself to others like a humble servant. Uppermost in the mind of every servant-leader like Jesus, then, is the welfare of others over personal power and perquisites. "Son of man" was Jesus' favorite self-designation and occurs over eighty times in the four Gospels, nearly seventy of which are in the three Synoptics. The background to the designation Son of man comes primarily from Daniel 7:9-14. The scene is one of final judgment as the Ancient of Days takes his seat before the court of heaven. One "like a son of man" approaches the throne and is given authority, glory, and sovereign power. He is worshipped by people of all nations and given an everlasting dominion and an indestructible kingdom. Daniel's imagery of a glorious Son of man who receives authority to rule the nations is clearly behind many of the texts where Jesus referred to the return of the Son of man to consummate the kingdom (Mt 13:41; 16:27, 28; 19:28; 24:27, 30, 37; 25:31; 26:64; Lk 17:22, 30; 18:8; 21:27). However, in many other places Jesus referred to himself as the Son of man who walks among people offering redemption to lost sinners, proclaiming God's inaugural rule, and experiencing loss, persecution, and betrayal (Mt 8:20; 9:6; 11:19; 12:8, 32; 13:37; 16:13; Lk 19:10; 22:48). Even more graphic are those passages, such as the present one, where the Son of man is one who will be betrayed by the religious authorities, suffer the shameful death of crucifixion, and be vindicated in resurrection (Mk 8:31; 9:9, 12, 31; 10:33, 45; 14:21, 41; Lk 9:22; 11:30). How could Daniel's Son of man, who is an exalted figure with direct access to the heavenly throne and invested with everlasting authority to rule the nations, fulfill the role of an earthly servant who makes authoritative claims, suffers an ignominious death, and is vindicated by being raised from the dead?

The most plausible explanation is that Jesus intentionally poured into the designation Son of man both phases of his redemptive mission, humiliation from Isaiah 52:13-53:12 and exaltation from Daniel 7:9-14. The Son of man, then, is the one who first comes as a suffering Servant to provide redemption through his vicarious death, is raised from the dead, and will some day return in glory to

---

[15] The Greek words for servant, διακονος and δουλος, are used interchangeably in Mt 20:26-27 (and the parallel in Mk 10:43-44).

[16] In the two accounts Jesus' example of servanthood is both the template of service with which the disciples should compare themselves (Mt 20:28, ὥσπερ), and the ground or reason for his call to serve (Mk 10:45, γαρ).

judge and to rule over the nations. The fourth servant song of Isaiah (52:13-53:12; cf. 42:1-7; 49:1-7; 50:4-11) develops the motif of the suffering of the messianic Servant touched on in the second and third songs (49:4, 7; 50:6-8). The fourth song introduces the servant as one who suffers extreme disgrace, but provides cleansing from sin and is highly exalted by the Lord (52:13-15). The song progressively expounds the servant's lowly demeanor and career of sorrows (53:1-3), his vicarious death as the Lord places on him the sins of wayward people (53:4-6), his silence before the accusers (53:7-9), and his satisfaction at the results of his death, namely, the justification of many transgressors (53:10-12). The fourth servant song of Isaiah is seen fulfilled by the Gospel writers in many incidents in Jesus' life and preeminently in his Passion.

Isaianic Servant of the Lord	Fulfillment in the Suffering of Jesus
53:1: "Who has believed our message?"	**Jn 12:38**: rejection by Israel's religious leaders
53:2: no beauty, no majesty, nothing desirable	**Mt 2:23**: a Nazarene, that is, a despised one (cf. Jn 1:46)
53:3a: despised and rejected by people	**Mk 9:12**: the Son of man must suffer and be rejected
53:3b: man of sorrows, and familiar with suffering	**Mt 16:21; Lk 18:31-33**: predictions of his Passion
53:4: "He took up our infirmities and carried our sorrows"	**Mt 8:17**: healing and exorcising ministry in Galilee
53:5: pierced, crushed, his wounds	**Mt 26:67**: they spit upon him and struck him with fists **Mt 27:26**: Pilate had Jesus flogged
53:6-7: iniquity laid on him; lamb to the slaughter	**Jn 1:29, 36**: John the Baptist's confession: lamb of God
53:7a, c: as a sheep before shearers, he did not open his mouth	**Mt 26:62-63a; 27:13-14** trials before the Sanhedrin and Pilate
53:7b: led like a lamb to the slaughter	**Mt 27:31**: soldiers led him away to be crucified
53:9: assigned a grave with the rich in his death	**Mt 27:57-60**: burial in the tomb of Joseph of Arimathea
53:12b, d: poured out his life unto death; bore the sin of many, and made intercession for the transgressors	**Mt 26:28**: Lord's supper: cup is blood poured out for many for the forgiveness of sins **Mt 26:38-39**: Gethsemane prayers for the cup he must drink, representing the Father's wrath poured out on him
53:12c: numbered with the transgressors	**Lk 22:37**: arrested in Gethsemane as a criminal **Lk 23:33** (cf. Mt 27:38): crucified between two robbers

At his baptism and at his transfiguration the Father's voice of authentication declares, "This is my beloved Son, with whom I am well pleased" (Mt 3:17; 17:5). This declaration combines Isaiah 42:1 ("here is my servant in whom I delight") with Psalm 2:7 ("you are my Son; today I have begotten you"). The Father identifies Jesus both as the servant whose faithfulness to the redemptive mission brings God delight, as well as the messianic Son who is exalted as King and Lord at his resurrection (cf. Acts 13:33; Rom 1:4; Heb 1:5; 5:5).[17] As the initial phase of Jesus' Galilean ministry draws to a close, Matthew notes that Jesus' healing ministry fulfilled Isaiah 42:1-4 from the first servant song (Mt 12:15-21). Jesus is the servant upon whom God has poured out his Spirit to fulfill the mission of bringing justice and hope to the nations. The servant does not cry out or quarrel. In spite of intense opposition he trusts in God and is gentle in heart to reveal the kingdom to his disciples (cf. Mt 11:28-29). He is not harsh toward the weak (bruised reed, smoldering wick), but reveals his salvation to child-like hearts (cf. Mt 11:27). The justice he brings is the present gift of righteousness to the repentant who hope in his name.

The clearest reference in the Synoptic Gospels to the substitutionary nature of Jesus' death is found in the present text where his life is given as a "ransom for many" (Mt 20:28/Mk 10:45).[18] The one who believes and repents is freed from slavery to sin by the ransom payment of Jesus' blood shed on the cross. Though this text anticipates the fuller theology of redemption developed in the New Testament epistles (cf. Tit 2:14; 1 Pet 1:18-19), it occurs here to support Jesus' challenge to his disciples to imitate his pattern of servanthood. Theirs will not be a redemptive, vicarious suffering. The imitation is one of degree not kind: just as he sacrificed comfort, security, and status in order to redeem others, so they must set aside career prospects, monetary gain, personal prestige and other such natural human pursuits for the promotion of God's rule among people. They must constantly remind themselves that they are servants, not lords, and that leadership in the kingdom of God must take on a wholly distinct and contrastive character from leadership in the secular world. Their authority as vice-regents will come later (Mt 19:28). The present age, however, is the salvation historical phase of sacrifice, suffering, and perhaps even death to promote first God's kingdom and righteousness (Mt 6:33). Their recollection of the life and death of Jesus, Son of man, the suffering Servant and coming King, will provide the pattern and motivation to pursue their calling to lead by serving.

---

[17] These passages, which quote Psalm 2:7, indicate that the Psalmist is not referring to Jesus' divine ontological Sonship (which is clearly taught in many other places, e.g. Mt 11:27; 22:41-45), but to his functional, messianic Sonship. Having completed the work of redemption, Jesus takes his seat at the right hand of the Father where he is invested with royal authority as King and Lord.

[18] The self-offering of Jesus' life, by the means of his death on the cross, is to provide a "ransom for many" (λυτρον ἀντι πολλων). Morris, *Apostolic Preaching of the Cross*, 29-38, definitively establishes that the term λυτρον means, in its present context of the Passion, the ransom payment made to purchase the freedom of slaves from captivity to sin. Jesus' death is set forth as voluntary ("to give his life"), substitutionary ("ransom payment"), and universal in its potential efficacy ("for many").

Washing the feet of the disciples (Jn 13:1-20)

Jesus and the twelve disciples arrived at the upper room on Thursday evening and reclined at the table to begin their Passover meal together (Mt 26:20; Mk 14:17; Lk 22:14). Jesus spoke of this final meal with his disciples as a harbinger of the messianic feast he would enjoy with them in the consummated kingdom (Lk 22:15-16; cf. Rev 19:9). Jesus had poured out his love to his disciples over the past three years and now was moving to complete his appointed work by his redemptive death (Jn 17:4; 19:30). No greater love than this could he show to his friends than laying down his life for them (Jn 15:13). Having loved them, he would love them to the end of his earthly life and to the fullest extent (13:1).[19] The Satan-inspired betrayal by Judas Iscariot was already set in motion (13:2). Fully aware that the fulfillment of the Father's earthly mission for him was rapidly drawing near (13:3), Jesus bequeathed to his disciples one final visual lesson. Without saying a word, Jesus would inscribe indelibly on their memories the significance of all of the previous verbal lessons about servanthood (Mt 18:1-4; 19:13-14; 20:25-28). Jesus rose from supper, removed his outer tunic, wrapped himself with a towel, filled the basin with water, and began to wash his disciples' feet one by one, drying them with the towel (13:4-5).

Peter represented the other embarrassed disciples when he attempted to dissuade the Lord from such a menial act of cleansing his dirty feet. He once again assumed the foolish station of issuing a negative command to his Lord: "You shall in no way at any time wash my feet" (13:8a; cf. Mt 16:22). And as before Jesus responded to the well-intentioned but misguided words of Peter with a sound retort: "Unless I wash you, you have no part with me" (13:8b; cf. Mt 16:23). Jesus' explanation that followed indicates that the portion Peter would forfeit by refusing to have his feet washed was not his salvific connection to Jesus, but the joy of unbroken fellowship. Peter was driven by emotion and shifted from refusal of the foot washing one moment to a request for an entire bathing of his body the next. Jesus said that those who have been bathed all over, an anticipatory reference to the forgiveness of sins through his coming death, only need to have their feet washed, symbolizing removal of defilement from contact with the world. All of the disciples, save Judas (13:10b-11), were receiving an essential lesson for successful Christian living and leadership: when sinful thoughts and actions arise, and arise they will, regular confession would bring cleansing and restore their joyful experience of fellowship with God (13:9-10a; cf. 1 Jn 1:9-2:2).

After he completed washing the twenty-four dirty feet, the Lord returned to his place at the table and pressed the disciples for the meaning of his action. He made the application clear through a greater to lesser argument: If I have done this to you, how much more should you do this for one another (13:12-14). Jesus, rightly elevated as Teacher and Lord and Sender, set his disciples an example (13:15) by serving them so that they, mere students and servants and messengers, might prove their identification with him by serving one another. Deliberate choices to give preference to others above themselves, followed up by menial acts of service, would demonstrate that they have submitted to the rule of the servant-King. Pursuit of privileged positions

---

[19] The phrase εἰς τέλος is taken with both temporal ("to the end") and qualitative ("fully") meanings.

which seal them off them from the discomforts that always attend the servant's task, would place them in a role "greater" than their Lord, and disqualify them from becoming leaders enfolded by the divine benediction (13:16-17).

Contrastive patterns of leadership (Lk 22:24-30)

If one follows the order of Luke's Gospel, the argument between the disciples over who would assume the highest position in the kingdom occurred, unbelievably, after the Lord washed their feet. Luke's simple account places the dispute after the identification of the betrayer (Lk 22:20-23), which according to John took place after the foot washing and during the meal proper (Jn 13:18-30).[20] It almost defies reason that the disciples could observe their Lord wash their feet and press the application to them so clearly (Jn 13:12-17), and then immediately engage in a fresh dispute over who would be the greatest in the coming kingdom (Lk 22:24). However, worldly ambition is not exorcised from the human heart easily and the disciples had already shown a pattern of internecine conflict over such matters (cf. Mk 9:33; 10:13; 10:35-37, 41).[21]

Jesus addressed the disputants by making a studied contrast ("but not so with you" [Lk 22:26; cf. Mk 10:43]) between secular models of leadership and the posture his kingdom leaders should assume if they wish to receive the divine approbation (Lk 22:25-27).

Worldly leadership	Kingdom leadership
1. Secular rulers exercise unquestioned lordship over their subjects (Lk 22:25a; cf. Mk 10:42; Mt 8:9).	1. Kingdom leaders are willing to occupy less esteemed roles and to undertake menial tasks in order to facilitate the success of others through their service (Lk 22:26).
2. Those who exercise secular authority are given the title Benefactor,[22] and thus bind their subjects to an obligatory relationship for favors distributed (22:25b).	2. Kingdom leadership is voluntary, free of binding obligations, and unconcerned with titles of respect. Like Jesus at the table serving the reclining disciples, the kingdom leader promotes the welfare of others over personal privilege (Lk 22:27).

[20] A plausible case can also be made that Luke's account is not strictly chronological (or John's account for that matter), and that the dispute took place before the foot washing incident. However, John seems to indicate that Jesus interrupted the meal just as it was being served (13:2-4) and then returned to the table to enjoy the meal proper at which time he identified the betrayer (13:12, 26-27).
[21] The noun rendered "dispute," φιλονεικια (Lk 22:24), occurs only here in the New Testament. However, its cognate adjective φιλονεικος means "contentious" in 1 Cor 11:16. The disciples were engaged in apparently much more than a gentle disagreement.
[22] The title Benefactor (ευεργετης) was applied throughout the Greco-Roman world to rulers and prominent persons to identify them as those whose good deeds benefit culture and contribute to the prosperity of civilization (EDNT, 2: 76-77). The title brought with it respect, material prosperity, and influence over others. The verb καλουνται could be middle rather than passive, in which case the authorities actively sought the title of respect, Benefactor, for themselves.

To obey Jesus' call to servanthood would involve a radical surrender of one's natural pursuit of comfort, wealth, and recognition. The leadership training program of Jesus was not to end in a specified period with graduation, credentials, and a secure vocational setting. The disciples were thus feeling the weight of their sacrifices (cf. Mt 19:27). Though these aspiring leaders deserved a sound rebuke for such shocking insensitivity that they could engage in intramural disputes right after the Lord washed their feet, Jesus ended by affirming their sacrifices (Lk 22:28) and promising them special roles in the coming kingdom (22:29-30). When the present rule of God assumes its universal and uncontested realm, the disciples will take their place at the table of the messianic feast (cf. Mt 26:29; Mk 14:27; Lk 13:29; 22:18) and sit on thrones as participants in Messiah's reign over Israel and the nations (cf. Mt 19:28; cf. 1 Cor 6:2; 2 Tim 2:12a; Rev 20:4). The path to promotion, then, is the way of the servant both for Jesus (cf. Php 2:6-11) and for his followers.

Leadership Profile of Jesus: Kingdom greatness through servanthood

1. *Example of the suffering Servant: The exalted Son of man of Daniel's vision was, first, the suffering Servant of Isaiah's prophecy. Jesus fulfilled the role of the Servant in the greatest act of self-abnegation this world has or ever will witness. It is, surprisingly, John's Gospel that records the scene in the upper room on the night before his death when Jesus filled the basin with water, wrapped himself with a towel, and washed the dirty feet of his disciples (Jn 13:4-12). Surprising because this is the Gospel that begins by introducing Jesus as the Word who is both with God and is himself divine (1:1-2). It is in John's Gospel that Thomas cries out to the risen Jesus, "my Lord and my God" (20:28). However, John's record gives a corresponding emphasis to the humanity of Jesus, the divine Word who became flesh (1:14). The God-man sits down by a well in Samaria, exhausted from the trip north, and asks a woman for a drink of water to quench his thirst (4:6). Jesus weeps at the tomb of his friend Lazarus (11:35). And now he takes the place of a common slave and performs the most menial of tasks. This time he will not allow the disciples to miss the application, though their penchant for rivalry will soon rear its ugly head once again. "I have set you an example that you should do as I have done for you" (Jn 13:15). For unworthy sinners and, at best, unprofitable servants to adopt a sense of entitlement and a belief in their own importance reveals an abysmal failure to ponder the mysterious depths of the self-humbling of the man who is God.*

2. *Radically different model of leadership: Jesus twice warned his disciples not to build their philosophy of leadership around the secular models of the day: "But not so with you" (Mk 10:43; Lk 22:26). Secular leaders operated on the basis of unquestioned, and often arbitrary, exercise of power over their subjects, binding obligations, and titles of respect. Leadership positions were invested with power, prestige, and perquisites. The New Testament vignettes of such first century leaders as Herod the Great, Antipas, Pilate, Agrippa I, Felix, Festus and Agrippa II reveal patterns of paranoia, manipulation, unjust use of power, political maneuvering, megalomania,*

bribery, self-aggrandizement, vanity and indulgence (Mt 2:1-8, 16-18; 14:1-12; 27:11-26; Lk 13:31-32; 23:6-12; Acts 12:19b-23; 24:24-27; 25:23; 26:24-32).[23] That the disciples repeatedly bickered over places of prominence in the coming kingdom proves they were imitating those models with which they were familiar. All aspiring kingdom leaders should pause to remember Jesus' words when they encounter the latest proposal in leadership theory: "But not so with you."

[23] This must be balanced by noting that Luke's record in Acts often provides a positive picture of secular authorities who carried out their duties with fairness in accordance with Roman law (Acts 13:7; 16:37-39; 18:12-17; 19:35-41; 22:22-23:35; 26:30-32; 28:30-31). Paul and Peter similarly enjoin believers to obey the secular rulers because they generally act with justice to commend those who do good and to punish wrongdoers (Rom 13:1-7; 1 Pet 2:13-17; cf. 1 Tim 2:1-2). Jesus' command to "render to Caesar the things which are Caesar's, and to God the things which are God's" conditions the attitude of the early church toward civil leaders (Mk 12:17).

PART FOUR

New Testament Profiles
in Leadership

Chapter 17.
Peter: A broken rock becomes a foundation stone

Preliminary questions to consider:
1. *What stabilizing truth can a leader who has experienced periodic failures reaffirm through the study of Peter's spiritual pilgrimage?*
2. *What mandate has the Lord clearly set forth for his new covenant leaders?*
3. *What must be the foundation of the work of any spiritual leader who desires lasting fruit?*

Call of the fisherman

Jesus gave to the leader of his apostolic team the name Cephas, which is the Aramaic word for rock (Jn 1:42; cf. 1 Cor 1:12; 3:22; 9:5). The New Testament normally knows him by its Greek equivalent, Peter (Mk 3:16; Mt 16:18). His Semitic name is Simon or, more precisely, Simeon (Acts 15:14; 2 Pet 1:1). His father's name was Jonah (Mt 16:17) or, in abbreviated form, John (Jn 1:42; 21:15-17). He would eventually become the "rock" of the church, but only after a long arduous journey with many stumbles and falls. He and his brother Andrew were fishermen and natives of the small town of Bethsaida, slightly north and east of the Sea of Galilee (Jn 1:44)

Peter was introduced to Jesus by his brother Andrew who, along with their friend John, had been stirred by the preaching of John the Baptist (Jn 1:35, 40). The Baptizer invited his listeners to turn their attention away from him to Jesus, "the lamb of God" (Jn 1:36). Andrew announced that "we have found the Messiah" and brought Peter to Jesus. Was it with a prophetic sense, that is, in terms of what he would become, that Jesus attached to Simon the name Cephas/Peter meaning "rock" (Jn 1:42)? Six to nine months later Peter and Andrew, while casting their fishing net into the water, heard and responded to Jesus' invitation to follow him and to become fishers for people (Mk 1:16-20). Later Peter will recall the great sacrifice he and the others made when they abandoned everything to follow Jesus (Mt 19:27). The Lord would in turn remind Peter that no one can outgive God and that no sacrifice would go unrewarded (Mt 19:28-29). Peter was living at that time with his wife and mother-in-law in their home in Capernaum (Mk 1:29-30; cf. 1 Cor 9:5).

Luke's narrative provides fresh details about that decisive meeting with Jesus (Lk 5:1-11).[1] Jesus stepped into Simon's boat and began teaching the people gathered on the shore of Lake Galilee. When Jesus commanded Simon to cast out

---

[1] This assumes that the incident in Luke 5:1-11 took place the same day as the call of the fishermen in Mark 1:16-20 / Matthew 4:18-22. Alternatively, this miracle occurred a little later in the multi-staged call to discipleship.

206

the nets he did so out of deference because they had toiled all night and had caught nothing. The miraculous catch of fish was too heavy for even two boats. As the boats began to sink, Peter fell to his knees and cried out, "Depart from me, Lord, for I am a sinful man" (5:8). Peter began his journey of faith with a deep understanding of his own sinful heart and his unworthiness to stand in the presence of such a majestic person. In all the vicissitudes of the coming days this conviction will never leave Peter. Contrition was the prelude to his decision to follow (5:10-11).

Uneven steps in the development of faith

When Jesus set apart the twelve to be his apostles, that is, commissioned representatives of the kingdom, Peter must have soon been identified as the primus inter pares, the first among equals. All four of the New Testament lists of the twelve apostles begin with Peter, followed by the other three fishermen, though not in the same order (Mt 10:2-4; Mk 3:16-19; Lk 6:14-16; Acts 1:13b). Peter regularly becomes the spokesman for the group (Mt 15:15; 16:16; 18:21; 19:27; Mk 11:21; Lk 12:41) though, admittedly, he sometimes speaks without thinking (Mk 9:6b; Lk 9:33b). He is the one approached by the Jewish authorities who want to inquire about Jesus' position on paying the half-shekel temple tax (Mt 17:24-25). Peter is brought into the inner circle along with James and John where they witness firsthand the raising of Jairus' daughter from the dead, the Transfiguration, and the intercession in Gethsemane (Mk 5:37; 9:2; 14:33). Years later Peter's memory remains vivid of that mountain-top experience where he was eyewitness of the Lord's majesty and earwitness of the thundering voice from heaven declaring his Sonship (2 Pet 1:16-18).

Peter figures prominently in so many of the scenes recorded in the Gospels. His intentions are always good, but his understanding of Jesus' mission is faulty and his expressive nature displays those faults for all to see. His faith grows as he observes his Lord in many situations, but is hindered by a mind that is easily distracted. While Peter is hosting Jesus in his home in Capernaum, his mother-in-law becomes sick with a fever. Jesus does as requested of him, healing her with a touch (Mk 1:31) and the authoritative word (Lk 4:39). That evening large numbers of people thronged Peter's house so that Jesus healed the sick and demon possessed (Mk 1:32-34). Peter is one of the privileged three to witness Jesus raise the young daughter of Jairus from the dead (Mk 1:40-42). Following the exorcisms in Peter's house, Jesus had refused to allow demonic testimony to his person (Mk 1:34). After he raised the girl he also prohibited the eyewitnesses to spread news of the miracle (Mk 5:43). Peter and the other disciples would continue to struggle with Jesus' reluctance to step forward and assert the authority that he clearly possessed.

Jesus' pattern of ministry was one of engagement and withdrawal. After one particularly busy period of traveling and preaching through the villages of Galilee (Mk 6:6b, 7, 30), Jesus invited his disciples to come apart with him and rest from the demanding crowds and incessant pressures. They withdrew to a solitary place in the hills north of Bethsaida (Mk 6:31-32; Lk 9:10). However, the crowds soon discover his location and throng the hills. When the disciples express concern that the crowds be sent home lest they be stranded at night in such a desolate place,

Jesus tests them: "you (pl.) give them something to eat" (Mk 6:37). Both Philip and Peter respond with incredulity. Peter notices the five loaves of bread and two fish brought by a young boy and asks, "What are they among so many?" (Jn 6:7-9). Jesus then blesses God for this small provision and multiples it to the full satisfaction of the multitude. The disciples are left to gather the remaining fragments and to reflect (Jn 6:12-13).

Jesus is forced to withdraw from the crowds who are demanding that he establish an earthly kingdom (Jn 6:14-15). He will not be drawn into their socio-political notions of his kingship so he dismisses them, sends the disciples ahead to Capernaum by boat, and withdraws to a mountain to pray (Mt 14:22-23). The disciples make painful headway against a strong contrary wind from the northeast. In the early morning hours Jesus comes to them walking on the lake and wishing to pass them by (Mk 6:48). He is testing their faith. Can they, in light of their past experiences, recognize his authority over nature and implore him for help? After Jesus calms their fears that it is he and not a ghost, Peter asks to come to him on the water (Mt 14:28). He boldly steps out and begins to walk, but when he looks at the wind and waves he begins to sink and cries for help. Peter's faith can get him walking on the water and moves him to cry to Jesus for help as he sinks, but cannot overcome his fear in the storm. He and his fellow disciples are a mixture of worshipping adoration for the Son of God (Mt 14:33) and yet stubborn insensitivity toward what they have seen both with the loaves and with the waves (Mk 6:51-52).

In the aftermath of the miracle of the feeding of the five thousand, many in the wider circle of Jesus' "disciples" began to turn away (Jn 6:60, 66). They could not understand his enigmatic teaching about eating his flesh and drinking his blood (6:53-58). Jesus refused to satisfy their political aspirations of a king who would rally the nation, cleanse the priesthood, and overthrow their Roman overlords.[2] As his followers begin to dissipate, he puts the question to the twelve: "You do not want to leave too, do you" (6:67). Now was the time of decision for his truest disciples. The initial excitement of following Jesus has long since worn off. He is talking more and more about suffering both for himself and his followers. Peter steps forward as the group's representative: "Lord, to whom shall we go? You have the words of eternal life. We believe and know that you are the Holy One of God" (6:68-69). Apostasy is unthinkable. A decisive commitment has been made and there is no turning back. The disciples have entered into a knowledge that Jesus is the Messiah and their faith is settled.[3] Peter's faith would continue to be tested and to grow, but not in a neat linear progression.

Rock of the church

At the end of the Galilean phase of ministry Jesus brought his disciples to the far north in the region near Caesarea Philippi. Away from the adoring crowds and

---

[2] Such were the current expectations of a conquering Messiah in intertestamental and New Testament era Judaism. See Emil Schurer, *The History of the Jewish People in the Age of Jesus Christ* (175 B.C.-A.D. 135), rev. and ed. G. Vermes, F. Millar, M. Black (Edinburgh: T. & T. Clark, 1979): II: 517-530.

[3] The perfect tense verbs in John 6:69, believe (πεπιστευκαμεν) and know (ἐγνωκαμεν), denote completed decisions in the past with continuing effects to the very time of the confession.

the scoffing religious leaders, he once again probes the twelve about his identity: "Who do people say the Son of man is?" (Mt 16:13). They reply that popular opinion identifies him as a prophet, but that there is no consensus. What was clear is that no group in Israel was openly confessing him as the Messiah (16:14). He asks them: "But who do you (pl.) say that I am?" (16:15). Once again Peter speaks up: "You are the Christ, the Son of the living God" (16:16). There is no ambiguity here. Peter has drawn a settled assurance from his direct exposure to Jesus' words and deeds for nearly two years.

Jesus affirms Peter's confession as springing not from human initiative, but from God-given insight (Mt 16:17). He makes a word play on the name Peter (Gk. *petros*) and identifies the leader of the apostles as the "rock" (*petra*) upon which he will build his church (16:18). The natural sense of Jesus' language is that Peter himself is the rock who will become the foundational apostle of the new covenant community.[4] This role finds its fulfillment in the early chapters of Acts (1-12; cf. Eph 2:20). In his role as foundation-laying apostle, as first among equals, he wields the keys of the kingdom, which signify the power to exclude or permit entrance based on response to his preaching. "It is the Church on earth carrying out heaven's decisions, communicated by the Spirit, and not heaven ratifying the Church's decisions."[5] The disciples, and believers of all ages, represented by Peter, are entrusted with proclaiming the kingdom, warning of exclusion and judgment, offering entrance and forgiveness. It is in this sifting process that they become instruments of building the church (cf. Mt 4:19; 5:13-16; 10:6-42; 28:18-20; loosing in Acts 2:14-39; 3:11-26; binding in Acts 4:11-12; 8:20-23).

Peter's confession of Jesus as Messiah leads immediately to a fuller self-disclosure as Jesus begins to speak "from that time on" in unmistakable terms of his suffering, death and resurrection (16:21). This is not the first reference to his death (cf. Mt 9:15; 10:38; 12:40; Jn 2:19; 3:14; 6:53-58), but now he expounds it openly to the disciples, without veiled allusions and symbols. The "Son of man" is not only the sovereign king of Daniel 7:13-14, but also the suffering servant of Psalm 22 and Isaiah 53. Peter has apprehended the former, but has no thought of the latter. He dares to rebuke Jesus and dissuade him from such dire predictions: "Never, Lord. This shall never happen to you" (16:22). "Peter's strong will and warm heart linked to his ignorance produce a shocking bit of arrogance. He confesses that Jesus is the Messiah and then speaks in a way implying that he knows more of God's will than the Messiah himself."[6] Jesus turns toward Peter in a face to face confrontation: "Get behind me, Satan. You are a stumbling block to me; you do not have in mind the things of God, but the things of people" (16:23). Peter is being manipulated by Satan to turn Jesus aside from the cross-way of the Father's will. Peter is blocking Jesus from his ordained path, exalting him as

[4] Though there are two distinct Greek words in the Matthean account (πετρος—-πετρα), the spoken Aramaic words behind them (kepha') would have been identical and the wordplay more direct.
[5] W. F. Albright and C.S. Mann, *Matthew*, The Anchor Bible (Garden City, NY: Doubleday, 1971): 197. The verbs bind and loose in Mt 16:19 are periphrastic future perfects and are best rendered: "shall have been bound/loosed," indicating Peter's role in confirming what heaven has determined.
[6] Carson, *Matthew*, 377.

King, but without recognizing him as the suffering Servant. Jesus' radically different assessments of Peter in this interchange are shocking. Peter moves from a confession that springs from divine revelation (Mt 16:17) to active opposition to the purpose of God and an unconscious alignment with Satan (16:23)! This mixture of insight and confusion is characteristic of Peter's responses to Jesus throughout the latter's earthly ministry.

Growing pressures and audacious claims

Peter, like John and the other apostles, was overtaken by the events of Passion week even though Jesus had predicted what would happen on at least three occasions (Mt 16:21; 17:22-23; 20:17-19). Even after the Lord's denunciation of Peter for failing to grasp his mission, these passion predictions grieved (Mt 17:23b) and utterly mystified the disciples (Lk 18:34). Peter and John made preparations for the Passover meal that Thursday evening (Lk 22:8). During the supper Jesus rose, removed his tunic and wrapped himself with a towel, filled the basin with water, and began to wash the disciples' feet one by one, drying them with the towel (Jn 13:2-5). The reader is not surprised to find that Peter is the one disciple who objected: "No, you shall never wash my feet" (13:8a). Peter was humble enough to feel that his Lord should not perform such menial service on him, but too proud to remain quiet and learn a valuable lesson. When Jesus made washing the precondition of fellowship with him, Peter blurted out, "Then, Lord, not just my feet, but my hands and my head as well" (13:8b-9). This time Peter was gently corrected but not rebuked, for his recognition of the need for cleansing was commendable. Jesus was performing not a bathing of the entire body, pointing to salvation, but the cleansing of the feet, symbolizing removal of defilement from contact with the world, that is, the restoration of personal purity and unbroken fellowship with God. He then pressed upon the disciples the meaning of his actions, namely, to imitate him in serving one another (Jn 13:12-17).

Even while washing their feet, Jesus intimated at betrayal by one of their number (Jn 13:10b-11, 18-19). But now, returning to the meal, he speaks more directly: "I tell you the truth, one of you is going to betray me" (13:21). The disciples were completely at a loss (13:22) and began to ask one another, "Is it I?" (Mt 26:22). Peter goaded John, sitting next to Jesus, to ask of whom he was speaking (Jn 13:23-24). No one seemed to understand why Judas suddenly departed (13:28-29). Before leaving the upper room Jesus addresses Peter: "Satan has asked to sift you (pl.) as wheat. But I have prayed for you (sg.) that your (sg.) faith may not fail. And when you (sg.) have turned back, strengthen your brothers" (Lk 22:31-32). Satan's attempt to undermine the faith of the eleven will not succeed. Jesus' intercession will, in spite of Peter's coming setback, prevail and enable him to be the means of strengthening his faltering brothers. Peter's characteristic response is to deny the implications of Jesus' intended meaning: "Lord, I am ready to go with you to prison and to death" (22:33). Still stinging from the Lord's earlier rebuke (Mt 16:23), he will no longer attempt to persuade his headstrong Lord that death and Messiahship are irreconcilable concepts. Peter's thought of suffering here is one of martyrdom like the Old Testament prophets or Maccabean heroes of old, not the voluntary sacrifice in his Lord's mind. Peter is grieved when the Lord says he will be with them "only a little longer" and that where he is going they cannot follow now, but will follow later (Jn 13:33, 36). He replies with unjustified confidence, asserting his willingness to follow Jesus even if it means death (Lk 22:37; Jn 13:37). In Peter's heart is a mixture of sincere love that yearns to be with Jesus and not be separated even for a moment, and an ignorance that overestimates both his own grasp of the situation and underestimates his own capacity for cowardice. The Lord predicts that before the rooster crows in the early morning hour, Peter will deny him three times (Jn 13:38).

When the group arrives at the Mount of Olives Jesus predicts the scattering of all of his disciples, in fulfillment of Zechariah 13:7, and anticipates his coming resurrection appearance to them in Galilee (Mt 26:31-32). Peter repeats his exaggerated claim of courage against Jesus' repeated statements to the contrary. He thinks he knows more than his Lord and is more steadfast than his brothers, of whom he concedes might indeed be offended (26:33). The other disciples are not to be outdone as they also insist on their undying loyalty (26:35). Taking Peter, John and James into the garden, Jesus enjoins them to be watchful while he moves to a quiet place to pray to his Father. But the events of the past week have taken their toll. The three disciples fall asleep from a sorrow-induced exhaustion (Lk 22:45). Each time Jesus returns he finds them sleeping (Mt 26:40, 43, 45), until they are brutally awakened by the arrival of the temple police led by Judas. Peter draws a sword and cuts off the ear of the servant of the high priest, one named Malchus (Jn 18:10). Peter had slept through the Lord's prayers in Gethsemane or he might have understood that suffering and death were the Father's will and the Son's choice. As at other critical times, Peter's actions are met with a rebuke: "Put your sword away" (Jn 18:11). Jesus' final miracle of healing is to restore Malchus' ear (Lk 22:51). Jesus is bound and escorted off. All of the disciples desert him and flee into the darkness (Mt 26:56).

The bitter setback

An unnamed disciple, almost certainly John, and Peter followed from a distance. John helped secure access for Peter to the courtyard of the high priest as the first two phases of the Jewish trial proceeded in the chambers inside (Jn 18:15-16). Peter's denials took place during the formal inquiry before Annas, still influential father-in-law of Caiaphas the high priest, and during the first hearing before the Sanhedrin that Caiaphas presided over. First, a girl on duty at the gate allows Peter entrance to the courtyard. As Peter is warming himself in the light of the fire, she identifies him as one who was with the Galilean. She and others call Peter "one of his disciples." Peter responds: "I am not" (Mt 26:69-70; Jn 18:17-18, 25). Next, another servant girl at the entryway to where Peter has withdrawn identifies him as "one of them" who was with the Nazarene. Peter denies it with an oath: "I do not know the man" (Mt 26:71-72). Finally, still in the courtyard about one hour later, a bystander identifies Peter as one of Jesus' Galilean followers, betrayed by his accent (Mt 27:73). This man was a relative of Malchus and claims he saw Peter in the olive grove at the time of arrest (Jn 18:26). Peter spews out curses and swears, "I do not know the man" (Mt 27:74). The denials are forceful and progress with increasing vehemence. At the third denial the rooster crowed and Peter recalled the words of the Lord, left the courtyard, and wept bitterly (Mt 26:75). Luke adds that between Peter's third denial and his departure "the Lord turned and looked straight at Peter" (Lk 22:61), perhaps as Jesus was being led across the courtyard bound for the formal trial of the Sanhedrin in the temple courts. Here is the darkest moment of Peter's life. His boisterous claims of loyalty have proven hollow. His exalted confession of Jesus' Sonship appears as a sham. He disappointed himself, failed in his leadership role in the team, and, above all, dishonored the one who meant more to him than life itself.

Restoration and reinstatement of the fallen leader[7]

On the early morning of the first day of the week four of the women disciples came to the tomb to anoint Jesus' body with spices. When they arrive the stone has been rolled from the entrance, the guards are nowhere to be found, and the body of Jesus is missing (Mk 16:1-4). Mary Magdalene rushes off to tell Peter and John that the body has been stolen (Jn 20:2). Suddenly the three women who remain encounter two angels in dazzling apparel. The angels remind the women of Jesus' words that he would rise (Lk 24:4-8) and that he will meet them in Galilee (Mk 16:6-7). The women flee from the tomb, filled with fear and joyful amazement at what they have seen and heard, speaking to no one about their encounter (Mk 16:8). Meanwhile, Peter and John, having been informed by Mary Magdalene of the missing body, run to the tomb after the three women have left. Peter bolts into the tomb and finds the linen strips lying on the ground and the head wrapping folded separately (Jn 20:2-7). Peter's understanding is limited, while John's is growing (20:8-10). Jesus then appears to a weeping Mary Magdalene who has come back to the tomb (20:11-13). Some of the disciples, including Peter and John, have now gathered together and hear the report of the three women who break their silence about their encounter with the two angels. The words seem like nonsense to the listeners (Lk 24:9-11). Then Mary Magdalene comes in and claims that Jesus appeared to her in the garden (Jn 20:18).

Sometime Sunday afternoon the Lord makes a special appearance to Peter (Lk 24:34; cf. 1 Cor 15:5a). The reader of the narrative would long to know what words, if any, were exchanged between the Lord, whom Peter had last seen as Jesus glanced in his direction in the courtyard following his denials (Lk 22:61), and the apostle he promised to restore (Lk 22:31-32). Alas, the record of Holy Scripture is silent. Later in the day Jesus appears to these three women and tells them to inform "my brothers" that he will meet them in Galilee (Mt 28:9-10). By now the eleven have gathered and are joined by two disciples who claim they met the risen Lord as they were walking to Emmaus. Jesus entered into conversation, opened up the Scriptures, broke bread with them, and suddenly disappeared (Lk 24:13-35). Now the converging testimonies of the three women (Mt 28:8; Lk 24:9-11), of Peter and John (Jn 20:8-10), of Mary (Jn 20:18; Lk 24:10), and finally of the two Emmaus disciples (Lk 24:33-35) have created an atmosphere charged

---

[7] The sequence of events traced here follows the simple reconstruction of the post-resurrection appearances set forth in George Eldon Ladd, *I Believe in the Resurrection of Jesus* (London: Hodder and Stoughton, 1975): 91-93.

with excitement. Suddenly on that Sunday evening Jesus appears to ten disciples who are gathered in the closed room due to fear of the Jews. For some unknown reason Thomas is absent. In an acted parable Jesus anticipates the definitive event of Pentecost by commissioning them to go and preach forgiveness and judgment in the power of the Spirit as his ambassadors (Jn 20:19-23). One week later the Lord accommodates doubting Thomas who has made the noble demand for objective evidence to substantiate the verbal claims of his friends. Even without touching the Lord, his earlier precondition for believing (Jn 20:25b), Thomas confesses Jesus as "my Lord and my God" (20:28).

Jesus promised before his death (Mt 26:32), and in his appearance to the three women (Mt 28:9-10; cf. 28:7), that he would meet his disciples in Galilee. Seven disciples have returned to Galilee and are fishing together on the Sea of Tiberius (21:1-3). At dawn Jesus appears, though unrecognized, and instructs them to cast the net on the right side of the boat (Jn 21:1-6a). Peter and the two sons of Zebedee must have recalled a similar incident three years before (Lk 5:1-11). Now as then they have toiled all night without success, but at a stranger's command they make a catch so large they cannot haul it in (21:6b). John recognizes it is the Lord. Peter reacts by wrapping up with his outer garment and jumping into the water (21:7). Is he so eager to greet the Lord that he cannot wait and must quickly swim ashore? Does the garment, even drenched, prepare him to greet the Lord more acceptably? However one interprets Peter's impulsive response, the sequel is a breakfast of bread and roasted fish with his favorite companion (21:8-13).

After they finished eating, Jesus and Peter entered into an emotional interchange (Jn 21:15-23). Three times Jesus directs the same question to his disciple: "Do you love me (more than these)?" The basis of the comparison "than these" in the first question, and assumed in the following two, is unclear; Peter does not take it up and Jesus never interprets it.[8] With each affirmative answer comes the same question, which the third time grieves Peter (21:17). The Lord knows his heart and cannot be doubting his sincere love, despite all the foolish chatter, impulsive actions, bombastic claims, and bitter setbacks of the past. What Jesus underscores with such sanctified redundancy is that if, as it is true, Peter loves him, then that love must be translated into the ministry of caring for his spiritual lambs. At the outset of his pilgrimage Peter is called to fish for people (Mt 4:19); at the conclusion he is commissioned to shepherd the lambs. The two metaphors for evangelistic and pastoral roles respectively will be Peter's life work as the foundational "rock" of the church. Jesus' reinstatement of Peter involves

---

[8] The demonstrative pronoun τουτων in the comparative phrase πλεον τουτων (Jn 21:15) can be either masculine or neuter genitive plural. If masculine, Jesus may be comparing Peter's devotion to that of the other disciples: "Do you love me more than these other disciples do?" This writer doubts Jesus would invite such a comparative assessment, especially in light of the rivalry among the disciples that earned his rebuke (Mk 10:41-43), as well as Peter's past tendencies toward overconfidence (Mt 26:33; Jn 13:37). Further, in the follow-up conversation Jesus mildly reproves Peter for being distracted with John's destiny (Jn 20:20-23). If the pronoun is neuter, the rendering is, "Do you love me more than these things?" This would be a reference to his fishing gear, which represents his previous career with its material provisions and security. Jesus, then, may be calling Peter to reaffirm his commitment, made over three years before on this same shore of Lake Galilee, to fish for (and feed) people rather than catch fish (cf. Mt 4:18-20).

more than forgiveness of the past; it dignifies his future with a role of supreme importance. This is the fullest measure of restoration there could be. Peter's tendency to be distracted emerges again when Jesus speaks in cryptic terms about his disciple's coming violent death (Jn 21:18-19).[9] He turns to see John and asks, "What about him?" Peter must stay focused on his role in God's redemptive program and leave Jesus' other choice servants to the sovereign disposition of the Lord (21:20-23). Years later as his life draws to a close, Peter, the rock, recalls the Lord's words and will make his "exodus" with perfect composure (2 Pet 1:13-15).[10]

Two final appearances follow, one on a mountain in Galilee (Mt 28:16-20) and one on the Mount of Olives east of Jerusalem (Lk 24:44-53; Acts 1:3-12). Peter would draw much from the Lord's exposition of the Old Testament as he pointed to text after text that spoke of his sufferings, death, resurrection, and proclamation of forgiveness of sins to all nations (24:44-47). Christological fulfillment of Old Testament types, images, and prophecies pervade Peter's two letters (1 Pet 1:10-12, 19, 24-25; 2:4-8, 9-10, 22, 25; 5:4; 2 Pet 1:19-21; 3:10-13). Particularly fitting are the three stone testimonia (Isa 28:16; Ps 118:22; Isa 8:14): the rock-apostle clarifies that Jesus Christ is the sole foundation of the church's faith and confession (1 Pet 2:4-8).

'Pentecostal' proclaimer of the risen Lord

Peter's dramatic failure of faith is behind him now. After the Lord's ascension he takes his place as leader of the renewed apostolic team as they pray and wait for the gift of the Holy Spirit (Acts 1:12-14). Peter takes the initiative to call for a replacement for Judas Iscariot. Matthias is chosen by lots (Acts 1:15-26). The new Israel requires twelve apostolic witnesses to the resurrection (1:22). On the fiftieth day after Sabbath of Passover week, the Feast of Pentecost, the Spirit of God descended upon the 120 believers. They began to declare the praises of God in the languages of the diaspora Jews assembled from all over the world for the festival (2:1-11). The crowd's response varied from perplexity to mockery (2:12-13). Peter stands up with the eleven at his side and proclaims in this event the fulfillment of Joel 2:28-32. The Spirit's arrival as prophetic fulfillment is the gift of the crucified, risen, and exalted Lord Jesus. His resurrection and exaltation to the right hand of God, adumbrated in Psalms 16:8-11 and 110:1 respectively, signal the inauguration of the new covenant (Acts 2:14-36). The climactic gift of the covenant, the forgiveness of sins, is offered to any and all who will repent and believe (Acts 2:38-39; cf. Jer 31:31-34). About three thousand people respond to

---

[9] C. K. Barrett, *The Gospel According to John*, 2nd ed. (London: SPCK, 1978): 585, lists the patristic evidence that takes the language of Jn 21:18b ("you will stretch out your hands, but another will bind you") to refer to crucifixion. Barrett concludes: "This passage must be taken as comparatively early and good evidence for the martyrdom of Peter by crucifixion, which it presupposes."

[10] Peter writes of his death as an "exodus" (ἔξοδος) or "departure" (NIV) from this world (2 Pet 1:15), which is at the same time for the believer an "entrance" (εἴσοδος) or "welcome" (NIV) into the eternal kingdom of the Lord Jesus Christ (1:11). The meaning for the Greek ἔξοδος of death or departure from this life is well attested in Hellenistic Jewish literature and in the early church fathers (*EDNT*, 2: 8).

Chapter 17. Peter: A broken rock becomes a foundation stone

Peter's Pentecost sermon and are baptized. Devoted attention to the apostolic teaching becomes the first order of business for the new community (2:42). Peter's other sermons recorded in the early chapters of Acts contain the same basic four elements as the Pentecost sermon: (1) The death and resurrection of Jesus as the (2) messianic fulfillment of the Old Testament provides (3) the gift of forgiveness and salvation when a person (4) repents and believes (Acts 3:11-26; 4:8-12; 5:29-32; 10:34-43).

Peter, John, and later James, the half-brother of the Lord, will serve as the "pillars" of the church in Jerusalem in its formative years (Gal 2:9). Peter's proclamation of the gospel in the aftermath of Pentecost is the divine instrument of building the new community of several thousand believers in Jerusalem (2:41; 4:4; 5:14; 6:1, 7). The apostle who was once snared by the fear of man now stands as a rock, boldly proclaiming the gospel before crowds in the temple court (Acts 3:11-12), to the hostile priests and Sadducees (4:7-8), and before the powerful Sanhedrin (5:27-29). The religious leaders are at a loss to explain the boldness of Peter and John, simple Galilean fisherman without rabbinical training, except that they "had been with Jesus" (Acts 4:13). Peter is the leader in exercising discipline on duplicitous members of the community such as Ananias and Sapphira (Acts 5:3, 9). Peter and John set the spiritual tone for the growing church, that is, praise, prayer, holiness, joy in adversity, and bold witness (Acts 2:42-47; 4:23-31; 5:11, 41-42).

Cultural blinders and the law-free gospel

Peter and the other apostles continued even after the resurrection to worship in the temple courts and to observe Jewish customs, such as the stated times for prayer, Sabbath, and the food laws (Acts 2:46; 3:1; 5:21, 42). Greek-speaking believers like Stephen who grew up outside of Palestine carried their faith in Jesus to its logical conclusion at a much earlier stage. The temple system with its sacrifices, along with the Mosaic law, was abrogated in Jesus' death and resurrection, and is thus no longer binding on the people of God (Acts 6:11-14; 7:48-50). For this reason persecution fell upon the Hellenistic members of the church who were driven north, while the apostles remained in Jerusalem (Acts 8:1). The Hellenists became missionaries in the northern territories, extending the gospel to Jews in Judea (Acts 8:1), to the Samaritans (8:1, 4), to diaspora Jews in Phoenicia and Cyprus (Acts 11:19), and even to uncircumcised Greeks as far north as Antioch (11:20-21). How will the leadership of the mother church in Jerusalem, represented by Peter, react to such developments?

When Philip's preaching in Samaria meets with a great response, Peter and John are dispatched to check on the work. They lay hands on the believers who receive the Holy Spirit (Acts 8:14-17). The delay between faith and the gift of the Spirit is probably to seal, through apostolic verification, the unity of the one church of Christ both Jew and Samaritan. Still, these Samaritans are circumcised part-Jews who observe, in their own way, the Mosaic customs. How can Peter reject a work so manifestly authenticated by the Spirit of God? His reverence for the Spirit as mediator of the blessings of the risen Lord explains his angry denunciation of Simon the sorcerer, who seeks to purchase God's free gift for money (8:18-24).

215

He and John are liberated enough to proclaim Jesus to Samaritan villagers on their return to Jerusalem (8:25).

Luke's narrative next finds Peter healing the paralytic Aeneas in Lydda and raising from the dead the pious Tabitha in the coastal city of Joppa. In both places many turned to the Lord (Acts 9:32-42). What is curious is that Peter is hosted in Joppa in the home of Simon the tanner, an occupation despised by strict Jews because of ritual defilement contacted through skinning dead animals (9:43).[11] Is this a further hint that Peter's understanding of the gospel is releasing him from Jewish scruples over such matters?

The decisive breakthrough comes through an encounter with a Roman centurion in Caesarea. But first Peter must be prepared. One afternoon Peter ascends to the roof to pray while waiting for lunch. He falls into a trance and sees a large sheet lowered from heaven by its four corners containing all kinds of animals, clean and unclean (Acts 10:9-12). When commanded to "kill and eat," Peter adamantly refuses: "Surely not, Lord. I have never eaten anything impure or unclean" (Acts 10:13-14). Peter has reverted to his former pattern of deflecting Jesus' agenda by dictating one of his own. The voice returns: "Do not call anything impure that God has made clean" (10:15). The lesson is hammered home to the stubborn apostle three times. Upon reflection Peter understands that the vision applies to his reticent attitude toward uncircumcised Gentiles contrasted with God's acceptance of them (10:28-29, 34-35).

Peter cannot help but recognize that his entire encounter with the Roman centurion is providentially directed. First, a vision comes to Cornelius to send for one Peter staying with Simon the tanner in Joppa (10:1-8, 30-33). Second, there is the preparatory vision of the sheet. Third, the Spirit helps Peter overcome his hesitation when Cornelius's servants arrive (10:19-20). Fourth, Peter arrives in Caesarea to a people spiritually prepared to receive the gospel (10:25-33). The decisive event, however, one that confirms to Peter that salvation is a free gift of God through faith and wholly apart from obedience to the law, is the manifest presence of the Spirit given to these Gentiles (10:44-46). Peter administers water baptism to the new believers (10:47-48). When he returns to Jerusalem, Peter immediately faces the criticism of the Judaizers for having enjoyed table fellowship with uncircumcised people (11:1-3). His reply begins with the experiential preparation of the vision (11:4-10), but climaxes with the definitive theological proof of the law-free gospel: "As I began to speak, the Holy Spirit came on them as he had come on us at the beginning" (11:15). The baptism of the Spirit, predicted by Jesus (Acts 1:5; 11:16), brought life both to the Jewish believers in Jerusalem and, without distinction, to the Gentile believers in Caesarea (11:17-18). His course of action was the only one possible.

---

[11] The vocation of tanner (βυρσευς), one who skinned animal hides to turn them into usable material such as leather for clothing or household goods, was one considered ritually unclean by strict Jews. Jeremias, *Jerusalem in the Time of Jesus*, 304, 308-10, lists the tanner as one of the repugnant, though not dishonorable, trades due largely to the foul smell connected with the tanning process. Jeremias notes, with rabbinical evidence, the restrictions and ostracism that tanners faced.

Chapter 17. Peter: A broken rock becomes a foundation stone

Apologist for the gospel of grace

After his miraculous release from prison following the death of the apostle James (Acts 12:1-19), Peter appears in the Acts narrative on one final occasion. The Jerusalem council convenes to deal with the controversy that has broken out between Paul, who insists on a law-free gospel, and the Judaizers who are demanding that the Gentile believers be circumcised and obey the Mosaic law (Acts 15:1-4). A few months previous to this Peter had visited Antioch. His purpose was probably to encourage the work of Barnabas, a member of the Jerusalem church, and of Paul, whom he had met face to face twelve years earlier when the latter interviewed him during a brief trip to Jerusalem (Acts 9:26-30; Gal 1:18-19).[12] When Peter arrived in Antioch he gladly entered into table fellowship with the Gentiles. However, when members of the Judaizing wing of the Jerusalem church arrived, purporting to be from James, he reversed his course and withdrew. Paul was forced to confront Peter for hypocrisy that affected, of all people, Barnabas (Gal 2:11-14). This disturbing incident underscores the difficult time Peter had in overcoming ethno-centrism and fully embracing his Gentile brothers. When the Jerusalem council convenes a few weeks or months later, he has returned to his first principles and resolutely defends Paul's law-free gospel in the face of the stern demands of the Judaizers (Acts 15:5). He recalls that defining experience when he witnessed the Spirit fall on the household of Cornelius, makes the rhetorical appeal that the yoke of the law is and always has been a burden too heavy to bear, and asserts that salvation is through the grace of the Lord Jesus (15:7-11). Peter's final appearance in the narrative portion of the New Testament is as an eloquent apologist for the gospel of grace.

Servant and elder of the churches

Peter wrote two letters to the believers scattered through five northern provinces of Asia minor (1 Pet 1:1-2; 2 Pet 1:1). Here one can discover the mature Peter, tempered by three decades of evangelistic and pastoral ministry. Peter stands forth as first and foremost a teacher of the word of God. He views the Old Testament text through the lens of christological fulfillment, one that at times transcends the immediate sense intended by the prophetic writers (1 Pet 1:10-12). He has studied its types and images and has discovered Jesus as paschal lamb (1:19; Ex 12:3, 6), suffering servant (2:22; Isa 53:9), chief shepherd of the sheep (2:25 and 5:4; Ps 23:1), precious cornerstone (2:4, 6; Isa 28:16), capstone (2:7; Ps 118:22), stumbling stone (2:8; Isa 8:14), and morning star (2 Pet 1:19; Num 24:17). The apostolic message of salvation through Jesus Christ, grounded in actual historical events like the Transfiguration (2 Pet 1:16-18), is the culmination of the divinely

---

[12] This assumes Galatians was written prior to the Jerusalem council in Acts 15. The following is a suggested chronology: Paul's first post-conversion visit to Jerusalem to interview Peter (Gal 1:18-19; A.D. 37); Peter's ministry in Joppa and Caesarea (Acts 9:32-11:18; A.D. 40-41); death of James, escape of Peter, and death of Agrippa I (Acts 12:1-23; A.D. 44); first missionary journey to Galatia (Acts 13:4-14:28; April 48-September 49); visit of Peter to Antioch (Gal 2:11-14; Autumn A.D. 49); Jerusalem council (Acts 15:1-35; late Autumn A.D. 49). Even if Galatians was written after the Jerusalem council, Paul is most likely referring in Gal 2:11-14 to a visit to Antioch by Peter prior to his defense of Paul's law free gospel on that occasion (Acts 15:7-11).

superintended record of prophetic Scripture (2 Pet 1:19-21). The Spirit carried along the human authors and ensured a trustworthy product. It is the word of the Lord that stands forever, as Isaiah declares (1 Pet 1:24-25; Isa 40:6-8). Peter wants the believers to cultivate wholesome thinking by saturating their minds with the words of the holy prophets, words that agree with apostolic doctrine (2 Pet 3:1-2). Paul's writings qualify as Scripture, though parts are difficult to understand (2 Pet 3:15-16). Peter's moral exhortations are uniformly grounded in the teaching of Scripture: holiness (1 Pet 1:16; Lev 19:2); patient suffering like Jesus (2:21-22; Is 53:9); forgiveness not retaliation (3:8-12; Ps 34:12-16); endurance in suffering (4:17-19; Prov 11:31); humility (5:5-7; Prov 3:34); and expectation of the Lord's return (2 Pet 3:10-13; Isa 66:22). A life of moral excellence is nurtured through meditation on the great and precious promises of God's Word (2 Pet 1:4). Peter, despite his exclusive role as chief apostle, primus inter pares, and designated rock of the church, directs the allegiance of the believers away from himself to the authority of Scripture properly interpreted.

His proclamation of the Word finds its center in the death (1 Pet 1:11, 19; 2:4; 2:21-24; 3:18; 4:1, 13; 5:1) and resurrection (1 Pet 1:3, 11; 3:21-22) of Jesus Christ. What God has accomplished through Christ one receives by grace (1 Pet 1:2, 10, 13; 4:10; 5:5, 10; 2 Pet 1:2; 3:18), the unconstrained favor of God which Peter experienced so many times as Jesus' disciple.

Peter's refusal to become an unquestioned authority figure or to assume some kind of primacy in the church is seen most clearly in his self-designations. "Rock" and "pillar" are designations applied to him by others (Mt 16:18; Gal 2:9). Peter calls himself an apostle, a servant, an elder, and a witness (1 Pet 1:1; 5:1; 2 Pet 1:1). His role is both special and common. He possesses unique authority as Jesus' commissioned representative, alongside the other apostles, to establish the church upon revealed truth. As an eyewitness to Jesus' sufferings and resurrection glory, his apostolic testimony is trustworthy (1 Pet 5:1b). His formal status, however, is as an elder of the churches (1 Pet 5:1a; cf. 2 Jn 1, 3 Jn 1). He reminds his fellow elders to keep their attention fixed on the Chief Shepherd, before whom he and they will give an account (5:4). Peter is one who has been commissioned to feed God's flock (Jn 21:15-17). He appeals to his fellow elders to do the same with the proper mood, motive, and manner (1 Pet 5:2-3). First, their mood or attitude in shepherding is to be that of volunteers, not conscripts: "not under compulsion, but willingly."[13] Second, their motive is to be that of servants, not mercenaries: "not for financial gain, but eagerly."[14] Third, their manner of leadership is to be exemplary, not authoritarian: "not behaving like overlords, but being examples

---

[13] This is our rendering of the contrastive phrase, μη ἀναγκαστως ἀλλα ἑκουσιως. The adverb ἀναγκαστως is cognate with the verb ἀναγκαζω, which means to compel someone to do something, often against their will (Mt 14:22; Acts 26:11; Gal 2:3, 14; 6:12). The adverb ἑκουσιως (Heb 10:26) and the cognate adjective ἑκουσιος (Phm 14) refer to willing, deliberate action.

[14] This is our translation of the phrase, μηδε αἰσχροκερδως ἀλλα προθυμως. The adverb αἰσχροκερδως literally means "shamefully greedy." Both elders (Tit 1:7) and deacons (1 Tim 3:8) are to be free from the controlling desire for material gain (cognate adjective: αἰσχροκερδης). The adverb προθυμως possesses the nuance of eagerness, as do its cognate noun προθυμια (Acts 17:11; 2 Cor 8: 11, 12, 19; 9:2) and adjective προθυμος (Mt 26:41/Mk 14:38; Rom 1:15).

(of humility and sacrifice)."[15] The younger believers are next addressed, perhaps because they aspire to leadership. Peter commands them to be submissive and in God's time he will exalt them to places of greater influence (1 Pet 5:5-6). Peter's philosophy of leadership is that of (1) a servant who promotes the welfare of the church (2 Pet 1:1) and (2) a steward who must render an account of his work (1 Pet 5:3b-4). The welfare of the flock and the approbation of the Lord are the consuming ambitions that keep at bay all concerns for formal positioning, personal recognition, and monetary gain.

Leadership profile of Peter

1. *The patience and faithfulness of Jesus toward his leader-in-training: Many terms have been used to describe the character of Peter: erratic, unreliable, well-meaning, eager, fervent, bold, overconfident, rash, devoted, affectionate, impulsive. The New Testament portrays him as a bundle of conflicting thoughts and emotions so tangled as to defy any attempt at classification. From Peter's initial appearance (Jn 1:41) until his impending death (2 Pet 1:13-15), the reader can trace the superintending care of a faithful Lord who calls, disciplines, rebukes, affirms, restores, and employs the flawed instrument. Whether Peter is sinking in the waters of Galilee, attempting to correct predictions of suffering and death, objecting to having his feet washed, falling asleep in the garden, hacking off the ear of the high priest's servant, or vehemently denying any connections to the Nazarene, Jesus' stubborn commitment to his servant is undaunted. Jesus intercedes for Peter's restoration even before he falls, and his prayers are effectual (Lk 22:31-32). The risen Jesus appears to Peter individually (Lk 24:34). The Lord personally restores Peter and assigns him a role to shepherd the believers (Jn 21:15-17). Just as the gates of hell cannot prevail against the church because Jesus has determined to build it (Mt 16:18), so Satan's sifting of Peter cannot prevail for Jesus has determined to use him. Jesus has designated him Peter, "the rock," and a rock he will be. Peter's story should be a powerful encouragement to any and all of God's servants who deeply recognize their own numerous liabilities, but aspire to impact others for the glory of God.*

2. *Dual roles to fish and to shepherd: The Lord arrests Peter's attention by using two familiar metaphors to specify his mission, one at the beginning and one at the end of the earthly ministry. Peter will fish for people (Mt 4:19) and he will feed God's flock (Jn 21:15-17). He is thus the comprehensive leader with both evangelistic and pastoral roles. The former is especially seen in the early chapters of Acts, as Peter's proclamation becomes the means of drawing thousands to faith and repentance (Acts 2:41; 4:4; 5:14; 8:25;*

---

[15] This is how we translate the phrase, μηδ ὡς κατακυριευοντες . . . ἀλλα τυποι γινομενοι. The authoritarian manner of secular leaders, described by κατακυριευω (parallel with κατεξουσιαζω), is censured by Jesus in Mt 20:25/Mk 10:42. It is a strong term, one that is used graphically in Acts 19:16 to record the incident where a demonized man "overpowered" seven Jewish exorcists. Paul employs the simple form of the verb in 2 Cor 1:24: "not that we lord (κυριευω) it over your faith, but we are fellow workers for your joy" (cf. Lk 22:25). The noun τυπος is commonly used for an example, pattern, or model to imitate (Php 3:17; 1 Thess 1:7; 2 Thess 3:9; 1 Tim 4:12; Tit 2:7).

10:48). The authoritative word spoken by Peter and the apostles looses or binds the listeners according to their response (Mt 16:19). The latter role of pastor is seen in his two letters to the churches of Asia Minor where he provides instruction in doctrine and ethics (1, 2 Peter). He urges his fellow elders to become worthy shepherds of God's people (1 Pet 5:1-4). Before his ascension the Lord assigned to the eleven apostles, who represent succeeding generations of believers until the "end of the ages," the task of discipling the nations. This mandate comprises both evangelism of the lost ("baptizing them") and instruction of new disciples ("teaching them"). All leaders, regardless of their primary calling and gifting, are commanded to dedicate their energies to fulfilling their Lord's final testamentary charge.

3. ***The centrality of the word of God****: We have catalogued above Peter's fixation on Scripture as he sets forth doctrinal and moral teaching for the churches of Asia Minor. Peter is the confessional leader. His faith has settled on Jesus as the Holy One of God, the Messiah, the Son of the living God (Jn 6:68-69; Mt 16:16). His struggle to take off his cultural blinders is complete only when he turns to a full-orbed study and exposition of Old Testament Scripture as it finds fulfillment in Jesus. He can now put Isaiah 53 beside Daniel 7 in his understanding of the Son of man, the suffering servant who will one day be ruler of the universe. Peter could have used his intimacy with the historical Jesus to nurture a cult-like following among the second generation of believers. However, he placed his entire ministry under the authority of God's word and nurtured Berean-like disciples who would examine the Scriptures to see for themselves if what Peter said was true (cf. Acts 17:11). This is the commitment of any leader who desires a lasting legacy.*

Chapter 18.
John the Apostle: The taming of ambition

Preliminary questions to consider:
1. *Why and how does the cross of Jesus have the power to transform a sinful person into a useful instrument for the kingdom of God?*
2. *What natural weaknesses and proven flaws do you acknowledge in yourself? In what way have you committed these to God's faithful work of character renewal?*

Call to fellowship and mission
John had first been attracted to the ministry of the desert prophet. He heard the astounding testimony of the Baptizer as Jesus approached the waters of the Jordan: "Behold the lamb of God" (Jn 1:35-40). John had been reflecting on that confession for months when Jesus arrived at the shore of Lake Galilee. He and his brother James, along with their father Zebedee, were in a boat preparing to cast their nets into the water when they heard Jesus' invitation to a deeper purpose: "Come, follow me, and I will make you fishers of people." Here was the call to companionship with one who must surely be God's Messiah. So with his brother James he left his family, his career, and a secure future to follow Jesus into the unknown (Mt 4:18-22; Mk 1:16-20). It would be a thrilling and perplexing three years journey of faith with One who lived unlike any other man, as John would later write: the Word of life "which was from the beginning, which we have heard, which we have seen with our eyes, which we have looked at and our hands have touched" (1 Jn 1:1).

Inner circle of intimacy
The ensuing years were certainly a change from his years fishing the Sea of Galilee—the preaching trips through Galilee, the healings and miracles, bitter interchanges with the Pharisees, the parables, quiet times of prayer, the laughter and tears, meals together in friends' homes. John was present in Peter's home in Capernaum when Jesus healed his friend's mother-in-law of a fever and then watched as practically the entire town gathered at the door. Jesus healed their diseases and exorcised their demons with authority (Mk 1:29-34). Jesus appointed twelve to be his apostles, or "sent ones," to be with him, to proclaim the kingdom of God, and to perform authenticating signs (Mk 3:13-15).

Peter became the representative leader of the group, but John and his brother James joined him in an inner circle of three to whom Jesus gave special attention (Mk 3:16-17). Perhaps this privilege was given, in spite of their shortcomings, because they were his initial followers. Or was it because they evidenced a deeper yearning for intimacy with Jesus than the others? On three occasions Jesus separated Peter,

James and John from the others for unusual glimpses of God's power. In Capernaum the lay supervisor of the synagogue, Jairus, made a desperate plea to Jesus for his twelve-year-old daughter who was on the verge of death. By the time they arrived at his home, the girl had died and the mourners had gathered. The crowd laughed in mockery when Jesus expressed hope for the girl's restoration. The three disciples and her two parents watched as Jesus spoke to the girl and tenderly raised her to life. All, including John, were completely astonished (Mk 5:35-43).

On a second occasion Jesus took with him Peter, James, and John up a high mountain (Mt 17:1). A week earlier he had spoken of an ominous trip to Jerusalem where he would suffer, be killed, and be raised to life (Mt 16:21). Peter had rebuked the Lord for such thinking and was in turn sternly rebuked. Now as they stood on the mountain the Lord was transformed so that his face shone like the sun and his garments became dazzling white. Then Moses and Elijah appeared, and spoke with Jesus. The voice of the Father endorsed his beloved Son (17:1-5). John, unlike Peter, remained silent throughout. All three disciples fell to the ground in abject terror and confusion until Jesus calmed their fears (17:6-8). Suffering and glory had somehow intermingled in these scenes, but John could not put it together

Thirdly, on the night before his crucifixion Jesus ushered the three into the garden of Gethsemane where he withdrew to pray to his Father. John and the others were enjoined to watch and pray, but they soon fell asleep from exhaustion (Lk 22:45). The Lord reproved them for resting at a time that required spiritual vigilance (Mt 26:40-41, 45).

Son of thunder

Jesus attached to John and James the Aramaic nickname Boanerges, meaning "sons of thunder" (Mk 3:17). Several incidents do confirm that indeed these brothers could be fiery and aggressive. Returning to Galilee after the trip north to Caesarea Philippi, the disciples encountered one who was outside their circle exorcising demons in Jesus' name (Mk 9:38). John is singled out as the disciple who objected and sought to restrain the individual "because he is not one of us" (Lk 9:49). Ironically several disciples had recently been unable to effectively exercise their authority over a demon due to lack of believing prayer (Mk 9:17-18; cf. Mt 10:1, 8). Jesus rebukes the narrowness of John and the others and tells them to stop forbidding him. At least the strange exorcist recognizes Jesus' authority and is placing himself on the side of God's kingdom, against Satan. Such recognition will lead to a deeper understanding and must not be quenched (Mk 9:39-40).

Several months later Jesus and his apostles met a nasty reception as they were passing through a Samaritan village, "because his face was set toward Jerusalem" (Lk 9:52-53). The racial tensions between Jews and Samaritans had a long history (cf. Jn 4:9). For this reason Jewish pilgrims to the annual religious feasts would avoid Samaria and travel from Galilee to Jerusalem via Transjordan. James and John react with vengeful indignation, showing how faint their grasp of the lessons of humility and forgiveness the Lord had set forth in recent days (Mt 18:1-9, 21-35). Perhaps overly impressed with their own delegated authority, the "sons of thunder" viewed themselves as prophetic spokesmen like Elijah and ask Jesus if they might call down fire on their adversaries (Lk 9:54; cf. 2 Kg 1:10-12).

Jesus rebuked them because they utterly failed to discern that Jesus' present mission was to redeem not to destroy (Lk 9:55; cf. 19:10). The issues at stake now and in Elijah's day were utterly different. Elijah was defending the claim of Yahweh to Israel's exclusive loyalty; the disciples were suffering from injured pride.

Shortly before Jesus' final ascent to Jerusalem as he passes through Perea, James and John, along with their mother (Mt 20:20),[1] make a startling request of Jesus. They desire positions of prominence in the glorious kingdom he will establish (Mk 10:35-37). There is an element of faith in this request, for Jesus had just spoken of his enthronement as Son of man and the disciples' share in his coming rule (Mt 19:28). However, these two brothers, who were among his earliest disciples, have made little advancement in the core kingdom values of humility and servanthood. Jesus challenges their presuppositions. They are thinking only of glory, but have overlooked the suffering that must precede it. They envisage a crown without a cross and thus "you do not know what you are asking" (Mk 10:38). Still they confidently assert that "we are able" to do whatever is required of them. The Lord responds gently by affirming that suffering will indeed be their portion, but that kingdom position is determined not by him, but by the Father from whom he derives his authority (10:39-40; cf. Mt 24:36; 28:18). The ambition of James and John incites the indignation of the other ten disciples (10:41). Jesus must correct their false notions of leadership in his kingdom (10:41-45). The twelve had earlier squabbled about who was the greatest among them (Mk 9:33-34). This incident shows that they still have not progressed in their ability to embrace a kingdom where the humble servant would become the first citizen (Mk 9:35-37).

The disciple whom Jesus loved

There was, however, another side of John besides the myopic, vengeful and ambitious ones. In recent months the Lord had spoken often about the suffering of the Son of man. Surely he was not speaking about himself, or was he? The disciples arrived in Jerusalem for the Passover festival after the long journey south. The events of that week had been particularly exhausting for John and the others. Their Lord's actions and words left them bewildered. How could he weep over Jerusalem's coming destruction (Lk 19:41-44) when moments earlier the Passover multitudes hailed his triumphant entry into the city with the acclamation, "Hosanna to the Son of David" (Mt 21:9; Lk 19:38-40)? On Monday they watched him boil over with rage at the temple authorities, openly attacking them for turning his Father's house of prayer for all nations into a market of Jewish profit and privilege (Mt 21:12-13). Tuesday was filled with intense debate with the religious leaders in the temple courts. They finally stalked out shamed, silenced, and hardened in their resolve to silence Jesus (Mt 22:46). Wednesday, a day of silence, and Thursday, a day of preparation for the Passover celebration, were the calms before the storm. Peter and John were entrusted with the task of making everything ready for their communal meal that evening (Lk 22:8). The meal climaxed with Jesus speaking

---

[1] Zebedee's wife was probably Jesus' aunt on his mother's side. Salome, sister of Mary, supported Jesus' ministry (Mt 27:55-56; Mk 15:40-41; 16:1; Lk 8:3; Jn 19:25-27) and thus was asking special favors for his two first cousins.

enigmatic language about his body broken and his blood poured out for them, followed by predictions of betrayal and denial (Mt 26:20-35). John, "the disciple whom Jesus loved," reclined closest to Jesus, perhaps sensing such opportunities for intimacy were rapidly fading (Jn 13:23).[2]

John walked to the Mount of Olives, accompanied Jesus inside the entrance, and observed his Lord's tortured facial expression as he retreated to pray in Gethsemane. A garden that had over the years been a place of rest and release from the pressures of ministry (Jn 18:1-2) now became a scene of conflict. In rapid-fire succession the temple police arrived, his fellow disciple Judas reappeared and identified Jesus with a kiss, and the Lord was bound and taken to the city for trial. John is almost certainly the unnamed disciple who, known to the high priest, entered the courtyard and secured access for Peter (Jn 18:15-18). After that everything seemed like a blur. Peter's denials, Pilate's vacillation, the bloodthirsty cries of the priests and crowds for Jesus' death, the release of Barabbas, the verdict of condemnation, and the final walk to Golgotha all unfolded rapidly in the early hours of that Friday morning.

Eyewitness of the cross

So John stood before the cross—a painful present sandwiched between a thrilling past and a cloudy future. He was the one, and only one, of the original twelve who was with Jesus until the end. Devastated but loyal, he stood before the cross and must have pondered what all this could mean (Jn 19:25-27). All the disciples had fled into the darkness at Jesus' arrest in the garden (Mt 26:56b). One had openly betrayed the Lord (Mt 26:47-50). Even their outspoken spokesman, and John's closest friend, Peter, had repeatedly denied any connections to the Nazarene (Mt 26:69-75). So there stood John with the women from Galilee—Mary, the mother of Jesus; his own mother and sister of Jesus' mother, Salome; Mary Magdalene; and the third Mary, the wife of Clopas (Mt 27:55-56; Mk 15:40-41; Jn 19:25; cf. Mk 16:1). As Jesus hung naked on a Roman cross, rejected by his people and cursed by God (Deut 21:23), John surely agonized over how it could all be ending this way. At times of crisis, it is said, people turn to the past to find an anchor for their turbulent present. There at the cross John must have recalled those incredible experiences with Jesus and wondered how a mission that began so gloriously could end so tragically.

Westcott perceptively comments that "all who were present at the scene acted according to their true natures."[3] Vain priests demanded that Pilate change the

---

[2] The assumption that John the apostle is the "beloved disciple" of the fourth Gospel (5 times: 13:23; 19:26; 20:2; 21:7, 20) is based on several lines of converging evidence. First, John the apostle is never mentioned by name in the fourth Gospel, a striking contrast with the Synoptics where he is frequently specified. Second, the "beloved disciple" texts occur in critical scenes where only the apostles would have been present: the Lord's supper (13:23); the cross (19:26); the empty tomb (20:2); the post-resurrection appearance by the Sea of Tiberius (21:7); and the reinstatement of Peter (21:20). Third, this very disciple is stated to be the writer of the fourth Gospel (21:24), which fits with the traditional view of Johannine authorship. Fourth, the name John occurs twenty times in the fourth Gospel with reference to the Baptizer and four times with reference to Peter's father (1:42; 21:15-17).
[3] B. F. Westcott, *The Gospel according to St. John* (Grand Rapids: Eerdmans, reprint 1975): 276.

embarrassing inscription above his head: "This is the king of the Jews" (Jn 19:19-21). The mercenary soldiers bargained for his garments (Jn 19:23-24). The fickle, manipulated crowds derided his claims to be the Son of God (Mk 15:29-30). The faithful women from Galilee mourned him (Mt 27:55-56). One loyal disciple remained to carry out his Lord's testamentary charge: "Behold your mother." In obedience John would bring Mary into his home and care for her as his own mother (Jn 19:27).

Easter perspective[4]

Before sunrise on the first day of the week, four of the believing women came to the tomb in order to anoint Jesus' body with spices. They wondered on the way whether someone might be found to help them move the heavy stone from the entrance (Mk 16:1-3). However, when they arrived the stone had already been rolled away and the tomb was empty (Jn 20:1). Mary Magdalene rushed off to tell Peter and John that the body of Jesus had been stolen (Jn 20:2). Peter and John rushed to the tomb, but arrived after the other three women had left. John reached the tomb first and peered in to see the burial strips. When Peter arrived John followed his bolder friend into the tomb and saw the head wrapping neatly folded by itself (Jn 20:3-8a). John now began to understand some of what the Lord had said about his resurrection (20:8b). Later he would grasp the Old Testament predictions of the event that until now he had overlooked (20:9). Then they returned to their homes wondering what had happened (Jn 20:10; Lk 24:12). Later in the day the eleven disciples had gathered and heard the report of Mary Magdalene's personal encounter with the risen Lord in the garden (Jn 20:18). The other three women break their silence and relate that angels' appeared to them at the tomb who announced "(Jesus) is not here; he has risen," just as he told us (Lk 24:6). The disciples cannot fathom what they are hearing from these credible witnesses (Lk 24:9-11). Later that afternoon two followers of Jesus, one named Clopas, arrive and claim that the risen Jesus walked along the road to Emmaus with them, expounded the Scriptures, and broke bread. They hear that Jesus also made an appearance to Peter (Lk 24:33-35). Now a series of independent confirmations is emerging—three women, Mary Magdalene, the two Emmaus followers, and Peter.

Now John will see for himself what he has only heard from others. In the evening Jesus appeared suddenly to ten disciples (minus Thomas) gathered in the closed room due to fear of the Jews. He calms their initial fright that they have seen a ghost, shows them his wounded hands and feet, eats fish before them, expounds the Scriptures, and anticipates their coming proclamation of the kingdom by the Spirit (Lk 24:36-43; Jn 20:19-25). John and the others are filled with joyful disbelief and wonder (Lk 24:41). Eight days later Jesus appeared to the eleven gathered disciples in the house. Doubting Thomas becomes worshipping Thomas, as he falls down and confesses Jesus as "my Lord and my God" (Jn 20:28).

---

[4] We follow here the simple reconstruction of the post-resurrection appearances of Jesus set forth in Ladd, *I Believe in the Resurrection of Jesus*, 91-93.

The next appearance of the Lord is to seven disciples, including John, by the Sea of Tiberius while they are fishing (Jn 21:1-14). They have returned to Galilee as the Lord instructed them (Mt 26:32; 28:7, 10). The beloved disciple is the first to recognize the stranger at whose beckoning they caught such a large haul of fish (21:6-7). None of the disciples doubted with whom they were enjoying a breakfast of fish on the shore (21:12-14). Later that day Jesus would say in response to Peter's question, "Lord, what about him?," that he would deal with John according to his sovereign determination (Jn 21:21-22). John's record of this conversation is, in part, to dispel the rumor that he would be spared death. Jesus only meant that Peter's responsibility is to follow him and leave John and the future in his Lord's capable hands (21:23).

The eleven apostles went to a designated mountain in Galilee as Jesus had instructed them (Mt 28:16). When he appeared they worshipped him, "but some doubted" (28:17). The doubters are most likely some of "my brothers" (28:10), that is, the larger crowd of disciples who had followed him from Galilee. The Lord issues his Great Commission. They are to go out in his authority, disciple all the nations by baptizing and teaching them to obey all of his commands, and are promised his presence each and every day until the end of time (28:18-20).

The forty days of Jesus' appearances (Acts 1:3) conclude with Jesus' visible ascension to heaven from the Mount of Olives (Lk 24:50-51). Before his departure the Lord told them not to be overly taken up with the future fulfillment of prophetic events, but to dedicate their energies to being his witnesses to the ends of the earth (Acts 1:6-8). John and the others worshipped Jesus and returned with great joy to Jerusalem to wait for the promised baptism of the Holy Spirit (Lk 24:52-53; Acts 1:4-5, 12).

Transformation at Pentecost

When John appears in the Acts narrative he always accompanies Peter. If there is a trace of rivalry between these two in the interchange of John 21:20-23, it has long since disappeared. Though Peter's denials of the Lord were a bitter setback for the designated leader of the apostolic band, John never let it affect their relationship. A lesser man might have used it as a means of self-promotion by discrediting his rival for leadership. The Lord's full reinstatement of Peter was sufficient for John and in Acts, like the Gospels, John is content to be the number-two man behind his more aggressive friend. After Jesus' ascension we find Peter, John and the others situated in the upper room praying and waiting (Acts 1:13). The coming of the Spirit at Pentecost brings power to their witness and the messianic community in Jerusalem is born (Acts 2:42-47). Peter and John continued to worship in the temple as law-abiding Jews, though they now see the Old Testament as fulfilled by Jesus (Acts 2:46; 3:1; 5:42). While they are proceeding to the temple to pray, they encounter at the Beautiful Gate a man crippled from birth (Acts 3:1, 3, 4). He is healed by the power of the exalted Jesus, leaps to his feet, and holds fast to the two apostles to the astonishment of the crowds (Acts 3:11). John is arrested with Peter in Solomon's Colonnade, a series of chambers on the eastern outer wall of the temple complex, as they are speaking to the people about Jesus (Acts 4:1, 3, 7). The Jewish leaders are impressed by the two apostles' bold articulation of the Old Testament Scriptures.[5] They could only account for this by the apostles' association with Jesus, for Peter and John were "unschooled, ordinary men" (4:13).[6] Like their Master, their courageous and skilled exposition of Scripture far surpassed their cultural and educational backgrounds. Their report of this encounter moved the assembled brothers to pray for greater boldness and authenticating signs in spreading the message of Jesus (4:23-31).

Peter and John, along with James the half-brother of the Lord, became the reputed "pillars" of the mother church in Jerusalem (Gal 2:9). As law-keeping, messianic Jews, they comprised the central leadership of the church, moderating between the more conservative Judaizers and the more liberal Hellenistic believers represented by Stephen and Philip. The persecution that fell on the church in the aftermath of Stephen's death drove out the Hellenists who then went north preaching the gospel (Acts 8:1-3; 11:19-21). The apostles remained in Jerusalem (8:1). When word came of response to Philip's preaching in Samaria, the apostles sent Peter and John to substantiate and shepherd the new work (8:14). The two men laid hands on the believers who received the Holy Spirit (8:17), probably delayed in this instance in order to confirm the unity of the one church of Christ, whether Samaritan or Jew. Peter and John returned to Jerusalem, preaching the gospel to Samaritan villages en route (8:25). John is not mentioned again in Acts except as the brother of James, the first of the apostolic band to be martyred (Acts 12:2). He was no doubt present at the important Jerusalem council where his theological affinities would have aligned with his fellow pillars, Peter and James, in their defense of Paul's law-free gospel (Acts 15:6-21).

Elder to the churches

There is consistent, though not abundant, patristic evidence that John the Apostle spent the final decades of his life in Ephesus, where he continued to teach and shepherd the emerging Christian communities of Asia minor.[7] A strong case can be made for the Johannine authorship of 2, 3 John where the author begins by identifying himself as the "elder," probably of the church in Ephesus.[8] Peter came to hold the same title of "elder" in the church of Rome (1 Pet 5:1). If the "John" of Revelation (Rev 1:1, 4, 9; 22:8) is the beloved apostle,[9] then he is God's messenger of encouragement and rebuke to the seven churches of Asia minor beginning with

---

[5] The noun παρρησια (Acts 2:29; 4:13, 29, 31; 28:31) and its cognate verb παρρησιαζομαι (Acts 9:27, 28; 13:46; 14:3; 18:26; 19:8; 26:26) are Luke's chosen terms in the book of Acts for denoting confident and courageous articulation of the gospel in the face of hostility.
[6] The Greek terms behind the NIV rendering are αγραμματος and ιδιωτης. The first term literally means "without letters," that is, illiterate. In this context, where it is the Jewish religious leaders who pronounce this assessment of the apostles (Acts 4:1, 5, 8), the term probably takes on the sense of one without formal schooling in the matters of the law (i.e. not a scribe [cf. 4:5, γραμματευς]). The second term, ιδιωτης, can take on the general sense of "uneducated" (cf. 2 Cor 11:6), or more specifically denotes a layperson rather than an expert in the law (*TDNT*, III: 215-217).
[7] The patristic testimony is conveniently summarized and assessed in Barrett, *John*, 100-105.
[8] D. A. Carson, Douglas J. Moo, and Leon Morris, *An Introduction to the New Testament* (Grand Rapids: Zondervan, 1992): 446-450.
[9] Ibid, 468-473.

Ephesus (1:4; 2:1-3:29). He identifies himself as a servant to God's servants (1:1), a brother and companion in the suffering and the kingdom and the endurance of all those who belong to Jesus (1:9). The majestic angel before whom John falls identifies himself as a fellow servant of John and of his brothers (22:8-9). Elder, servant, brother are the titles John feels most comfortable with, remarkable for one who was probably the last link of the churches to the apostolic age. If there was a primacy with John and Peter, it was a primacy of privilege, for they refused to arrogate to themselves titles of ecclesiastical supremacy.

Leadership profile of John the Apostle

1. **Transforming power of the cross**: *The cross not only reveals one's nature, as the Passion narratives prove, it also transforms those who gaze at it intently. It transformed the centurion who at the moment of Jesus' death confessed that this was surely the Son of God (Mt 27:54). It transformed the thief crucified beside Jesus who pleaded for mercy and received the promise of paradise (Lk 23:42-43). John himself would be radically changed by what he witnessed. True, it was only with the resurrection that all of the confusion would be swept away and a new perspective gained. Then John would recall the scene and reflect deeply upon it. A shameful death of unimaginable cruelty, one that signified the curse of God upon a blasphemer (Deut 21:23), became for John the revelation of the glory of God (Jn 12:23; 13:31-32; 17:1). And what a metamorphosis took place! From an impetuous and hot tempered "son of thunder" who asked for fire to consume a village of Samaritans, from a myopic, threatened disciple who forbade one outside their circle from casting out demons in Jesus' name, from an ambitious self-promoter who sought prestige in the coming kingdom—from all that he was in his natural self—John became the gentle apostle who more than any other expounds agape($\alpha\gamma\alpha\pi\eta$), unconditional self-sacrificing love, as the essence of God's being and the mark of those who know him. "This is love: not that we loved God, but that he loved us and sent his Son as an atoning sacrifice for our sins. Beloved, since God so loved us, we also ought to love one another" (1 Jn 4:10-11). John became a transformational leader because he was, first and foremost, a transformed leader.*

2. **In the leadership training school of Jesus**: *The maturation process as a disciple and as an equipper of others is never a straight line. Though not as bumpy as that of Peter, John's path had its curves and obstacles. He moved from initial exposure and reflection to full commitment. As part of the kingdom team he received special training in the inner circle. He enjoyed exceptional intimacy as one upon whom Jesus particularly showered his love. The hopes that were shattered at the cross were restored at the resurrection and empowered at Pentecost. John responded to Jesus in these experiences with a full array of emotions: astonishment (Mk 5:42), terror (Mt 17:6), exhaustion (Lk 22:45), faith (Jn 20:8), joyful amazement (Lk 24:41), and certainty (Jn 21:7, 12). Jesus faithfully brings along all of his beloved children who aspire to kingdom usefulness and who share John's uneven forward steps. Through their experiences of his faithfulness, he molds them into people of influence*

far beyond their cultural limitations. He turned the near-sighted, easily angered Galilean fisherman into the apostle of love, elder and pillar of the churches, and mediator of his revelation of the coming kingdom.

Chapter 19.
Barnabas: Power of the mentor

Preliminary questions to consider:
1. *How would you define the gift of exhortation and how does one develop it?*
2. *What is it about the process of personal mentoring that leaves such a lasting imprint on the life of its beneficiary?*

Sacrificial giver

Joseph, a Levite from Cyprus, is introduced in the narrative of Acts as a sterling example of the spirit of generosity that pervaded the early church in Jerusalem (Acts 4:32-35). His sacrificial gift of the proceeds from the sale of a field he owned (4:36-37) forms the contrastive backdrop to the pretentious actions of Ananias and Sapphira (5:1-11). Though Levites historically did not own real estate in Israel (Josh 13:14; 14:4), the Mosaic restrictions had apparently been relaxed by New Testament times.[1] His Cypriot background helps account for Joseph's more tolerant attitudes with respect to external matters. His theological affinities aligned with the more liberated Hellenistic wing of the Jewish church, but he also had the full confidence of the apostles. The latter appended to him the nickname Barnabas, literally in Aramaic, "son of prophecy," but explained by Luke as "son of encouragement." Barnabas, then, acted like a prophet who brought consolation and hope to those under his influence (cf. Isa 40:1-2; Jer 31:10-14; Zeph 3:14-17). His monetary gift to the church is just the first in a series of ministries of encouragement to which Barnabas dedicated himself.

Trusted bridge-builder in suspicious times

Luke's second vignette of Barnabas comes at a critical point in the life of the newly converted Saul. After his transforming encounter with the risen Lord as he neared Damascus, Saul spent three years in Arabia probably engaged in evangelistic activity (Gal 1:17-18).[2] This accounts for the hostility he aroused from King Aretas of Nabatea (Arabia) who, when Paul returned to Damascus, ordered the governor of the city to seize him (2 Cor 11:32). Paul had also made the Jews angry by his preaching and so a plot was made to ambush and kill him (Acts 9:20-23).

Somehow the plot was discovered and Saul made a daring escape under the cover of darkness when his friends lowered him in a basket through an opening in the city wall (Acts 9:24-25; 2 Cor 11:33). Saul made his way to Jerusalem. His

---

[1] As early as the sixth century B.C. the prophet-priest Jeremiah was able to purchase a field in his hometown of Anathoth (Jer 32:6-15). If the property that Barnabas sold was in Cyprus, it may be that the Mosaic legislation was not strictly applied to diaspora Jews.
[2] Martin Hengel and Anna Maria Schwemer, *Paul Between Damascus and Antioch*, transl. John Bowden (London: SCM, 1997): 106-113.

purpose for this first visit to the holy city since his conversion was to interview Peter, almost certainly to learn details about the earthly life of the Lord Jesus (Gal 1:18). He also spent time with James, the Lord's brother (Gal 1:19). However, when he first arrived the Jerusalem disciples were unwilling to receive him. Saul was their former persecutor and was responsible for the incarceration, torture and even death of many of their fellow believers (Acts 7:58; 8:1-3; 9:1; 22:3-5; 26:9-11). The disciples feared Saul was pretending conversion in order to infiltrate their ranks and wreak even greater havoc upon the Christian community (Acts 9:26).

Saul stood in a veritable no-man's land. On the one side were his former Jewish colleagues, now incensed at him for openly advocating the cursed Nazarene as risen Lord and Messiah (Acts 9:20-23). On the other side was the naturally suspicious Christian community that doubted his intentions. At the critical moment Barnabas steps in, literally "laying hold of" Saul and bringing him to the apostles (9:27a). How or whether Barnabas knew Saul firsthand is unclear. He did, however, relay the report of Saul's conversion and that he had fearlessly proclaimed Jesus in Damascus (9:27b). The fact that suspicions were removed and that Saul became a trusted fellow-witness in Jerusalem (9:28-29) speaks to the level of esteem that Barnabas was held by the apostles. He embodied the love which "always protects, always trusts, always hopes, always perseveres" (1 Cor 13:7). Was it not from Barnabas that Paul experienced the reality of unconditional love described in this poetic masterpiece? As in Damascus, Saul's preaching in Jerusalem aroused murderous hostility and he was quickly spirited off to Caesarea, then to Tarsus where he disappears from the narrative (Acts 9:30). Probably these 'silent years' were spent in tent-making and church planting (Gal 1:20-24).[3]

Teaching elder in an expanding ministry

Earlier persecution had broken out against the Hellenistic wing of the Jerusalem church in the aftermath of Stephen's death (Acts 8:1-3). These Greek-speaking Jewish believers were driven north and "preached the word wherever they went" (8:4). Through Philip, followed up by Peter and John, the gospel spread to Samaria (8:5, 17, 25). The Hellenistic missionaries evangelized the Jews of Phoenicia, Cyprus and Antioch (Acts 11:19). However, in the city of Antioch, largest city in the eastern reaches of the Roman empire, and second only to Rome and Alexandria, the Hellenists preached Jesus to uncircumcised Greeks for the first time (11:20). The response was overwhelming and "a great number of people believed and turned to the Lord" (11:21). What policy would the mother church in Jerusalem adopt toward these new fellow believers who were uncircumcised, pork-eating, former idolaters? Earlier the Samaritans had embraced the faith, but they were at least part-Jews who held to the Mosaic stipulations in their own way (Acts 8:14-17). The Ethiopian eunuch was either a full-fledged proselyte to Judaism or, at the least, a pious worshipper of the Lord (8:27). The household of Cornelius

---

[3] Ibid, 151-158. A suggested chronology is as follows: Paul's conversion, Summer A.D. 35; return to Damascus from Arabia, early Summer 37; first post-conversion visit to Jerusalem, Summer 37; silent years in Tarsus, Autumn 37 until Spring 43.

was the first group of Gentile converts to embrace Jesus, but their head was a Gentile God-fearer who attended and supported the synagogue in Caesarea (10:2, 22, 30-31). Now a large number of pagan Greeks had embraced the faith of Jesus and needed follow up and teaching.

The choice of Barnabas as the Jerusalem church's representative to lead and develop the new work was a stroke of genius (11:22). One shudders to think how differently the outcome would have been if a representative of the Judaizing wing had been selected. Upon his arrival Barnabas "saw the evidence of the grace of God" at work in the lives of the new believers and it gladdened his heart (Acts 11:23a). He fixed his attention not on the eating habits, cultural distinctives, and external appearance, but on the transformed life-orientation brought about by their encounter with Jesus. He thus was free to encourage them "to remain true to the Lord with all their hearts" (11:23b). Barnabas, as a true new covenant leader, was concerned not about external matters, but about the heart. Three qualities are listed to account for Barnabas' response (11:24).[4] First, he was a good man, that is, a morally upright and generous-hearted man.[5] Second, his personality was under the controlling influence of the Holy Spirit.[6] Third, confident trust in the Lord directed his words and deeds. By gently stoking the embers of faith, Barnabas saw the work in Antioch expand as "a great number of people were brought to the Lord" (11:24b).

Barnabas needed help to disciple the growing number of converts and so he went to Tarsus to find Saul. For the second time Barnabas entered Saul's life at a critical moment (Acts 11:25-26; cf. 9:27). Barnabas brought Saul out of nearly six years of obscurity in Tarsus and incorporated him into the dynamic leadership team of prophets and teachers in Antioch under his guidance (Acts 13:1). Here Saul had the opportunity to invest his energies in a growing congregation, to hone his teaching skills, and to rub shoulders on a daily basis with these beloved Greek brothers. Barnabas, whose own personality and gifting would before long be eclipsed by his younger coworker, had the humility to place the welfare of the work above his individual standing. The personal agendas of both men, if there were any, were sublimated to the common task of edifying the church. Their team-teaching ministry was signally blessed. Antioch became the mother church of Gentile Christianity and the place where the "people of the way" (Acts 9:2; cf. 19:9, 23; 22:4; 24:14, 22) became known as "Christians," that is, the ones who confess, follow and belong to Christ (11:26b; cf. 26:28; 1 Pet 4:16).

---

[4] The causal conjunction ὅτι makes the connection explicit. It is, unfortunately, omitted in the NIV.
[5] The adjective here, ἀγαθος (good), appears in intimate connection with, and thus overlaps with, the semantic range of other adjectives such as καλος (attractive or noble; Rom 12:17, 21); ἁγιος (holy; Rom 7:12); δικαιος (upright or righteous; Rom 7:12; Lk 23:50); εὐαρεστος (acceptable or pleasing [to God]; Rom 12:2); τελειος (perfect or complete; Rom 12:2); πιστος (faithful; Mt 25:21); and ἐπιεικης (gentle or forbearing; 1 Pet 2:18). Luke seems to have chosen this comprehensive term to indicate that Barnabas' character evidenced the manifold fruit of the Spirit (Gal 5:22-23). See EDNT, 1: 5-7.
[6] The governing adjective πληρης is normally followed by a qualitative noun such as faith or wisdom (or the person of the Holy Spirit or good works) to indicate that the quality is possessed in abundance or full measure (Lk 4:1; Jn 1:14; Acts 6:3, 5, 8; 7:55; 9:36). The same combination of the fullness of faith and the Holy Spirit is also attributed to Stephen (Acts 6:5).

Mentor of a developing leader

The leadership team of five in Antioch was led by Barnabas with Saul perhaps the youngest member since he is mentioned last (Acts 13:1). The group that Barnabas assembled was quite diverse and included a Hellenistic Jew from the church in Jerusalem (Barnabas), one Simeon called Niger, Lucius of Cyrene in north Africa, Menahem, a Palestinian and foster brother of Herod Antipas, and the former strict Pharisee from Tarsus, Saul. Paul the missionary would build similarly diverse, multi-cultural teams for his church planting enterprise. After several years of teaching ministry, the Holy Spirit intervened during a time of worship and fasting and commanded the congregation to "set apart for me Barnabas and Saul for the work to which I have called them" (13:2). The congregation as a whole confirmed the direction of the Spirit through prayer and fasting and then set apart and sent forth their first missionaries. The pattern of the 'missionary call' was a worshipping community, sensitive to the voice of the Spirit, corporately commissioning already proven workers. Barnabas demonstrates his selfless character by leaving the promising work in Antioch, where he was the recognized leader, to undertake a difficult pioneering work in Cyprus and Galatia. John Mark, the young cousin of Barnabas (Col 4:10), had come north with the two men following their famine relief visit to Jerusalem (12:25) and now joined the two missionaries as their helper (13:5).

When the missionaries completed their work in Cyprus, they sailed north and came to Perga near the southern coast of Asia Minor. There John Mark left them and returned to his home in Jerusalem (13:13). Many suggestions have been made to explain Mark's departure: homesickness, physical illness, a sudden emergency, inability to withstand the rigors of missionary work. The narrative, however, perhaps points to the change in leadership of the team from Barnabas to Paul to explain Mark's action. A shift in terminology occurs in Acts 13:9 where Saul is designated for the first time by his Roman name, Paul. Until this point the two are always referred to as "Barnabas and Saul" (Acts 11:26, 30; 12:25; 13:2, 7; cf. 13:1). Upon arrival in Perga the group is identified as "Paul and his companions" (13:13). After this the regular order becomes "Paul and Barnabas" (13:42, 43, 46, 50; 14:1, 3, 20, 23; 15:2, 22, 35). The exceptions to the rule are when Barnabas and Paul are designated by the Lystran animists as the incarnations of Zeus and Hermes respectively (14:12, 14) and when they are viewed from the vantage point of the Jerusalem church (15:12, 25), Barnabas' home church.

The scene in Lystra is particularly revealing. Barnabas is equated with Zeus, the fatherly head of the Greek pantheon. Zeus (the Roman Jupiter) can intervene in human affairs with ferocity in tempest, thunder and lightning, but more often orchestrates the activity of other gods, behaving more like a just king than a capricious tyrant.[7] Hermes (the Roman Mercury) is the chief spokesman who carries out the instructions of Zeus with speed and diligence. He is also the active, charming and youthful god of the athletes.[8] The pagan identification by the Lystrans

---

[7] S. Hornblower and A. Spawforth, eds. *The Oxford Classical Dictionary*, 3rd ed. (Oxford University Press, 1996): 1636-1638.
[8] Ibid., 690-691.

of Barnabas with Zeus and Paul with Hermes confirms that the older Barnabas was taking a supportive role as teacher and mentor, while Paul was in the forefront as evangelist and preacher. What is remarkable is that until their falling out over Mark (Acts 15:36-41) there is not a hint of rivalry between the two men. They work harmoniously over a period of seven years, which includes five years teaching together in Antioch, eighteen months of rigorous missionary work in Cyprus and Galatia, a unified stand both in Antioch and at the Jerusalem council against the Judaizers, and a further period of furlough ministry in Antioch.[9] The success of their relationship and cooperative ministry must surely be attributed in large part to the magnanimous character of Barnabas. He introduced Saul to the work in Antioch, helped him develop and utilize his gifts of evangelism and teaching, and supported his gradual ascent to leadership of their missionary team. John Mark had likely been drawn to the work through his relationship with cousin Barnabas. When Paul began to step forward as the more dynamic preacher (cf. Acts 13:16; 14:8) and aggressive trail-blazer, Mark became disillusioned, only to return later to seek a second chance (15:37).

Resolute defender of the gospel of grace

Sometime after the missionaries' return to Antoich (Acts 14:26-28), the Judaizers infiltrated the promising work in Galatia and began to demand that the Gentile believers be circumcised and obey the law of Moses. Paul quickly responded with the letter to the Galatians in order to pull the churches back to their apostolic foundations and out of the tightening grip of the legalists (Gal 1:6-10; 3:1-5; 4:8-20). In that letter Paul recalls a recent incident when Peter visited Antioch. Paul had been forced to confront Peter for hypocrisy when, after enjoying table fellowship with the Gentile Christians, the chief apostle withdrew under pressure of the Judaizing faction that arrived from Jerusalem (Gal 2:11-14). Even more shocking is that "even Barnabas was led astray" (2:13b). Both men were committed to the principles of grace, but in this case they failed to act in accordance with those principles. When Paul writes "so that even Barnabas,"[10] it reveals his deep respect for his mentor and the fact that he knew in this instance Barnabas was acting completely out of character.

Whatever temporary disagreement there may have been, Paul and Barnabas stand shoulder to shoulder when Judaizers from Judea arrive at Antioch and demand that the Gentile believers be circumcised and obey the law of Moses as a precondition of salvation (Acts 15:1). They vigorously defend justification by faith alone, apart from the works of the law (15:2; cf. Gal 2:15-21). Paul and Barnabas are appointed by the church in Antioch to go to Jerusalem and settle this matter with the apostles and elders (15:2-4). After Peter addresses the leaders in defense of a law-free gospel (15:6-11), "Barnabas and Paul" report to the entire

[9] A suggested chronology is the following: Paul's arrival in Antioch after the years of silence, Spring A.D. 43; first missionary journey to Cyprus and Galatia, April 48-September 49; return to the home church in Antioch, October 49; Galatians written from Syrian Antioch, Autumn 49; the Jerusalem council, late Autumn 49; launching of second missionary journey, April 50.

[10] The result clause (ὥστε) with the ascensive καὶ makes Barnabas' action even more shocking than the hypocrisy of Peter and of the other Jews.

assembly the great wonders "that God had done among the Gentiles through them" (15:12). Barnabas is mentioned first because of his standing in the Jerusalem church and probably because he was the natural one to take the lead in this report. James, the half-brother of the Lord and recognized leader of the Jerusalem church, concluded with an eloquent defense of the integrity of the Gentile ministry (15:13-19). He proposed four accommodating measures to facilitate Jew-Gentile relations in the churches, measures to which Paul and Barnabas conceded (15:20-31).

Second chance for a failed brother

After an extended furlough of approximately six months (October A.D. 49 until April 50), Paul proposed to Barnabas that they return to Galatia to look after the spiritual needs of the young churches planted during their first journey (Acts 15:36). Barnabas was receptive, but wanted to take John Mark along with them (15:37). Mark had apparently returned to Antioch from his home in Jerusalem and asked his cousin for a fresh opportunity to serve. Paul was adamant against restoring Mark to the team, since "he had deserted them" during the first journey and thus had not demonstrated the perseverance required for such rigorous work (15:38; cf. 13:13).[11] Neither man was able to give way. The harsh disagreement[12] that resulted broke apart a partnership that had been greatly used by God over the past seven years (Spring A.D. 43 until April 50). The two men parted company: Paul chose Silas as Barnabas' replacement and left for Galatia; Barnabas left for Cyprus with John Mark (15:39-41).

It is difficult to objectively assess the relational disruption between Paul and Barnabas over John Mark. Luke records the matter of fact incident without interpretation. It may well be that, as is the case with most strained relationships, both men were partially at fault. Perhaps Paul was too severe in accusing the young Mark of desertion. His personal pride may have been injured if, as seems likely, Mark found it difficult when Barnabas began to cede leadership of the team to Paul. On the other hand, Barnabas may have treated Mark with undue leniency. People often lose all objectivity when dealing with their children or, in this case, one's young cousin. There is no mention of prayer or attempts at reconciliation, with both men apparently digging their heels in and refusing compromise. Whatever hard feelings there were initially, Paul has certainly lost them when a few years later (A.D. 55) he salutes Barnabas as an example of one who, like himself, has relinquished his right to have a wife for the sake of the ministry (1 Cor 9:6).

---

[11] The language is strong, literally "the one who turned away (or turned back) from them" (τον ἀποσταντα ἀπ᾽ αὐτων). Barnabas would not have shared Paul's assessment, recorded by Luke, of Mark's action as one of willful desertion (see NIV).

[12] The term παροξυσμος, rendered in Acts 15:39 "sharp disagreement" (NIV), is used one other time in the New Testament, in the positive sense of "provoking" or "stimulating" other believers to love and good works (Heb 10:24). In the LXX it twice refers to the furious anger of the Lord (Deut 29:28; Jer 32:37). The cognate verb παροξυνω occurs twice in the New Testament, once of Paul's inner distress over the idolatry in Athens (Acts 17:16), and once to describe the opposite of ἀγαπη: it is not easily provoked (i.e. to anger; 1 Cor 13:5). The verb occurs in Prov 27:17 (LXX) to denote constructive provocation. The capacity for righteous anger, as well as healthy provocation, which both men possessed, in this case degenerated into personal hostility and disrupted their working relationship.

Fortunately the New Testament provides a sequel to this incident and it is a happy one. Paul refers to John Mark in three of his subsequent letters. About twelve years later (A.D. 62) Paul sends greetings from Mark, who is with him in Rome, to the church in Colossae (4:10) and to Philemon (24). Paul commands the Colossians to receive Mark when he comes to them. Then, in his final correspondence (A.D. 67?), Paul asks Timothy to come to him in Rome and to bring along Mark who is "profitable for the ministry" (2 Tim 4:11).[13] This is a striking commendation of a fellow servant of the gospel whom he regarded years before as an unreliable deserter. Patristic evidence uniformly indicates that Mark became the amanuensis of Peter during the final years of the chief apostle's life.[14] John Mark drew from Peter's sermons to the church in Rome, along with other oral and written sources, to compile the second Gospel.[15] Even without taking sides in the Paul-Barnabas paroxysm, it seems that in the end Barnabas' policy of giving the young man a second chance produced salutary results both in his life and in the churches, a legacy that Paul acknowledges.

Leadership profile of Barnabas
1. *The tribe of the encouragers: Barnabas was the exhortational leader. His nickname, "son of encouragement," had been attached to him even before the glowing incidents of his life preserved in Acts. Encouragement was a habit for Barnabas, cultivated over the years in many situations with many people. Luke notes the outcomes of his ministry of encouragement. His sacrificial gift to the church in Jerusalem is one reason "there were no needy persons among them" (Acts 4:34). It is his intercession with the apostles that enables Paul to move about freely in Jerusalem and boldly to proclaim the Lord Jesus (9:28). His glad heart and encouraging words contributed to the great number of people that were brought to the Lord in Antioch (11:24). By encouraging Paul to use without hindrance his evangelistic and preaching gifts, the pioneering work in Galatia was established (14:21-23). His second-chance policy helped turn a young deserter into a fruitful minister (2 Tim 4:11). It takes little foresight or creativity to carp at, criticize, and deflate the struggling hopes of brothers and sisters engaged in spiritual warfare. The encourager is one who nurtures hope by drawing on the resources of a Lord who transcends all human limitations. In that he or she imitates the Paraclete himself.*
2. *The power of the mentor: One wonders how the church in Antioch would have developed if someone other than Barnabas had been sent to check on the developments there. One could speculate whether Paul would have become the great pioneer to the Gentiles if Barnabas had not taken him to the apostles in Jerusalem, had not rescued him from obscurity in Tarsus, had not fully*

---

[13] The adjective εὐχρηστος can mean useful, profitable, or helpful (cf. 2 Tim 2:21; Phm 11). John Mark is now being warmly commended by his former critic as one who is making a positive contribution to the ministry of proclaiming the gospel and establishing the churches.

[14] Carson, Moo, Morris, *An Introduction to the New Testament*, 92-95.

[15] R. T. France, *The Gospel of Mark*, NIGTC (Grand Rapids: Eerdmans, 2002): 35-41.

incorporated him into the leadership team in Antioch, and had squelched rather than facilitated the dynamic gifts of a younger colleague in the missionary enterprise. One wonders whether John Mark would have recovered from his early failure to become a profitable servant of Paul, amanuensis of Peter, and author of the second Gospel, if Barnabas had not given him a second chance. Though Luke provides only five vignettes of Barnabas, his influence far outweighs his coverage. Fourteen of the twenty-seven books of the New Testament were written by men helped on their way by Barnabas. We see in the life of Barnabas the incredible power of the servant-leader who facilitates the success of others.

Chapter 20.
Timothy: Extraordinary usefulness of an ordinary vessel

Preliminary questions to consider:
1. *What should be the attitude of the leader who is called to undertake tasks and to perform roles that he/she does not feel particularly suited for?*
2. *How does the young leader of a church (or parachurch ministry) win the respect of older members who may question his/her leadership qualifications?*

New member of the missionary team
During their first missionary journey to Galatia, Paul and Barnabas planted a church in the town of Lystra (Acts 14:6-20). It was apparently at this time that a young man was brought to Christ, one who would become the most trusted member of Paul's mission team. Paul indicates the spiritual lineage when he later calls Timothy "my beloved and faithful son in the Lord" (1 Cor 4:17), "my true son in the faith" (1 Tim1:2), "my son" (1 Tim 1:18; 2 Tim 2:1), and "my dear son" (2 Tim 1:2). Luke introduces Timothy as a young believer in the church of Lystra who joins Paul and Silas when they make a return trip to the Galatian churches (16:1-3).

Several salient facts illumine Timothy's background. First, his mother was Jewish, but his father was Greek (16:1). This explains Timothy's uncircumcised condition. Both his mother Eunice and his grandmother Lois preceded Timothy in the faith, ostensibly at the time of Paul's first visit (2 Tim 1:5). As a child Timothy had been instructed by his pious Jewish mother in the Old Testament Scriptures (2 Tim 3:15). Timothy must have been in his late teens at the time of his conversion, for he is addressed as a "young man" about fourteen years later (1 Tim 4:12).[1] Second, even at this early stage, perhaps a year separating Paul's two visits, Timothy had acquired a positive reputation among the brothers at Lystra and nearby Iconium (16:2). Timothy wasted no time in discovering ways to express his Christian faith. Third, Paul saw great potential in the young man for missionary work. Perhaps he saw Timothy as the helper who could replace the disappointing John Mark. At any rate, he first had Timothy circumcised in order to remove any potential obstacle to his ministry in the synagogues, his normal base for evangelism (16:3). This policy of 'sanctified expediency' was to remove barriers and to enhance unhindered communication of the gospel to Jewish listeners (cf. 1 Cor 9:19-20; Acts 18:18; 21:20-26). In the earlier case of the Greek Titus, Paul had refused to give ground to the Judaizers who insisted on his circumcision (Gal 2:1-5). The Judaizing faction made circumcision a matter of religious principle (Acts 15:1).

---

[1] We date Paul's visit to Lystra during his first missionary journey in March/April A.D. 49. The approximate date of the writing of 1 Timothy is A.D. 63.

But when principle was not at stake, Paul was the most flexible of people. Circumcision or uncircumcision made no difference to him (Gal 5:6; 6:15; 1 Cor 7:19).

In his two letters to Timothy written years later, Paul refers to prophecies made about Timothy at the time of his ordination to missionary work (1 Tim 1:18; 4:14). Prophetic utterances related to his calling and gifting took place at the time that Paul and the elders set him apart through the laying on of hands (2 Tim 1:6-7). Three factors, then, converged in Timothy's call to missionary work: the personal sense of leading and gifting which was confirmed by Spirit-directed prophecies; the endorsement of the members of his home church; and the corroborating assessment of a veteran leader, Paul. In the hardships of evangelistic and pastoral work Timothy would need to regularly return to these foundational elements of his call.

Discipler of new believers
Timothy does not appear in Luke's record of Paul's ministry in Philippi or Thessalonica. He next appears with Silas in Berea, while Paul moves on alone to Athens (Acts 17:14-15). Then a few weeks or months later Paul writes two letters to the church in Thessalonica, with Timothy and Silas as co-sponsors (1 Thess 1:1; 2 Thess 1:1). He explains the reason for Timothy's recent visit to them and the encouraging report that Timothy has just brought back (1 Thess 3:1-6). The following is one plausible reconstruction of the movements of the missionary band in Macedonia before and after Paul's arrival in Corinth:

1. Timothy (and Luke) remains at Philippi, then rejoins Paul and Silas at Berea (Acts 16:40; 17:4, 10, 14). October A.D. 50-February 51
2. Silas and Timothy remain in Berea; Paul travels alone to Athens (Acts 17:14-15). Late February A.D. 51
3. Silas and Timothy rejoin Paul in Athens at some point (1 Thess 3:1; cf. Acts 17:15). Timothy is sent back to Thessalonica (1 Thess 3:2); Silas is perhaps sent back to Philippi (Acts 18:5). March A.D. 51
4. Paul relocates from Athens to Corinth and is rejoined there by Silas and Timothy on their return from Macedonia (Acts 18:5; 1 Thess 3:6). Late Spring A.D. 51
5. After Timothy's arrival and good report (1 Thess 3:6) Paul, along with his two co-workers, writes 1 Thessalonians (early summer A.D. 51) from Corinth (note Achaia in 1:7-8, thus Athens is a possibility). A few weeks later (late Summer 51) he writes 2 Thessalonians over fresh misunderstandings in the area of eschatology. Paul ministers in Corinth (Acts 18:1-18a) from late Spring A.D. 51 until the first of September 52.

Paul expresses his deep love for the fledgling church in Thessalonica and his implicit trust in Timothy as his envoy. He was "torn away" from the church "in person not in thought" and had made every effort to return to these who are his glory and joy (1 Thess 2:17-20). When his plans to return were thwarted and he "could stand it no longer" (3:1, 5), he sent Timothy in order to strengthen and encourage their faith (3:2) and to assess their spiritual health lest Satan should get the upper hand (3:5). Paul's language is full of emotion and discloses a deep pastoral concern for the Thessalonian church, his confidence in Timothy to meet their needs, and yet a desire to hold on to Timothy as long as possible. This passage (1 Thess 2:17-3:10) is labeled the "apostolic parousia" because Paul both writes and sends his representative as dynamic substitutes for his own coming.[2] Paul commits this sensitive mission to Timothy whom he commends as a brother and fellow worker of God in spreading the gospel (3:2). The church is facing severe persecution, primarily from Jewish quarters, and the apostle is fearful that their embryonic faith could be overturned and his work in Thessalonica rendered futile (3:3-5; cf. 2:14-16).

When Timothy returned to Paul in Corinth he brought an encouraging report, which brought great relief to the apostle (1 Thess 3:6-7). Timothy relayed news of a church that was fervent in evangelism and resilient in suffering (1:2-10; 3:7-10). He also illumined Paul about issues that needed to be addressed such as infiltrators who were attacking Paul's integrity (2:1-12), ethical problems (4:1-12), confusion about eschatological matters (4:13-5:11), and the regulation of worship (5:12-22). The Macedonians' care for Paul was expressed by the monetary gifts they sent to him through Timothy and Silas. This allowed him to put aside tent-making for a time and to devote full attention to the ministry of preaching in Corinth (Acts 18:5; 2 Cor 11:9; Phil 4:15).

Trusted envoy to a troubled church

No church caused Paul more sleepless nights than the church in Corinth. Both the two extant letters to the church and other correspondence referred to that is no longer extant reveal a church with an ongoing history of relational, moral, and doctrinal inequities. The following is a plausible reconstruction of the communication of Paul with the church in Corinth during his second and third missionary journeys:

1. Paul's first stay in Corinth on the second journey lasted eighteen months (Acts 18:1-18a; late Spring A.D. 51-first of September 52). During this period he wrote 1, 2 Thessalonians. He leaves Corinth, makes a brief visit to Ephesus where he left Priscilla and Aquila, then descends to Jerusalem and finally returns to Antioch (Acts 18:18b-22; first of September A.D. 52-first of November, 52). Meanwhile, Apollos comes to Ephesus, then moves on to Corinth (Acts 18:24-19:1; 1 Cor 1:12; 3:4-6, 22; 4:6; 16:12). Cephas also makes a visit to Corinth (1 Cor 1:12; 3:22; 9:5).

2. Paul arrives at Ephesus on the third journey and stays about three years (Acts 19:1-41; cf. 19:8, 10; 20:31; September A.D. 53-first of May 56). The Ephesian period is one of extreme adversity and great fruitfulness for Paul (Acts 20:18-20; 1 Cor 4:11-13; 15:30-32; 16:4-9; 2 Cor 1:8-11; cf. 2 Cor 11:23-28; Rev 2-3).

---

[2] Charles A. Wanamaker, *The Epistles to the Thessalonians*, NIGTC (Grand Rapids: Eerdmans, 1990): 119-120.

3. Paul hears of moral problems in the church in Corinth and writes the "previous letter" (1 Cor 5:9). This letter apparently dealt with two issues: idolatry and fornication (5:10-11).

4. Paul receives reports from Chloe's household (1 Cor 1:11; cf. 5:1; 11:18). Later a delegation of three men led by Stephanus (1 Cor 16:15-18) come to Paul in Ephesus and bring a letter of questions ("Now concerning:" 7:1, 25; 8:1; 12:1; 16:1, 12). He writes the letter of 1 Corinthians in early Spring A.D. 56, shortly before the riot in Ephesus: 1:1-6:20 is in response to reports from Chloe and others; 7:1-16:12 is in response to the letter from Corinth brought by Stephanus.

5. The first letter to the Corinthians reveals a church being torn apart by personality- centered factions (1:10-4:21). There is growing anti-Pauline sentiment in the church, although it has not grown to the levels of agitation evident in 2 Corinthians.

6. At this point Paul dispatches **Timothy** to Corinth to confront those responsible for the unhealthy developments. He wanted to go himself, but was forced to delay his travel plans (1 Cor 4:18-21; 16:5-9; 2 Cor 1:15-17). His characteristic commendation of Timothy is in order to prepare the church for his arrival: He is Paul's beloved son, faithful in the Lord (4:17a). Timothy's mission is to remind the church of the apostolic teaching that is the standard for all the churches (4:17b). Then at the end of the letter Paul warns the church to welcome and not intimidate his young colleague, for he "is carrying on the work of the Lord, just as I am" (16:10-11). Timothy's visit, however, ends without positive results. Could it be that Timothy's age and/or his gentle and perhaps retiring personality, hinted at in several places (1 Cor 16:10; 1 Tim 4:12; 2 Tim 1:7), was not suitable for the volatile, charged atmosphere he encountered in the church? Titus would later prove a more effective ambassador to Corinth than Timothy (2 Cor 2:13; 7:6-7, 13-16).

7. Paul makes a "painful visit" to Corinth (2 Cor 2:1; 12:14, 21; 13:1-2). 2 Corinthians 2:5-11; 7:12 probably refer to the ringleader who opposed and insulted Paul on this visit. Paul then writes a "severe letter" (or "tearful/ sorrowful letter") carried by Titus to Corinth (2 Cor 2:3, 4, 9; 7:8, 12). In the "severe letter" he demands that the church punish the offender who had maliciously spoken against him. By the time of 2 Corinthians the offender has been duly disciplined and has shown true repentance; so Paul appeals to the church to restore the individual in loving forgiveness (2 Cor 2:3-9; 7:8-12).

8. Paul leaves Ephesus (May A.D. 56) and anxiously travels to Troas, then to Macedonia where he receives good news from Titus about the state of the church in Corinth (2 Cor 2:12-13; 7:5-16; cf. Acts 19:21; 20:1-2). Before leaving Ephesus he sent **Timothy** and Erastus ahead to Macedonia, ostensibly to check on the churches and prepare for his arrival. These two members of the Pauline team are described as "two of those ministering with him" (Acts 19:22).

9. Paul writes 2 Corinthians from Macedonia (October A.D. 56; cf. 2 Cor 2:13; 7:5), sending it by Titus who is to ready the Corinthians for Paul's coming

visit, especially with regard to the Jerusalem collection (2 Cor 8-9).[3] **Timothy** is named in the opening salutation of the letter, as he is in 1, 2 Thessalonians (with Silas), Philippians, Colossians, and Philemon. Paul's unhesitant way of associating young Timothy with himself in the salutations is remarkable. It reveals both the apostle's humility and his unwavering confidence in a co-worker who shares his message, motives, and mission (cf. Php 2:19-24). Against those who attack him for duplicity due to his change of travel plans, Paul reminds them that he, Timothy, and Silas have been wholly consistent preachers of God's promises in Christ (2 Cor 1:19-20).

10. Paul arrives in Corinth (his third visit: 2 Cor 12:14; 13:1), and spends three months there (end of November A.D. 56- end of February 57). He writes his magnum opus, the epistle to the Romans, from Corinth or its port Cenchrae (Acts 20:2-3; 1 Cor 16:6-7; Rom 16:1-2). Paul relays greetings to the church in Rome from several members of his mission team, his amanuensis Tertius, his host Gaius, and two local believers (Rom 16:21-24). Of these **Timothy** is the first mentioned and is distinguished as Paul's "fellow worker" (16:21). Paul departs Corinth at the end of February A.D. 57 and heads to Jerusalem to deliver the funds collected from the Gentile churches (1 Cor 16:1-4; 2 Cor 8-9; Rom 15:25-32; cf. Acts 20:4; 24:17).

Delegate of the Jerusalem fund

During the past several years Paul has urged his Gentile churches to take up a voluntary collection to aid the suffering brothers in Judea. Famine, political chaos, and persecution had all contributed to the desperate condition of the church in Jerusalem. The churches responded and chose representatives to handle the funds that had been collected. The representatives who will accompany Paul to Jerusalem are listed in Acts 20:4. The list includes seven delegates, three from Macedonia, two from Galatia, one of which is Timothy, and two from Asia. The missing church is Corinth in the province of Achaia. Paul had given instructions to the Corinthians concerning the Jerusalem fund (1 Cor 16:4) and the church had pledged to contribute. But one year elapsed so Paul was compelled to urge the church, through Titus, to make good on its pledge (2 Cor 8:6-15). Paul was very sensitive about money matters (cf. 1 Thess 2:4-5; 1 Cor 9:7-15; 2 Cor 2:17; 11:7-12). The delegates would have had to be people of unquestioned integrity so that there would not even be a hint of impropriety. The Jerusalem fund, however, meant more than money; it was also a genuine expression of the Gentile believers' commitment to the unity of the one church of Christ, Jew and Gentile (Rom 15:25-27). Paul asks for prayer that the gifts will be received in the spirit in which they

---

[3] One must account for the markedly different tone between Chapters 1-9 (positive, affirming) and Chapters 10-13 (admonitory, sarcastic). F. F. Bruce, *Paul: Apostle of the Heart Set Free* (Grand Rapids: Eerdmans, 1977): 274-279, suggests that 2 Corinthians 1-9 ("letter of reconciliation") was sent via Titus. Then, with further news of false apostles encountered on Titus' second visit, Paul dispatched 2 Corinthians 10-13 ("letter of rebuke"). An alternative scenario is that Chapters 1-9 were written and, before sending the letter, fresh news came from Corinth of troubles from pseudo-apostles. In response, Paul added Chapters 10-13, and the entire extant letter was sent to Corinth (so Carson, Moo, Morris, *An Introduction to the New Testament*, 267-72).

have been offered, a voluntary expression of Christian love and unity (15:30-31; cf. Acts 24:17). Paul praises the delegates of the fund as being both "brothers" and "representatives of the churches and an honor to Christ" (2 Cor 8:23). It is not surprising that Timothy was the duly elected representative of the churches in Lystra and Iconium in light of his sterling reputation there (Acts 16:2).[4]

Loyal son in the faith

Timothy was with Paul during his two years under house arrest (Acts 28:30-31). He is named, as Paul's brother (Col 1:1; Phlm 1) and fellow servant of Christ Jesus (Php 1:1), in the salutations of three of the four prison epistles written during those years (Eph 1:1 names Paul alone).

One of Paul's purposes behind the writing of Philippians is to inform the church of Epaphroditus' recovery, to praise his dedicated service, and to appeal to the church to receive its envoy back with honor (Php 2:25-30). It is helpful to briefly reconstruct the events leading up to the writing of the letter:

1. The Philippians receive news of Paul's imprisonment in Rome.
2. Epaphroditus arrives in Rome with a gift from the Philippian church for their beloved apostle (4:14, 18).
3. Epaphroditus falls ill to the point of death, but by God's mercy, recovers (2:27). Paul receives word from Philippi of their distress over the news of Epaphroditus' illness (2:26). The latter is sent back home with the epistle to the Philippians (2:28-30).
4. Paul hopes to be released soon (1:19-26). When he is able he will send Timothy to Philippi and receive him back with good news (2:19). It may well be that the church had been expecting Timothy and thus Paul explains why Timothy will not come until later (2:19-23). Eventually Paul plans to visit Philippi himself (1:26-27; 2:24).

Paul's description of Timothy in Philippians 2:19-24 is one of the highest complements paid by one individual to another in all of Holy Scripture. Paul is exhorting the church in Philippi to conduct itself in a manner worthy of the gospel of Christ (1:27-2:30). Under pressure from persecuting opponents (1:28-29), Judaizing interlopers (Php 3:2, 17-19), extreme teachers advocating a form of perfectionism (3:12-16), and divisive personalities (4:2-3), Paul urges the believers to maintain unity through humility (1:28; 2:1-4). The supreme example of humility to emulate is Christ Jesus (2:5-11). Then Paul cites himself, Timothy and Epaphroditus as leaders who have been steadfast and self-defacing in adversity (2:17-30). In the middle of this final section stands Paul's unparalleled commendation of his now seasoned coworker. He says five things about Timothy (2:20-22):

1. "I have no one of equal soul." The Greek term is not used elsewhere in the New Testament, but is cognate with the term rendered "one in spirit" (NIV)

---

[4] Timothy's province and home church are not listed in Acts 20:4, perhaps because in one sense he represented all the churches as a core member of the Pauline mission team.

in 2:2 and forms a wordplay with the verb rendered "I may be cheered" (NIV) in 2:19.[5] The sense in the context is that Timothy is a kindred spirit with Paul in his concern first and foremost for the welfare of the church.

2. "He will sincerely care for the things concerning you." Although the main verb can take on the negative meaning of worry or anxiety (Mt 6:34; 10:19; Php 4:6), it can also denote proper concern for matters that are vital (1 Cor 7:32, 34; 12:25).[6] When Timothy arrives the Philippian church can expect a sincere servant of God whose primary concern will not be his own physical comfort, personal recognition, or monetary remuneration, but the spiritual and practical needs of the church. Paul presumes Timothy's ability to both perceive those needs and his integrity to offer the encouragement, reproof, or challenge that is fitting.

3. Unlike all others he seeks the things of Christ Jesus, not his own things (literally, "for all seek the things of themselves, not the things of Christ Jesus, but [Timothy]"). The main verb denotes active pursuit out of an engaged will (cf. Mt 6:33; 13:45; Rom 2:7; 10:3; 1 Cor 10:24, 33; 13:5; 2 Cor 12:14; Col 3:1).[7] Paul had clearly been stung by other coworkers and envoys whose motives were mixed.[8] That is why his appreciation of Timothy is so strong. Timothy is different; his motivation is to glorify Jesus Christ and that is the ground of his concern for the church of his Lord.[9]

4. "You know the proven character of him." The Philippians knew Timothy well. He had come to them initially during the second missionary journey with Paul and remained to help them after Paul was driven south (Acts 16:6, 12, 40; 17:4, 10; A.D. 50). During the third journey he was sent with Erastus to Macedonia ahead of Paul who remained for a while longer in Ephesus (Acts 19:22; 20:1-2; A.D. 56). Then Timothy returned, after wintering in Corinth, with Paul and the other Jerusalem fund delegates to Macedonia en route to Troas (Acts 20:3-6; A.D. 57). Timothy has now served with Paul for over a decade and has proven his worth. The term rendered "proven character" is used seven times in the New Testament, all in Paul's letters, and denotes the refined product that emerges from a process of testing (Rom 5:4 twice; 2 Cor 2:9; 8:2; 9:13; 13:3; Php 2:22).[10] Though still a young man, Timothy has faced numerous hardships as Paul's assistant and has come through the testing with a solidity of character which outweighs his years. Adversity was God's refining tool to make Timothy a vessel of usefulness.

[5] The term in Php 2:20 is ἰσόψυχος, which is used once in the Septuagint (Ps 54:14 [ET 55:13], ἄνθρωπε ἰσόψυχε: "a man like myself" [NIV]). The cognate terms in the near context are σύμψυχος (2:2) and εὐψυχῶ (2:19).

[6] μεριμνάω (see *EDNT*, 2: 408).

[7] ζητέω (see *EDNT*, 2:102-103).

[8] O'Brien, *Philippians*, 321, argues convincingly that this is not a universal indictment of all of Paul's coworkers, but an indication that in his present circumstances there is no one suitable whom he could send to Philippi other than Timothy. Paul has referred earlier to brothers in Rome who were preaching Christ from wrong motives (Php 1:15-18).

[9] The post-positive conjunction γάρ in v. 21 makes this causal connection explicit.

[10] O'Brien, *Philippians*, 323, provides a useful summary of the Greek term δοκιμή and its sense in Php 2:22.

5. "As a son with a father he has served with me for the gospel." Here Paul spells out the manner in which Timothy has demonstrated such proven character.[11] Paul's affection for Timothy is that of a father for an obedient son. These kindred spirits have served together with the same purpose, namely, to promote the gospel. Their motivation, the glorification of God through the building of Christ's church, was perfectly aligned and that made them, along with Silas, Luke, and other part-time associates, a "cord not quickly broken" (Eccles 4:12).

"This one," Paul says, the one who has proven that his life's pursuit is the glory of Christ and the edification of his church, he will send "as soon as I see how things go with me" (2:23). Whether Paul is referring to the outcome of his trial (1:19-26) or to pressing pastoral concerns in Rome (Acts 28:30-31), it is clear that Timothy is of immense value to Paul and that he is reluctant to release him. Timothy has become a rare and invaluable leader because he is first a servant of Christ (Php 1:1; 2:22).

Young pastor of a strategic congregation

The evidence of the three Pastoral epistles confirms that Paul's expectation of being released from his house arrest in Rome was realized (Php 1:24-26; 2:24). He engaged in several years of further missionary work in the east before being arrested again under Nero and executed (A.D. 62-67).[12] One of Paul's first tasks was to appoint Timothy as his pastoral envoy to the strategic church in Ephesus. Paul had spent three years in Ephesus, which became the base for wider evangelism in the province (Acts 19:1-41; A.D. 53-56). His moving farewell address to the Ephesian elders took place in Miletus en route to Jerusalem (Acts 20:17-38; A.D. 57). He wrote the epistle to the Ephesians during his Roman incarceration (A.D. 61). Thus the church had a ten-year history, but it had been five or six years since Paul had personally been with them when he made the return visit (1 Tim 1:3; A.D. 62).

1 Timothy

The first letter to Timothy is written to the trusted colleague whom Paul left in charge at Ephesus while he moved on to Macedonia (1 Tim 1:3; 4:12-14). This private correspondence is written to instruct Timothy in his manifold pastoral duties, though its contents would be communicated to the congregation as a whole in Timothy's teaching ministry.[13] The general purpose statement is found in 3:15: "You will know how people ought to conduct themselves in God's household, which is the church of the living God." Paul is particularly concerned that Timothy

---

[11] The epexegetical ὅτι introduces concrete evidence of the δοκιμή (proven character) of Timothy (contra NIV, which takes ὅτι as a causal conjunction in v. 22b).

[12] Paul was either acquitted or his first trial passed the two-year statute of limitations and he was released. Church tradition uniformly associates the martyrdom of Paul and Peter with Nero's persecution of Christians in the aftermath of the fire in Rome, A.D. 64 (for a survey of the evidence, see Bruce, *Apostle of the Heart Set Free*, 441-455). After a further period of missionary activity, perhaps five years (A.D. 62-67), Paul was arrested again in Rome where he was executed under Nero (A.D. 67/68).

[13] The final benediction, "grace be with you (pl.)" (6:21b), probably indicates that the letter is to be read to the whole congregation.

carry out the following assignments: (1) the refutation of dangerous heretical teachings that have crept in (1:3-11; 4:1-8; 6:3-5, 20-21); (2) the maintenance of propriety in public worship (2:1-15); (3) the appointment of church officers who possess the highest of spiritual standards (3:1-13); and (4) the sensitive pastoral care of various socio-cultural groups in the church (5:1-6:2).

This would be a daunting task for any pastor, especially one like Timothy who was young, perhaps 30 years of age (1 Tim 4:12; cf. 2 Tim 2:22), and timid by nature (2 Tim 1:7; cf. 1 Cor 16:10). The key to his success will be to win the respect of the older members of the congregation by being a godly example (1 Tim 4:12). Five areas are spelled out for Timothy to set an example for others to observe and imitate: speech, manner of conduct, self-sacrificing love, trust in God, and personal purity. "Godliness" is a major motif of 1 Timothy and denotes God-like character and behavior that spring from a deep reverence for God (2:2; 3:16; 4:7, 8; 6:3, 5, 6, 11).[14] By setting a godly example Timothy will win the confidence of reticent older believers, defuse their tendency to doubt him, and thereby become an agent for constructive change.

2 Timothy

When Paul writes his second letter to Timothy he is once again in Rome, this time confined in the Mamertime prison without the freedom he had in his earlier house arrest (2 Tim 1:8, 16-17; 2:9; 4:6, 13, 16-18). Many of his former friends have abandoned both him and his message (1:15; 2:17-18; 4:10a, 14-15). Other trusted colleagues have been called to places of need (4:10b, 12, 20). Luke alone is with Paul (4:11a), although he relates greetings from several friends (4:21). Paul desires that Timothy, "my dear son" (1:2a), come to him soon, if possible, before winter (4:9, 21). He is to bring John Mark with him, now a profitable servant (4:11b). Paul is cold and longs for his mind to be occupied with Scripture. Timothy should bring the cloak he left with Carpus in Troas and the papyrus scrolls, especially the skin parchments of the Old Testament (4:12-13). Paul knows his life is drawing to an end and he longs to bid farewell to his beloved son in the faith (4:16-18). Paul recalls the tears Timothy shed when they last parted and his coming to Rome will produce great joy (1:4).

Here, then, is Paul's testamentary charge to the maturing pastor of the church in Ephesus. The apostle's paramount concern is the preservation and proclamation of the gospel in all of its fullness, as set forth in Scripture (1:8, 10; 2:8). Paul charges Timothy to guard this good deposit entrusted to him (1:14), to persevere in studying, teaching, and applying it (3:14-17), to preach it at all times (4:2), and to be willing to suffer for it as Paul has (1:8, 12; 2:9, 12; 3:11-12). The gospel was entrusted by God to Paul (1:8-11) and now passes to Timothy to entrust to others (1:13-14; 2:2).[15]

---

[14] The term εὐσέβεια occurs fifteen times in the New Testament, of which eight are in 1 Timothy (above).

[15] The noun παραθήκη means something committed or entrusted to another for safekeeping, that is, a deposit (1 Tim 6:20; 2 Tim 1:12, 14). It is one of many related terms in the New Testament that refers to a sound body or corpus of authoritative teaching handed down by the Lord to his church through the apostles (see *NIDNTT*, 3: 60-62). The usage of παραθήκη in 2 Tim 1:12 seems to differ from its other two occurrences (where it refers to the gospel); in this case it is Paul who has entrusted his life and destiny as a deposit for God's safekeeping.

Though the admonitions are highly personal (cf. 2:1-2, 22-26; 3:14; 4:2, 5), Paul intends the contents of the letter to affect the church's life through Timothy's teaching.[16]

Manifold tasks of the congregational leader

The instructions Paul gives through these two letters to the young pastor of a local congregation can be organized around four major categories:

1. **Discipline over oneself:**
   (i) Maintain courage, faith and a good conscience (1 Tim 1:18-19).
   (ii) Discipline oneself for the goal of godliness (4:7b-8).
   (iii) Set an example in five crucial areas (4:12).
   (iv) Develop and do not neglect one's spiritual gift (4:14, 15; 2 Tim 1:6-7).
   (v) Give careful attention to one's behavior and doctrine (4:16).
   (vi) Give proper attention to one's physical health (5:23).
   (vii) Cultivate contentment and flee from the dangerous pursuit of material wealth (6:6-11a).
   (viii) Pursue the qualities of righteousness, godliness, faith, love, endurance, gentleness, peace; flee youthful lusts (6:11b-12a; 2 Tim 2:22).
   (ix) Persevere in one's confession of faith to the consummation of eternal life (6:12b).
   (x) Be strong in the grace in Christ Jesus (2 Tim 2:1).
2. **Discharge of one's duties:**
   (i) Refute false teachings and command and teach true doctrine (1 Tim 1:3-11; 3:14-16; 4:1-11; 6:3-5).
   (ii) Intercede publicly for those in secular authority that calm will prevail and the gospel can be spread (2:1-4).
   (iii) Ensure proper order and unity between men and women in public worship (2:8-15).
   (iv) Administer the fund for widows with proper conditions so that there may not be abuse (5:3-16).
   (v) Keep the commands to preach the gospel and shepherd the church, with a constant focus on one's final accountability at Christ's return (6:13-16).
   (vi) Six metaphors for the role of the leader and their meaning:
      (1) Good soldier (2 Tim 2:3-4): endure hardship and seek only to please one's commanding officer, the Lord.
      (2) Competitive athlete (2:5): maintain self-discipline and personal integrity.
      (3) Diligent farmer (2:6): work with diligence.
      (4) Approved workman (2:14-19): study and accurately expound the Word of truth, avoiding verbal disputations and godless chatter.
      (5) Sanctified vessel (2:20-21): embrace all that enhances and turn away from all that detracts from one's growth in purity.

---

[16] The second letter to Timothy ends with the identical congregational benediction that concluded the first letter: "grace be with you (pl.)" (4:22b; cf. 1 Tim 6:21b).

    (6) Patient servant (2:23-26): avoid quarreling and gently instruct those who oppose one's message.

  (vii) Separate from those who profess religion but deny their confession through immoral conduct (3:1-9).

 (viii) Keep one's head in all situations, endure hardship, do the work of an evangelist, discharge all the duties of the ministry (4:5).

3. **Development of and delegation to others:**

   (i) Evaluate and appoint overseers and deacons based on the established criteria (1 Tim 3:1-13); be patient, not hasty, in ordaining officers (5:22).

  (ii) Provide sensitive pastoral care appropriate for older and younger men, and for older and younger women (5:1-2).

 (iii) Maintain respect and proper provision for elders with a high degree of accountability (5:17-20).

 (iv) Manage one's relationships and decisions without partiality or favoritism (5:21).

  (v) Nurture respect and compassion between slaves and masters (6:1-2).

 (vi) Command the rich members of the congregation to place their hope in God, not in fleeting material wealth, and to give generously to others (6:17-19).

 (vii) Take the apostolic teaching and pass it on to reliable people who will in turn teach it to others (2 Tim 2:2).

4. **Devotion to the Word of God:**

   (i) Devote oneself to the public reading of Scripture, to preaching, and to teaching (1 Tim 4:13, 15).

  (ii) Guard the deposit that has been entrusted to you, namely, the gospel (6:20a; 2 Tim 1:14).

 (iii) Keep the pattern of sound teaching based on apostolic instruction (2 Tim 1:13).

 (iv) Remember the gospel of Jesus Christ, the God-man, and its unrestrained power (2 Tim 2:8-9) and keep reminding others (2:14a).

  (v) Be willing to suffer to proclaim the gospel of salvation (1:8, 12; 2:9-13; 3:11-12).

 (vi) Continue in the study, application, and teaching of the Scriptures (3:14-17).

 (vii) Preach the Word on all occasions with a view to correct, rebuke, and encourage the hearers (4:2-4).

In summary, Timothy has been appointed to be the multi-task leader of a local church. His success will depend on how he disciplines himself, communicates the truth to God's people, and handles relational challenges. 1 Timothy places great emphasis on the pastor's self-management. 2 Timothy focuses on the primacy of God's word. Paul is at peace that the church in Ephesus, strategic to the evangelization of the province of Asia, is in reliable hands.

Chapter 20. Timothy: Extraordinary usefulness of an ordinary vessel

Leadership profile of Timothy

1. *Minister for all seasons: Timothy is the paradigmatic missionary who is called on to do a variety of tasks, some of which he feels well-qualified to fulfill and others that are clearly out of his comfort zone. His evident ability to teach and encourage young believers began in his home church in Galatia (Acts 16:2) and was used to strengthen the Macedonian churches (1 Thess 3:1-6; Php 2:22). When it came to confronting the recalcitrant opponents in Corinth, however, his gentle manner was inadequate (1 Cor 4:17; 16:10-11). Still, he was willing to go to Corinth, as he was to serve in the Jerusalem fund delegation, as he was to step in the historic congregation of Ephesus as pastoral envoy. In the church in Ephesus he would be required to carry out the roles of teacher, watchman, intercessor, administrator, treasurer, evangelist, and mentor. Timothy was the flexible leader, willing to do what needed to be done whether it was his primary gifting or not.*

2. ***Ordinary ability, extraordinary usefulness****: Several texts imply that Timothy was timid by nature and needed encouragement to step forth and assume the leadership roles Paul needed him to fulfill. Paul prepares the church in Corinth for Timothy's visit by commanding them to receive him warmly and do nothing to intimidate the young man (1 Cor 16:10-11). Paul instructs Timothy to not allow older members of the Ephesian congregation to shake his confidence or undermine his leadership (1 Tim 4:12). Later he must remind Timothy to continue utilizing and developing his gifts because God intends his servant to be powerful, loving and disciplined, not timid (2 Tim 1:6-7). Whereas Paul explodes on the New Testament canvas as the dynamic, unflappable (albeit vulnerable), pioneering evangelist, Timothy eases on to the scene. He follows in the background, appears where needed, and contributes, always positively contributes, to the success of the work. One needs only to read the array of New Testament texts where Timothy is commended to see how this ordinary man became extraordinarily useful (Acts 16:2; 1 Cor 4:17; 16:10b; 2 Cor 8:23; 1 Thess 3:2; 2 Cor 1:1; Rom 16:21; Col 1:1; Php 1:1; 2:20-22; 3:17; Phlm 1; cf. Heb 13:23).[17] No wonder Paul could say, "I have no one else like him" (Php 2:20a).*

---

[17] A wide array of designations are used of Timothy in these texts: disciple (μαθητης; Acts 16:1); one who ministers or helps (διακονεω; Acts 19:22); brother (αδελφος; 2 Cor 1:1; 8:23b; 1 Thess 3:2; Col 1:1; Phlm 1; cf. Heb 13:23); fellow worker (συνεργος; Rom 16:21; 1 Thess 3:2); son or child (τεκνον; 1 Cor 4:17; Php 2:22; 1 Tim 1:2, 18; 2 Tim 1:2; 2:1); servant (δουλος; Php 1:1) or one who serves (δουλευω; Php 2:22); example (τυπος; Phil 3:17: ημας follows and must include at least Paul, Timothy and Epaphroditus).

Chapter 21.
Titus: Paul's troubleshooter

Preliminary question to consider:
What qualities should a leader look for in a person needed to undertake a task fraught with difficulty and uncertainty?

Resolute defender of the gospel

The expanding ministry in Antioch made the Judaizers nervous from the start. Large numbers of Greeks were responding to the message of salvation through faith in the Lord Jesus Christ (Acts 11:19-26). This reactionary wing of the Jerusalem church would demand of these Greek believers obedience to the Mosaic law, including circumcision and the Levitical food laws. During the years while Barnabas and Paul were discipling the young believers, some from the Judaizing faction came to Antioch and, in Paul's words, "had infiltrated our ranks to spy on the freedom we have in Christ Jesus and to make us slaves" (Gal 2:4b). Paul learned of their activity and, in the first of a long series of battles, defeated their efforts to undermine the promising work in Antioch (2:5). During those years Paul and Barnabas organized a collection from the disciples in Antioch for the brothers in Judea who were suffering from severe famine (Acts 11:27-29). The two men went to Jerusalem to deliver the gift to the Jerusalem elders (11:30).

During their visit to Jerusalem Paul and Barnabas met with the elders to deliberate the nature of the gospel. If the Judaizers' demands prevailed, Paul knew, the gospel as he proclaimed it—salvation by faith in Christ wholly apart from Jewish legal matters—would be undermined and his work rendered futile (Gal 2:1-2). Paul could reflect on this visit several years later when writing to the church in Galatia, which had now been infiltrated by the same pernicious teaching. He recalls that Titus, an uncircumcised Greek believer representing the Antioch church, had accompanied him on that visit and stood his ground. The natural sense of Paul's language is that Titus himself was resolute against any attempts to compel his circumcision, because to do so would compromise the gospel of salvation by grace through faith alone (Gal 2:3, 5).[1] The so-called pillars of the Jerusalem church, Peter, James, and John, affirmed Paul's understanding of salvation and committed to him the primary responsibility of reaching the Gentiles, while they focused on Jewish evangelism (Gal 2:6-10). For the moment the Judaizers were silenced.[2]

---

[1] Paul says that Titus himself "was not compelled to be circumcised" (Gal 2:3) and that "we did not give in to them for a moment" (2:5). The first text indicates that the Jerusalem church leaders refused to concede to the Judaizers' demands. The first person plural "we" in v. 5 surely includes the entire visiting team of Paul, Barnabas, and Titus.

[2] This reconstruction assumes that the epistle to the Galatians was written before the Jerusalem

Courageous envoy to a troubled church

It is in connection with the church in Corinth that Titus now emerges as a core member of the Pauline mission team.[3] The church in Corinth was planted during the eighteen months Paul worked there during the second missionary journey (Acts18:1-11; v. 11, a year and a half: middle of March A.D. 51-first of September 52). On the third missionary journey Paul settles for three years in Ephesus, situated on the coast of Asia minor just across the southern Aegean from Corinth (19:8, 10; 20:31; September A.D. 53-first of May 56).

During these busy years in Ephesus Paul is forced to deal with a series of troubling developments in the church in Corinth. First, he hears of moral problems and writes the "previous letter" (1 Cor 5:9). He reminds the church that it must reach out to all sorts of people regardless of their lifestyle, but when someone professes faith in Christ that person must no longer commit idolatry or fornication (5:10-11). Secondly, reports come to Ephesus from two Corinthian delegations about vexing relational, moral, and doctrinal problems that need to be addressed (1 Cor 1:11; 5:1; 11:18; 16:15-18). Paul writes 1 Corinthians as his theologically grounded response to these situational concerns (early Spring A.D. 56). Third, the influence of the anti-Pauline faction in the church (cf. 1 Cor 1:12) threatens to undermine its apostolic foundations. Paul dispatches Timothy to Corinth, but he is forced to return without positive results (1 Cor 4:17; 16:10-11). It is very possible that Timothy's gentle temperament proved no match for the recalcitrant faction leaders. Fourth, Paul then makes a "painful visit" to Corinth (2 Cor 2:1) and is maligned by the ringleader.[4] Fifth, he follows up this visit with a "severe letter," which is carried by Titus to Corinth. This was a letter of tough love designed to bring the church to a brutally honest self-assessment, a letter which caused grief both to Paul and to his readers (2 Cor 2:3-4, 9; 7:8, 12). Titus was sent as the bearer of unpleasant news to a church that had already turned away Timothy and had insulted its own apostolic founder. Did Paul recognize that the resolute individual who had stood his ground against the legalists in Judea could similarly face off with the opponents in Corinth? As Titus departed Paul must have worried if this was the last opportunity to reclaim the wayward congregation.

Titus and Paul had agreed on a timetable for his return to Corinth and specified Troas as the meeting place. However, when Titus did not appear, Paul left the promising work in Troas for Macedonia hoping to find Titus there (2 Cor 2:12-13). For Paul to leave first Ephesus and now Troas, both of which were growing ministries, reveals his firm commitment both to the welfare of his young coworker and to the resolution of the troubles in Corinth. Paul the pioneer was also Paul the team leader and Paul the pastor. Titus performed his difficult assignment admirably. As Paul came to Macedonia he was "harassed at every turn—conflicts on the

council of Acts 15:6-35. Thus the Jerusalem visit of Galatians 2:1-10 aligns with the famine visit of Acts 11:27-30. If, however, Galatians 2 refers to the Jerusalem council visit (Acts 15), then the controversy referred to in Gal 2:4-5 took place when Judaizers came to Antioch after Paul and Barnabas had returned from their first missionary journey (Acts 15:1-2).

[3] Surprisingly, Titus never appears in the record of Acts. It has been suggested that Luke is for some reason reluctant to mention Titus because he is his brother. This is impossible to substantiate.

[4] This individual is probably referred to in 2 Cor 2:5-11; 7:12.

outside, fears within" (2 Cor 7:5). Then Titus appeared and Paul's heart was comforted, not only because his coworker was safe, but also because of the report that Titus brought (7:6-7a). The "severe letter," along with Titus's diplomatic yet firm handling of the delicate situation, became God's tool to bring the church back to its senses. In Paul's words, Titus "told us about your longing for me, your deep sorrow, your ardent concern for me, so that my joy was greater than ever" (7:7b). The church was moved to godly sorrow that produced repentance (7:8-10). The anti-Pauline ringleader was discredited and the church recovered its devotion to its apostolic founder (7:11-12).

Titus shared Paul's shepherd's heart. He took no pleasure in a mission of confrontation, though he was willing to undertake it. The church received him with fear and trembling and proved obedient to the apostle's commands, contained both in 1 Corinthians and in the "severe letter." Titus was moved and communicated his affection for the church to Paul (7:15). He returned to Paul refreshed, which delighted Paul's heart (7:13). Paul's anticipatory boasting to Titus that the Corinthians would in the end turn back was vindicated (7:14).

Leader of a delegation on a sensitive mission

Paul now wrote 2 Corinthians from Macedonia, sending it by Titus who is to ready the Corinthians for Paul's coming visit (2 Cor 2:13; 7:5; October, A.D. 56). Titus' particular assignment is to ensure that the church in Corinth follow through on the pledge it made the previous year to contribute to the Jerusalem fund (2 Cor 8:10-12). Paul in recent years has been gathering voluntary gifts from the Gentile churches to alleviate the poverty of the brothers in Judea due to famine, persecution, and political instability. He earlier gave instruction to the Corinthians on the logistics of the fund (1 Cor 16:1-4). Titus had made further preparations for the collection on his first visit (2 Cor 8:6). Now it is time that good beginnings translate into completion. For the second time Titus is Paul's choice for a sensitive task.

Paul begins his appeal by setting forth the example of the sacrificial giving of the Macedonians (2 Cor 8:1-5). Next he urges the Corinthians to bring to completion their pledge (8:6-15). Finally, he explains the mission of Titus and the two unnamed brothers who will accompany him (8:16-9:5). Paul has complete confidence in Titus whom he praises for being a kindred spirit. The following words of commendation compare favorably with what Paul later has to say about Timothy (cf. Php 2:20-22):

1. Titus shares Paul's pastoral concern for the church because both share God's heart (2 Cor 8:16)
2. Titus is undertaking this ministry not out of compulsion, but enthusiastically and on his own initiative (8:17).
3. Paul is sending with Titus two other unnamed brothers who have proven in other assignments, along with Titus, their blameless character (8:18, 22). Only people of the highest integrity would be chosen for this task, for Paul takes pains "to avoid any criticism of the way we administer this liberal gift" (8:20).
4. Titus, a partner and fellow worker, and the brothers, an honor to Christ, are to be welcomed upon their arrival (8:23-24).

5. Paul has boasted to these three men that their ministry will successfully complete what has been sincerely pledged. He reminds the Corinthians that it will not be to their credit if they disappoint these expectations (9:1-5).

6. Against fresh slanders raised against him, Paul reminds the Corinthians with a series of rhetorical questions that neither he nor Titus ever exploited them (12:17). Paul's envoy was a faithful representative of the apostle's interests: "Did we not act in the same spirit and follow the same course?" (12:18; cf. Php 2:20). Paul and Titus spoke as accountable servants of Christ with a view to the edification of the believers (12:19). Their motive and manner were in perfect alignment.

Paul followed Titus to Corinth and spent the winter of A.D. 56/57 there before making his way to Jerusalem. During these months of reflection Paul wrote the epistle to the Romans. Titus' second visit proved fruitful, for Paul writes that "Macedonia and Achaia were pleased to make a contribution for the poor among the saints in Jerusalem" (Rom 15:26). Though no representative from Achaia is mentioned in the list of delegates in Acts 20:4, perhaps Timothy was designated steward of these funds. He was with Paul in Corinth (Rom 16:21) and then accompanied him to Jerusalem (Acts 20:4). Titus is not mentioned in Acts or Romans so he may have been sent on another assignment at this time.

Pastor to a church in an unpromising setting

Titus reappears as the recipient of the pastoral letter that bears his name. Paul has been released from his house arrest in Rome and is once again active in missionary work in the east.[5] Paul appoints Titus as leader of the church on the island of Crete. Paul addresses Titus as "my true son in our common faith" (1:4), much like he does Timothy (2 Tim 1:2) and Onesimus (Phlm 10). Titus' task is specific, namely, to "straighten out what was left unfinished and appoint elders in every town" (1:5). When his mission is completed Paul plans to send replacements so that Titus can join him in Nicopolis (in Epirus on the west coast of Greece) where he plans to winter (3:12). Zenas the lawyer and Apollos are probably the bearers of the letter to Titus. He is instructed to help these travelers on their way by providing whatever needs they have (3:13).

The contents of the letter underscore that Titus' work in Crete would not have been easy. Paul's words describing Cretan character are not exactly flattering. He endorses the testimony of one of their own poets, Epimenides: "Cretans are always liars, evil brutes, lazy gluttons" (Tit 1:12-13).[6] Titus will need to draw upon a wide array of pastoral skills to set the church in order. First, he will need wisdom to appoint godly overseers in each town, according to the established criteria (1:5-9). Second, courage will be required to silence the ruinous teaching of the Judaizers (1:10-16), to warn the unruly to be good citizens and neighbors (3:1-2), and to

---

[5] The place of writing is unclear: Corinth, Philippi, or possibly Asia Minor are reasonable conjectures. The date is likewise impossible to establish with precision; the period of A.D. 63-65 is likely.

[6] According to the testimony of several early Christian writers, the quotation in Tit 1:12 is from the sixth century B.C. Cretan poet Epimenides. See I. Howard Marshall, *A Critical and Exegetical Commentary on the Pastoral Epistles*, ICC (Edinburgh: T & T Clark, 1999): 198-201.

discipline those who are divisive (3:9-11). Third, Titus must address the needs of each socio-cultural group in the church with sensitivity and sound teaching (2:1-14). He must speak with exhortation and rebuke as the authorized representative of Paul (2:15). Teaching of sound doctrine (1:1-3; 2:11-14; 3:4-7) and exhortation to do good works (2:14; 3:1, 8, 14) would require thoughtful preparation, study and articulation. Titus, like Timothy, must defuse the doubts of his detractors by being an example of good works and sound speech (2:7-8; cf. 1 Tim 4:12). The final benediction is pronounced upon the whole church (3:15b).[7] Paul intends that this private correspondence benefit the entire community of believers through Titus' teaching ministry. The final reference to Titus in the New Testament finds him sent by Paul on still another mission, this time to Dalmatia (2 Tim 4:10).

Leadership profile of Titus

Titus can be called Paul's troubleshooter. He was the member of the mission team that was assigned the most difficult and unpleasant tasks. His courage to stand firm in a difficult situation was first evidenced when the Judaizers attempted to compel his circumcision (Gal 2:1, 3). Perhaps here Paul recognized the stability of character that could handle tough assignments. Titus was dispatched to Corinth after the church had dismissed Timothy and humiliated Paul. Paul's praise for Titus after that visit indicates he possessed a tenderness to go along with his toughness (2 Cor 7:7, 13-15). He is now coming, Paul writes to the Corinthians, to help them translate their pledge to the Jerusalem fund into an actual offering, another challenge for the troubleshooter (2 Cor 8:6). Titus stands alongside Timothy as one in whom Paul has complete confidence, because he shares the same motives and purposes as his mentor (2 Cor 12:17-18; cf. Php 2:20-22). Titus becomes the pastoral envoy to Crete, by all indications another mission fraught with difficulties (Tit 1:10-16). Later he will be sent on a mission to Dalmatia which, one might conjecture, would likewise require a resilient and resourceful leader (2 Tim 4:10). Paul praises this man as his brother (2 Cor 2:13), partner and fellow worker (2 Cor 8:23), and true son in the faith (Tit 1:4).[8]

---

[7] The final benediction in the epistle to Titus, "grace be with you all" (ἡ χαρις μετα παντων ὑμων), bears the same basic meaning as the benediction in the other two Pastoral letters (1 Tim 6:21b; 2 Tim 4:22b: ἡ χαρις μεθ' ὑμων). All three benedictions, addressed to the churches as a whole, indicate that the instructions given to the individual recipient, in this case Titus, are to be communicated to the entire congregation.

[8] The following are the designations applied to Titus: ἀδελφος (2 Cor 2:13); κοινωνος and συνεργος (2 Cor 8:23); γνησιον τεκνον (Tit 1:4).

PART FIVE

Paul:
Builder of Faith Communities

Chapter 22.
Characteristics of his leadership

Preliminary questions to consider:

1. *When a leader takes on the mantle of Paul and makes the glory of God and the edification of the church one's first priority, how will this condition the way one's leadership role is carried out?*
    Does your approach to leadership embody the same characteristics as Paul's? Which of these do you consider areas of personal strength and which do you consider areas that need to be developed?

2. *What is really behind the paternalistic and authoritarian approaches to leadership that one often encounters in the church and in parachurch ministries?*
    How does one learn to act consistently with the conviction that the Spirit of God indwells and endows with spiritual gifts all born-again believers?

1. AUTHORITATIVE

Paul occupied a unique place of leadership in the early church through his direct commissioning by the risen Lord to be the apostle to the Gentiles (Gal 2:8; 1 Cor 9:2; Rom 1:5).[1] He defends his apostolic authority[2] as being granted directly by the risen Lord (Gal 1:15-16), wholly independent of Jerusalem and the original apostles (Gal 1:17-2:10). Paul was a witness of the resurrection, just as the Jerusalem apostles were, though he was "as one abnormally born" (1 Cor 15:7-8; 9:1). As an apostle he is conscious of being a mediator of divinely revealed truth to the churches. This apostolic tradition (or teaching or deposit)[3] is the established doctrinal and ethical charter for the emerging churches. He faithfully delivers to the churches that which he received from the Lord Jesus.[4] The direct line of transmission and its faithful delivery means that Paul's teaching possesses authority for the faith and life of the new covenant communities.

Though succeeding generations of church leaders do not bear the stamp of

---

[1] Paul refers to himself as an apostle (ἀπόστολος) in the solemn technical sense twenty-four times in ten of his extant letters (Rom 1:1; 11:13; 1 Cor 1:1; 4:9; 9:1, 2, 5; 12:28; 15:9 [twice]; 2 Cor 1:1; 12:12; Gal 1:1; Eph 1:1; 2:20; 3:5; 4:11; Col 1:1; 1 Thess 2:7; 1 Tim 1:1; 2:7; 2 Tim 1:1, 11; Tit 1:1). Three times he refers to his apostolate (ἀποστολη: Rom 1:5; 1 Cor 9:2; Gal 2:8).

[2] Twice he employs the term ἐξουσια to refer to the authority delegated to him by the risen Lord (2 Cor 10:8; 13:10).

[3] These three terms are: παραδοσις (1 Cor 11:2; 2 Thess 2:15; 3:6); διδαχη (Rom 6:17; 16:17; Tit 1:9); and παραθηκη (1 Tim 6:20; 2 Tim1:14).

[4] The technical terms for reception and delivery of the tradition are παραλαμβανω (1 Cor 11:23; 15:1, 3; cf. Gal 1:9, 12; Php 4:9; 1 Thess 4:1; 2 Thess 3:6) and παραδιδωμι (1 Cor 11:2, 23; 15:3) respectively.

apostolic authority,[5] they do submit to the apostolic teaching and call the churches to faithful obedience to those teachings preserved in the canonical record. Paul's unbending allegiance to the corpus of revealed truth and his bold confrontation of those who depart from it serve as a model for authentic leadership of all ages.

Compliance

Paul employs a number of verbs of compliance where he demonstrates his firm commitment to the established rule of faith, and his demand (or his directive that the church leaders so demand) that the churches submit to the its authority: **command** (1 Cor 7:10; 11:17; 1 Thess 4:11; 2 Thess 3:4, 6, 10, 12; 1 Tim 1:3; 4:11; 5:7; 6:13, 17);[6] **solemnly charge** (1 Tim 5:21; 2 Tim 4:1);[7] **adjure** (1 Thess 5:27);[8] **direct** or **lay down a rule** (1 Cor 7:17; 11:34; 16:1; Tit 1:5);[9] **warn** (1 Thess 4:6; 5:12, 14; 2 Thess 3:15; 1 Cor 4:14; Col 1:28; 2 Tim 2:14);[10] **declare** or **testify** (Gal 5:3; 1 Thess 2:12; Eph 4:17);[11] **strongly affirm** (Tit 3:8; cf. 1 Tim 1:7);[12] **convince** or **convict** (Eph 5:11; 1 Tim 5:20; 2 Tim 4:2; Tit 1:9, 13; 2:15);[13] **rebuke** (2 Tim 4:2);[14] and **guard** (1 Tim 6:20; 2 Tim 1:14).[15]

Confrontation

Paul is not afraid to directly confront individuals or groups of individuals who seek to undermine the apostolic foundation of the churches. He uses the strongest language to censure the motives and conduct of the Judaizers who are pulling the Galatian church away from the doctrine of justification by faith not works (Gal 1:8-9; 4:17; 5:12; 6:12-13). Paul expresses his astonishment that the Galatians have been so quickly influenced by such teaching (1:6-7), probes their illogic and foolishness by a series of rhetorical questions (3:1-5), admits his perplexity and frustration over the rapidity of their defection (4:16-20), and spells out the disastrous consequences that such a Judaizing theology will produce (5:2-4, 7-11, 15; 6:7-8). Even his colleagues Peter and Barnabas were deserving of rebuke when they acted hypocritically under pressure from Judaizers who came to Antioch from Jerusalem (Gal 2:11-14). When he and Barnabas traveled to Jerusalem to deliver money for famine relief, Paul

---

[5] Both Luke and Paul occasionally employ the term ἀπόστολος in a functional, nontechnical sense for a pioneering church planter who introduces the gospel to unreached areas, including Barnabas (Acts 14:4, 14), Silas and Timothy (1 Thess 2:6b), and the couple Andronicus and Junias (Rom 16:7). The term is also applied to those who are sent on special missions as representatives of churches, such as the Jerusalem fund delegation (2 Cor 8:23) and Epaphroditus from Philippi to Rome (Php 2:25).

[6] παραγγελλω and the cognate noun παραγγελια (1 Thess 4:2; 1 Tim 1:5, 18)

[7] διαμαρτυρομαι

[8] ἐνορκιζω

[9] διατασσω

[10] νουθετεω (1 Thess 5:12, 14; 2 Thess 3:15; 1 Cor 4:14; Col 1:28) and the cognate noun νουθεσια (1 Cor 10:11; Tit 3:10); διαμαρτυρομαι (1 Thess 4:6; 2 Tim 2:14)

[11] μαρτυρομαι

[12] διαβεβαιοομαι

[13] ἐλεγχω

[14] ἐπιτιμαω

[15] The verb φυλασσω is used here in the sense of preserve or maintain in all of its integrity; the object is the "deposit" (παραθηκη), that is, the gospel which God has entrusted to the church.

refused to give an inch to those who demanded that Titus be circumcised (Gal 2:3, 5). Paul has even stronger words of condemnation for the Jewish opponents in Macedonia who are hindering the spread of the gospel (1 Thess 2:15-16).

In the church in Thessalonica a misunderstanding regarding the imminence of the Lord's return caused some brothers to begin abandoning their proper work and to meddle in other people's affairs. Paul addresses the problem gently in the first letter to that church (1 Thess 4:11-12). When the situation has deteriorated by the time of the writing of the second letter, he targets the abusers with direct commands to start working and stop meddling (2 Thess 3:6-13). Those who refuse to comply are to be singled out for discipline, yet admonished as brothers (3:14-15). Paul urges the church leaders to adapt their pastoral approach to the types of individuals they are addressing: the idle must be warned; the timid encouraged; the weak helped; and all treated with patience with no hint of recrimination (1 Thess 5:14-15).

No church tested Paul's patience more than the church in Corinth. With the Corinthians Paul was forced to exercise a confrontational pattern of leadership over a long period, one that required iron resolve. First, when Paul heard of moral problems in the church, he wrote the "previous letter" that addressed issues such as idolatry and fornication (1 Cor 5:9). Second, while at Ephesus he wrote the extant letter of 1 Corinthians in response to issues brought to his attention by two delegations from Corinth (1 Cor 1:11; 16:15-18). Paul tackled head on a number of disturbing relational, moral and doctrinal problems with strong rebuke and warning. Those who destroy God's church will themselves be destroyed (1 Cor 3:16-17). The incestuous individual is to be severed from church fellowship (5:5). Though it is Paul's intent to warn not to shame them (4:14), he is forced to shame those who are involved in lawsuits with fellow believers (6:5), as well as those who are denying the bodily resurrection of Christ (15:34). Those who participate in banquets in idol temples are arousing the jealousy of the Lord (10:22). Physical sickness and premature death are visiting those who are partaking of the Lord's Supper in an unworthy manner (11:30).

Third, following Timothy's unsuccessful mission to Corinth (1 Cor 4:17; 16:10-11) Paul made a "painful visit" there. He earlier warned the church that he would face off with his arrogant opponents and wield the whip of rebuke (1 Cor 4:18-21). On that visit Paul was maliciously insulted by the ringleader of the opposition faction (2 Cor 2:1, 5; 7:12). Fourth, Paul followed up the painful visit with a "severe letter," designed to test the church's obedience (2 Cor 2:9), but which was written out of distress, anguish, and tears (2:3-4). The letter, carried by Titus to Corinth (and which is not extant), was effective in discrediting his opponents and bringing the church to repentance (7:8-12). Fifth, Paul left Ephesus, traveled anxiously to Troas, and then to Macedonia where he met Titus, who brought him great relief with news of a reconciled church (2 Cor 2:12-13; 7:13-16). He wrote 2 Corinthians 1-9 to express his joy over their restoration and to instruct them on fulfilling their pledge to give to the Jerusalem fund. However, fresh news came of troubles in Corinth from interlopers claiming superior Jewish credentials. Paul wrote Chapters 10-13 to address this shocking development. Paul ridiculed the claims of these pseudo-apostles (2 Cor 11:13) or self-claimed "super-apostles" (11:5; 12:11). He also warned the church that upon his coming third visit to them (12:14; 13:1-2) he would not spare any and all who were seeking to undermine the apostolic character of the church (13:1-4). Titus carried the extant letter of 2 Corinthians to Corinth. Paul finally arrived in Corinth to spend the winter of A.D. 56-57 before proceeding to Jerusalem (Acts 20:2-3; Rom 15:25-27). Thus over a period of five and one-half years,[16] with four letters, three dispatches of his two most trusted colleagues, and three personal visits, Paul administered the protective crook and the corrective rod of a loving shepherd.

Warning and rebuke

The church in Rome was being divided along racial lines due to an anti-Semitic strain of teaching among the majority Gentile believers. Paul warns them against boastful arrogance over Israel's fall. He reminds them that God will not spare them either if they fall into unbelief (Rom 11:18-22). The apostle issues a stern warning to the brothers to separate from those who would cause divisions in the church (16:17-18). The Philippian church is commanded to watch out for Judaizers, who compel circumcision as a precondition of salvation (3:2), and for antinomians who espouse a hedonistic ethic (3:18-19). Paul exposes the sham of asceticism and an unhealthy fascination with angels that have crept into the church at Colossae (Col 2:4, 8, 16-23). Archippus is warned to complete the work the Lord assigned him to do (Col 4:17).

The pastoral duties that Timothy and Titus must fulfill to the churches of Ephesus and Crete respectively include admonition and rebuke. Paul earlier warned the elders of the church in Ephesus that they must be on guard against false teachers who would arise even within their ranks and distort the truth (Acts 20:28-31). By seeking "to draw away disciples after them" (20:30), these heretics were the opposite of servant-leaders who were to eschew personal allegiances for loyalty to the apostolic teaching. In his first letter Paul instructs Timothy to confront those who promote controversies surrounding Jewish myths rather than God's work (1 Tim 1:3-7), to expose the hypocrisy of those promoting asceticism (4:1-7), to publicly rebuke elders who sin "so that the others may take warning" (5:20), to unmask the arrogance of those who teach a prosperity form of theology (6:3-5), and to preserve the integrity of the gospel and turn away from the ideology of the proto-gnostics (6:20-21). His second letter to Timothy is similarly full of warning against those who pervert sound teaching and endorse libertarian ethics (2 Tim 2:17-18; 3:1-9, 13; 4:3-4). Paul does not hesitate to censure individuals who have turned away from their earlier profession of faith (1 Tim 1:19-20; 2 Tim 1:15; 4:10a, 14-15). Paul condemns both the motives and the doctrine of the Judaizers who have infiltrated the church in Crete (1:10-16). He commands Titus to sharply rebuke any who are falling prey to their pernicious teachings (Tit 1:13). Titus' pastoral ministry must combine teaching, exhortation and rebuke, all

---

[16] We date Paul's initial arrival in Corinth during the second missionary journey in March, A.D. 51. His arrival in Corinth for the third visit is dated approximately October, A.D. 56. Paul comes to Corinth, spends three months in the Winter of 56-57, during which he writes his magnum opus, Romans (Acts 20:2-3; 1 Cor 16:6-7). He departs Corinth at the end of February A.D. 57 and heads to Jerusalem to deliver the funds collected from the Gentile churches (1 Cor 16:1-4; 2 Cor 8-9; Rom 15:25-32; cf. Acts 20:4; 24:17).

administered with delegated authority from the Lord (2:15).[17]

In summary, when unsound teaching threatens to undermine the established doctrinal and ethical foundation of the churches, Paul is confrontational. Paul knows where to draw the line between what is essential and what is negotiable. When the integrity of the gospel is at stake, Paul is the most unbending of leaders.

2. EXHORTATIONAL

While the ethical sections of Paul's letters are replete with imperatives, these commands are more than balanced by exhortations that appeal to the minds and wills of believers to respond with a voluntary obedience to the lordship of Christ. Though Paul is an authoritative leader, he is not authoritarian, demanding compliance to satisfy a psychological need to lord it over others. He is respectful, gracious and non-coercive, never controlling, manipulative or threatening. Paul is deeply conscious that the apostolic authority delegated to him is for building up the churches, never for tearing them down (2 Cor 10:8; 13:10).

Encouragement

The language of exhortation begins with Paul's favorite verb, παρακαλεω,[18] which normally means "**encourage**" or "**exhort**" (1 Thess 4:1; Rom 12:1; Eph 4:1), but can be rendered "**appeal**" or "**plead**" when addressing relational issues with deep emotion (1 Cor 1:10; Php 4:2; Phlm 9-10), or even the stronger "**urge**" when his exhortation approximates the force of a command (Rom 16:17; 1 Tim 1:3; 2:1; Tit 2:6, 15). Paul often employs this verb in the first person (singular or plural) to encourage the believers to freely respond to God's grace. In light of the "mercies of God," so eloquently expounded in the first eleven chapters of Romans, Paul exhorts the believers to dedicate their whole selves to God as a living sacrifice, which is their reasonable act of worship (Rom 12:1). He encourages the believers to live to please God (1 Thess 4:1), to love one another more and more (1 Thess 4:10), to administer sensitive and patient pastoral care of people in the church (1 Thess 5:14), to agree with one another (1 Cor 1:10), to imitate him (1 Cor 4:16), to reaffirm their love for a fallen and repentant brother (2 Cor 2:8), to not receive the grace of God in vain (2 Cor 6:1), and to live worthy of their calling (Eph 4:1). He does not warn, but rather exhorts two squabbling sisters to come together in the Lord (Php 4:2). Even to a church that is pulling away from him, Paul appeals to the Corinthians "through the meekness and gentleness of Christ"[19] to reclaim their true apostolic heritage (2 Cor 10:1). Though Paul could have demanded that Philemon restore Onesimus, he makes an appeal to the slave-owner based on the slave's new standing in Christ (Phm 9-11). Timothy and Titus are enjoined

---

[17] The prepositional phrase μετα πασης επιταγης is taken to modify all three preceding imperatives. The noun επιταγη is elsewhere used of the divine command (Rom 16:26; 1 Cor 7:6, 25; 1 Tim 1:1; Tit 1:3) or of an apostolic command (2 Cor 8:8). Here it refers to the delegated authority from the Lord invested in the apostolic envoy to the church.

[18] Paul employs the verb παρακαλεω fifty-four times, distributed throughout all of his letters with the single exception of Galatians. In addition, he uses the cognate noun παρακλησις twenty times.

[19] The prepositional phrase, δια της πραυτητος και επιεικειας, is used adverbially to indicate the manner of Paul's appeal. He takes on the mantle of Christ who in his earthly life was meek (πραυς) and humble (ταπεινος, very close in meaning to επιεικια [gentleness, forbearance]) in heart (Mt 11:29).

to imitate Paul and to carry on a ministry of exhortation in the churches assigned to them (1 Tim 5:1; 6:2; 2 Tim 4:2; Tit 2:6,15; cf. Tit 1:9 [elders]). Mutual exhortation, in fact, is to characterize community life in the churches (Rom 1:12;[20] 12:8; 1 Cor 14:3, 31; 2 Cor 2:7; 1 Thess 4:18; 5:11).

Other verbs of appeal, of cognitive recollection, and of cognitive information are sprinkled in the ethical sections of Paul's epistles: **plead** or **beg** (Gal 4:12; 2 Cor 5:20; 10:2);[21] **ask** or **request** (1 Thess 4:1; 5:12; 2 Thess 2:1; Php 4:3; Eph 3:13);[22] **inform** or **make known** (Gal 1:11; 1 Cor 12:3; 15:1; 2 Cor 8:1; Col 4:7, 9; Eph 6:21);[23] **remind** (1 Cor 4:17; Rom 15:15; 2 Tim 1:6; 2:14; Tit 3:1; cf. Eph 2:11; 2 Tim 2:8);[24] **want** (you [pl.]) **to know** or **not to be ignorant** (1 Cor 10:1; 11:3; 12:1; Rom 11:25; Php 1:12; Col 2:1);[25] and **commend** (Rom 16:1).[26]

To conclude, Paul's language targets the thinking and volition of the believers for a rational and voluntary response to the gracious work that God has done in Christ on their behalf. Paul is an exhortational leader who knows that true obedience, the kind that elicits God's pleasure, is that which flows "from the heart," not that which is compelled by the demands of a forceful taskmaster (Rom 6:17; Eph 6:6).

Exercise of spiritual gifts

As a leader committed to building self-governing and self-propagating churches, Paul encourages believers to develop and use their spiritual gifts for the good of the whole. Paul provides four lists of representative gifts given by the Spirit to the church:

1 Cor 12:8-10	1 Cor 12:28-30	Rom 12:6-8	Eph 4:11
word of wisdom	apostles	prophesying	apostles
word of knowledge	prophets	serving	prophets
faith	teachers	teaching	evangelists
healing	workers of miracles	encouraging	pastor-teachers
miraculous powers	healing	contributing to needs of others	
prophecy	able to help others	leadership[27]	
distinguishing spirits	administration	showing mercy	
speaking in tongues	speaking in tongues		
interpretation of tongues	interpretation		

[20] συμπαρακαλεω

[21] δεομαι

[22] ἐρωταω (αἰτεω in Eph 3:13)

[23] γνωριζω

[24] ἀναμιμνησκω (1 Cor 4:17; 2 Tim 1:6); ἐπαναμιμνησκω (Rom 15:15); and ὑπομιμνησκω (2 Tim 2:14; Tit 3:1). The transitive verb μνημονευω (remember) is used as an imperative in Eph 2:11; 2 Tim 2:8.

[25] οὐ θελω ἀγνοειν (1 Cor 10:1; 12:1; Rom 11:25); θελω εἰδεναι (1 Cor 11:3; Col 2:1); and βουλομαι γινωσκειν (Php 1:12)

[26] συνιστημι

[27] The verb προιστημι can refer to the pastoral and/or governance function of elders (1 Thess 5:12; 1 Tim 5:17) and the management of one's earthly family, which is a qualifying criterion for church leadership (1 Tim 3:4, 5, 12). The usage in Rom 12:8 may be another reference to the elder/overseer who is to exercise this office "with eagerness." Alternatively, since this is one of a number of χαρισματα (12:6), it may designate informal leadership functions in the church not related to a particular office that was subject to appointment.

Paul seeks to lead the churches into a balanced exercise of their gifts. There is a pastoral symmetry about his approach to gifts that encourages freedom, but within a theological framework that places corporate edification as the goal of individual expression. The Thessalonians are commanded to not show contempt for the gift of prophecy and, at the same time, to test all things by apostolic tradition (1 Thess 5:19-22). Paul trusts the believers to exercise their powers of discernment, based on the revealed canon of truth, to sift that which is genuine from that which is spurious. He does not, however, lay down a draconian measure to prevent abuse of the gift of prophecy by commanding its disuse. His concern over spurious prophecies is balanced by an equal concern that the church must not quench the energizing and illuminating ministry of the Holy Spirit among them.

In the case of the troubled church in Corinth, it was the gift of tongues that began to occupy a place of unhealthy prominence. Paul addresses the problem by establishing parameters for the proper exercise of the gift. Again, Paul appeals to their faculty of reasoning (1 Cor 14:20) and trusts the church to take corrective action. First, prophecy is the greater gift because, unlike tongues, it is an intelligible message that brings corporate edification (14:1-5). Second, speaking in tongues is unintelligible and cannot edify the hearer unless it is interpreted (14:6-12). Paul is careful not to denigrate the gift of tongues; in fact, he affirms the private practice of tongues as contributing to his own prayer life (14:5, 18, 39). Third, though private praying in tongues edifies the individual (14:2, 4, 5, 14-15, 18, 19, 28), in the assembly the speaker should seek the gift of interpretation so that the message can be understood and edify others (14:13-19). Fourth, uninterpreted tongues are a negative sign of judgment on unbelievers, who are shielded from the intelligible word of salvation (14:21-23), but prophecy is a positive sign of blessing on believers and can thereby lead to the conversion of unbelievers (14:24-25). Fifth, all gifts should be exercised in an orderly manner (14:26-40). Both prophecy and tongues are regulated during times of corporate worship so that individual expression contributes to the building up of the body. Though Paul gently scolds the Corinthians with a series of rhetorical questions for letting the situation get out of hand (14:36-38), he closes with a command to pursue the gift of prophecy and to stop hindering others from exercising the gift of tongues (14:39).[28] Once again Paul tackles the problem of abuse not by commanding disuse, but by correcting the abuse.

Voluntary offering

Paul's exhortational pattern of leadership is clearly illustrated in his instructions to the church in Corinth regarding their participation in the Jerusalem fund (2 Cor 8:1-9:15). He had earlier instructed them to take up a voluntary offering over a number of weeks and to appoint representatives to handle the money. When he arrived he would provide letters of introduction for those who would then accompany him to Jerusalem to deliver the gifts (1 Cor 16:1-4). By the time he writes 2 Corinthians, Paul must remind them to fulfill the pledge they had made

---

[28] The present imperatival prohibition (μη κωλυετε) indicates a command to desist from a course of action that is already occurring.

the previous year (2 Cor 8:10-12; 9:1-5). Though Paul is bold to urge the Corinthians to keep their promises, the entire argument is one of appeal, not of coercion (8:8). First, the Macedonians provide a sterling example of the principle that giving is a volitional expression of one's dedication to the Lord (8:1-5). Second, giving is a response to the grace of the Lord Jesus Christ who enriched them by his poverty (8:6-9). Third, the willingness of the heart must be translated into concrete action (8:10-12; 9:1-5). Fourth, the collection will be organized by proven men of integrity, Titus and the two brothers (8:16-24). Fifth, true giving is voluntary, premeditated and heart-determined, not out of compulsion or grudging release (9:6-7). The amount of money given is clearly less important to Paul than the motivation behind the gift.

Finally, the glory of God and the edification of the believers are the complimentary aims of the entire project, beautifully set forth in a doxological chain of events. First, God's abounding grace provides them with the ability to give generously (9:8-11a). Second, the recipients then overflow with thanksgiving to God for such generosity (9:11b-12). Third, God is then praised and the gospel commended (9:13, 15). Fourth, God's people become united in prayers of thanksgiving for God's grace—those who give for the ability to do so, and those who receive for the loving concern of their brothers (9:14). While the Jerusalem fund had a deeper theological significance, namely, to strengthen the unity of the one church of Christ both Jew and Gentile (cf. Rom 15:25-27; 31b), its immediate significance was its potential for blessing in one local congregation. He sees their participation in the fund as an opportunity to experience and express the reality of God's grace in Christ Jesus.[29]

Liberty in nonessentials

The church in Rome was an exemplary church whose sterling reputation for fidelity to the gospel was widely acclaimed (Rom1:8). However, there was a growing division between two groups in the church over external practices unrelated to the essential content of the gospel. The issues over which the two sets of believers were divided were the eating of meat such as pork, which contravened the food laws of Leviticus 11 (Rom 14:2, 3, 6, 14, 15, 20, 21, 23), the drinking of wine (14:21), and the observing of special days in the religious calendar (14:5, 6). The one group, self-designated "strong ones" (15:1), were probably Gentile believers who felt no compulsion to abstain from pork and wine, or to retain calendrical distinctions drawn from the Old Testament. The "weak ones" (14:1, 2), a pejorative label attached to them by their disputants, were most likely Jewish believers conditioned by their background to have a sensitive conscience toward such external matters. There is no evidence that either group departed from the crucial doctrine of justification by faith apart from the works of the law. Rather, disagreement over external practices unrelated to the truth of the gospel was fracturing the testimony of the church in Rome.

Paul clearly states that his theological affinities lie with the strong (15:1), for

[29] The thematic term of 2 Corinthians 8-9 is grace (χαρις), which occurs ten times in these two chapters (8:1, 4, 6, 7, 9, 16, 19; 9:8, 14, 15).

he inherited from Jesus the view that the Old Testament ceremonial legislation has been abrogated in the new covenant (14:14; cf. Mk 7:19). Since his transforming encounter with the risen Lord near Damascus, Paul has been liberated from the binding shackles of a law-based approach to God (cf. Gal 5:6; 6:15; 1 Cor 7:19; Php 3:4-8). But Paul will not take sides in the dispute, for to do so would be to ride roughshod over the consciences of sensitive believers and to embolden his fellow "strong ones" (15:1) to do the same. The problem here is not one of theology, but one of attitude. The strong are despising the weak as immature, overly scrupulous brothers who need to be liberated from their infantile convictions (14:3a). The weak are condemning the strong as compromising brothers with low ethical standards (14:3b).

Paul's exhortational leadership again emerges as he tackles this vexing relational disturbance. He sets forth six principles aimed not at changing their convictions or conduct, but at transforming their attitudes. Each principle summons the proper mindset with its supporting rationale.

1. Principle of equality: Because all believers are fellow servants of God, to judge one's brother is to usurp the exclusive right of the one Master who takes full responsibility for his own (Rom 14:1-4).
2. Principle of motivation: One must respect the motives behind the actions of one's brother, for each makes their choice on the basis of what they believe is pleasing to the Lord (14:5-8).
3. Principle of accountability: Premature assessment of one's brother preempts the divine appointment, where each individual will give an account of one's actions at the judgment seat of the risen Lord Christ (14:9-12).
4. Principle of restraint: One must refrain from exercising one's liberty when it will embolden another to violate their conscience,[30] for to do so will bring them irreparable spiritual harm (14:13-21).
5. Principle of faith: Convictions about nonessential matters should be mutually respected and embraced as a private matter, because each person's inner freedom to undertake or not to undertake a certain course of action determines its legitimacy before God (14:22-23).
6. Principle of sacrifice: One should act in a way that edifies one's brother, for Christ set us an example of sacrificial concern for others (15:1-4).

Paul feels no need to demand uniformity of standards among the brothers in Rome, as long as the fundamental principles of the gospel are not compromised. Both the insensitive arrogance of the strong and the vulnerability of the weak call forth a pastoral approach that requires clear commands (14:1, 22), strict warnings (14:15b, 16, 20a), moral appeals (14:5b; 15:1, 2), and earnest exhortations (14:13, 19).

---

[30] The Greek term for conscience, συνείδησις, is not used in Romans 14, though it is prominent in the similar passage in 1 Corinthians 8 and 10 (8:7, 10, 12; 10:25, 27, 28, 29 [twice]). The dynamic equivalent for conscience in Romans 14 is faith (πίστις: 14:1, 22, 23 [twice]; cognate verb πιστεύω: 14:2), which in this context means the inner freedom (because one's faith allows it) to undertake a certain course of action.

3. ACCOUNTABLE

Paul maintains the highest standards of personal integrity because he is deeply conscious of his accountability to the God who set him apart for ministry to the Gentiles (Gal 1:15-16). He confidently summons the churches to imitate his pattern of life because he wants them to share his life purpose of glorifying God and edifying others (Rom 15:9-12; Col 1:28-29). Paul often must defend his character against attacks because his authority as God's commissioned representative is inextricably tied to the integrity of his message. Paul is a leader driven by a sense of stewardship and the account he must render to his Master at a great future day when motives will be unmasked and actions will be weighed (1 Cor 4:1-5).

Clear conscience

Integrity is the coherence of motive and action that characterizes all authentic leadership. Paul's term for integrity is conscience and he strives to maintain a clear conscience both before God and people (Acts 24:16; 2 Cor 8:21 cf. Acts 23:1). Conscience is one's dialogue with oneself, the inner voice that testifies to the adherence to or violation of one's moral standards. The conscience functions as accuser or defendant in all people, depending on whether or not they live up to their innate awareness of what is right or wrong implanted in their constitutions by God himself (Rom 2:15). Because the conscience is deeply affected by one's cultural conditioning (cf. 1 Cor 10:25, 27), Paul sees its renewal by the Holy Spirit based on faith in the gospel as part of the sanctifying process (Rom 9:1; 1 Tim 1:5, 19a). The testimonial function of the conscience, whether with affirmation or conviction, is central to one's spiritual health. Those who damage it by violating it or, in extreme cases, sear the conscience suffer irreparable spiritual harm (1 Cor 8:9-12; 1 Tim 1:19b-20; 4:2; Tit 1:15; cf. Eph 4:19). Paul aims for a clean and clear conscience, an inner congruity between intent, thought, and action, that both pleases God and commends the gospel to people (2 Cor 1:12; 4:2; 5:11; 2 Tim 1:3). He urges Timothy to maintain personal integrity in his pastoral ministry in Ephesus, that is, a conscience that verifies his freedom from duplicity and hidden agendas (1 Tim 1:5; cf. 3:9 [deacons]).

Pattern to imitate

Though Paul is fully aware that he has by no means attained complete victory over sin (1 Cor 9:26-27; Php 3:12-14), he calls on the churches to imitate his pattern of life.[31] Paul puts himself forward as an example to the churches because of the confidence that his motives, actions, and teaching are in imitation of God's love revealed in Christ's sacrifice (1 Thess 2:4-6a; 1 Cor 11:1; Eph 5:1-2). The believers are to imitate his joy in suffering (1 Thess 1:6), his diligence to provide for his own needs through hard work (2 Thess 3:7, 9), his sacrificial way of life (1 Cor 4:16-17), and his zealous and undistracted pursuit of Christ (Php 3:17). He

---

[31] The language of imitation occurs in three cognate terms: μιμητης (1 Cor 4:16; 11:1; Eph 5:1; 1 Thess 1:6; 2:14); μιμεομαι (2 Thess 3:7, 9); συμμιμητης (Php 3:17). The term τυπος can be rendered pattern, model, or example, which in Paul's case deserves imitation (Php 3:17; 1 Thess 1:7; 2 Thess 3:9; 1 Tim 4:12).

commands the Philippians and Timothy to imitate his soundness of faith, speech and doctrine (Php 4:9; 2 Tim 1:13). Strictly speaking, Paul does not call on the churches to "follow" his leadership, for Christ alone is their leader, whereas he is a servant commissioned to enhance their allegiance to Christ.[32] Paul sets forth himself not as a leader to follow, but as a fellow servant to imitate. He forges several chains of imitation that bind the doctrine and conduct of the churches and their leaders to the apostolic pattern: Paul—Thessalonians—churches in Macedonia and Achaia (1 Thess 1:6-7); Paul—Timothy—believers in Ephesus (1 Tim 4:12, 16); Paul—Titus—believers in Crete (Tit 2:7-8). Paul wants Timothy, Titus, and the believers in the emerging churches to share his deep sense of responsibility for how they are influencing others.

Defense of integrity

Paul was often attacked with ad hominem arguments. His opponents sought to undermine his message of justification by faith apart from the law by discrediting the messenger. Paul's defenses are not attempts to salve a wounded ego. Rather, Paul's apologetic is driven by a holy zeal to preserve the integrity of the gospel that God has entrusted him with. To a church troubled by Judaizing infiltrators, he writes that a true servant of Christ seeks the approbation of God not of people (Gal 1:10). To please God who tests the heart, and to whom he must give an account, is Paul's singular ambition in life (1 Thess 2:4a; 2 Cor 5:9; 2 Tim 2:4). Though he does seek to please others in the sense of serving their spiritual needs (1 Cor 10:33; Rom 15:1-2), he is not a man-pleaser who pursues self-aggrandizement through flattery (Gal 1:10; 1 Thess 2:4b-6). Against attacks on his personal integrity Paul invites the Thessalonians to recall his demeanor when he was among them: forthright appeals free from manipulation (1 Thess 2:3); speech free from flattery and pretense (2:5); gentle motherly care (2:7); wholehearted devotion (2:8); sacrificial labors (2:9); holy, righteous and blameless conduct (2:10); and fatherly encouragement (2:11). Paul makes his final appeal to God who stands as witness to the truthfulness of his defense (2:5, 10; cf. Gal 1:20; 2 Cor 1:23; Rom 1:9; Php 1:8).

It is to the church in Corinth, which is under the assault of anti-Paul interlopers, that the apostle launches his most vigorous defense. He is forced, because of the severity of the attacks and the danger they present to the church, to "commend"[33] himself as the Lord's true servant. The proofs of the veracity of Paul's claim to be God's authorized leader include the Corinthians themselves (2 Cor 3:1-2), his plain exposition of the gospel to the consciences of people (4:2), the testimony of their own consciences (5:11-12), his resilience in manifold hardships (6:4-10), and ultimately the commendation of the Lord himself (10:18). Paul is somewhat

---

[32]The normal term in the New Testament for "follow" in the sense of committed discipleship, ἀκολουθεω (cf. Mt 4:20, 22; 8:19, 22, 23; 9:9; 10:38; 16:24; 19:21, 27-28), is found only once in Paul's letters (1 Cor 10:4: the spiritual rock that "accompanied" [NIV] Israel in the wilderness).

[33] Of the sixteen occurrences of the verb συνιστημι in the New Testament, all but two are in Paul's writings, and nine of those fourteen appear in 2 Corinthians (3:1; 4:2; 5:12; 6:4; 7:11; 10:12, 18 [twice]; 12:11).

embarrassed by having to make a defense of his character to those who ought to be his strongest defenders (10:13-14; 11:1; 12:11).

Paul is eager to distance himself from the motives and methods of the infiltrators who have come to Corinth and are seeking to pull the church away from its apostolic founder. First, he does not peddle the word of God for profit, but speaks before God with sincerity (2 Cor 2:17). Paul's deep sense of accountability, of one whose thoughts, words, and actions are assessed under the searchlight of God's holiness, finds expression in his frequent "before God/the Lord" posture (Gal 1:20; 2 Cor 2:17; 4:2; 7:12; 8:21; 12:19; Rom 14:22; Eph 1:4; Col 1:22; 1 Tim 2:3; 5:4, 21; 6:13; 2 Tim 2:14; 4:1).[34] In organizing the Jerusalem fund, Paul takes pains to ensure that his conduct is above reproach by having representatives appointed by the churches directly handle the money (1 Cor 16:3-4; 2 Cor 8:19-21; Acts 20:4). Second, he denounces secret and deceptive techniques in favor of a plain exposition of the truth aimed at the consciences of his listeners (2 Cor 4:2; 5:11). Third, unlike the false teachers who are caught up with oratorical eloquence (1 Cor 2:4), self-absorbed claims to wisdom and knowledge (1 Cor 1:19-25; 8:1-2), and physical appearance (2 Cor 10:10), Paul is concerned with heart motivation (2 Cor 5:12). Fourth, Paul refuses to engage in personal comparisons with others as the false apostles do, or to interfere in the work appointed by God to others as these intruders are doing by cutting into his assigned field of ministry in Corinth (2 Cor 10:12-16). Fifth, Paul chides the Corinthians for tolerating self-promoting leaders who enslave, exploit, take advantage of, and treat them rudely (11:20-21). He ridicules the claims of his opponents to be servants of Christ, and chronicles the resume of sufferings that are his credentials as a genuine servant (11:23-29). Sixth, Paul asserts it is he, and not the pseudo-apostles who feign a higher spirituality, that had a third-heaven revelatory experience where he heard inexpressible mysteries, an encounter which were it not for divine discipline he would be tempted to boast about (12:1-7).

It is helpful to list from 2 Corinthians the points of defense Paul raises against his accusers. To read Paul's responses and seek to reconstruct the precise attacks being made against him is admittedly a difficult task, somewhat like listening in to one end of a telephone conversation and piecing together what the person on the other end of the line is saying. The following reconstruction draws first on arguments in the immediate context in 2 Corinthians and, second, on data from 1 Corinthians that might shed light on what was a fluid situation.

---

[34] There is no appreciable difference of meaning in the various prepositions he employs: κατεναντι θεου (2 Cor 2:17; 12:19); κατενωπιον θεου (Eph 1:4; Col 1:22); ἐνωπιον θεου (Rom 14:22; 2 Cor 4:2; 7:12; 8:21; Gal 1:20; 1 Tim 2:3; 5:4, 21; 6:13; 2 Tim 2:14; 4:1).

Accusation	Defense
1. Paul is untrustworthy and fickle, and makes his plans based on worldly wisdom. This is proven by his failure to visit Corinth as he pledged (2 Cor 1:12, 17).	1. My conduct toward both outsiders and with you is holy and sincere. My plans are made and revised not in a worldly way, but with dependence on God's grace (1:12, 15-17). I delayed my visit from a desire to spare you grief from a fresh confrontation (1:23-2:2).
2. Paul is delusional. His religious mania is expressed by the sensational accounts he gives of an encounter with Jesus near Damascus (5:13). His mental imbalance accounts for his refusal to accept monetary support for his services and his preference for denying himself normal pleasures.	2. I have seen Jesus our Lord (1 Cor 9:1) and am equally qualified with the other apostles as a witness of the resurrection (1 Cor 15:8). I plead guilty to the charge of working to support myself and living a sacrificial life (11:7-15, 23-29). All of this mania, as they call it, is for your benefit and for God's glory (5:13).
3. Paul has wronged, corrupted, and exploited the church by his endeavor to collect funds for Jewish believers in far off Judea (7:2). The whole endeavor is a trick because the funds will never reach their purported destination (12:16). The collection is just a pretext for Paul to enrich himself.	3. Neither have I nor those I have appointed to organize the collection ever exploited anyone (7:2). Titus and the two brothers are men of honor and the entire project is being administered in a way that is above reproach (8:16-23a; 12:17-18). Those whom the church appoints to take up the collection will accompany me to Jerusalem, and personally deliver the funds to the suffering brothers (8:23b-24; cf. 1 Cor 16:1-4; Acts 20:4).
4. Paul is courageous to confront when he writes letters from a distance, but is weak and vacillating when physically present (10:1, 2, 10). This is proof that his warnings are merely human arguments without the evident authority of Christ behind them (13:3).	4. Do not mistake my meekness and gentleness, in imitation of Christ, as weakness (10:1). Though I do not relish confrontation, I am thoroughly prepared to demolish the arguments of my opponents and to punish all that are taken captive by their deceit (10:2-6). You will soon find out when I arrive how powerfully the presence of Christ is working through me (10:11; 13:1-4).
5. Since all worthy religious instructors receive payment in accordance with the value of their imparted wisdom, Paul's refusal to accept support is proof that his message is worthless (11:7).	5. These so-called wise men are no more than religious peddlers who use religion as a means of financial gain (2:17). My reasons for not accepting monetary support from you are, first, to model the gospel which is an offer of salvation through grace, freely given and freely received (11:7; cf. 1 Cor 9:15-18), and, second, to relieve you of financial burdens (11:8-12; 12:13-15; cf. 1 Thess 2:9; 2 Thess 3:8).

Stewardship

Underlying the appeals to preserve a clear conscience, to imitate his pattern of life, to reject the inflated claims of false teachers, and to reaffirm the integrity of his leadership is Paul's sense of stewardship. He has been "entrusted" with the gospel and the mandate to proclaim it in all of its purity to the Gentiles (Gal 2:7; 1 Cor 9:17; 1 Thess 2:4; 1 Tim 1:11; Tit 1:3; cf. Col 1:25; Eph 3:7). His pastoral envoys like Timothy and Titus and the elders they appoint have been delegated with responsibility to preserve the integrity of the gospel against all attempts to distort it either by subtraction or addition (1 Tim 6:20; 2 Tim 1:14; Tit 1:7). As one who has been given a trust, namely, to establish the churches among the Gentiles on the foundation of the revealed gospel, Paul will be judged for his faithfulness not by a human court nor even by his own conscience, but by the Lord himself (1 Cor 4:1-4). The divine assessment will take place at the appointed time of the Lord's return (1 Cor 4:5a). All hidden agendas will be exposed (4:5b). Only that which meets the criterion of faithfulness to the charge will receive God's approval (4:5c).

Judgment seat of Christ

Paul thus exercises his leadership of the churches with an overwhelming sense that the day of Christ's return is rapidly approaching when he will stand before the judgment seat and give a full account of his actions to God (2 Cor 5:10; Rom 14:10-12). Paul's faithfulness to his call is conditioned by this great future event toward which he strains with reverent expectation. He describes the coming event of the personal return of Christ as a "revelation" of his majesty, his glorious "appearing," and the royal "arrival" of the King to consummate his rule.[35] The day of judgment is the reason he makes it his singular ambition to please God in life and ministry (2 Cor 5:9; cf. 1 Thess 4:1; Rom 14:18; Eph 5:10; Col 1:10).[36] His reverential fear of the Lord, to whom he is accountable, is also the driving force behind the passionate defense of his apostolic authority, a defense aimed at striking the consciences of the Corinthian believers with the present danger they face from the false apostles (2 Cor 5:11).[37] Paul's emphasis on a life that is holy, blameless, and pure (1 Thess 5:23a; Eph 1:4; 5:27; Php 2:15; Col 1:22) is grounded in his conviction that the Lord's near return cannot be precisely timed and that believers must be prepared and not ashamed when that day comes (1 Thess 5:23b; 1 Cor 1:8; Php 3:13-14; 1 Tim 6:14).

While two major texts refer to the judgment of all believers including Paul (2 Cor 5:10; Rom 14:12: 1st p. pl.), there is one passage in Paul's epistles that specifically addresses those in formal church leadership, namely, 1 Corinthians 3:13-15. This text is in the middle of the section where Paul is dealing with the

---

[35] These are the basic meanings of the three terms Paul employs for the second coming, namely, ἀποκάλυψις (1 Cor 1:7; 2 Thess 1:7), ἐπιφάνεια (2 Thess 2:8; 1 Tim 6:14; 2 Tim 4:1, 8; Tit 2:13), and παρουσια (1 Cor 15:23; 1 Thess 2:19; 3:13; 4:15; 5:23; 2 Thess 2:1, 8) respectively.
[36] The conjunction γαρ in v. 10 provides the causal connection between accountability (2 Cor 5:10) and the singular ambition to please God (5:9).
[37] The inferential conjunction οὖν introduces v. 11: Paul's pastoral persuasion of the church gains its motivation from reverential fear of the Lord to whom he must give an account.

disturbing problem of factions that have developed in the church in Corinth (1 Cor 1:10-4:21). Personality-centered sloganeering characterized these rival groups who divided over special allegiances to Paul, Apollos, Cephas, or Christ, the latter probably a prideful contrarian group separating from all the others (1:10-12).

In the present section Paul reminds the Corinthians that he and Apollos are merely servants who are God's instruments to build his church (3:5). Paul employs both the agricultural metaphor of planting and watering, and the architectural metaphor of an expert builder who lays a foundation, to underscore that their attention should be focused on God who makes the plant to grow and on Christ who is alone the church's foundation (3:6-11). Those who plant or water will be rewarded according to the diligence of their labors (3:8). The one who builds will be assessed according to the materials used, whether perishable materials like wood, hay and straw, or lasting materials like gold, silver, and costly stones (3:12). The solid building materials are a metaphor for sound doctrine based on apostolic tradition and a blameless moral life that produces a clear conscience (cf. 1 Tim 4:16).[38] The quality of the leader's work will be revealed in the light of God's blazing holiness (3:13a). Ministries built upon the centrality of Christ and fidelity to the Word of God will bring reward. Those centered on the dynamism of the human instrument, motivated by the desire for material riches or personal prestige, or built by showmanship, will be consumed by the divine splendor (3:13b-15a). The final expression, "he himself will be saved, but only as one escaping through the flames" (3:15b), underscores the gravity of the warning, namely, that a hollow kind of leadership can be exercised even by genuinely regenerate people. It is a severe admonition directed not at those who profess faith but destroy the church through false teaching,[39] but at those whose salvation is secure and yet whose work proves utterly worthless. This text is not intended to teach a full-orbed theology of the carnal Christian, but to warn those who undertake church planting and church building ministries to make sure their motivation, conduct, and teaching are wholly submitted to the lordship of Christ.

4. AFFIRMATORY

The portrait of Paul as the indefatigable missionary whose undaunted faith triumphs over every obstacle, of a pioneering maverick whose singular pursuit of his divine calling overshadows personal relationships, is a caricature. To study carefully his extant thirteen-letter personal correspondence to churches and

---

[38] When Paul instructs Timothy, who has been appointed pastor of the church in Ephesus (thus a waterer and continuing builder), he repeatedly commands him to maintain strict adherence to the Word of God. First, Timothy must devote himself to the public reading of Scripture, to preaching, and to teaching (1 Tim 4:13, 15). Second, he is to guard the deposit that has been entrusted to him, namely, the gospel (6:20a; 2 Tim 1:14). Third, he is to keep the pattern of sound teaching based on apostolic instruction (2 Tim 1:13). Fourth, he must remember the gospel of Jesus Christ, the God-man, and its unrestrained power (2 Tim 2:8-9), and keep reminding others (2:14a). Fifth, he is commanded to continue in the study, application, and teaching of the Scriptures (2 Tim 3:14-17). Sixth, Timothy must preach the Word on all occasions with a view to correct, rebuke, and encourage the hearers (4:2-4). Here is a later testimony to what Paul views as establishing the church on the foundation of Christ and building on the foundation with lasting materials.

[39] We understand the subsequent warning in 1 Cor 3:17 to address the false teacher, one who is far more sinister than the foolish laborer of 3:15.

individuals is to discover a man that is emotionally sensitive, vulnerable to failure, tenderly affectionate, and affirming of others. Paul is not hesitant to praise the sterling qualities of individuals and of churches. As one who has been overwhelmed by God's redeeming mercies (Rom 12:1; 1 Tim 1:12-17), Paul is free to exhort, affirm, and facilitate others. He disdains every form of flattery, which aims only at ingratiating oneself through falsely inflating another (1 Thess 2:5; Rom 16:18).[40] His words are sincere, truthful expressions of appreciation for what God has done in and through his coworkers and the lives of ordinary believers in the churches. Relationships clearly are important to Paul. The modern dichotomy between the task-oriented leader and the relational leader would have mystified him.

Family of God

Paul's favorite designation for his fellow believers is "brothers," a term which signifies familial intimacy with God as beloved members of his covenant family (1 Thess 1:4; 2 Thess 2:13).[41] This accounts for his other common designation, "beloved ones," where Paul seems to mean that those chosen and beloved by God (Rom 1:7; 11:28) are beloved to him (Rom 12:19; 1 Cor 4:14; 10:14; 15:58; 2 Cor 7:1; 12:19; Eph 5:1; Php 2:12; 4:1; 1 Thess 2:8).[42] Paul also calls the believers in the churches he has planted his "children," for he is in one sense their father and feels a deep sense of responsibility for their spiritual nurture (1 Cor 4:14; Gal 4:19; 1 Thess 2:7, 11). Similarly he addresses Timothy, as he does Titus and Onesimus, affectionately as his "child" in the faith (1 Cor 4:17; 1 Tim 1:2, 18; 2 Tim 1:2; 2:1; Tit 1:4; Phm 10).[43] Phoebe is commended, just as Apphia is saluted, as "our sister" (Rom 16:1; Phm 2). In many cases the personal pronoun "my" accompanies these three designations, brother(s), beloved one(s), and child(ren), to stress Paul's personal solidarity with fellow members of God's family.

Personal greetings

Ten of his thirteen letters close with greetings to the church as a whole (or to Timothy, Titus, Philemon) and/or to individual members (Rom 16:3-16, 21-24; 1 Cor 16:19-20; 2 Cor 13:12-13; Php 4:21-22; Col 4:10-15; 1 Thess 5:26; 2 Thess 3:17; 2 Tim 4:19-21; Tit 3:15; Phlm 23-24).[44] Three times he authenticates the

---

[40] The related terms for flattering speech are: κολακεια (1 Thess 2:5); χρηστολογια (Rom 16:18); and εὐλογια (Rom 16:18).

[41] The designation ἀδελφοι is modified by the perfect passive participle of ἀγαπαω (1 Thess 1:4; 2 Thess 2:13), which is drawn from the Septuagint of Hosea 2:23 (quot. in Rom 9:25), and signifies God's sovereign choice of those far removed from his saving mercies (cf. Col 3:12). This author counted sixty-eight occurrences in the Pauline corpus where ἀδελφοι occurs as a direct address (nominative for vocative). Twice he addresses Philemon as "brother" (Phm 7, 20: true vocative ἀδελφε).

[42] The substantival use of the adjective ἀγαπητοι (pl.) in these texts seems to be almost interchangeable with ἀδελφοι in Paul's letters, as well as the material equivalent of the perfect passive participle ἠγαπημενοι.

[43] The Greek term in both instances is τεκνον. The term for son, υἱος, is used of God's children (pl. υἱοι) a number of times, but never in direct address (Rom 8:14, 19; 9:26; 2 Cor 6:18; Gal 3:7, 26; 4:6, 7 [sg.]; 1 Thess 5:5).

[44] The only exceptions are Galatians, Ephesians and 1 Timothy, all of which do conclude with a benediction of grace (Gal 6:18; Eph 6:23-24; 1 Tim 6:21b).

integrity of the letter by writing the greeting with his own hand (2 Thess 3:17; 1 Cor 16:21; Col 4:18). The extended greetings in Romans 16:3-16 are remarkable because this is a letter written to a church Paul did not plant in a city he has not yet visited. Nevertheless, he warmly greets twenty-six individuals by name, including at least nine women, and five households. These are friends he has known in his itinerant ministry in the eastern Mediterranean that have now settled in the capital city. Paul is often surrounded by others who share with him in extending greetings to the churches: the Asian churches, Priscilla and Aquila with their house church, and all the brothers in Ephesus (1 Cor 16:19-20); all the saints in Macedonia (2 Cor 13:13); Timothy and three other coworkers (Rom 16:21), including his host in Corinth, Gaius (16:23a); six brothers who are with him during his house arrest in Rome (Col 4:10-14; Phlm 23-24; cf. Acts 28:30-31); the saints in Rome, including some members of the imperial household (Php 4:22); four brothers among many others who have located him in the Mamertime prison in Rome (2 Tim 4:21b; cf. 1:17). Though Paul is the singular author of the thirteen letters attributed to him, he incorporates his coworkers Timothy and Silas in the initial address of the two letters to Thessalonica (1 Thess 1:1; 2 Thess 1:1) and Timothy alone in three more letters (2 Cor 1:1; Php 1:1; Col 1:1). This is a man who relishes the company of others and has drawn them into his collaborative approach to ministry.

Thanksgiving

Paul's letters reveal a leader who is not hesitant to affirm churches and individuals where praise is due, who shares their griefs, joys, and longings, who is transparent in disclosing his inner turmoils, and who possesses a deep affection for his spiritual children. He normally begins his letters with an expression of thanksgiving to God for his evident work in the lives of the believers. Though each church has its faults that require correction, Paul nearly always finds something distinctive about the church that causes his heart to well up with gratitude: (1) the resilience of the Thessalonians who became a model to the other churches of joy in the midst of suffering (1 Thess 1:2, 6-8) and whose faith and love is ever increasing (2 Thess 1:3-4); (2) the abundant spiritual gifts of the Corinthians (1 Cor 1:4-7); (3) the spreading reputation of the sterling faith of the Romans (Rom 1:8); (4) the Ephesians' faith in the Lord and love for the saints (Eph 1:15-16); (5) the Philippians' generous gifts that signify their partnership in his ministry (Php 1:3-5; 4:10-19); (6) the faith, love, and increasing fruitfulness of the Colossians (Col 1:3-6). Paul thanks God for the faith and love of Philemon (Phm 4-5) and the sincere faith of Timothy, his grandmother, and mother (2 Tim 1:4-5). Thanksgiving is one of Paul's ways of offering affirmation, free of flattery, for he is conscious that the entire work of planting the church depends on God's power operative in people's lives (1 Cor 3:6-9). The author who begins his letters with thanksgiving or praise (cf. 2 Cor 1:3; Eph 1:3; 1 Tim 1:12)[45] is a leader

[45] The only letters of the Pauline corpus that do not contain a praise or thanksgiving period in their prologue are Galatians and Titus. In the former he is drawn from the outset into an expression of astonishment at the Galatians' rapid defection from the gospel (Gal 1:6-10); in the latter Paul launches into instructing Titus how to handle the difficult situation in Crete (Tit 1:5ff). These exceptions to the rule prove that Paul disdains artificial complements or expresses thanks or praise simply as a formality.

whose mind is saturated with meditations of people who have been transformed by God's gracious work in Christ.

Transparency

Though full of profound doctrinal exposition and incisive moral application, Paul's letters contain numerous personal glimpses into the heart of a leader who cherishes those whom God has brought into his appointed sphere of ministry. He is especially transparent in expressing his loving affirmation for the Thessalonian church and the Corinthian church. This is somewhat surprising, since his time spent in Thessalonica was brief due to his premature departure due to persecution. He clearly had the capacity to bond with these fellow believers over a few short weeks or months.[46] No church caused Paul more heartache than the one in Corinth, yet his tender overtures of love more than match his necessary words of rebuke. We now offer a contextual reading (or broad interpretive paraphrase) of several representative texts in the Thessalonian and Corinthian correspondence. These texts disclose a leader who deeply loves those under his pastoral care and is not hesitant to say so.

1. "We were gentle among you, like a mother who tenderly nurtures her children. And so because we deeply cherish you, we delighted to impart to you not only the gospel, but our very lives as well, because we loved you dearly" (1 Thess 2:7-8).
2. "Brothers, when we were torn away from you for a short time, in person but not in thought, out of deep desire we made every effort to return and be reunited with you face to face (1 Thess 2:17). For who else expands our hope, brings us such joy, or will be the object of our exultation at the coming of the Lord Jesus, if it is not you (2:19)? Indeed, you yourselves are the ones we glory in and rejoice over even now (2:20). So when I could no longer endure not knowing how you were bearing up under your many trials, I was willing to be left alone in Athens and I released Timothy to go to you in my place (3:1-2a). I sent him to find out about your faith, because I feared that the tempter might undermine the work that we invested in you (3:5). But now Timothy has just returned, and he reported to us that your faith and love are strong, and that you have pleasant memories of us, and that you long to see us, just as we long for you (3:6).[47] I can say that we truly live as long as you are standing fast in the Lord (3:8). We cannot even begin to thank God for all the abounding joy we have in the presence of our God because of you (3:9)."

---

[46] We propose a chronology that has Paul in Thessalonica on his second missionary journey from November A.D. 50 until January 51 (Acts 17:1-9). After Timothy's arrival and good report (1 Thess 3:6), Paul, along with his two co-workers in the salutations, writes 1 Thessalonians (early Summer A.D. 51) from Corinth (note Achaia in 1:7-8; thus Athens is a possibility). A few weeks later (late Summer 51) he writes 2 Thessalonians to address fresh misunderstandings in eschatology.

[47] The language of "longing" captures the pastoral heart of one who relishes the company of his fellow believers and yearns to contribute to their spiritual welfare: ἐπιποθέω (Rom 1:11; Php 1:8; 1 Thess 3:6; 2 Tim 1:4); ἐπιπόθητος (Php 4:1); ἐπιποθία (Rom 15:23). The Corinthians finally responded to such love with a reciprocal longing for him (2 Cor 7:7, 11: ἐπιπόθησις).

3. "Now we stand persuaded in the Lord concerning you that you are both doing and will continue to do the things we are commanding" (2 Thess 3:4).[48]

4. "I followed up my painful visit to you with a letter to prepare you for my coming visit (2 Cor 2:1). I wrote strong words of rebuke to you, as tears flowed from an anguished and distressed heart, not to cause you grief, but that you might recognize the deep love I have for you, that is, the love of a father chastising his children (2:4)."

5. "We have opened our mouths to express our love for you, Corinthians; our hearts stand opened wide and fully exposed. Our love for you is not being withheld, but you are withholding your affections from us. As a mutual exchange of love, I am appealing to you as to my children, open wide your hearts to us also (2 Cor 6:11-13). Make room in your hearts for us (7:2a). I said before that you occupy such a place in our hearts that we would gladly live with you or die with you (7:3)."

6. "No one is going to prevent me from 'boasting' in the fact that I did not receive money from you, but supported myself through tent-making. Why would I support myself and not seek money from you? Is it because I do not love you? On the contrary, as God himself will testify, I love you more than you can imagine. My policy of self-support is designed to relieve you of financial burdens and to distance myself from those who peddle their religious wares for financial gain and all at your expense (2 Cor 11:9b-12). I will gladly spend for your benefit every penny I earn, and expend all my energies for you as well. If I love you more (by making such sacrifices), can you explain to me why you love me less (by turning to those who only exploit you) (12:15)?"

Many more texts from the entire corpus could be added to this representative sample from Paul's correspondence to two churches (e.g. Php 1:6-8; 4:1). But these are sufficient to disclose the heart of a leader who cannot help but express his love for and confidence in those for whose sake he has labored.

Commendation of fellow workers

Paul is abundant in his affirmation of fellow workers who have helped shoulder the burden of his apostolic ministry. He openly honors all whose motives and methods have commended them as true servants of Christ. His brothers and sisters are "beloved" both to God and to him (Rom 16:5b, 8, 9, 12b; 1 Cor 4:14, 17; Eph 6:21; Col 1:7; 4:7, 9, 14; 2 Tim 1:2; Phlm 1b, 16).[49] His words of commendation continue to reverberate as generation after generation of their spiritual heirs learn of and are encouraged by the record of these ancient witnesses.

---

[48] Paul often uses the verb πειθω ("persuade") in the perfect tense to express his settled confidence in the good work that God is doing in the lives of believers (Gal 5:10a; 2 Cor 2:3b; Rom 15:14; Php 1:6; Phm 21; 2 Tim 1:5; cf. 2 Cor 8:22: πεποιθησις). This is another way, similar to the thanksgiving periods, of affirming them while attributing its effective cause to divine grace.

[49] These texts employ the singular form of the adjective ἀγαπητος.

Person commended	Word of commendation[50]
Timothy	our brother and God's fellow worker in the gospel of Christ (1 Thess 3:2) beloved and faithful child in the Lord (1 Cor 4:17) He works the work of the Lord, even as I do (1 Cor 16:10). my fellow worker (Rom 16:21) I have no one of such a kindred spirit, who will genuinely care for your needs. You know of his proven character, that as a son with his father he served with me in the work of the gospel (Php 2:20, 22). my true son on the faith (1 Tim 1:2; cf. 1:18; 2 Tim 1:2) being reminded of the sincere faith which is in you (2 Tim 1:5a)
Stephanus, F. and A.	They refreshed my spirit and yours. Therefore, give recognition to such people as them (1 Cor 16:17-18).
"the brother"	who is praised by all the churches for his service to the gospel (2 Cor 8:18)
"our brother"	whom we have often proved in many situations to be zealous, and now much more so because of his great confidence in you (2 Cor 8:22)
Titus	my partner and fellow worker among you (2 Cor 8:23a) Our brothers are apostles of the churches and an honor to Christ (8:23b). my true son according to our common faith (Tit 1:4)
Phoebe	our sister, who is a servant of the church in Cenchrae (Rom 16:1) She was a great help to many people and to me (16:2).
Priscilla and Aquila	my fellow workers in Christ Jesus (Rom 16:3) They risked their lives (lit. "lowered their own necks" [for the executioner's sword]) for my sake, for whom not only I give thanks, but also all the churches of the Gentiles (16:4).
Mary	who worked very hard for you (16:6)
Andronicus and Junias	my fellow Jewish believers and my fellow prisoners (16:7a) They are outstanding among the apostles, who also have been in Christ before me (16:7b).
Urbanus	our fellow worker in Christ (16:9)
Apelles	the one who has been tested and approved in Christ (16:10a)
Tryphena and Tryphosa	the women who work hard in the Lord (16:12a)
Persis	the beloved woman who worked very hard in the Lord (16:12b)
mother of Rufus	his mother and mine (16:13a)
Epaphras	our dear fellow servant (Col 1:7a) who is a faithful minister of Christ on our behalf (1:7b) who is one of you, a servant of Christ Jesus, always wrestling for you in his prayers (Col 4:12) He toils earnestly for you and for those in Laodicea and in Hierapolis (4:13). my fellow prisoner (Phm 23)

[50] Paul's common use of συν-compounds ("fellow") underscores how much he values those who are his partners in ministry: συνεργος (Rom 16:3, 9, 21; 1 Cor 3:9; 2 Cor 1:24; 8:23; Php 2:25; 4:3; Col 4:11; 1 Thess 3:2; Phm 1, 24); συναιχμαλωτος (Rom 16:7; Col 4:10; Phm 23); συνδουλος (Col 1:7; 4:7); συστρατιωτης (Php 2:25; Phm 2); συζυγος (Php 4:3).

Tychicus	the beloved brother and faithful minister in the Lord (Eph 6:21)
	the beloved brother and faithful minister and fellow servant in the Lord (Col 4:7)
Onesimus	the faithful and beloved brother, who is one of you (Col 4:9)
	my son, who became my son while I was in chains (Phm 10)
	Formerly he was useless to you, but now he is useful to you and to me (Phm 11).
	the one who is my very heart (lit. "my affections") (Phm 12)
	no longer as a slave but more than a slave, a beloved brother; both to me and even more to you he is beloved both as a person and as one in the Lord (Phm 16)
Philemon	our beloved friend and fellow worker (Phm 1b)
	I gained much joy and encouragement because of your love, because the hearts of the saints have been refreshed by you, brother (Phm 7).
Archippus	our fellow soldier (Phm 2)
	[Speak to Archippus: "See to the ministry that you received in the Lord, that you might fulfill it" (Col 4:17).]
Epaphroditus	my brother and fellow worker and fellow soldier, and your apostle (Php 2:25)
	He was longing for you all and was feeling distressed because you heard that he was ill (Php 2:26).
	Hold such people (like him) in high esteem, because he nearly died for the work of Christ, risking his life in order that he might supply the service you were unable to render to me (Php 2:29b-30).
Euodia and Syntyche	[Help] these women [to reconcile] who have contended by my side in the cause of the gospel, along with Clement and the rest of my fellow workers (Php 4:3).
Onesiphorus	He often refreshed my soul and was not ashamed of my chains, but when he was in Rome he searched eagerly for me and found me (2 Tim 1:16-17).
	And how many ways he ministered to me in Ephesus, you know very well (1:18b).
Mark	He is helpful to me for the ministry (2 Tim 4:11).

It is no surprise, then, that Paul could elicit profound loyalty from others (Acts 20:36-38; Gal 4:15; 2 Cor 7:7, 11), for they knew they were genuinely loved by their apostle. Because Paul is so deeply committed to these fellow workers in the gospel, and so open in affirming them, it is also understandable how deeply he was hurt by those who betrayed his trust (2 Tim 1:15; 4:10a, 14, 15, 16). Affirmatory leadership can be lonely and painful, especially when one openly expresses affection for and affirmation of others but, as was the case with the Corinthians, there is no reciprocation (2 Cor 6:11-13; 12:15b). The potential of open betrayal by a trusted coworker or simply the deafening silence from those one has sacrificed much for will always be present. The leader who would imitate Paul (1 Cor 11:1), nevertheless, will be cautious in rebuke and generous in affirmation because in doing so he is reflecting a gracious God (Eph 4:31-5:2).

5. SACRIFICIAL

What sets Paul apart as a leader is the extent to which he was willing to sacrifice physical comforts, personal security, and normative life expectations, such as a family and a career with ample material support (1 Cor 9:3-15), in order to fulfill his divine calling to establish churches among the Gentiles. His encounter with the risen Lord as he approached Damascus reversed his life direction. Each of his autobiographical memoirs focuses on the radical transformation wrought in his heart by the grace of the Lord Jesus Christ (Gal 1:15-16; 2:15-16; Php 3:4-11; 1 Tim 1:12-17). In his letters we discover a man whose growing appreciation of God's redeeming grace produces a deepening humility and a mellowing sweetness. His humility enables him to be magnanimous toward others, especially those who struggle and fail. The result is a facilitative pattern of leadership that is never dictatorial, but always seeks to propel others to spiritual fruitfulness (2 Cor 1:24). Such a posture brings him adversity, suffering, and eventually a martyr's death. Yet to offer himself to God as a living sacrifice is but his reasonable act of worship when he ponders the incomparable "mercies of God" (Rom 12:1).

Humble self-assessment

Paul is a model of his own injunction to the Romans: "Do not think of yourself more highly than you ought, but rather think of yourself with sober judgment" (Rom 12:3a). One can trace a deepening sense of unworthiness as his hardships break and conform Paul into the image of his suffering Lord (Php 3:10). He progresses downward, in his own estimation, from the least of the apostles (1 Cor 15:9) to the least of all saints (Eph 3:8) to the chief of sinners (1 Tim 1:15). Especially to the church in Corinth, a continually seething cauldron of relational disturbances that tried the limits of his patience, does the apostle willingly admit his inadequacies and expose his insecurities. Paul states that he first arrived in Corinth "in weakness and fear and with much trembling" (1 Cor 2:3). He had been forced to leave the promising work in Macedonia due to persecution both from secular and Jewish quarters (Acts 16:38-40; 17:5-9, 13-15). Upon his arrival in Athens he found the response discouraging (17:32-33). He then came to the capital of the province of Achaia, a large multiracial city full of idols and immorality, yet with a culture fascinated by itinerant teachers who espoused Greek wisdom and delivered impressive oratory. Paul refrained from imitating the rhetorical style of these sophists and set forth the gospel with clarity and in dependence on the Holy Spirit (1 Cor 1:17; 2:4-5). He warns the church that knowledge in and of itself, unless conditioned by love, puffs one up with a distorted view of one's importance (8:1-2). The Corinthians' fascination with human wisdom and oratorical style helps account for the personality-centered factions that developed in the church (1:10-17). Paul is shocked most by the group that claims allegiance to him; he intentionally distances himself from all attempts to elevate him beyond his appointed place as a servant and steward of the gospel (1 Cor 1:12-13; 3:4-9, 21-23; 4:1-2, 6-7).

Vulnerability

When he addresses the area of moral temptation, Paul is conscious of his own vulnerability to fall into sin (1 Cor 10:12-13). He therefore exercises rigorous self-discipline lest he himself become disqualified for eschatological reward (9:26-27).[51] Paul's deep sense of self-distrust is similarly expressed in Philippians 3:10-11. He makes the experiential knowledge of Christ's resurrection power and continual conformity to his sufferings his singular pursuit, "if perhaps I might attain to the resurrection of the dead" (3:11).[52] This text should not be understood to cast doubt on Paul's assurance of final salvation, which he boldly articulates in many places (e.g. 1 Thess 4:17-18; 2 Cor 5:6-10; Rom 8:28-30; Php 1:20-24; 2 Tim 1:12). Nor, however, should Paul's language be emptied of its force. He recognizes his own capacity for sin and unbelief, and maintains a conscious dependence on God's strength to enable him to persevere in faith, which is a precondition for eschatological salvation.[53] After nearly three decades of Christian ministry we find Paul still following hard after Christ, refusing to be handicapped by past failures, and deeply aware that he has not attained to spiritual perfection (Php 3:12-14).

Strength in weakness

The second epistle to the Corinthians discloses an apostle who actually delights in his weaknesses because the human extremity affords God's power the opportunity to rest upon his life. The pressures Paul faced in Ephesus reached a level where he "despaired even of life" and "felt the sentence of death" (2 Cor 1:8-9a). This near-death experience broke him of self-reliance and made him God-dependent (1:9b). Now the trials of Ephesus are behind him. As Paul writes this letter from Macedonia, Paul is filled with gratitude at what God has been producing in his life through suffering. What level of confidence he has as a privileged servant of the new covenant comes from the God who makes him competent (2 Cor 3:4-6). He is, as it were, nothing more than a clay jar, unattractive and of little value, yet smudged with the divine fingerprints and filled with the divine power (4:7). He witnesses an aging body that is gradually wasting away, but refuses to lose heart because God's mercy has placed him in his present ministry and has pledged a glorious eternity (4:1, 16-18). The unknown physical malady that he calls the "thorn in my flesh" (12:7) he now views as God's way of preventing him from becoming conceited over a unique revelatory experience granted to him (12:1-6). God's refusal to answer his earnest plea for its removal carries with it a promise: "My grace is sufficient for you, for my power is made perfect in weakness" (12:9a).

[51] The term rendered "disqualified" (ἀδόκιμος) in 1 Cor 9:27 may take on the meaning of loss of reward for one who undertakes building the church, but who uses inferior materials so that the work is consumed (1 Cor 3:10-15). On the other hand, the same term is used in 2 Cor 13:5 for those who are found upon closer examination to be outside of the sphere of Christ's salvation. As with Php 3:11 (see below), this would underscore Paul's deep sense of self-distrust and utter dependence on God's power rather than a lack of assurance of salvation.

[52] The much anticipated experience of resurrection is expressed with several elements of contingency (3:11): the conditional particle "if" (εἰ), compounded with the indefinite adverb "somehow" or "in some way" (πως), governs an aorist subjunctive (mood of probability) verb (καταντήσω).

[53] Silva, *Philippians*, 191-193, comments with balance and insight on this text.

Thus Paul will "boast" in his physical infirmities, unlike the supremely confident "super-apostles" who took pride in oratory and knowledge (11:5-6; 12:11), because his weakness drives him to fuller reliance on God's strength (12:9b-10; cf. 11:30).

Boasting

It may seem surprising that a leader marked by humility and sacrifice would choose the term "boast" as one of his favorite words, but such is the case with Paul. The three related terms rendered "boast" (verb) or "boasting" (nouns) occur 59 times in the New Testament, of which 55 are in Paul's letters.[54] The prominence of the term "boast," as well as the term "puff up," in the Corinthian letters[55] indicates that pride in such things as the accumulation of human knowledge and its articulation through impressive oratory characterized that church in general and made the sophists who exemplified such qualities more attractive to them than Paul. The apostle will boast, but only in the saving wisdom imparted by virtue of his union with Christ Jesus (1 Cor 1:30-31; 2 Cor 10:17: quot. Jer 9:24; cf; Gal 6:14; Php 3:3). When Paul does, for the sake of argument, adopt the stance of the super-apostles and dare to boast about human accomplishments, he admits he is taking the posture of a "fool" (2 Cor 11:16-21). One detects here Paul's feeling of uneasiness about offering such a resume, but the false apostles have forced him into such counter-boasting (11:18). The credentials that authenticate him as a true servant of Christ, however, are not academic degrees, accumulated knowledge, or rhetorical skills, but sacrificial labor, physical deprivation, imprisonment and torture, exposure to constant danger, internal pressure growing out of his concern for the churches, and heart-wrenching empathy for his brothers who fall into sin (11:22-29). Yes, Paul says, if I must boast I will boast in these realities, which expose my frailty and drive me to depend on God's power rather than on human qualifications (11:30).

Magnanimity

Paul's humble self-assessment prevents him from treating others harshly and liberates him to be magnanimous with others, especially those who fail and even those who cause him grief. He instructs the Galatians that when a believer falls into sin and subsequently repents the mature believers must remember their own vulnerability to temptation and restore such a one with a spirit of meekness (Gal 6:1). He counsels the Thessalonians to exercise patient pastoral care of all the brothers, even when such care requires strict admonition (1 Thess 5:14). When a believer stubbornly persists in idleness, the remedy should take on the character of household discipline of a brother, rather than condemnation of an enemy (2 Thess 3:14-15). Paul reveals his generosity of spirit when he urges the Corinthians to forgive and comfort a sorrowing individual who has been duly chastened by

---

[54] The three terms are the verb καυχαομαι (35 of 37 in Paul), and the cognate nouns καυχημα (10 of 11) and καυχησις (10 of 11).

[55] The three terms for "boasting" occur thirty-nine times in 1 and 2 Corinthians. Just as impressive is the attestation of the verb "puff up" (i.e with conceit, pride, or arrogance; φυσιοω): six of its seven New Testament occurrences are in 1 Corinthians (4:6, 18, 19; 5:2; 8:1; 13:4).

the discipline imposed by the congregation (2 Cor 2:5-11). This probably refers to the ringleader who maliciously attacked Paul at the time of his "painful visit" to Corinth (2:1). In the "severe letter" that followed he demanded that the church punish this offender (2:3-4, 9). But now is the time for restoration. They should affirm their love for him lest this individual should become swallowed up by excessive grief, and a spirit of unforgiveness provide Satan the opportunity to exploit the situation to great harm (2:7-8, 10-11). When Paul was placed under house arrest in Rome, certain brothers saw this as an opportunity to usurp his position of authority. They began to preach Christ while filled with envy, rivalry, and selfish ambition. In fact, their actions were even designed to increase the pain of his imprisonment by pulling the loyalty of the churches to them and away from Paul (Php 1:15-17). But whatever the motives, whether in sincere exposition of the truth or as a pretext for self-promotion, Paul rejoiced that Christ was being proclaimed (1:18). Here is a leader who does not view himself as indispensable, but whose chief concern is the fulfillment of the evangelistic mission, whether through him or through others.

Suffering servant

From the time of his conversion Paul was appointed to suffer for the sake of the name of Jesus (Acts 9:16). Paul takes on the posture of Isaiah's suffering servant, not like the messianic Servant whose vicarious sacrifice is unique and unrepeatable, but in the sense of a witness whose sufferings bear the image of the Servant-Lord whose person and work he proclaims to the Gentiles (Isa 42:1, 6-7; 49:6b; Acts 9:15-16; 22:21; 26:15-18). Paul's sacrifices are representative and testimonial. The epistles of Paul are replete with the language of hardship. One of the great interpretive hurdles for the 21st century western commentator (less of a hurdle for those who write out of a contemporary setting of persecution) is to capture the full force of language written to churches whose normal life setting was one of personal harassment, societal marginalization, and material loss. The key to Paul's resilience, and that of the churches he planted, was a confidence in the divine purposes being worked out through their sufferings.

Paul expounds a theology of Christian suffering that includes three overlapping dimensions of significance. First, his sufferings are endured for the edification of the church, the body of Christ. Paul writes to the Colossians that he could joyfully endure his physical sufferings on their behalf because they "fill up what is still lacking in regard to Christ's afflictions, for the sake of his body, the church" (Col 1:24). We can forthrightly dismiss any idea that there is something insufficient in the redemptive sufferings of Christ that the apostle must in some way compensate for. The undiminished deity of Jesus (Col 1:15-19; 2:9-10) and the fully efficacious benefits of his death on the cross (1:20-22; 2:11-15) are points of emphasis in this epistle designed to correct a defective Christology afflicting the church. On a number of occasions Paul, drawing on dominical tradition, states that God in his sovereign purposes has appointed the church and its apostles to suffer as a witness to the person and work of their Lord, who is himself the suffering Servant (Acts 14:22; 1 Thess 3:3-4; Php 1:29-30; cf. Mt 5:11-12; 10:17-25; 24:9-14; Jn 15:18-25; 16:33; Acts 5:41). The meaning of the enigmatic language of Colossians 1:24 seems to be that Paul acts as a shield to absorb some of the appointed number of blows aimed at the body of Christ. God has designed suffering to confirm the churches' solidarity with her Lord as she communicates the gospel of the crucified and risen Christ to the Gentile world (Col 1:25-27). Paul stands in as a protector and defender of the young, vulnerable churches. He receives in their stead a portion of the hardships and persecutions which otherwise might cause the people of God to become disheartened. All the suffering that Paul endures is for the strengthening and comfort of the churches (1 Thess 2:2; 3:7-10; 2 Cor 1:3-7; Rom 5:3-5; Eph 3:13; Php 2:17; 2 Tim 4:6).

Therefore, secondly, the suffering of the apostle, and by extension that of the churches, authenticates their <u>identification</u> with Jesus, the suffering Servant. Suffering brings the witness into a participation in the humiliation experienced by Jesus which, by breaking down all levels of trust in human resources, releases the power of the risen Lord to become operative in one's life (2 Cor 1:5; 4:7-12). Paul's theology of weakness is not a self-deprecating delight in personal pain for its own sake. Rather, harsh realities such as physical ailments, aggressive opponents, malicious verbal attacks, and even physical assaults crush every fiber of self-reliance, so that he becomes an empty vessel through which God's triumphant power can flow (2 Cor 12:7-10). Further, his hardships bring him into a closer fellowship with the Lord who suffered in his place (Php 3:8, 10b-c). To know, in his personal experience, Christ's sufferings is to know his resurrection power (Php 3:10a). These coordinate areas of identification with Christ, namely, his death and resurrection, promote Paul's sanctification and prepare him for the glory of Christ's unmediated presence in the kingdom of God to be ushered in at the resurrection (Php 3:11; 2 Cor 4:16-18; Rom 8:17b-18).

Third, the apostle's sufferings are marks of <u>authentication</u> as a true servant of Christ. His physical sufferings brand him as one who belongs to Jesus (Gal 6:17)[56] and distinguish him from the Judaizers. The latter sought to avoid persecution from their fellow Jews by proclaiming a legalistic message more palatable than Paul's offensive doctrine of salvation through faith alone in the finished work of the crucified Messiah (Gal 6:12; cf. Gal 2:21; 3:13; 5:11-12). To a church divided by personality-centered factions, Paul reminds the Corinthians that he, Apollos, and Cephas are but servants of Christ and stewards of the gospel who will render an account of their stewardship (1 Cor 4:1-5). To authenticate his true servants God has put the apostles on display like prisoners of war who march in chains to the place of execution behind their conquerors (1 Cor 4:9a). This "spectacle" serves as a testimony to the entire universe of people and angels that these are servants of the Servant (4:9b-10).[57] The solidarity is found not in the common experiences of physical deprivation and brutal treatment alone (4:11-12a), but also in how the apostles emulate the Lord's nonretaliatory posture when he suffered (4:12b-13). In two extended catalogues of trials Paul provides the Corinthian church with a set of criteria by which they can determine whose claims to authentic servanthood are credible (2 Cor 6:3-10; 11:23-33). The first catalogue, a portrait

---

[56] The term στιγμα was used of the branding of animals to certify ownership. Judged from the near context (Gal 5:11-12; 6:12-15), Paul is likely contrasting his "marks" (from his beatings and tortures [Acts 14:19; 2 Cor 6:5; 11:23-25]) that authenticate him as a servant of the gospel of grace with the marks of circumcision that confirm the Judaizers as slaves of the law (*EDNT*, 3:276-277).

[57] Richard B. Hays, *First Corinthians*, Interpretation (Louisville: John Knox, 1997): 71-72.

of godly conduct in a context of trouble, establishes the credibility of his claim to be the true servant of God. The second catalogue is offered as a 'foolish boast' (11:16-18, 21b) to counteract the ridiculous claim of the super-apostles to be servants of Christ (11:23a). If you want to recognize true servants, Paul says, look at the level of their sacrificial imitation of the suffering Servant. Paul's resume lists no academic degrees, published works, or human accolades, only imprisonments (11:23), tortures (11:23-25), dangers (11:25-26), physical deprivations (11:27), internal pressures (11:28), and heartaches (11:29).

To conclude, Paul's sufferings authenticate him as God's servant, identify him with the crucified and risen Lord, and edify the church. One who aspires to lead, that is, to influence others for the kingdom of God, must imitate Paul who himself imitates Christ (1 Cor 11:1).[58]

6. MISSIONAL

Paul's conversion was at the same time a commission. His call to evangelize the Gentiles and, by extension, to gather them into communities for edification and witness was clearly defined at the outset of his apostolic ministry. The passion to pioneer among the unreached and the need to shepherd the emerging churches produced a healthy tension that drove him to deeper dependence on God's guidance (cf. 2 Cor 2:12-13; 10:15-16; 11:28). Paul is an example of a leader who has a clearly defined mission and maintains a laser-like focus on its accomplishment. Paul is not a visionary who devises a brilliant plan and then through personal charisma draws others into his ambitions, but an obedient servant who embraces the divine agenda and then through sacrificial devotion mobilizes others to join him as God's coworkers (1 Cor 3:5-9).

Gentile evangelism

From the moment of his conversion Paul's mission in life is set. He is now Christ's apostle, "sent one," commissioned to declare the good news of the forgiveness of sin through Christ's death and resurrection (1 Cor 15:3-4)[59] to the Gentiles (Gal 1:15-16; 2:2; Rom 1:5, 9, 14-15; 15:9-12; Eph 3:1, 8; Col 1:25-27; 1 Thess 2:16; 1 Tim 2:7; 3:16; 2 Tim 4:17).[60] All three of the conversion accounts

[58] A fine treatment of Paul's theology of sufferings is found in Thomas R. Schreiner, *Paul: Apostle of God's Glory in Christ* (Downers Grove, IL: InterVarsity, 2001): 87-102.

[59] Both the noun "gospel" (εὐαγγελιον) and the cognate verb "proclaim the good news" (εὐαγγελιζομαι) confirm through their usage Paul's constant attention to his evangelistic mission: the noun, often a nomen actionis meaning the proclamation of the message (e.g. Rom 1:1, 16; 15:19), occurs a total of sixty times and in all of Paul's letters except Titus; the verb occurs twenty-one times. The general verb "to proclaim" (κηρυσσω) most often refers to evangelistic proclamation in Paul's letters (Rom 10:8, 14, 15; 1 Cor 1:23; 9:27; 15:11-12; 2 Cor 1:19; 4:5; Gal 2:2; Col 1:23; 1 Thess 2:9; 1 Tim 3:16; cf. 2 Tim 4:2 [expository preaching?]). Paul's "proclaimed message" (κηρυγμα) brings to its hearers an undivided focus on the crucified and risen Lord Jesus Christ (Rom 16:25; 1 Cor 1:21; 2:4; 15:4; 2 Tim 4:17; Tit 1:3). Twice Paul designates himself a "herald" (κηρυξ) of the good news (1 Tim 2:7; 2 Tim 1:11).

[60] The Greek term rendered "Gentiles," ἐθνη (pl. of ἐθνος), signifies the non-Jewish peoples who are outside of and wholly unrelated to the covenant promises to Israel. It occurs fifty-four times in Paul's letters, nearly always in the plural (only exception is Rom 10:19, which is a quotation of Deut 32:21). The references to Gentiles are concentrated in Romans and Galatians where Paul is forging his theology of Gentile inclusion in the people of God (39 times).

in the book of Acts specify the Gentiles as the sphere of Paul's evangelistic mission (Acts 9:15-16; 22:21; 26:15-18). The third account draws on the language of the first and second servant songs of Isaiah (42:7; 49:6b), where the prophet anticipates the Lord's servant bringing light to the Gentiles and salvation to the ends of the earth (Acts 26:17-18). Paul is the Lord's appointed servant (Acts 26:16)[61] and witness (Acts 9:16) whose sufferings imitate the Servant whom he proclaims. Paul's church planting strategy is to first enter the synagogues where he addresses both Jews, who were privileged with receiving the offer of the kingdom first (Rom 1:16b), and the Gentile God-fearers who attended worship on the Sabbath (Acts 13:5, 43, 50; 14:1; 15:21; 17:1, 4, 17; 18:4; 19:8). Nevertheless, Paul's specific call is to evangelize the Gentiles. Luke traces the shift to an exclusive focus on Gentile evangelism that occurred due to the obstinacy of the Jews (Acts 13:46-48; 18:6; 22:21; 26:20; 28:28). The comity arrangement that Paul and Peter agreed to was not a rigid sealing off of two separate groups, but a demarcation of strategic priorities: Paul would concentrate on Gentile evangelism, while Peter would target Jewish communities (Gal 2:7-9).

During the fourteen intensive years beginning with his arrival in Antioch (Acts 11:25-26) until his departure from Corinth at the end of the third journey (20:3-6),[62] Paul and his mission team became the instrument of establishing Gentile churches in the major urban centers of six Roman provinces: Syria (Antioch); Cyprus (Salamis); Galatia (four towns); Macedonia (Philippi, Thessalonica, Berea); Achaia (Corinth); and Asia (Ephesus). During those final months in Corinth he writes his magnum opus, the Epistle to the Romans, and makes the claim that "there is no more place for me to work in these regions" (Rom 15:23; cf. 15:19). This cannot mean that there were no more unevangelized areas in the eastern Mediterranean world, but that the beachhead has now been established and the "churches of the Gentiles" (Rom 16:4) can now carry on the task of reaching the remaining rural frontiers for the gospel. Paul is pulled by his chief ambition of pioneering in the places where the name of Christ has not yet been made known (Rom 15:20-21; cf. 2 Cor 10:16). Therefore, when he has delivered the funds collected from the Gentile churches for the impoverished brethren in Judea, the eastern phase of his ministry will be completed. His plan is to shift his support base from Antioch to Rome and have that great church in the imperial capital assist him in the new evangelistic venture to Spain (Rom 15:24-29).

Pastoral care of the Gentile churches

Evangelism of the Gentiles, though Paul's primary calling, is but one

---

[61] The term translated "servant" in Acts 26:16 is ὑπηρετης, used similarly in 1 Cor 4:1 of the Lord's attendant or helper (cf. Acts 13:5). The term originally meant a rower or galley slave and is used perhaps to underscore the humble station that Paul assumes in the Lord's work. Since it differs from the terms used in the Septuagint to translate עֶבֶד in the Isaianic servant songs (δουλος: Isa 49:3, 5, 7; substantival participle of δουλευω: Isa 53:11; παις: Isa 42:1; 45:4; 49:6; 50:10; 52:13), perhaps this is Luke's way of distinguishing Paul's servant status from that of the messianic Servant who suffers a vicarious death (Isa 53:6, 8, 10-12).

[62] We date Paul's arrival in Antioch in Spring, A.D. 43 and his departure from Corinth at the end of his third missionary journey in Spring, A.D. 57.

dimension of a full-orbed mission that includes the pastoral care of new believers. Paul is a builder of faith communities (1 Cor 3:10). He always leaves churches behind in the cities he has evangelized. In the record of his commission in Romans Paul clarifies his objective for the Gentiles: to lead them to "the obedience of faith," which we understand to mean faith in Jesus Christ, which produces a life of obedient submission to his lordship (Rom 1:5; cf. 16:26).[63] The nine letters to congregations and the four letters to individuals are testimony to Paul's commitment to follow up those who have come to Christ in the sphere of his ministry (2 Cor 10:13-16).[64] He frames his mission statements (sample below) in terms of presenting the believers to Christ as mature and fully equipped disciples:

1. "I am again in the travail of childbirth until Christ should be formed in you" (Gal 4:19).
2. "Night and day we pray most earnestly that we might see your face and supply the parts of your faith that are lacking" (1 Thess 3:10).
3. "For I am jealous over you with the jealousy of God, for I pledged you to one husband, to Christ, as a pure virgin" (2 Cor 11:2; cf. Eph 5:27).
4. "I long to see you in order that I might impart some spiritual gift so that you might be established" (Rom 1:11).
5. "We proclaim him, admonishing every person and teaching every person with all wisdom, so that we might present every person mature in Christ, for which purpose I indeed labor, striving according to his energy which is working effectively in me with power" (Col 1:28-29).
6. "And (God) himself gave some as apostles, some as prophets, some as evangelists, some as pastors and teachers for the equipping of the saints for the work of the ministry, for the edification of the body of Christ, until we all might attain to the unity of the faith and to the knowledge of the son of God to become a mature man, to attain to the measure of the stature of the fullness of Christ" (Eph 4:11-13).

These representative mission statements confirm the pastoral dimension of Paul's calling, even though his primary task is the evangelization of the Gentiles. His pastoral mindset can be seen in the terms he employs for the churches' spiritual upbuilding: **edify**;[65] **perfect** or **equip**;[66] **strengthen**;[67] and **establish**.[68] Along with

---

[63] In the prepositional phrase εἰς ὑπακοην πιστεως the genitive πιστεως is understood as subjective. Thus the noun ὑπακοη is taken to signify the life of obedience that springs from and evidences true faith.

[64] Though Paul did not found the church in Rome, he knows many of the believers there (Rom 16:3-16). He feels a responsibility to address some of the relational issues that are troubling them (Rom 11:13-24; 14:1-15:4). Paul views the church in Rome, as a predominately Gentile church, legitimately within the sphere of his apostolic domain (Rom 1:11-15; 15:23, 24, 28, 29).

[65] The verb οἰκοδομεω (1 Cor 8:1; 10:23; 14:4, 17; 1 Thess 5:11; cf. Acts 20:32) and the cognate noun οἰκοδομη (Rom 14:19; 15:2; 1 Cor 14:3, 5, 12, 26; 2 Cor 10:8; 12:19; 13:10; Eph 4:12, 16, 29) signify the edification or building up of the faith of the believers individually and corporately.

[66] The verb καταρτιζω (1 Cor 1:10; 2 Cor 13:11; 1 Thess 3:10) and the cognate noun καταρτισμος (Eph 4:12) signify the perfecting of believers both doctrinally and morally to reflect the character of Christ and/or the fitting or equipping of believers, as mature disciples, to carry out the work of ministry.

being a herald of the good news, he is also a teacher employed to instruct the people of God in sound doctrine and godly conduct (1 Tim 2:7; 2 Tim 1:11).[69]

7. Summary of the leadership approach of Paul

We conclude this section with a functional definition of the six characteristics of Paul's approach in leading individuals and congregations:

Characteristic	Definition
1. Authoritative	Demands conformity to the doctrinal and ethical teaching of the faithfully transmitted gospel, and confronts, warns, and rebukes those who compromise its basic principles.
2. Exhortational	Appeals without coercion or pressure to the consciences and wills of believers to respond with wholehearted obedience to the manifold grace of God.
3. Accountable	Pursues first and foremost the divine approbation, while also maintaining a clear conscience before people, always conscious that a day is approaching when one's motives and actions will be assessed by the Lord, who is the righteous Judge.
4. Affirmatory	Takes the initiative at every opportunity to express sincere praise of and affection for one's brothers in Christ.
5. Sacrificial	Bears up under adversity and hardship with a buoyant resilience, with full awareness that such sufferings nurture humility, foster magnanimity, and deepen the level of one's fellowship with the suffering Servant.
6. Missional	Maintains a laser-like concentration on God's agenda, that is, the evangelization of the lost, the edification of the saints, and the establishment of vital churches.

Leadership profile of Paul: Characteristics of his leadership

1. *Building up of God's people: Paul's multi-faceted leadership style is geared toward one purpose, namely, the edification of the communities of faith. The apostolic authority he uniquely possesses, even when it must be exercised forcefully, is for building up, not tearing down, the spiritual fabric of the congregations (2 Cor 10:8; 13:10). Paul is deeply conscious that he is above all a builder and will be held fully accountable for the quality of his work (1 Cor 3:8-15).[70] He will*

[67] The verb στηρίζω (Rom 1:11; 16:25; 1 Thess 3:2, 13; 2 Thess 2:17; 3:3) signifies the strengthening of the faith of believers so they might remain resolute and holy in a hostile and immoral setting.
[68] The verb βεβαιόω (1 Cor 1:8; 2 Cor 1:21; Col 2:7) means the firm establishment of one in a settled faith or a blameless moral life.
[69] The teacher (διδάσκαλος) is one who exercises the ministry of sound instruction of the people of God (1 Cor 12:28-29; Eph 4:11; 1 Tim 2:7; 2 Tim 1:11; cf. Acts Acts 13:1; Heb 5:12; Jas 3:1). Though not as frequently attested in Paul's letters as the verb εὐαγγελίζομαι, the verb for teaching (διδάσκω) occurs in nine of thirteen letters with the meaning of instruction in the content and moral implications of the gospel (Rom 12:7; 1 Cor 4:17; Gal 1:12; Eph 4:21; Col 1:28; 2:7; 3:16; 2 Thess 2:15; 1 Tim 2:12; 4:11; 6:2; 2 Tim 2:2; cf. Tit 1:11 of false teachers).
[70] The term Paul uses in 1 Cor 3:10 (ἀρχιτέκτων) means a "master (expert) builder." In this architectural metaphor Paul lays the foundation, which is Christ, and others build upon the foundation (ἐποικοδομέω

stand beside the believers to facilitate their growth, rather than reign over them to compel their submission (2 Cor 1:24). He will gladly spend all of his material resources and expend all of his physical energies for the building up of his spiritual children (2 Cor 12:14-15). The concern that weighs heaviest upon him is the welfare of the churches (2 Cor 11:28). Even as he faces the immediate prospect of a violent death, Paul can only think of the needs of the Philippian church, and how he hopes to be released for a further period of serving them (Php 1:22-26). Paul-like leaders are consumed with fulfilling God's purpose for them, completing their appointed race, and receiving the divine approbation of their motives, methods, and activities (2 Tim 4:6-8, 17-18).

2. ***Coworker with God the Holy Spirit***: *Paternalistic approaches to the training of new believers and the development of churches remain all too painful a reality as we enter the twenty-first century. Reluctance to pass the baton of responsibility to local leaders, reticence to allow contextualized patterns of worship to emerge in new settings, and unwillingness to challenge the believers to sacrificially support their own work free from dependence on mission financing and structures are symptoms of a paucity of confidence in the Spirit of God who indwells, guides, and empowers his church. Such confidence in the Spirit does not mean the mission leader's abdication of prayerful concern for and ongoing pastoral communication to freshly planted churches. Such conviction, however, will translate into willing retirement and withdrawal accompanied by gradual and real hand-over of responsibility to the local leadership. For the apostle Paul, and the other apostles, what signaled the inauguration of the eschatological age, grounded in the redemptive benefits of Christ's death and resurrection, was the outpouring of the Spirit upon the church of both Jew and Gentile (Acts 10:44-48; 11:15-17; 15:8). The promised age of the Spirit has begun now that Jesus has taken his lordly position at the right hand of the Father in fulfillment of Psalm 110:1 (Rom 8:34; Eph 1:20; Col 3:1). The exalted Lord is now mediating his presence to his new covenant people by the Holy Spirit (1 Cor 15:45; 2 Cor 3:17-18). Paul's post-Damascus life was dedicated to building the new community of God's people, who by the leading of the Spirit declare God's salvation to the nations still in darkness. His confidence in the Spirit liberates him to be a leader who can 'peacefully strive' for the edification of the churches, value his colleagues as trusted instruments of God's grace, and intercede with joyful hope.*[71]

[1 Cor 3:10, 12, 14; cf. Eph 2:20]). The church is the building (οἰκοδομή) and thus even as master builder Paul labors as God's fellow worker (1 Cor 3:9; cf. Eph 2:21). His most common terms for edification are the verb οἰκοδομέω and its cognate noun οἰκοδομή. Believers must seek to conduct themselves in a way that produces the edification or "building up" (οἰκοδομή as a nomen actionis: the process of edification) of others (Rom 14:19; 15:2; Eph 4:29); prophecy is a superior gift because it contributes to the edification of the assembled body of believers (1 Cor 14:3, 5, 12, 26); Paul's apostolic authority is exercised always for the edification of the church (2 Cor 10:8; 12:19; 13:10); God has given apostles and others to the church to equip all believers to contribute to the edification of the whole (Eph 4:12, 16). Paul similarly employs the cognate verb οἰκοδομέω (and ἐποικοδομέω [Col 2:7]) in parenetic sections to impress upon the believers their responsibility to act in a way that contributes to the building up of the faith of their brothers in the church (1 Cor 8:1; 10:23; 14:4, 17; 1 Thess 5:11).

[71] For a full development of this crucial dimension of Paul's approach to leadership, see Don N. Howell, Jr., "Mission in Paul's Epistles: Genesis, Pattern and Dynamics," in *Mission in the New Testament*, eds. W. J. Larkin and J. F. Williams (Maryknoll, NY: Orbis, 1998): 77-91.

Chapter 23.
Criteria for community leaders

Preliminary questions to consider:
When you study the qualifying criteria that Paul sets forth for elders and deacons,
does the contemporary church utilize the same criteria when it assesses and chooses
its leaders?
If not, what alternative criteria are given prominence that Paul shows little regard
for?

It is striking that Paul's letters contain relatively little instruction on formal structures of church governance, and what there is seems more descriptive than prescriptive. His greatest concern is the spiritual maturity and emotional stability of those who are appointed to leadership. It is probably fair to say that Paul felt comfortable leaving the specifics of church government to the local leadership whom the Spirit of God was more than capable of guiding. It was his practice to appoint elders or overseers to direct the affairs of the emerging churches.[1] The interchangeable usage of these two terms in the Pastoral letters indicates that they refer to the same office (Tit 1:5, 7; 1 Tim 3:2; 5:17, 19). The term "elder," drawn from its usage for respected members of the Jewish community, refers to the dignity of the office, while "overseer" captures the function of the office, namely, to supervise the corporate life of the congregation (cf. 1 Pet 5:1-4).[2] A secondary level of leadership, the deacons, probably served under the authority of the elders and carried out certain administrative tasks and practical ministries other than teaching and governance (Php 1:1; 1 Tim 3:8, 12).[3]

Paul instructs the Thessalonians to hold in high regard those who are serving the church as leaders, probably elders (1 Thess 5:12-13; cf. 1 Cor 16:15-18; Heb 13:17). He praises the leaders as diligent laborers who stand over the church in a position of delegated authority.[4] This same term is used elsewhere of the ruling function of elders (1 Tim 5:17), the spiritual gift of leadership (Rom 12:8 [not necessarily formal]), and the effective management of one's family both by elders

---

[1] The Greek terms for elder and overseer are πρεσβυτερος (Acts 11:30; 14:23; 15:2, 4, 6, 22, 23; 16:4; 20:17; 21:18; 1 Tim 5:17, 19; Tit 1:5; Jas 5:14; 1 Pet 5:1; also πρεσβυτεριον: 1 Tim 4:14) and ἐπισκοπος (Acts 20:28; Php 1:1; 1 Tim 3:2; Tit 1:7; also ἐπισκοπη: 1 Tim 3:1) respectively.
[2] The cognate verb ἐπισκοπεω is in brackets in the UBS text of 1 Peter 5:2, but still attests to one of the functions of the elders, namely, providing pastoral oversight.
[3] It is unclear whether διακονος in Rom 16:1 is used in its frequent general sense of servant (e.g. 1 Cor 3:5; Eph 6:21; Php 1:1; 1 Tim 4:6) or with the technical meaning of deaconess.
[4] The term for formal leadership in this context is the verb προιστημι (literally "stand before"), which means "to rule, direct, be at the head of" (*BDAG*, 870). A different term, ἡγεομαι, is used in Hebrews, which perhaps gives even greater force to the governing authority of the leaders (Heb 13:7, 17, 24; cf. Mt 2:6; Lk 22:26; Acts 7:10).

(1 Tim 3:4-5) and by deacons (1 Tim 3:12). The task of admonishing the church (1 Thess 5:12b) indicates that one of the most important functions of leaders was teaching the church to obey apostolic doctrine (cf. 1 Tim 3:2; 5:17; Tit 1:9). Elders who serve well are to be accorded double honor and supported financially (1 Tim 5:17-18; cf. Gal 6:6; 1 Cor 9:14). When an elder is accused of some breach of the sacred trust of the congregation, the accusation must be established by multiple witnesses and, if proven, public rebuke must follow as a deterrent against further violators (5:19-20). Clearly the congregational leaders possessed a high degree of accountability for their conduct because of the privileged position they assumed in governance and teaching (cf. Heb 13:17; Jas 3:1).

Below is one way of categorizing and functionally defining the criteria Paul sets forth for church leaders, first elders and then deacons. One can readily contrast the scarcity of information Paul provides with respect to the structures of governance, with his detailed concern for the type of people appointed to leadership. Would it not be safe to conclude that, at least in Paul's mind, the quality of the people who oversee the spiritual life of the congregation is far more crucial to the accomplishment of its mission than the particular form of church government?

Overseers (1 Tim 3:1-7) or **elders/overseers** (Tit 1:5-9)
1. **Reputation with others, including outsiders**
    (i) Above reproach (1 Tim 3:2)[5] or blameless (Tit 1:6, 7):[6] Not vulnerable to criticism for character or conduct deficiencies, and thus one who contributes in a positive manner to the testimony of the church in the community. These two basically synonymous terms may be summative qualities that stand at the head of the two lists, that is, the overseer must be without blame or reproach with respect to the criteria that follow.[7]
    (ii) Good reputation with outsiders so that one will not fall into disgrace and the trap of the devil (3:7): Nonbelievers view the church and its leaders either with cynicism, due to the failure of its members, or with esteem for the high moral standards they profess. A leader without an unblemished moral record provides the devil with an opportunity to attack and weaken both the leader and the church, harming its mission in the community.
2. **Character virtues**
    (i) Temperate (3:2):[8] A stable and balanced individual, whose clear thinking protects one from all forms of addictive behavior, including but not limited to alcoholism.
    (ii) Self-controlled (3:2; Tit 1:8):[9] One who possesses that sensible, prudent caution that leads to a temperate lifestyle.
    (iii) Attractive or honorable (3:2):[10] A person who cultivates wholesome

---

[5] The adjective ἀνεπιλημπτος also occurs in 1 Tim 5:7; 6:14.
[6] The adjective ἀνεγκλητος also occurs in 1 Cor 1:8; Col 1:22; 1 Tim 3:10 (deacons).
[7] Marshall, *Pastoral Epistles*, 477.
[8] This quality (νηφαλιος) is also required of deacons' wives (1 Tim 3:11) and older men (Tit 2:2).
[9] Titus is to teach older men (Tit 2:2) and younger women (2:5) to manifest this quality (σωφρων).
[10] In 1 Tim 2:9 the term κοσμιος refers to the "modest" attire appropriate for godly women.

attitudes and winsome behavior, never coarse or crude, which command the respect of others and enhance both the spiritual life and reputation of the church.

(iv) Gentle or forbearing (3:3):[11] The opposite of being pugnacious or overly aggressive, this individual is peaceable, humble and gentle like his Lord (2 Cor 10:1) in responding to difficult situations and in relating to others (Php 4:5).

(v) Not a recent convert lest one become conceited and fall into the trap of the devil (3:6): Time always provides humbling experiences which temper one's self-confidence and foster dependence on divine grace. Pride can easily arise in the heart of one who is exalted to a position of influence too soon and so bring about a great fall (1 Pet 5:5-6).

(vi) Lover of what is good (Tit 1:8): A person who highly values and cultivates virtuous qualities that reflect the character of God who alone is good (Php 4:8).

(vii) Upright (Tit 1:8):[12] One who has been declared righteous by faith and then evidences the new standing by an upright life that obeys God's commands (1 Jn 3:7).

(viii) Holy (Tit 1:8):[13] Devoted to a life of purity and separation from defiling influences.

3. **Self-management**

(i) Disciplined (Tit 1:8):[14] An individual who maintains strict control over one's thought life and physical actions, especially with regard to areas such as exercise, appetite, and sexual drive (1 Cor 9:25-27).

(ii) Not given to drunkenness (3:3; Tit 1:7): A person who knows their own limits with fermented drink and avoids any approaches to inebriation (cf. Eph 5:18a; Tit 2:3; 1 Tim 5:23).

(iii) Not a lover of money (3:3)[15] or not greedy for material gain (Tit 1:7):[16] One whose value system centers around the kingdom of God rather than material things and who is content with God's provision (Heb 13:5-6); making money or hoarding money, whether successful or not, are not one's controlling ambitions (1 Tim 6:6-10, 17-19). The elder is a willing and eager servant of God, one whose sole interest is the welfare of the church not monetary gain (1 Pet 5:2), though the faithful elder deserves material support (1 Tim 5:17-18).

---

[11] The New Testament occurrences of the adjective ἐπιεικης (Php 4:5; Tit 3:2; Jas 3:17; 1 Pet 2:18; cf. Acts 24:4; 2 Cor 10:1: cognate noun ἐπιεικεια) enjoins all believers to be gentle or forbearing.

[12] This is the meaning of the adjective δικαιος in texts such as Php 4:8; 1 Tim 1:9; 1 Jn 3:12.

[13] Moral purity is denoted by this word group: ὁσιος (1 Tim 2:8; Heb 7:26; Rev 15:4; 16:5); ὁσιοτης (Lk 1:75; Eph 4:24); ὁσιως (1 Thess 2:10). Cf. ἀνοσιος ("unholy"): 1 Tim 1:9; 2 Tim 3:2.

[14] The cognates of this adjective, ἐγκρατης, occur in the New Testament with the same meaning of self-discipline: ἐγκρατευομαι (1 Cor 7:9; 9:25); ἐγκρατεια (Acts 24:25; Gal 5:23; 2 Pet 1:6).

[15] The adjective ἀφιλαργυρος occurs also in Heb 13:5. The root terms without the α-privative, φιλαργυρια (1 Tim 6:10) and φιλαργυρος (Lk 16:14; 2 Tim 3:2), specify the danger of greed.

[16] The same quality, μη αἰσχροκερδης, appears in the criteria for deacons (1 Tim 3:8) and in Peter's appeal to his fellow elders (1 Pet 5:2, μηδε αἰσχροκερδως [adv.]).

(iv) Not quick-tempered (Tit 1:7):[17] One who does not easily anger, but maintains composure even when accorded unfair treatment (Jas 1:19-20).

4. **Relations with others**
   (i) Hospitable (3:2; Tit 1:8):[18] One whose heart and home is open to all, including those outside one's circle of familiarity, and especially to traveling believers who need security, lodging and food (3 Jn 5-8).
   (ii) Not pugnacious (3:3; Tit 1:7):[19] Not only a person with no record of abusive and violent conduct, but one who is not abrasive and contentious so that there is a history of strained relations with others.
   (iii) Not quarrelsome (3:3):[20] Not a person who causes division often over peripheral issues and unprofitable controversies (2 Tim 2:23-24; Jas 4:1-2), but is peaceable and conciliatory without compromising principle (Rom 12:18; Jas 3:17-18).
   (iv) Not self-willed (Tit 1:7):[21] Not one who proudly insists on having one's way or cannot submit to authority (2 Pet 2:10), but can yield in order to promote the interests of others (Php 2:3-4).

5. **Family**
   (i) Husband of one wife (3:2; Tit 1:6; cf. 1 Tim 3:12 [deacons]; 5:9 [widows]):[22] A person who is faithful to one's marriage vows and thus has not been engaged in sexual promiscuity of any kind. This would not rule out those who have experienced divorce as the wronged party in cases of adultery (Mt 19:9) or desertion by an unbeliever (1 Cor 7:15). Certainly widowers who remarry in the Lord can stand for church leaders (1 Cor 7:39; Rom 7:2-3).
   (ii) Manages his own family well (3:4-5):[23] This qualification is proven by the behavior of one's children (and, in the case of deacons [probably also assumed of elders], the godly character of one's wife [3:11 below]).

---

[17] The adjective ὀργιλος occurs only here in the New Testament. However, its nominal root ὀργη is the common term used in warnings against anger (Eph 4:31; Col 3:8; 1 Tim 2:8; Jas 1:19-20; cf. Eph 4:26, ὀργιζομαι [vb.]).

[18] The adjective φιλοξενος occurs also in 1 Pet 4:9 and the cognate noun φιλοξενια (lit. "love of strangers") in Rom 12:13; Heb 13:2.

[19] These are the only two occurrences of this term, (μη) πληκτης, in the New Testament. See *BDAG*, 826; *LS*, 1418.

[20] Titus is to instruct the believers in Crete to live out this quality (Tit 3:2, ἀμαχος). The root terms without the α-privative, μαχη (2 Tim 2:23; Tit 3:9; Jas 4:1) and μαχομαι (2 Tim 2:24; Jas 4:2), specify the vice of contentiousness.

[21] The corrupt heretics condemned by Peter embody this quality of arrogant self-will (2 Pet 2:10, αὐθαδης).

[22] Marshall, *Pastoral Epistles*, 155-157, discusses the five major interpretations of this criterion. He concludes: "It is positive in tone and stresses faithfulness in marriage, rather than prohibiting some specific unsanctioned form of marriage" (p. 478).

[23] The verb προιστημι is Paul's preferred term (8 times in the NT, all in Paul) to express the function of leadership in the church (1 Thess 5:12; Rom 12:8; 1 Tim 5:17). The "management" of one's family is thus viewed by Paul as a test case for leading the church, both for elders (1 Tim 3:4-5) and for deacons (1 Tim 3:12). The verb occurs twice in Titus with the meaning of "give attention to" or "devote oneself to" (3:8, 14).

The children of the elder obey him[24] with proper respect (3:4).[25] Their obedient behavior and respectful attitudes confirm that this is a parent who has not embittered the children by harsh treatment, but has carefully brought up them up to love and reverence the Lord (Eph 6:1-4; Col 3:20-21). Another way of expressing the same standard is having trustworthy (or believing)[26] children, not accused of dissipation[27] or rebellious[28] (Tit 1:6). Although parents cannot always be blamed for the rebellious behavior of children, the elder must meet the standard of being "without reproach" for the sake of the church and its reputation. The special tasks of teaching and governance over the church of God can only be effectively fulfilled by those who prove capable of governing the family (1 Tim 3:5). Family stewardship becomes the testing ground for church leadership.

6. **Ministry skill**

   (i) Able to teach (3:2; cf. 1 Tim 5:17; Tit 1:9):[29] This quality is also required of Timothy in his pastoral ministry (2 Tim 2:24), and is spelled out there as the ability to gently and prayerfully instruct those who are hostile with a view to their repentance. The responsibility of at least some elders is preaching and teaching, which together combine instruction in content and its moral application (1 Tim 5:17). The elders in Crete must be faithful teachers of apostolic doctrine, able both to encourage believers and to rebuke those who oppose the truth, either through advocating false teaching or through refusal to submit to its moral authority in their lives (Tit 1:9). The elder, then, is a person who studies and can articulate the truths of the Word of God in a way that edifies the church (2 Tim 2:15; 3:14-17).

Deacons (1 Tim 3:8-13)

1. **Reputation with others, including outsiders**

   (i) Tested and proven to be blameless (3:10): There is to be a period of evaluation to determine whether the individual evidences the criteria set

---

[24] Obedience or submission to divinely ordained authority is central to the New Testament uses of the noun ὑποταγη (2 Cor 9:13; Gal 2:5; 1 Tim 2:11; 3:4) and its cognate verb ὑποτασσω (38 times; e.g. Rom 13:1, 5; Eph 5:21, 24; Col 3:18; Tit 2:9; 3:1).

[25] The noun σεμνοτης (1 Tim 2:2; 3:4; Tit 2:7) and its cognate adjective σεμνος (Php 4:8; 1 Tim 3:8, 11 [deacons and wives]; Tit 2:2 [older women]) denote the dignified and honorable manner of life that commands the respect of others, in this case one's children.

[26] Either meaning can draw support from the use of πιστος in the Pastoral epistles: trustworthy/faithful (1 Tim 1:12, 15; 3:1, 11 [wives]; 4:9; 2 Tim 2:2, 11, 13; Tit 1:9; 3:8); and believing (1 Tim 4:3, 10, 12; 5:16; 6:2).

[27] The noun ἀσωτια denotes debauchery or reckless living (Eph 5:18; 1 Pet 4:4). The adverb ἀσωτως is used to describe the "wild" (NIV) lifestyle of the prodigal son (Lk 15:13).

[28] The adjective ἀνυποτακτος designates those who refuse to submit to divinely ordained authority (1 Tim 1:9; Tit 1:6, 10; Heb 2:8).

[29] The adjective διδακτικος (1 Tim 3:2; 2 Tim 2:24) combines with the noun διδασκαλια (15 times in the Pastoral epistles; e.g. 1 Tim 5:17; Tit 1:9), the noun διδασκαλος (1 Tim 2:7; 2 Tim 1:11; 4:3), and the verb διδασκω (1 Tim 2:12; 4:11; 6:2; 2 Tim 2:2; Tit 1:11) to provide an impressive accent in the Pastoral letters on the critical importance of sound teaching for the health of the church.

forth for deacons. As with elders, this is probably a cautionary note not to appoint a person to this office hastily (1 Tim 5:22). A person who is blameless, that is, free from any substantive basis of criticism for failure to meet these standards, commends the church to the outside community (cf. Tit 1:6-7). A period of testing allows time for one's character to be revealed, as it inevitably will, through concrete actions (1 Tim 5:24-25).

2. **Character virtues**
   (i) Worthy of respect (3:8):[30] This person evidences a dignity and seriousness of manner that commands the respect of others.
3. **Self-management**
   (i) Not engaging in double talk (3:8):[31] One whose speech is sincere, straightforward, not duplicitous or deceiving (2 Cor 1:17-18).
   (ii) Not indulging in much wine (3:8): Equivalent to that required of elders (1 Tim 3:3; Tit 1:7; cf. Eph 5:18a; Tit 2:3), that is, one who does not even approach the limits of inebriation.
   (iii) Not greedy for material gain (3:8): The same criterion as that for elders (Tit 1:7), that is, a person who does not allow material wealth to usurp the kingdom of God as the defining pursuit of one's life.
4. **Family**
   (i) **Deacon's wife** (3:11):
       (1) Worthy of respect: Equally required of the deacon (3:8), namely, the dignity of manner that commands the respect of others.
       (2) Not a malicious talker:[32] This includes but is not limited to slanderous speech.
       (3) Temperate: This quality is also listed for elders (3:2). It refers to the stability of character that prevents engagement in all forms of addictive behavior such as overindulgence in alcohol.
       (4) Trustworthy in all things: One who is dependable and faithful "in all things," perhaps denoting the practical ministries in the church, which she will help fulfill alongside her deacon husband.
   (ii) Husband of one wife (3:12a): Same criterion required for elders (1 Tim 3:2; Tit 1:6), namely, one who is morally without reproach, has remained faithful to his spouse, and who has not been divorced outside of Scriptural parameters.
   (iii) Manages his children and household well (3:12b): Same criterion for elders (1 Tim 3:4-5), that is, an individual whose godly management of his family is evidenced by a stable, loving marriage and obedient, respectful children.

---

[30] This quality (σεμνός) is also required of deacons' wives (1 Tim 3:11) and of older women in the church (Tit 2:2; see f.n. 104).
[31] This is the only occurrence of (μη) διλογος in the New Testament. Its literal sense of "saying something twice" took on the meaning of speech that was contradictory, insincere or deceitful, perhaps like the native American saying, "speak with a forked tongue." See *BDAG*, 250; *LS*, 431.
[32] The adjective διαβολος, often employed in its substantival form for "the devil" (1 Tim 3:6-7), occurs two other times in the New Testament with the meaning of "slanderous" (2 Tim 3:3; Tit 2:3 [older women]).

5. **Ministry skill**
    (i) Keeps hold of the deep truths of the faith with a clear conscience (3:9; cf. 1 Tim 1:5, 19; 2 Tim 1:3): An individual that holds firmly to sound apostolic doctrine and who lives in light of that revealed truth with a clear conscience, that is, with an inner moral sensibility that validates the profession.

Summary of criteria for church leaders

The criteria that Paul sets forth for elders and deacons place priority on godly character. Both elders and deacons are to be people whose sterling reputation for moral excellence commends the church to the outside world. The eight character virtues listed for elders could be compared to the fruit of the Spirit in Galatians 5:22-23. Elders are to be people who have progressed on the road to maturity far enough that their Spirit-polished character is evident to all. Paul specifically forbids a recent convert to serve as an elder, though he does not repeat this criterion for deacons. It might be that the diaconate would serve as a testing ground for the development of younger potential leaders who might later qualify as elders. Both sets of leaders must be people who successfully manage their emotions, drives, speech, and finances. Further, in both cases the earthly family is set forth as the sphere of assessment to determine whether one is truly qualified to lead the family of God. A stable and loving marriage that produces respectful children often reveals the hidden character of the kind of person who will develop into an effective leader in the church.

There are two areas that are especially singled out for elders that are not listed as qualifying criteria for deacons. First, the elder must be a person who can get along well with others. The relational qualities—hospitable, not pugnacious, quarrelsome or self-willed—of the upper echelon of leadership will set the tone for the rest of the church. While Paul had to occasionally address doctrinal (Galatia, Corinth, Colossae) and moral (Corinth) aberrations in the churches, it was the relational issues that taxed his pastoral energies the most: bitter disputes fostered by legalism in Galatia (Gal 5:15, 20); personality-centered factions and socio-economic divisions in Corinth (1 Cor 1:10-13; 11:18-22, 27-32); so-called strong and weak brothers judging one another over disputable matters in Rome (Rom 14:3-4); two influential women squabbling with one another in the church at Philippi (Php 4:2); teachers engaged in unhealthy controversies that created strife and friction both in Ephesus (1 Tim 6:3-5) and in Crete (Tit 3:9-11). Paul's greatest pastoral challenge was helping the people of God get along with one another. Elders with the requisite skill to relate to different types of personalities and to foster unity in the midst of diversity would enhance the church's reputation in the community. It would be this loving unity that would arrest the attention of unbelievers and draw them to the gospel message (Jn 13:34-35; Eph 4:1-6). Second, the elder must be able to teach, a criterion that assumes a thorough knowledge of the fulfillment of Old Testament Scripture in apostolic doctrine (2 Tim 2:15; 3:14-17). In short, the elder must be a person who is skilled in the relational and didactic areas of ministry. A truth-grounded unity would characterize the congregation so signally blessed to have leadership of this caliber.

Leadership profile of Paul: Criteria for community leaders
The leader in leadership: *When Paul sets forth the established criteria for church leadership he says very little about function, role, personality type, or spiritual gifting. True, the elder must be one who understands and can effectively teach the Word of God. But Paul's primary focus is on the underlying spiritual and moral constitution of the leader. Paul's philosophy of leadership is character-grounded rather than role-defined. Are the fruits of the Holy Spirit springing forth in manifest beauty from the soil of the heart of this individual? Does this person successfully manage their emotions, drives, appetites, actions, and reactions in a way that pleases God and sets an example for younger believers? Is this person, if married, nurturing a loving, stable and healthy family life? Is there a pattern of harmonious relationships with others? These are the questions Paul implores Timothy and Titus to ask as they assess potential leaders for the churches in Ephesus and Crete respectively. The standards are exacting, for the quality of the church, and thus its effectiveness in witness, inevitably springs from the quality of its leaders.*

PART SIX

Profile of the
Servant-Leader

Profile of the Servant-Leader

The Bible is a book that tells it like it is. The God of perfection who planned, supervises and will one day consummate the plan of redemption employs flawed human vessels to accomplish his purposes. The biblical record applauds the successes of its greatest leaders without magnifying them, and censures their failures without excoriating them. Divine grace is at work and the human instruments are but servants whose vocation is to magnify a majestic Lord. One way we might construct a profile of the servant-leader in Holy Scripture would be to assemble the individual profiles into a composite whole, a sum of the parts. This method would produce an extensive list of virtues, a kind of profile that would rival the most idealized portrait found in romantic novels about super heroes. But God does not depend upon heroes, he uses smudged and unattractive "jars of clay" (2 Cor 4:7)—a betrayed brother, a reluctant desert herdsman, a fearful wheat thresher, an overlooked shepherd boy, a burdened cupbearer, and an ethnocentric Galilean fisherman. Rather than compile an extensive list of desirable attributes, this profile plots three trajectories that penetrate the fundamental identity of all servant leaders—character, motive and agenda. Who the leader is and is becoming in one's essential being (character), why the leader undertakes a course of action (motive), and what the leader pursues as the defined mission (agenda) are, we believe, the core constituents and interrelated foci of the kind of leadership enjoined in Holy Scripture.

Proven Character

Character can be defined as a person's moral constitution, in which is embedded a stable set of values. For the biblical leader these values are conditioned by revealed truth recorded in Holy Scripture. The apostle Paul establishes a set of criteria for elders and deacons that centers around moral virtues that spring from and evidence godly character (1 Tim 3:1-13; Tit 1:5-9). Paul's philosophy of leadership is character-grounded rather than geared around personality, role, temperament, or gifting. This is because character possesses the staying power and impact potential necessary for a lasting legacy. Timothy and Titus will succeed in their pastoral ministries to the degree that they give careful attention to growing in godliness and setting an example for the believers in faith (Godward), love (manward) and integrity (selfward) (1 Tim 4:7-8, 12, 16; Tit 2:7-8, 15; 3:8). These three areas intersect in the character of the godly leader. Faith is steadfast confidence in the goodness and sovereignty of God, especially in difficult circumstances. Love is the daily choice to sacrifice one's personal preferences for the welfare of others. Integrity is that congruity of claim, character and conduct that wins respect and provides the moral authority to lead others.

How does one develop the character that is the prerequisite for effective leadership? Paul refers to "proven character" as the refined product that emerges from a process of testing (Rom 5:3-4).[1] Suffering endured from the perspective of faith is the soil in which perseverance grows, and from perseverance blooms character. Proven character is evidenced by a buoyant hope that has experienced the faithfulness of God to be more than adequate for the crisis (5:4b-5). The tested servant is more than a survivor, but is one who views future challenges as fresh opportunities to prove the sufficiency of God's grace. "Suffering" in the context of Paul's ministry is a broad term, one that encompasses all kinds of adversity, including physical hardship, emotional distress, and persecution encountered in obedience to God's mission.[2] These refining experiences are the marks of credibility that commend him as a servant of Christ (2 Cor 6:4-10; 11:23-29). Those individuals that Scripture honors as effective leaders were people whose characters were tested and refined in the crucible of hardship. It was in crisis that inherited values were personalized and internalized and that character was formed (cf. Jas 1:2-4; 1 Pet 1:6-7). Long years of soul-shaping in obscurity preceded their rise to prominence.

Joseph experienced betrayal, slavery, false accusation and imprisonment over a period of thirteen years before he was elevated as Vizier of Egypt. Moses felt he was ready to lead Israel at aged 40 (Ex 2:11; Acts 7:25), but God removed the pampered son of the Egyptian princess to the desert of Midian for forty years to tend the flocks of Jethro (Ex 3:1; 7:7). At aged 80 he was now prepared, even if reluctant, to confront Pharaoh. Joshua spent his youth as Moses' apprentice and then, in spite of his obedience, was consigned to watch his entire generation die off during the forty years of wilderness wandering (Ex 24:13; 33:11; Num 14:28-34). After his anointing by Samuel (1 Sam 16:13), David received not a crown, but fifteen years as a fugitive in desolate places trying to escape the murderous pursuit of Saul. A total of twenty-two years passed before David was crowned undisputed King of Israel (2 Sam 5:3). Upon his return to Jerusalem as governor,

---

[1] The Greek term is δοκιμη and all seven of its NT occurrences are in Paul's writings. This noun can mean one of three things: (1) a "test" or "trial," the outcome of which is uncertain (2 Cor 2:9; 8:2); (2) the demonstrable "proof" that what one claims is in fact true (2 Cor 9:13; 13:3); and (3) "proven character" that has been refined through hardship (Rom 5:4 [twice]; Php 2:22). These same three meanings can be plotted across the set of terms that are cognate with δοκιμη. The verb δοκιμαζω has the following meanings: (1) to "test" or "examine" something (or someone) in order to determine its quality (Lk 14:19; 1 Cor 3:13; 1 Thess 2:4b; 5:21; 1 Tim 3:10; 1 Pet 1:7; 1 Jn 4:1), which includes self-examination (1 Cor 11:28; 2 Cor 13:5; Gal 6:4); (2) to "prove" the genuineness of a claim to a given attribute (2 Cor 8:8, 22); and (3) to "approve," that is, to accept as trustworthy and to embrace its worth (Rom 1:28; 2:18; 12:2; 14:22; 1 Cor 16:3; Eph 5:10; Php 1:10). The adjective δοκιμος signifies the verdict of "approved," having passed the examination of its quality or worth (Rom 14:18; 16:10; 1 Cor 11:19; 2 Cor 10:18; 13:7; 2 Tim 2:15; Jas 1:12). The one who fails the test is rendered the verdict of "disapproved" or "rejected," signified by αδοκιμος (Rom 1:28; 1 Cor 9:27; 2 Cor 13:5, 6, 7; 2 Tim 3:8; Tit 1:16; Heb 6:8). The noun δοκιμιον in its two NT uses signifies a test (or refinement)—in each case through suffering—designed to prove the genuineness of one's faith (Jas 1:3; 1 Pet 1:7). Finally, the noun δοκιμασια refers to the "testing" of Israel's faith in the wilderness (Heb 3:9).

[2] Paul employs the term θλιψις in Rom 5:3 (twice) to refer to the hardships, pressures, tribulations, persecutions that accompany his apostolic witness to Jesus (Acts 20:23; 2 Cor 1:4, 8; 2:4; 4:17; 6:4; 7:4; Eph 3:13; Php 4:14; Col 1:24; 1 Thess 3:7) and is the lot of all true disciples (Acts 14:22; Rom 8:35; 12:12; 2 Cor 8:2, 13; 1 Thess 1:6; 3:3; 2 Thess 1:4, 6; cf. Jn 16:33; Heb 10:33). The endurance of affliction makes one an imitator of the Lord Jesus who endured great affliction in his obedience to the Father's will (Col 1:24; 1 Thess 1:6; cf. Rev 1:9).

Nehemiah was greeted by broken down walls, burned gates (Neh 2:13) and determined enemies (2:10). His pursuit of God's will brought with it threats of physical force (4:8), a demoralized work force (4:10), exploitation and internal dissension (5:1-5), and grave personal danger (6:2). Daniel's faithfulness landed him in a den of hungry lions; for their integrity his three friends were cast into a blazing furnace (Dan 3; 6). The apostles, including Peter and John, came to the end of their three years of leadership training by being "sifted as wheat" by the enemy of their souls (Lk 22:31). When Paul praises Timothy to the Philippians for his "proven character," he is commending one who has served for twelve years in the rough and tumble of missionary work as his most trusted associate (Php 2:22). Paul himself spent nearly a decade studying the Scriptures and developing his evangelistic gifts, first in Arabia then in Tarsus, before being rescued from obscurity by Barnabas and assuming a position of prominence in the church in Antioch (Acts 9:30; 11:25-26). Years of preparation preceded the elevation of these leaders to positions of influence. Adversity was God's refining tool to shape them into vessels of usefulness.[3] Those who are looking for a person of character to fill a leadership role in the church or parachurch organization would do well to examine when and how the candidate has handled adversity. Leaders with "proven character" are those who have learned to trust God in the hard experiences of life (Ps 119:71).

Doxological Motive

A passion for God's honor and a deep concern for the spiritual welfare of Israel drove forward the great leaders in the preparatory stage of the history of redemption. In the two watershed crises, the golden calf and report of the spies, Moses intercedes for the Lord to relent from his threat to destroy Israel. The basis of his plea is God's honor: to destroy the people you have redeemed and established a covenant with would damage your reputation among the nations (Ex 32:11-13; Num 14:13-16). Moses is zealous that God's abounding love and tender compassion be magnified in his granting of forgiveness to a repentant people (Num 14:17-19). When Achan's sin leads to a demoralizing defeat at Ai, Joshua imitates his mentor with a desperate plea for Israel's deliverance. If the Canaanites now mobilize and wipe out your people, Joshua prays, "what then will you do for your own great name" (Josh 7:9b)? More than a warrior, Joshua is the shepherd of Israel (Num 27:17) who reaffirms the nation's covenantal identity before, during, and after the military campaign (Josh 5; 8; 24). Samuel reminds the people, after granting their request for an earthly monarch, that the Lord whose good pleasure was to make them his own will abide with them "for the sake of his great name" (1 Sam 12:22). Samuel pledges to intercede for them and to teach them to fear the Lord and to serve him out of recognition of "what great things he has done for you" (12:23-24). David's dramatic arrival on the scene is as a shepherd boy who

---

[3] By contrast, one can observe the tragedy of those who grew up in privileged circumstances, without the character-forming experiences of hardship that had shaped their fathers, and who failed as leaders (or potential leaders): the sons of Eli (1 Sam 3:22-25); the sons of Samuel (1 Sam 8:1-4); and the sons of David—Solomon, Amnon, Absalom, and Adonijah. Saul's elevation was a meteoric rise from donkey wrangler (1 Sam 9:1-4) to anointed prince of Israel (10:1), with practically no period of preparation and no recorded instances of real adversity before his anointing.

dares to defend God's honor against the insults of the Philistine giant (1 Sam 17:45-47). The "man after God's own heart" (1 Sam 13:14), despite his colossal failures, is the shepherd-ruler (2 Sam 5:2) who brings the ark to Jerusalem, establishes the joyful worship of the Lord at the center of national life (2 Sam 6:12-22), and rules over the people with reverential fear (2 Sam 23:3). Daniel declares to Belshazzar, at the peril of his life, that the king has brazenly defied the true God by desecrating the sacred vessels of the Jerusalem temple. He announces that the sacred writing on the wall is a final declaration of judgment, for the king has failed to "honor the God who holds in his hand your life and all your ways" (5:23). Nehemiah works tirelessly for the physical and spiritual restoration of the exilic community "out of reverence for God" (Neh 5:15). He teams with Ezra to renew the covenant so that songs of thanksgiving and praise once again reverberate throughout the once desolate holy city (Neh 12:31, 40).

As redemption history reaches its intended goal and the ceremonies of the old covenant complete their course, there is an even more pronounced focus upon the interior life of God's servants. In his training of the twelve Jesus made a constant beeline to the matters of the heart, the center of the personality where motives and values mingle in the process of self-determination. It is not enough to do the right thing or even to have a stable and growing character. New covenant leaders must regularly assess why they are doing what they are doing. The inherent worth of "acts of righteousness" (Mt 6:1), such as giving to the poor, praying, or fasting, depends on the underlying motive behind them. Are they the expressions of a grateful heart that is attuned to the glory of God, or are they self-serving acts performed to attract the approbation of one's peers (Mt 6:2-4; 5-8; 16-18)? Jesus is warning his disciples to check their motives because even ministry can be carried out for the wrong reasons. It is the "pure in heart" who will have an undimmed vision of God's majesty.

Paul strains toward a day of judgment when hidden things will be uncovered and motives will be exposed (1 Cor 4:5). On that day the comparative assessments of others will mean nothing (4:3a). One's own self-appraisal will prove faulty (4:3b), for the heart has a remarkable capacity to deceive itself (Ps 19:12; Jer 17:9). Even the conscience, one's internal dialogue with oneself, can not be relied upon (4:4). The deep sense of accountability feeds his singular ambition to please the Lord in every facet of life and ministry (2 Cor 5:9-10). The doxological motive governs his holy ambition to seize the day of opportunity and to promote God's rule among the Gentiles (Rom 15:9-12, 16, 20-21). Peter commands the elders in the churches of Asia minor to test the driving forces behind their leadership, rooting out all manner of obligatory, self-aggrandizing and authoritarian inclinations (1 Pet 5:2-3).

How is a leader to act with initiative and boldness and not be paralyzed by a morbid introspection with constantly second-guessing one's elusive hidden motivations? The answer lies in the ruthless honesty to lay one's soul bare before the penetrating sword of Scripture, which has the power to penetrate, cut through, expose, and renew the "thoughts and intents of the heart" (Heb 4:12). Servant-leaders must undergo daily spiritual surgery under the Spirit-illumined exposure to God's word, undergirded by earnest prayer for God to search one's thoughts and meditations (Ps 19:14; 51:6; 139:23-24). This is the area where Jesus and the

Pharisees ended up on a collision course: they created a firewall between God and the soul with their traditions over the Sabbath, fasting, ritual washings, and tithing; he would remove these traditions and restore the direct interface between the heart and the Word. Jesus began his public ministry by modeling dependence on the word of God (Mt 4:4, 7, 10: "It is written"). He stripped away the layers of rabbinical casuistry and restored his disciples' direct exposure to the penetrating power of the Old Testament as fulfilled in his teaching (Mt 5:17-20). Paul commanded Timothy to study and to submit to the functional authority of Scripture with its ability to teach, rebuke, correct, and train in righteousness (2 Tim 3:16-17). This was a practice the young pastor was already accustomed to (3:14-15). The living word shaped the motives of the one singularly praised for his genuine concern for the Philippians' welfare and his pursuit of the things of Christ Jesus (Php 2:20-21).

The heart, the "wellspring of life" (Prov 4:23), is the place of decision and destiny. Careful and regular attention to one's heart motivation will prevent the servant-leader from the pitfalls that commonly attend positions of influence: concern for personal reputation, status, image, popularity, recognition, vocational "success" as defined by the prevailing culture, and the assessment of others based on external, extrabiblical criteria. A heart in pursuit of God's glory and the spiritual welfare of God's people nurtures resilience because it releases one from being inflated by triumphs or dismayed by setbacks. One who seeks to please God above all else possesses a kingdom perspective that facilitates partnerships with others of like faith, sublimating egocentric agendas and the need "to be someone" for a greater legacy—the building up of individuals into communities of worship and witness. Such a person shares the servant posture of the forerunner of the Messiah: "He must increase; I must decrease" (Jn 3:30). This kind of leader yearns not for a place in history or a visible monument to one's accomplishments, but for the divine benediction on a stewardship fulfilled: "Well done, good and faithful servant" (Mt 25:21, 23).

Divine Agenda

The God of creation moves to graciously reconcile the fallen human race to himself (2 Cor 5:19). He separates a man, Abraham, from his idolatrous clan and establishes a covenant with him and his family designed to reverberate into salvific blessing to all the peoples of the earth (Gen 12:1-3). The covenant family grows into a nation, Israel, whose calling is to testify to the holiness and majesty of the one true Lord of the nations (Ex 19:5-6; Deut 6:4-5: Isa 49:6b). This carefully planned and superintended history of redemption moves inexorably forward, despite the waywardness of the "stiff-necked" covenant people, toward its intended climax. In the fullness of time the one adumbrated by kings, sages and prophets is born to a Jewish girl in the town of Bethlehem, Jesus the Messiah, the son of David, the son of Abraham (Mt 1:1; Gal 4:4). His three brief years of public ministry are devoted to proclaiming the dawning of the kingdom of God (Mt 4:17). He commits his legacy to twelve men, one whose betrayal will lead to his death. As the only person ever born whose central purpose in life is to die, Jesus is rejected by the very covenant nation from which he sprang and is delivered to a shameful death (Jn 1:11). Vindicated by God, he is raised from the dead and

300

exalted to the right hand of the Father as Lord and King (Acts 2:32-36). The "good news" of salvation through the vicarious death and victorious resurrection of Jesus Messiah is proclaimed by the apostles, who go forth in obedience to his final commission (Acts 1:8). Until the Lord returns to consummate the inaugurated kingdom, his church, the new Israel, moves forth in obedience to the Spirit and the Word to extend God's dynamic rule over all who will respond in faith and repentance. The mandate is to teach all Jesus commanded, to all the nations, to the end of the age (Mt 28:19-20).

Servant-leaders are not visionaries who devise a brilliant plan, then by dint of personal charisma draw others to fulfill those ambitions. Rather they are faithful stewards of the divine mandate—to fish and to feed, to evangelize and to teach, to pioneer and to pastor. Biblical leadership maintains a laser-like concentration on God's clearly stated agenda, that is, the evangelization of the lost, the edification of the saved, and the establishment of vital churches. Servant leaders take the initiative to bring others to a passionate commitment to what is on the heart of God, the extension of his saving rule over individuals and communities both qualitatively (holiness of character) and quantitatively (expansion to the unreached frontiers). The apostle Paul stands before us as the premier example of the missional leader driven by the divine agenda. A clearly defined mission (1 Cor 1:17), a regular reaffirmation of its core values and message (1 Cor 11:23-26), and the ability to contextualize the message to different audiences (1 Cor 9:19-23) preserves Paul from three respective common pitfalls: (1) Mission ambiguity: failure to clarify from the outset one's purpose for existence; (2) Mission drift: subtle and gradual erosion of the sharp edges of the defining purpose; (3) Mission confusion: failure to adapt one's methodology and orient one's message to fit changing circumstances because the mission and its method for accomplishment are not clearly distinguished.

We conclude with a set of questions that can be used in regular self-assessment to determine whether one's ongoing practice of leadership is biblical or secular, that is, grounded in the principles and precepts of Holy Scripture or conditioned by the prevailing models
of one's culture.

1. *Do I take the **initiative** and actively seek opportunities to impact others for the sake of the kingdom of God?*

2. *Does my character evidence in increasing measure the virtues of **godliness** so that I impact others toward a life of holiness?*

3. *Has there been a posture of faith in God's sufficiency when facing hardship and adversity so that my **character** exhibits a refined solidarity and resiliency?*

4. *In the innermost core of my being do I sense a passion for God's glory and the welfare of others? Or do I detect self-aggrandizing **motives** that have not yet been honestly faced and staked to the cross? Am I conscious of exercising leadership of others before the Audience of one or the audience of many?*

5. *Do my activities point toward a singular focus on God's **mandate**—the discipling of the nations—or are other competing agendas displacing a kingdom perspective with an organizational or programmatic one?*

Bibliography of Works Cited

Abbreviations

BDB   Brown, Francis, with the cooperation of S. R. Driver and Charles A. Briggs. *The new Brown, Driver, Briggs, Gesenius Hebrew and English lexicon: with an appendix containing the Biblical Aramaic.* Peabody, MS: Hendrickson, 1979.

BDAG   Bauer, Walter. *A Greek-English Lexicon of the New Testament and other Early Christian Literature.* Rev. and ed. Frederick William Danker. 3rd ed. University of Chicago Press, 2000.

DJG   Green, Joel B. and Scot McKnight, eds. *Dictionary of Jesus and the Gospels.* Downers Grove, IL: InterVarsity, 1992.

DPHL   Hawthorne, Gerald F. and Ralph P. Martin, eds. *Dictionary of Paul and His Letters.* Downers Grove, IL: InterVarsity, 1993.

EDNT   Balz, Horst and Gerhard Schneider, eds. *Exegetical Dictionary of the New Testament.* 3 vols. Grand Rapids: Eerdmans, 1990-1993.

HALOT   Koehler, Ludwig and Walter Baumgartner. *The Hebrew and Aramaic Lexicon of the Old Testament.* 5 vols. Leiden: E. J. Brill, 1993-2000.

LS   Liddell, Henry George and Robert Scott. *A Greek-English Lexicon.* 9th ed. with revised supplement. Oxford: Clarendon, 1996.

NIDNTT   Brown, Colin, ed. *The New International Dictionary of New Testament Theology.* 3 vols. Exeter: Paternoster, 1975-78.

NIDOTTE VanGemeren, Willem A., ed. *New International Dictionary of Old Testament Theology and Exegesis.* 5 vols. Carlisle: Paternoster, 1996.

TDNT   Kittel, Gerhard. ed. *Theological Dictionary of the New Testament.* Transl. and ed. Geoffrey W. Bromiley. 10 vols. Grand Rapids: Eerdmans, 1964.

TDOT   Botterweck, G. Johannes. *Theological Dictionary of the Old Testament.* 11 vols. Grand Rapids: Eerdmans, 1974-2001.

TWOT   Harris, R. Laird, ed. *Theological Wordbook of the Old Testament.* 2 vols. Chicago: Moody, 1980.

Other Works Cited

Albright, W. F. and C. S. Mann. *Matthew.* The Anchor Bible. Garden City, NY: Doubleday, 1971.

Augustine. *Expositions on the Book of Psalms.* Nicene and Post-Nicene Fathers, vol. 8. Grand Rapids: Hendrickson, 1994.

Bruce, F. F. *Paul: Apostle of the Heart Set Free.* Grand Rapids: Eerdmans, 1977.

Barrett,, C. K. *The Gospel According to John.* 2nd ed. London: SPCK, 1978.

Beasley-Murray, G. R. *Jesus and the Kingdom of God.* Grand Rapids: Eerdmans, 1986.

Bergen, Robert D. *1, 2, Samuel.* Broadman and Holman, 1996.

Block, Daniel I. *Judges, Ruth.* Nashville, TN: Broadman, 1999.

Caird, G. B. *The Language and Imagery of the Bible.* London: Duckworth, 1980.

Carson, D. A. *Matthew.* Expositor's Bible Commentary, vol. 8. Grand Rapids: Eerdmans, 1984.

Carson, D. A., Douglas J. Moo, Leon Morris. *An Introduction to the New Testament.* Grand Rapids: Zondervan, 1992.

Davies, W. D. and Dale C. Allison. *A Critical and Exegetical Commentary on the Gospel according to Saint Matthew.* ICC. 3 vols. Edinburgh: T. & T. Clark, 1991.

de Vaux, Roland. *Ancient Israel: Its Life and Institutions.* Transl. John McHugh. London: Darton, Longman, and Todd, 1961.

Dunn, James D. G. *The Epistles to Colossians and to Philemon.* NIGTC. Grand Rapids: Eerdmans, 1996.

Durham, John I. *Exodus.* WBC. Waco, TX: Word, 1987.

Edersheim, Alfred. *The Life and Times of Jesus the Messiah.* 2 vols. London: Longmans, Green, and Co., 1900.

Fee, Gordon D. *God's Empowering Presence: The Holy Spirit in the Letters of Paul*. Peabody, MS: Hendrickson, 1994.

_____ . *Paul's Letter to the Philippians*. NICNT. Grand Rapids: Eerdmans, 1995.

France, R. T. *The Gospel of Mark*. NIGTC. Grand Rapids: Eerdmans, 2002.

Goldingay, John E. *Daniel*. WBC. Dallas, TX: Word, 1989.

Goppelt, Leonhard. *Theology of the New Testament*. Transl. John E. Alsup. Grand Rapids: Eerdmans, 1981.

Hartley, John E. *Leviticus*. WBC. Dallas, TX: Word, 1992.

Hawthorne, Gerald F. *Philippians*. WBC. Waco, TX: Word, 1983.

Hays, Richard B. *First Corinthians*. Interpretation. Louisville: John Knox, 1997.

Hengel, Martin and Anna Maria Schwemer. *Paul Between Damascus and Antioch*. Transl. John Bowden. London: SCM, 1997.

Hornblower, S. and A. Spawforth, eds. *The Oxford Classical Dictionary*. 3rd ed. Oxford University Press, 1996.

Hurst, L. D. "Re-enter the Pre-existent Christ in Philippians 2:5-11?" *New Testament Studies* 32:3 (1986): 449-457

Jeremias, Joachim. *Jerusalem in the Time of Jesus*. Transl. F. H. and C. H. Cave. 3rd ed. London: SCM, 1969.

Kitchen, K. A. *Ancient Orient and the Old Testament*. London: Tyndale, 1966.

Ladd, George Eldon. *A Theology of the New Testament*. Revised edition by Donald A. Hagner. Grand Rapids: Eerdmans, 1994.

_____ . *I Believe in the Resurrection of Jesus*. London: Hodder and Stoughton, 1975.

_____ . *The Presence of the Future*. Grand Rapids: Eerdmans, 1974.

Lane, William L. *The Gospel according to Mark*. NICNT. Grand Rapids: Eerdmans, 1974.

Larkin, William J. and Joel F. Williams, eds. *Mission in the New Testament. An Evangelical Approach*. Maryknoll, NY: Orbis, 1998.

Marshall, I. Howard. *A Critical and Exegetical Commentary on the Pastoral Epistles.* ICC. Edinburgh: T. & T. Clark, 1999.

Martin, Ralph P. *Carmen Christi. Philippians 2:5-11 In recent interpretation and in the setting of early Christian worship.* Grand Rapids: Eerdmans, 1983.

Metzger, Bruce M. *A Textual Commentary on the Greek New Testament.* 2nd ed. United Bible Societies, 1994.

Miller, Stephen R. *Daniel.* Broadman and Holman, 1994.

Morris, Leon. *The Apostolic Preaching of the Cross.* 3rd ed. London: Tyndale, 1965.

O'Brien, Peter T. *The Epistle to the Philippians.* NIGTC. Grand Rapids: Eerdmans, 1991.

Oswalt, John N. *The Book of Isaiah.* NICOT. 2 vols. Grand Rapids: Eerdmans, 1998.

Ridderbos, Herman. *The Coming of the Kingdom.* Transl. H. de Jongste. Philadelphia: Presbyterian and Reformed, 1962.

Schreiner, Thomas R. *Paul: Apostle of God's Glory in Christ.* Downers Grove, IL: InterVarsity, 2001.

Schurer, Emil. *The History of the Jewish People in the Age of Jesus Christ* (175 B.C.-A.D. 135). Rev. and ed., G. Vermes, F. Millar, M. Black. Edinburgh: T. & T. Clark, 1979.

Seow, Choon-Leong. *The First and Second Books of Kings.* The New Interpreter's Bible. Nashville: Abingdon, 1999.

Silva, Moises. *Philippians.* WEC. Chicago: Moody, 1988.

Thiselton, Anthony C. *The First Epistle to the Corinthians.* NIGTC. Grand Rapids: Eerdmans, 2000.

Wanamaker, Charles A. *The Epistles to the Thessalonians.* NIGTC. Grand Rapids: Eerdmans, 1990.

Wenham, Gordon J. *Genesis 16-50.* WBC. Dallas, TX: Word, 1994.

_____ . *Numbers.* TOTC. Downers Grove, IL: Inter-Varsity, 1981.

Westcott, B. F. *The Gospel According to St. John.* Grand Rapids: Eerdmans, reprinted 1975.

Whiston, William, transl. *The Complete Works of Josephus.* Grand Rapids: Kregel reprint, 1960.

Williamson, H. G. M. *Ezra, Nehemiah.* WBC. Waco, TX: Word, 1985.

Wood, Leon *The Holy Spirit in the Old Testament.* Grand Rapids: Zondervan, 1976.

Xenophon. *Cyropaedia.* Loeb Classical Library.

15829266R00168

Printed in Great Britain
by Amazon